Consensus and C
in African Societies

An Introduction to Sociology

Consensus and Conflict in African Societies

An Introduction to Sociology

Margaret Peil

Longman

LONGMAN GROUP LIMITED
LONDON

Associated companies, branches and
representatives throughout the world

First published 1977

ISBN 0 582 64173 x (Cased)
ISBN 0 582 64174 8 (Paper)

Printed in Great Britain by
T. & A. Constable Ltd, Edinburgh

Contents

Preface   xi

1 The Discipline of Sociology   1
    A science of society   2
    The social sciences   6
    Concepts   9
    The comparative method   21

2 Social Organisation   27
    Types of societies   27
    Primary groups   30
    Leadership   33
    Social order   41

3 Individual and Society   47
    Socialisation   47
    Social exchange   59
    Social networks   64

4 Social Differentiation   78
    Social stratification   79
    Differentiation, past and present   89
    Social mobility   110
    Ethnocentrism   116

5 The Family   133
    Kinship   133
    Marriage   138
    Marital roles   156
    Patterns of family change   163

6 Education   174
   Functions of education   175
   Education and social mobility   189
   Schools and universities as organisations   201
   The teaching profession   205

7 Religion   213
   The sociological meaning of religion   213
   Religion in society   215
   Belief systems   227
   Formal organisation   239

8 The Cities   252
   Urbanisation   252
   What is a city?   259
   Migration   272
   Associations   288

9 Social Problems   304
   Unemployment   304
   Housing   312
   Social control and deviance   321

10 Social change   336
   Theories of change   339
   Response to change   352

Bibliography   362
Index   388

Maps, Figures and Tables

Maps

1 Cities and geographic divisions   xiv
2 Ethnic groups mentioned in the text   xv
3 Long-distance labour migration   274

Figures

1 Variables influencing parental attitude towards Western education   2
2 Structured relationships in a democratic and an authoritarian society   6
3 Types of exchange   61
4 The network of primary and secondary relationships of an accomplished Kano entrepreneur   66
5 Types of networks   68
6 The shape of stratification systems   111
7 A multiracial stratification system   123
8 Forms of descent   134
9 Types of residential units   144
10 The relationship between socio-economic participation and polygyny   151
11 Population pyramids and the demand for education   186
12 The relationship between social background, educational attainment and occupational placement   198
13 A model of the migrant adaptation process   284
14 A typology of modes of adaptation   325
15 Dynamic equilibrium   343
16 Phases of social change   344

Tables

1 Reasons for approving or disapproving of polygyny   150
2 Marital status by sex and place of residence, Ghana 1960   153
3 Percentage who had attended school by age and sex, Ghana 1960 and 1970   178

4 The effect of education on children by educational
   attainment of respondent, Lagos 1971   180
5 The two most important things a person can gain with
   his education, East African university students   184
6 Occupations of students' fathers by country, university, entry year and sex   191
7 Education of children by parental education, Lagos 1971   194
8 Religious affiliation of respondents by country, sex
   and demographic background   248
9 National and urban population by country and city   255-6
10 Opportunities for interaction by density of population   261
11 Proportion of rural Ghanaian adults who migrated to
   town, by education and sex   281
12 Percent unemployed by background characteristics,
   town and sex   308
13 Ethnicity and religion of 3 friends, by place and sex,
   Kenya and Nigeria   319
14 Household density on two standards, by town   320
15 Crimes in Kampala and Ouagadougou   331

Acknowledgements

We are grateful to the following for permission to reproduce copyright material:

Centre for Migration Studies for a figure from 'A Multivariate Model of Immigrant Adaptation' by J. Goldlust and A. H. Richmond from the *International Migration Review*, vol. 8, no. 2, Summer 1974; East African Publishing House for a table by J. Barken from *Education And Political Values*; Heinemann Educational Books Ltd. and Basic Books Inc. for adapted tabular material from *Modern Social Theory* by P. S. Cohen (c) 1968 Percy S. Cohen, Basic Books Inc. (originally from *Class and Class Conflict in Industrial Society*); Oxford University Press for an adapted extract from *Schism and Renewal in Africa* by D. B. Barrett, 1968.

Preface

This book is primarily intended as an introductory sociology text for universities in tropical Africa. Although attempts have been made to make the social sciences more comparative in their approach, sociology tends to be tied to a single nation or cultural area because explaining social behaviour in a single society is a sufficiently complex task without bringing in factors which vary from one society to another. While the goal is to develop theories which are supported by data from many societies, in practice it is best to understand one's own society first. The teaching of sociology in African universities has been hampered by introductory texts which have been written for students in highly industrialised countries; these have little meaning for students with different values, norms and experiences. British students find some American texts difficult; it should cause no surprise that African students often find them incomprehensible. If, therefore, sociology remains basically ethnocentric, African students should have a text based on their own society.

This is not to say that all African societies are alike, for there are many important differences within individual countries and large variations between peoples in different parts of the continent. However, as African nations face many common problems of urbanisation and social change their societies may be becoming more similar over time. It is hoped that by studying sociological theory in the light of data from various parts of Africa and attempting to explain why their experience has been somewhat different from what is reported elsewhere, students will come to a better understanding of the structure and functioning of their own society and their place in it. Learning the basic principles of sociological analysis should make students better able to cope with the changes they will face throughout their lives and make them more competent teachers, civil servants, managers, or employers.

The discipline of sociology has grown so rapidly in recent years that it is no longer possible to cover all aspects of it in an introductory text. The topics selected for inclusion here seemed to be those most interesting to African students and/or have been the focus of most research by academics working in Africa. Many topics have had to be treated very briefly and without the analysis and criticism of research findings which they deserve. Since this book is mainly for students who are just starting their study of sociology, it was thought better to provide a broad background for scientifically examining their own society, leaving the fuller study of specific branches of the discipline for later courses. The bibliography is comprehensive so that students can read further on topics and societies which interest them.

Primary data have been included to strengthen the students' realisation that sociology applies to real people, to teach them to read tables and draw conclusions from them and to make them more aware of the possibilities of data collection and analysis all around them. Wherever possible, data from more than one country are used to encourage students to compare and suggest reasons for similarities and differences. Since it is essential for students to learn that in the social sciences no one theory provides a satisfactory answer for all our questions and that many things which are printed are open to serious question, varying points of view are examined and the student is encouraged to test what he reads against his own observations. The opportunity to criticise various parts of this book may also be a useful learning experience.

I am grateful to all those who have commented on drafts of the various chapters; to my students at Legon, Lagos and Birmingham, who have contributed so much to my understanding of African societies; and to the African Studies Association of the United Kingdom and Longmans for this opportunity to examine the relevance of sociological theories to present-day African societies and the contribution of studies made in Africa to the development of the discipline.

Centre of West African Studies,
Birmingham,
28 January 1976

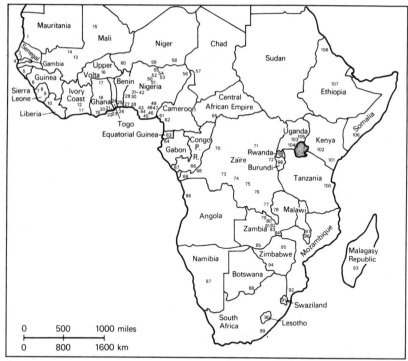

1	Nouakchott	37	Ilorin	73	Kikwit
2	Dakar	38	Iseyen	74	Kananga
3	Kaolack	39	Iwo	75	Mbuji-Mayi
4	Banjul	40	Ogbomosho	76	Likasi
5	Bissau	41	Oshogbo	77	Lubumbashi
6	Conakry	42	Oyo	78	Mansa
7	Freetown	43	Benin City	79	Chingola
8	Lunsar	44	Sapele	80	Mufilira
9	Kanema	45	Port Harcourt	81	Kitwe
10	Monrovia	46	Aba	82	Ndola
11	Abidjan	47	Umuahya	83	Luanshya
12	Bouake	48	Onitsha	84	Lusaka
13	Bamako	49	Enugu	85	Livingstone
14	Kita	50	Kaduna	86	Luanda
15	Timbuctoo	51	Kakuri/Makera	87	Windhoek
16	Ouagadougou	52	Zaria	88	Gaberone
17	Bolgatana	53	Jos	89	East London
18	Kumasi	54	Kano	90	Maseru
19	Sekondi/Takoradi	55	Katsina	91	Mbabane
20	Cape Coast	56	Maiduguri	92	Maputo
21	Accra	57	Ndjamena	93	Tananarive
22	Ashaiman	58	Zinder	94	Bulawayo
23	Tema	59	Maradi	95	Salisbury
24	Lome	60	Niamey	96	Blantyre-Limbe
25	Cotonou	61	Douala	97	Zomba
26	Porto-Nova	62	Yaounde	98	Bujumbura
27	Ajegunle	63	Bata	99	Kigali
28	Lagos	64	Libreville	100	Dar es Salaam
29	Abeokuta	65	Bangui	101	Mombasa
30	Ibadan	66	Brazzaville	102	Nairobi
31	Ado-Ekiti	67	Pointe-Noire	103	Jinja
32	Ede	68	Kinshasa	104	Kampala
33	Ile-Ife	69	Matadi	105	Mbale
34	Ikere-Ekiti	70	Mbandaka	106	Mogadishu
35	Ila	71	Kisangani	107	Addis Ababa
36	Ilesha	72	Bukavu	108	Asmara

Map 1 Cities and geographic divisions

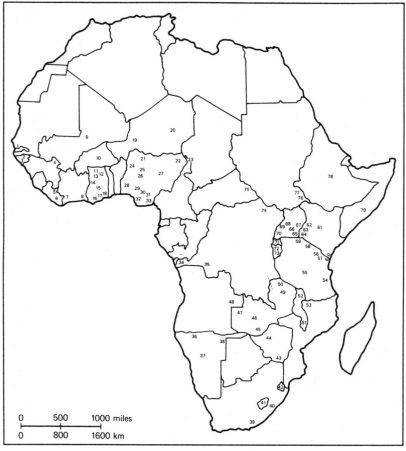

1	Wolof	28	Yoruba	55	Hadza
2	Temne	29	Weppa-Wano	56	Arusha
3	Mende	30	Yako	57	Chaga
4	Mandinka	31	Ibo	58	Masai
5	Kpelle	32	Ijaw	59	Gusii
6	Kru	33	Efik	60	Swahili
7	Bete	34	Yombe	61	Kikuyu
8	Abure	35	Kongo	62	Luhya
9	Bambara	36	Ambo	63	Margoli
10	Mossi	37	Herero	64	Luo
11	Sisala	38	Bushmen	65	Soga
12	Frafra	39	Xhosa	66	Ganda
13	Gonja	40	Zulu	67	Gisu
14	LoDegga	41	Sotho	68	Nyoro
15	Akan	42	Swazi	69	Ankole
16	Fante	43	Shona	70	Kiga
17	Ga	44	Ndebele	71	Hutu
18	Ewe	45	Tonga	72	Titsi
19	Fulani	46	Ila	73	Twa
20	Toureg	47	Lozi	74	Azande
21	Hausa	48	Luvale	75	Pygmie
22	Kanuri	49	Bemba	76	Dinka
23	Marghi	50	Lala	77	Nuer
24	Serkawa	51	Ngoni	78	Amhara
25	Gwari	52	Nyasa	79	Somali
26	Nupe	53	Yao		
27	Tiv	54	Guru		

Map 2 Ethnic map

1 The Discipline of Sociology

The word 'sociology' was created by Auguste Comte in 1837, when he combined the Latin word for society (*socio*) with the Greek word for science (*logy*). Thus, sociology is the science of society. This does not take us very far, as it is a science in a rather limited sense and there are many ideas on the precise meaning of the word society. A fuller definition is that sociology is a social science which studies the social relationships between people as individuals and as groups and the influence of social conditions on these relationships. The meaning of 'social science' and 'group' will be discussed below.

Sociology began at a time when the great changes of the industrial revolution made people more aware of their society than they had been in the past. It is easy to take things for granted when they differ little from one year to the next; the need for constant adjustment to change makes people think more about their position, and this makes sociology so relevant to Africa today. The first major thrust came from social and political philosophy, ideas about what society ought to be. Second, the new discipline was influenced by evolutionism, the attempt to trace animal and human history from its earliest origins. As a result of Charles Darwin's theories that the origins of all species of plants and animals alive in his day could be traced back to the earth's early history, philosophers (notably Herbert Spencer) became interested in the development of human society. Third, social reformers such as Charles Booth began using social surveys to provide information on the social conditions of the poor which would prod legislators into passing more equitable laws. Modern sociology continues to be concerned with social philosophy, social progress and social reform, though individual sociologists vary in which of these they emphasise.

Sociology became an independent academic discipline with the establishment of the first department of sociology at the University of Chicago in 1892. The first sociology department in tropical Africa was established at the University of Ghana in 1951. Most African departments have combined sociology with anthropology, and sometimes with demography as well. Since sociology developed in industrialised countries and anthropology mainly in non-industrialised countries, the combination of the two provides African students with a better understanding of their society than either could do separately. However, sociology has developed rapidly in recent years, as the research discussed in this book will show.

A science of society

In order to be scientific, we must apply the scientific method to our study of society. This involves careful definition of terms, the gathering of data to prove or disprove our hypotheses and the investigation and explanation of inconsistencies in these data. Many people assume that they know a good deal about society just from their experience of daily life, but 'common sense' ideas are often found to be incorrect, as are the sweeping generalisations common in the newspapers. Over time, a science grows as more data are accumulated on the way things work, theories are modified to suit new evidence and old ideas are proved to be incorrect or at least not the whole answer.

The scientific method requires the systematic collection of data rather than just casual observation of the passing scene. One way of organising these data is into independent, intervening and dependent variables. The factors which are considered to be the cause of the observed behaviour or attitudes are classed as independent variables, because they are free of the control of other variables. The results are dependent variables, because they are controlled by the others. In between, there are certain factors which modify the action of the independent on the dependent variables; these are known as intervening variables. Figure 1 shows some of the variables affecting parental acceptance or rejection of Western education.

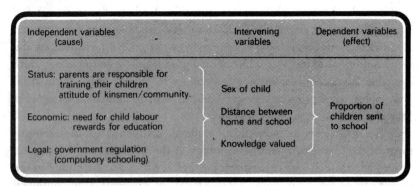

Independent variables (cause)	Intervening variables	Dependent variables (effect)
Status: parents are responsible for training their children attitude of kinsmen/community.	Sex of child	
Economic: need for child labour rewards for education	Distance between home and school	Proportion of children sent to school
Legal: government regulation (compulsory schooling)	Knowledge valued	

Figure 1 Variables influencing parental attitude toward Western education

The independent variables are the economic, political, and status pressures on the father. Intervening between these pressures and his decision on sending a child to school are the sex of the child (boys are more likely to be sent), the distance (the father may think the school is too far for the child to walk even though he would otherwise be sent) and his values (does he see education as a 'good thing'?).

The scientist develops hypotheses on what combination of independent and intervening variables will produce what results. He then tests these hypotheses by collecting data on the relationships between these variables, watching for any other variables which may affect the result. His goal is to develop theories which will explain why men behave as they do in their relationships with other men and predict their future behaviour. In working toward this goal, sociologists face three basic problems: the variability and unpredictability of human nature, confusion of terminology and bias due to their values.

First, humans are more variable than plants or animals. A chemist knows that the material he studies will always react in the same way (every sample of pure nitrogen is the same); he has only to discover the laws governing these reactions to be able to predict what will happen in any future test. Similarly, a biologist can be sure that what is true of plants today will be true tomorrow; even changes can be predicted once one understands the laws of biological cause and effect. A scientist studying human beings cannot have this security, because each person is different from all the others; they learn from each other and are constantly changing in reaction to their individual and group experiences.

Thus prediction, the goal of science, is very difficult if not impossible. We must be content with conditional statements: 'probably', 'likely', 'usually'. The only certain things are birth and death. Though many attempts have been made in recent years to translate human behaviour into scientifically approved numerical data, we continue to study many things which cannot be adequately quantified. Many of our findings are in terms of 'more' or 'less' or just 'different', without our being able to say precisely how much more or less or different. Why does violence break out in one situation and not in another which seems to be very similar? Why does one student do better than another in school when both have the same measured intelligence? Why is everyone in one village willing to try a new crop when the next village resists strongly? This variance forms the substance of further study.

Second, a science can only develop if it has clear and unambiguous terms which can be used in the development of theories. Sociologists face considerable difficulty here, because most of their terms have been taken over from ordinary speech and have varying meanings. You will find many definitions of society, institution, group, class, urban, etc. While these some-times mean roughly the same things, they may be based on a particular ideological or methodological orientation and thus differ considerably from one author to another. Much controversy within sociology is over the meaning of terms; this hinders the development of the discipline as a science.

Third, sociologists are necessarily influenced in their work by the values which they hold and the values of the society in which they work. Values enter research in the choice of problem and methods of study, the formation of hypotheses, the collection and analysis of data and the conclusions reached. Certain things are studied, in certain ways, because they are defined as proper items of study and means of approach, because knowledge of them is thought to be important and because it is felt that the findings will be useful either to the researcher, his employers, and/or the society as a whole.

Values can pose a serious problem for the scientist because it is often difficult to separate facts (the end of research) from values (the point of view which guides the research). This is particularly true when the researcher is an outsider; he may unconsciously assume that the people he is studying are not acting rationally because their attitudes and behaviour are different from his own. On the other hand, an outsider may be more able to put aside his assumptions and really look objectively at what is happening than someone who is a full member of the society he is studying and thus shares its biases. But it is always hard (many would say impossible) to study behaviour in a neutral way, without implying that it is either good or bad and without being affected by our relationship with the people we study. We are all biased by our values, and this means that we often ignore what Weber[1] calls 'inconvenient facts'. We tend to find things which confirm our opinions when as scientists we should be looking for contradictions which will prove our theory wrong.

There seem to be two possibilities for overcoming this problem: careful use of scientific methodology and an awareness of these biases and attempt to make values clear when reporting the findings. While the ultimate goal is full and objective knowledge of reality, one must be aware that this will never be reached. When you disagree with an author, consider whether this disagreement is based on facts, values, or both. What are the author's values and what are your own? Try to separate what the author has proved from what he has assumed and what you expect from what you have evidence to prove.

The subject of our scientific study, society, can be defined as a group of people with shared values, beliefs, symbols, patterns of behaviour and

(1) 1946, p.147.

territory. People usually become members of a society by birth, though there are also ways of assimilating outsiders who wish to join. Some authors define societies as politically independent entities (referred to today as nation states), but the word is also used for smaller entities which may have been politically independent in the past but are not so now. Thus, many African countries include several societies which are in the process of being incorporated into a national society; some of these might be independent nations but for the accident of colonial rule.

An individual on his own can be compared to man in society. A person can do many things by himself (eat, breathe, think), but only in rare cases does he live alone, because he is dependent on other people (family and kinsmen, but also neighbours and even people far away) for many things he cannot produce for himself. People usually live in groups and share their resources – they are interdependent – and in this way they constitute a society. Urban life has many examples of this interdependence. Think of the many people who make it possible for you to buy a cotton shirt. There are those who grew the cotton and transported it to the factory; those who made the machines which make cloth out of the cotton or which are used to sew the shirt; workers and managers in the textile and clothing factories; and the person who sells you the shirt. If this cooperation ceased, there would be no shirt to buy.

In order to develop a science of society, sociologists aim at generalising about average or normal behaviour rather than concentrating on individuals. Percentages or more complex statistics are used to summarise the information from large samples or censuses of all the people in a society. People who do not conform to the common patterns provide the ultimate test of whether a theory is correct, but if too much attention is paid to each individual we will never get a clear view of the whole society. In studying society, we include both its structural and functional aspects as well as the factors which cause change. The structure shows the framework at any one point in time, like the scaffolding or plan of a building. For example, the arrows in the two diagrams on page 6 show differing structures (patterns of relationships) in a democratic and an authoritarian society.

The social function is the purpose served by these structural arrangements. The functioning of some part of a society, such as the family or the economy, may aid in the integration of its members around certain values or goals or may lead to serious conflict over resources and rewards. The same structure may serve different functions for people in various positions in the society. For example, a highly selective educational system may help children who have well-educated parents to get ahead or maintain a high status but provide much less opportunity for children whose parents are illiterate (see Chapter 6).

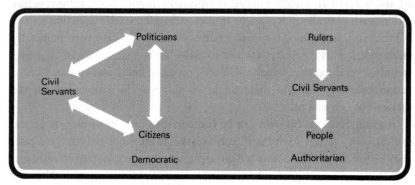

Figure 2 Structured relationships in a democratic and an authoritarian society

Sociologists look at society in a variety of ways; structuralism, functionalism, conflict theory, social interactionism and positivism are among the main approaches. There also tends to be some division between the theorists (who prefer to work at a high level of abstraction which may appear to have little to do with actual people) and the empiricists (who may be so concerned with everyday events that they cannot develop any theories or generalisations at all). However, most sociologists are somewhere in between, trying to combine theory and data to explain the patterns found in the society in which they live. As various theoretical and methodological approaches lead to somewhat different views of social reality, combining perspectives probably leads to the fullest view. For example, functionalists have tended to study the relative stability and integration of a society whereas conflict theorists have sought to explain discord and change. Structuralists mainly look at the macro-level (societies as a whole) whereas social interactionalists focus on the micro-level (the relations between individuals within that whole). For a full understanding of how a society works, all these aspects must be included.

The social sciences[2]

There are many ways of systematically studying society, including sociology, anthropology, ethnology, demography, geography, history, psychology, economics and political science. These differ in method and focus, but it is

(2) Smelser (1967) provides an extended commentary on the perspectives of various social sciences and their relationship to sociology.

sometimes difficult to draw strict boundaries between them. University departments usually specialise in a single discipline, such as history or economics, but people do not live their lives in such neat categories (economic in the morning, political in the afternoon, social in the evening). Rather, behaviour is influenced by many different factors at once. Therefore, the more one knows about all of the social sciences the better one is able to interpret social behaviour. Specialists in one of the social sciences should be aware of the intellectual currents and research findings of the others.

Anthropology, especially social anthropology, is sociology's nearest neighbour among the social sciences. Both are generalised sciences, attempting to look at society as a whole in contrast to the more specialised economics and political science. In the past, there tended to be a division of labour whereby anthropologists studied non-Western societies and sociologists studied industrialised societies. As non-Western societies have industrialised and as societies all over the world have developed many similar features, this distinction no longer applies; it was never very meaningful in Africa because so few trained sociologists were employed there. Anthropologists tend to favour long-term participant observation as a research method and are often more concerned with historical and symbolic variables than sociologists, but most researchers today use a variety of methods in order to get as full a view as possible of the section of society they are studying.

Anthropology in Africa got its start in the reports of missionaries and colonial officers who felt it was important to understand the society in which they worked. Colonial governments later encouraged and sometimes employed professional anthropologists to work in their territories. Though the authorities tended to assume that better knowledge of the peoples under their rule would facilitate their control, anthropologists generally used this opportunity to further much wider academic interests. As supporters of the customary way of life, they sometimes took on a social reformist role; where their findings showed that colonial rules seriously interfered with traditional customs, they sometimes pressed to get the rules changed or at least less rigorously enforced. Today's African sociologists and anthropologists are usually studying their own society rather than working among strangers. We have learned a good deal about ethnocentrism in the last fifty years, so that some of the mistakes of our predecessors are less likely today, but this does not mean that our work will have no errors. Science is ongoing, and each generation must improve on what has gone before by adding to the store of knowledge.

Early anthropologists were often unaware of or ignored social change in the societies they were studying. They concentrated on the lineage system, or witchcraft beliefs, or the traditional political hierarchy without checking on how these had been affected by the presence of a primary school, mission church, or colonial officer in the village. But even historically minded social scientists often find it difficult to trace and measure change because of the absence of earlier studies or periodic statistics. There is a great need for long-term studies and replication of earlier work to assess the changes which have taken place and the effect these have had on the people concerned. It is also important to keep in mind that in a rapidly changing society research is soon out of date. When you read reports, note when the research was done and keep in mind that there are many differences between societies of the 1950s and those of the 1970s because of the effects of independence, urban growth, an expanding educational system, increase in scale and communications, etc. Behavioural patterns reported as common in 1940 may be rare in 1980.

Social anthropology in Africa has been closely tied to ethnology, the descriptive study of peoples and their cultures. Similarly, sociology is related to demography, the quantitative study of population. Demographers use national and sample censuses to provide data on the size, territorial distribution and components of change in population (fertility, natality, migration, changes in status and mortality). Since most African countries are growing at rates of over 2 per cent per year and some cities at rates of over 10 per cent per year, accurate data on population are very important for understanding the nature of the society which is developing. Where the distribution of population becomes a tool for political conflict over the allocation of power and resources, as in Nigeria, the wealth of useful information provided by an accurate national census can be lost and sociologists must collect sample data for their own needs.

The work of geographers of most interest to sociologists is on the spatial factors of population distribution and particularly on migration and the growth of cities. The environment may have an important role in shaping society, as among pastoral peoples. Historians may be concerned only with the description of unique past events, but many look for common patterns found in several societies or in the past of the same society at different periods of time. Sociologists have not been very interested in the past, but they are gradually coming to realise that an understanding of what went before is of considerable help in understanding the present.

Psychologists have generally been more concerned with the instincts and mental processes of individuals – perception, learning, decision-making – than with the way these are shaped by the society of which the individual is a part. However, as the influence of society on these processes has become increasingly apparent, social psychology has grown in importance. Social psychologists study such topics as attitudes, small groups and crowd behaviour, focusing on individual personality and behaviour in particular social situations. The sociologist may study the same topics, though from a somewhat different point of view; he focuses on the individual in society, in his relationships with others, rather than as a unique personality.[3]

The differences between sociology, economics and political science are of domain rather than perspective. The economist concentrates on the economic relations of the society. His work is often highly quantitative, based on government and business statistics, and it may sometimes be questioned whether he has any interest in the people whose transactions are recorded in his data. Political scientists are concerned with power and the people who use it. Thus, they focus on a particular segment of the society and certain types of relationships between people. The boundaries between these fields and sociology are crossed by economic sociologists (studying the economic relations between individuals and organisations, as in employment, and the effect of social conditions on economic behaviour) and political sociologists (examining the social aspects of government and politics, including political attitudes of members of the public and the process of becoming a political leader). Lastly, social administration has the practical concern of applying sociological knowledge to the problems faced by members of a society, especially the disadvantaged.

Many topics studied by social scientists cut across disciplinary boundaries. Each looks at the problem in a somewhat different way; by working together, they can come to a fuller understanding of the subject than would be possible if each worked separately. For example, geographers look at the spatial aspects of migration, demographers at the shifts in population which result, anthropologists at its effect on kinship systems, sociologists at the changing interaction patterns of migrants and their problems of adjusting to their new environment, psychologists at the strains causing and resulting from the move, economists at the way migration affects the national and local economy, and political scientists at the effect of migration in redistributing political power.

Concepts

Concepts are ideas; they are expressed through certain words which are understood to have a particular meaning which defines an underlying reality. Many specific cases are grouped together and a word is used which expresses what representatives of this group or category have in common. All sciences have a vocabulary which combines words invented for their own use and

(3) Worsley 1970, pp.31-5.

other words which are used generally in the society, though the latter may have a special meaning for the scientist.

Sociologists and other social scientists are often accused of using jargon – changing the meaning of words so that outsiders cannot understand what they are talking about. For instance, if you read, 'The nAchievement of the elite is a result of systematic interdependencies and a cosmopolitan-participant culture.' you would heartily wish that the author would settle for plain English. Jargon is sometimes used to make a relatively simple statement sound more important, and an attempt will be made to avoid it in this book. But there are times when specialists must use a special vocabulary in order to communicate accurately with other specialists. As concepts are introduced, definitions will be provided which should help you to understand what you read. You may find it useful to make your own sociological dictionary as you go along, keeping track of varying definitions and eventually working out some of your own. A few basic concepts are introduced here: culture and civilisation, role, value, norm, institution, group and community, function and dysfunction.

Culture and civilisation

The general public often thinks of culture as the aesthetic side of society: art, music, drama and literature. Social scientists include much more, everything passed down by human society except its biology: language and technology, laws and customs, beliefs and moral standards. The child is born into a society and learns its culture in the process of growing up. For each individual, this is a specific culture, the social heritage of a particular society at a given time (Malawian society today, Hausa society in 1900). You can probably think of many ways in which the culture of the society in which you grew up is different from European culture or even from the special variant of culture which you find at university. The sense of time, for instance, provides interesting cultural differences. We are culturally and socially conditioned to divide our days and years into regularised patterns. The use of the sun and an orientation toward the rhythm of days and seasons as contrasted to the use of an accurate watch to precisely regulate the use of time result in the often-remarked differences between 'African time' and 'European time'. Even though watches are now available, punctuality has not yet acquired a cultural value for many Africans. The ethnic categorising we occasionally engage in (insofar as it is based on evidence) often relates to cultural rather than physical differences; this people are thought to be hardworking or willing to take risks; that people tend to be unfriendly or poor scholars.

There is sometimes considerable cultural diversity within a society. If boundaries can be drawn around certain groups, we may refer to them as subcultures – sets of beliefs, norms and customs supported by values, interpersonal networks and participation in common institutions which exist within a larger social system. Thus, students may feel that their elders do not understand them and express their need to set themselves apart by wearing certain hair or clothing styles and behaving in unconventional ways. Insofar as there is a national culture, there may be minority subcultures in which groups in a particular area continue to use their own language and follow other local customs even though most of their culture is similar to that of their fellow citizens. Most Tanzanians speak Swahili in addition to their local language; they share adherence to the national government and a common educational system; but there are subcultural differences between peoples who are mainly pastoral and those who are settled agriculturalists or town dwellers, between people who are Christian or Muslim and those who follow traditional religions, and so on. Some African nations, such as Somalia, are much more unified culturally than others, such as Nigeria. In the latter, it might be said that there are a number of cultures as well as subcultures and that a national culture is only gradually developing.

Some aspects of culture change much more rapidly than others (preferences in popular music as versus food preferences), but most aspects of culture shift gradually over the course of time. New words are introduced into the language and others are no longer used; new beliefs are accepted; people come to expect a greater say in running their own affairs; more members of the society are employed for wages rather than farming for themselves; increased income means that people can afford better housing and more material goods such as watches and radios; and so on. It is common to think of such changes as 'progress' or 'development', but this is a value judgment which those who prefer the old ways would deny.

All people have a tendency to think of their own culture as best. This is known as ethnocentrism (centring attention on one's own ethnic group). We tend to assume that the way we have learned to do things is the proper way and that other people are either ignorant or deliberately doing things wrong because they have no respect. This can cause difficulty when people of differing cultures meet, because each tends to look down on the others as inferior. There is a useful saying, 'When in Rome, do as the Romans do', but this may be of little help if one is living in a city where many different cultures or subcultures are represented. At least, one can try to be aware of what sort of behaviour various people expect and to avoid misunderstanding. Ability to use a common language can be a great help, since if people can communicate they can at least discuss their differences.

Language is especially important to culture because it allows human beings to express their symbols and meanings in a way which can be understood by others. Language must be learned; a child growing up with animals would have no language just as it would have no other culture. Language is the main means for passing on the cultural heritage; it allows the development of abstract principles in science and morality which would be impossible without it. Language use poses problems in many African countries, whose efforts to build a unified society are hindered because people find it difficult to communicate with each other. But language is such a fundamental aspect of local culture that no group wants to give up its language, even for one which is more widely used.

Civilisation was originally identified with the city, because the growth of cities ushered in improvements in man's standard of living which raised him from the 'primitive' subsistence state. The word comes from *civis*, the Latin word for citizen, which can be contrasted with the *pagani*, residents of country districts. In most parts of the world today, the city man still considers himself more 'civilised' than the 'bush man' on his farm. In French colonial territories, some people acquired the status of *civilisé*, which meant that they were French citizens under French law and therefore no longer subject to traditional law. A notable component of identification as 'civilised' in many English-speaking African countries is education. This idea is well developed in Liberia,[4] where being civilised implies not only formal education but also a good income which can be spent on Western dress, housing and other aspects of material culture. Although no one ever refers to himself as uncivilised, the use of 'civilised' to indicate a more prestigious cultural variant is fairly widespread (see Chapter 4).

Role

A society can be seen as a system of roles, each of which involves relationships between people, patterns of behaviour, rights and duties associated with a particular position.[5] Everyone has many roles. For example, you are a son or daughter, a student, a friend, a citizen. You also have other kinship, economic, political, religious and recreational roles. In each of these, certain relationships are established based on continued, reciprocal activities and expectations about future behaviour. The role of eldest son, for example, involves obedience and respect given to parents and older kinsmen and dominance over younger ones. Parents and kinsmen, in turn, behave in certain established ways towards an eldest son. In addition to every day

(4) Fraenkel 1964, pp.67–8.   (5) Southall 1959; Banton 1965.

behaviour, there are also rights and duties for specific occasions, such as the funeral of one's father.

The social structure of a society includes all of its roles and social organisations (established role clusters serving a particular purpose, such as bureaucracies). An individual's behaviour in society is structured by the roles which he fills and the organisations he belongs to. In the process of learning and carrying out his roles, he is subject to sanctions; he is rewarded for successful role performance and punished for deviation from what society expects of him. This is most evident in childhood socialisation (see Chapter 3), but continues throughout life.[6]

Role relationships may be specific or diffuse, broad or narrow, generic or proper; they also differ from one culture to another.[7] A relationship is specific if the rights and duties arc fully defined; it is diffuse if the activities involved are not well defined, as in friendship. Broad relationships are unspecialised, as when kinship, economic and religious/moral activities are included in the father/son role relationship. A relationship which is restricted to one area, such as the economic, is classed as narrow. Proper relationships are between named persons: trader Yosefu and his customer Comfort; generic roles belong to the post rather than to the individual holding it: president of the town improvement society, worker at Pioneer Mills. Whereas proper relationships depend on the personalities of those filling the roles and disappear when this particular relationship breaks down (i.e., if one of the parties leaves town), generic relationships are based on the content of the role independent of the occupant at any given time and continue from one individual to another. Lastly, because role relationships are based on cultural expectations, they differ from one culture to another and over time. The role of employee is more specific and narrower in England than in a small African factory. How would you characterise the differences between the role of kinsman in rural and urban areas?

All the relationships involved in a particular role can be summarised as the role-set. For example, the role of student involves relations with fellow students, lecturers, administration and hall personnel. These are the student's role-set. Some people share more than one role-set. If two brothers are also fellow students, their relationship will be broadened by the fact that they have both of these ties rather than just one.

Role conflict and role strain may arise if a person cannot meet all the demands of his various roles. For instance, many educated married women in West Africa face a conflict of roles. They are expected to hold a full-time job as well as caring for a household and several children. A woman may want to

(6) Smelser 1967, p.9.　(7) Southall 1959, pp.24–5.

13

give time to training her children (as is expected of the mother role), but she also feels that it is important to make a significant contribution to household expenses (as is expected of the wife role). She has considerable difficulty living up to both expectations without some help from her husband, whose idea of the husband/father roles often does not include being useful around the house.

In addition to conflict between roles which are wholly or partly incompatible, there may be psychological strain in carrying out a single role satisfactorily because various members of the role-set make conflicting demands. A worker promoted to supervisor is often under considerable role strain. His employers expect him to make the men under him work hard, but these were formerly his colleagues and expect him to be lenient with them. Somehow, he must maintain discipline and get the work done while at the same time keeping a good relationship so that the workers willingly obey his orders.

Merton[8] has pointed out various ways in which strains in the role-set can be handled:

1 Some members of the role-set are more important than others, and a person can pay more attention to these. The politician concentrates on community influentials, assuming that if he wins these over they will encourage others in the community to vote for him.

2 Interaction between members of a role-set is not continuous. Children can often do things they should not because their parents are not watching them. If everyone knew all about the behaviour of everyone else, pressure to fulfil the details of all one's roles would make social life impossible. Nevertheless, some accountability and observability is important if the values of the society are to be upheld. Secret policemen and others who are never observed are under no pressure to fulfil their roles in a socially approved manner.

3 Members of the role-set differ in power and the individual can assess how interested the more powerful members of his role-set are in his behaviour. If they are not very interested, they may safely be ignored. If an elder brother is actively demanding service, he may be obeyed even though this means delaying a task assigned by an absent parent. In the same way, the demands of a less important role can sometimes be neglected in the interests of a more important role. A man will take some days off from work (without permission if necessary) in order to attend the funeral of a parent.

4 If the members of the role-set can be made to see that their demands are conflicting, relief can often be obtained. The individual may be able to withdraw until members of his role-set have solved their conflict, as when a

(8) 1957, pp.371–9. Magid 1976 shows how Idoma local councillors handle role conflict.

villager says he will support whichever political leader can prove he is the most powerful.

5. People get social support from others of the same status who face similar problems with their role sets. This leads to the formation of organisations such as trade unions and professional associations, whose rules state clearly what behaviour is expected in particular roles ('conditions of work').

6. It may be necessary to break off role relationships if the conflict cannot be solved in any other way. The individual may be able to cut off some members of his role-set (as when a student avoids or ignores certain of his fellow students), but often he must move to a new site (a worker quits his job or a tenant finds a room in a different house).

Roles may be either ascribed or achieved. Ascribed roles are acquired without any activity on the individual's part, often at birth: sex, age, kinship, ethnicity. Achieved roles are open to effort and competition and must be won: educational qualifications, promotion. In small-scale societies, most roles are ascribed and relatively few roles are held by a large proportion of the members of the society. Most of the men, for instance, will be fathers and farmers or hunters, and will also have religious and political roles. The more technically and socially complex the society, the more roles are available and the more people are dependent on others in a complicated division of labour. These positions are largely achieved. Some interesting questions which might be asked about roles are: Who has access to leadership roles in this society? Why are roles more open to achievement in some societies than others? Why is it impossible to combine some roles and how does this prohibition differ in various societies?

Value, norm and institution

Kluckhohn[9] defines a value as 'a conception, explicit or implicit, distinctive of an individual or characteristic of a group, of the desirable, which influences the selection from available modes, means and ends of action.' The problems which arise from the sociologist's values have already been mentioned. But values are an important component of behaviour and must be studied if one is to understand the behaviour of people in society. Values are usually inferred from observed behaviour. If a man regularly associates with certain people, we assume that he values this relationship. If he regularly ignores or avoids others, we assume that he does not value their company. However, there is also a tendency to try to use values to explain behaviour. In the case just give, this would mean saying that the values cause the association or

(9) 1951, p.395.

non-association. This becomes a circular argument, because we are saying that what we observe is caused by something we have only guessed was present because of the observed behaviour. It is probably more correct to treat values as either a dependent variable (the values a person has are the result of his experiences and the society in which he lives) or an intervening variable (given certain causes or pressures, the result will vary according to the person's values) rather than as an independent variable (values directly cause people to act in certain ways). It is often difficult to distinguish causes and effects, since the result of one man's behaviour may cause another man to act. Nevertheless, given the difficulty of obtaining direct evidence on values, it seems reasonable to treat them as part of the equation but to be wary of seeing them as a cause. The value 'education is a good thing' is used as an intervening variable in Figure 1.

Norms are the standards which should govern behaviour in roles; they are the societal expectations of what is 'normal'. Sometimes they have been formalised as law, but most are less formal. Universities often hand out sheets of regulations to new students, but there are also unwritten norms for the student role which are ignored only at the risk of losing one's place or becoming unpopular with one's colleagues. However, many people do not follow the norms exactly in their daily lives because it is impossible or inconvenient to do so. Therefore, when studying a society it is necessary to distinguish between norms and behaviour; people tend to cite the norm unless questioned about what they actually do. A study of inheritance in a Ghanaian village found that the norm was very seldom followed completely, though everyone could say what should be done.

Sumner, an early sociologist, divided norms into folkways, mores and laws or stateways. Folkways are customary practices which are considered appropriate behaviour but are not rigidly enforced. If someone uses bad grammar or builds his house in a somewhat different shape from the others, he may be considered eccentric or an individualist, but people will not be particularly bothered by his behaviour. Mores are subject to stronger sanctions because they are considered much more important to the welfare of the society. Many are negative statements, such as rules which forbid murder and theft, but some are expressed both positively and negatively. Wives must be faithful to their husbands and not commit adultery. The mores mentioned so far are held by most societies, but some clans and families have taboos of their own; they may not eat certain animals, go fishing on a certain day, etc.

Some small-scale societies, such as the Bushmen of southern Africa, have only folkways and mores with which to exercise social control over their members. Most societies also have laws. A law may be customary or enacted.

When the chiefs or elders held court to deal with disputes over land or wives, they were enforcing customary law, based on tradition and public opinion about norms. Large-scale societies usually cannot rely on customary law because many people with differing norms live together; written rules are needed to deal quickly with a changing situation and to make clear to everyone what is expected of them. Thus, the political system gradually develops enacted law (the stateways). The mores may be embodied in an unwritten or a written constitution or a body of 'common law', but laws are also made about taxes, business behaviour, welfare rights, etc. The truth of Sumner's statement that people will not obey the stateways if they conflict with the folkways can be seen in the difficulty colonial governments had enforcing their laws when these went against local custom and in the trouble independent governments have rooting out corruption and smuggling.

An institution may be defined as an enduring complex of norms, roles, values and sanctions embracing a distinct segment of human life. When certain patterns of behaviour have become a well established part of the social structure, we say they are institutionalised.[10] For example, the formal educational system inherited from Europe has been institutionalised in patterns of roles (student, teacher), organisations (school, university), values (academic freedom), norms (standards of performance, rules against cheating) and sanctions (certificates). Various institutions of the society can be examined in order to compare societies and to look at interrelationships between institutions within one society. Family and kinship institutions are basic to social relations, as they give every member of the society a place at birth and are essential for the continuance of the society. Stratification differentiates members of the society in their relations with others, providing positions of superiority and inferiority. The institutions of property and exchange provide methods of access to and protection of material goods. Religious institutions involve the ultimate values of the society. Stratification, family, educational and religious institutions are discussed in Chapters 4 to 7.

The word institution is sometimes used when organisation or association would be better, for a specific group of individuals pursuing a common goal: Parliament, the Catholic Church, a university. These provide a focus for research on the political, religious and educational institutions of the society in which they are found. For example, we may study the effect of kinship and stratification institutions on the selection of students for the university, or the effect of participation in the university community on placement in the stratification system after graduation.

(10) Smelser 1967, p.9.

The study of social groups is fundamental to sociology because patterns of interpersonal behaviour are often structured by membership in one or more groups. The word group is given a variety of meanings in ordinary English. It may refer to a categoric group, any set of people which the speaker wants to treat as a unity. This can be an aggregate, people who share some attribute (such as football fans or readers of this book) or people who have the same social role, such as doctors, criminals, or people of the same ethnicity who may not even know each other. On the other hand, it is also used for corporate groups, people who interact over a period of time and who have some form of organisation (which establishes a division of labour and sets them apart from non-members), a sense of solidarity and common values, norms and goals which enable them to undertake joint action.

It is not always easy to decide which of these meanings is intended, as members of an aggregate or category may join together to form a corporate group – church members may organise a bible study group, and doctors usually belong to a medical association. Members of an ethnic group probably have some sense of solidarity and share many norms and values, but they may or may not form an ethnic association and, if they do, some people who belong to the category may not join this association. Social groups may be based on informal ties, as in a children's play group or a group of elderly men who meet regularly to gossip, or they may be more formal, as in a savings society or a master with his apprentices. The degree of formality will affect the way the group functions and the feelings the members have about each other and about the group.

Homans[11] has been particularly concerned with what he calls the human group. He sees the group as a social system operating in a particular environment. The group has activities (the behaviour of members), interaction (the reaction of one member to the behaviour of another which has meaning in terms of this action or past or future action) and sentiment (the internal state of the actor, which can be inferred from his expression, tone of voice, etc.). The group must solve certain problems within itself and other problems of its relations with its environment. Various theories about group behaviour, such as social differentiation and control, social conflict and integration, can be tested by careful study of different types of groups – a family, workmates in a factory, a peer group of schoolboys, residents of a village. Sometimes these studies cover only a short period of time; others follow changes in the group over months or years.

Study of the relations between individuals within the group provides

(11) 1950.

information on factors affecting role performance and the way power, authority and influence are exercised. We may also analyse relations between groups (as in competition for prestige and power between ethnic associations), the role of social groups in forcing institutional change (pressure from farmers' groups to make local or national government more responsive to their needs) or change in personal behaviour (peer group pressure to conform to group norms), or the way various social groups together form the building blocks (the social structure) of the society. Some of these are discussed in Chapter 2.

The word community usually implies some idea of locale, frequent social interaction and close ties between members of a group. These ties may be based on kinship, common occupation, the experience of living together, etc., so long as they are sufficiently important to provide the members of the community with common interests and goals. Some uses of community omit locale and argue that community interests ignore distance (a community of scientists, who might live all over the world). But residence in the same area is important in providing opportunities for interaction and working together for common goals; even though technology helps overcome distance, it seems more useful to keep the idea of common residence and use some other word for close-knit groups which lack this.

Wolpe[12] distinguishes the communal group as having three characteristics: a common identity and culture; male and female representatives of all age groups; and differentiation by power, status and wealth. They are a subsociety in that they represent a full demographic and socioeconomic segment of the wider society, with various subgroups and institutions to cater for their members' needs at any stage of life. Members have a sense of identity which allows them to contend with other groups for political and economic power. This identity may be based on race, religion, language, ethnicity, geographic area of origin, or common experience. Some strangers settling in a town, for example, living together in a slum, housing estate, *zongo* or *sabon gari*, develop a communal identity which is based on the need to defend their interests against the government or other sectors of the urban population. The stranger community often shares a common religion and *lingua franca*; other cultural similarities develop as they live together.[13] Other migrants never develop this new identity, but maintain a communal identity with the people of their home town.

Individuals do not necessarily belong to only one community, though one is probably more important than the others and in some aspects of life other identities may be more important than communal ones. Schildkrout shows

(12) 1974, p.6. (13) Schildkrout 1970; Bujra 1973.

that on some issues members of the *zongo* were united whereas in others they divided according to nationality, ethnicity or superethnicity, occupation, wealth, etc. Similarly, Wolpe found that in Port Harcourt communal groups based on religion displaced ethnic communalism on educational but not on political issues and that trade union groups which showed considerable strength on economic issues were ignored at election time. Communal conflict over power and status will be discussed in Chapter 4.

Function and dysfunction

Sociologists are concerned with how a society works as a whole and with how each of the parts fits together. They thus study the functions of norms, roles and institutions. It is easy to assume that any patterns one finds are functional (they help society to reach its goals), but one frequently finds patterns which give rise to conflict and seem to work contrary to what the participants intend. The concepts of manifest and latent function and of dysfunction have been used to explain this. While there are difficulties in assessing all of the functions of any particular activity, the functional approach does encourage us to look for real effects rather than accepting popular beliefs about why things are done.

Merton[14] suggested that many activities have both manifest and latent functions. Everyone recognises the purpose of certain activities, but there may also be consequences which are not intended or even known to the participants. For instance, the manifest function of a funeral is to bury the dead. The latent functions may be to affirm family ties, resolve quarrels, provide recreation for the village, etc. While manifest functions are usually seen positively (things are done for the good that is expected to result, at least for the doer), latent functions may be negative, preventing the achievement of goals. For example, a latent function of the distribution of an inheritance may be the beginning of a family quarrel which lasts for generations. The participants may be aware of the latent functions of their actions, or they may be unaware of the links between what they do and the long-term consequences.

Activities which are detrimental to the system are termed dysfunctions. A problem may arise for the observer in that behaviour which is functional in certain circumstances may be dysfunctional in other circumstances and behaviour which is functional for certain goals or individuals may be dysfunctional for other goals or individuals. For instance, a boy may be taught in school that standing in line and waiting his turn is good behaviour and pushing to get to the front is bad behaviour. This is functional for the school,

(14) 1957, p.51.

since it makes it easy to organise the pupils and control their movement. But such behaviour is dysfunctional if one wants to get on a city bus during the rush hour, since unless one pushes the goal cannot be achieved. Thus, a boy who learned his lesson well might always be late for school in the morning.

One way of studying change in a society is to look for signs of functional differentiation. Over time, institutions and patterns of behaviour (especially in the division of labour) tend to become more complex so that activities carried out by one individual or organisation are divided and each section is carried out by separate people or organisations. For example, the function of educating young people for their place in society was formerly carried out by the family. While the family still performs an important part of this function, there are now schools to teach literacy (among other things) and the government also sends out officers (members of the civil service and/or a political party) to teach people their role as citizens; the radio and newspapers also have educational functions. Thus, education is now much more differentiated than in the past.

The comparative method

Social science aims to generalise about human behaviour in all societies. Therefore, it is not enough to look at patterns in one place; only by comparing social behaviour in various societies can one find out which basic forms apply everywhere and which are culture-specific. Some of the first sociologists felt that studying behaviour patterns of earlier societies (which they assumed were simpler than their own) would give them an insight into the society of their own day. Their comparative studies were hindered by the lack of information, especially on non-European societies. As a result, they often had to speculate from very fragmentary evidence and were often wrong. Later sociologists reacted against this by concentrating on careful studies of their own societies. There has been a renewed interest in cross-cultural studies in recent years, because improved communications and the expansion of knowledge have vastly increased the possibility of fruitful work.

Durkheim[15] suggested that three types of comparisons can be made:
1 variations in a single society (permanency of migrants in Lusaka, Ndola and Livingstone);
2 contemporary societies which are basically similar but differ in certain respects (Senegal and the Gambia in 1977) or the same society at different times (Zaria in 1850 and 1900);

(15) 1938, p.136–40.

3 societies which differ considerably but have some common feature (industrial workers in Uganda and Brazil or the same society before and after a radical change (villages in northern Liberia before and after the opening of the iron mines). The first is often not considered really comparative; most comparative studies fall into the second category.

Generally, then, comparative sociology involves studying at least two different societies. In practice, the comparison has often been implicit rather than explicit. The researcher reports his findings on a lesser-known society, leaving the reader to make the comparison with his own and explain the differences; or findings from one society are shown next to data from another society, but the comparison is never really made. As data are often collected in slightly different form, it may be impossible to make a real comparison. (In one study, students are asked, 'What job do you think you will get if you leave school after completing your School Certificate?' In another they are asked, 'What job do you think you will get when you leave school?' and in a third, 'What job would you like to get when you leave school?' How will these results differ?)

Comparative sociology of types two or three is more difficult than working within a single society. Since the culture and environment have considerable influence on behaviour, researchers who try to explain behaviour without understanding the local context do so at their peril. It is both difficult and time-consuming to get a real comprehension of another culture, and the more different the second is the harder it is to do this. African students in Europe or America often feel that it takes several years to get beneath the surface. Trained social scientists may accomplish the task somewhat more quickly, but many do not appreciate the necessity of it or lack the time, and the quality of their analysis suffers. Present-day research tends to be based on the collaboration of a research team, with each collecting the same information in a different society. Nevertheless, collaborative analysis of the data is still rare.

There is often little thought about how close two societies really are, or realisation by non-Africans studying African societies of the wide differences within this category in comparison to the broad similarity of culture and behaviour in European societies. It is far too easy to choose one country in Europe, Latin America, Africa and Asia and assume that the findings can be generalised to the whole world. Reports on the attitudes and behaviour of Nigerians based on interviews in Lagos or Ibadan are sometimes written by people with little understanding of the society and culture of even this part of Nigeria. However, ethnocentricity is by no means limited to Europeans; Africans also often assume that their own experience is characteristic of everyone in their own society and sometimes even of all Africans. One function of a sociology course is to make students more aware of the variety within and between societies so that they develop a habit of comparison.

There have been several approaches to comparative research, including a search for evolutionary lines of development, for the means of social integration and for basic models of behaviour. Comparative studies are often seen implicitly or explicitly as an experiment in which most variables are held constant and only one is manipulated. For example, Weber was interested in the role of values in the development of capitalism. He examined the nature of society in countries which had accepted capitalism quickly and those which had been slower to adopt it, and developed a theory that certain religious values facilitated the change to a capitalist form of organisation (see Chapter 2). Some comparative studies have been based largely on speculation; others have involved elaborate field work or the use of data collected by others. None of these approaches has been completely satisfactory, but the work now being carried on has often been strongly influenced by them.[16]

The early evolutionists generally assumed unilinear evolution – that a direct line could be traced from 'primitive' societies of the past to the 'modern' societies of their day. They often based their conclusions on contemporary less-developed societies, such as the Australian aborigines. These societies were assumed to be very simple (the more we know of a society the more we can appreciate its complexity) and older than European society.[17] We now realise that all societies functioning today are of approximately the same age, though some may have changed more over time than others. The evolutionists did not have the evidence on the earliest men which is available today. They generally worked from the argument to the evidence, looking for ethnographic examples which were useful for proving their points rather than trying to study a society as a whole in relation to other societies.

Radcliffe-Brown was particularly interested in the social integration of society (i.e. what holds the society together). He was very influential in interesting British social anthropologists in collecting full ethnographic descriptions of societies and comparing aspects of social relations in neighbouring societies. However, the classifications developed from these comparisons have not been very useful for understanding the social structure of other societies. Early field-workers were often unaware that the societies they studied were by no means stable over time or that their informants tended to tell them about ideal rather than actual behaviour. A comparative method which ignores social change and the way the social system works in daily life has serious limitations. The emphasis on integration meant that many of the dysfunctions of the society, the factors leading to conflict, were ignored.

(16) Marsh 1967, pp.21–30.   (17) See Bohannan 1969, p.319.

In addition, most of Radcliffe-Brown's students worked in one society rather than several and their different approaches made true comparisons impossible.

Murdock is a herald of the computer age. With colleagues and students, he developed the Human Relations Area Files (HRAF) in an attempt to bring together all the ethnographic information ever produced so that scholars could test their theories on as large a sample as possible. There are several difficulties with this approach. Although data on some 4 000 societies have been included, there is far more information on some than on others and the data are of varying quality. Some are the product of careful research by trained anthropologists; others are casual reports of travellers. The data available to test a particular hypothesis may come from only a few, unrepresentative societies. Since even professionals collecting data often had quite different interests from later researchers, the lack of information on a specific topic does not mean that the phenomenon was absent from the soeiety and the way the data are recorded may not be comparable with data on a similar phenomenon in another society. Thus, the HRAF provide a good starting point for developing theories, but these need thorough testing in the field to prove their validity.

A great deal has been written about structural anthropology; there is room for only a brief mention of it here. Radcliffe-Brown's idea of structure was 'a network of actually existing relations.[18] The French structuralists, on the other hand, have generally thought of the whole as something more than the sum of the parts; a society as a collectivity is an entity beyond the contribution of each individual member.'[19] Levi-Strauss has been the leader of this new school, which seeks to get behind what can be seen empirically to the unconscious models on which men base their behaviour. They use the comparative method to find the common structural elements, especially of thought, which their theory predicts. However, their use of data is necessarily selective and their explanations of symbolism, based on theoretical models and intuition, are almost impossible to prove or disprove empirically. Thus, it is difficult to decide between the views of various structuralists or to assess their place in comparative studies.

Newer evolutionists have moved from the early consideration of unilinear evolution to studies by anthropologists such as White and Steward of the various stages passed through by historical societies and attempts by sociologists such as Parsons, Eisenstadt and their followers to trace the increasing functional differentiation of systems and subsystems over time (see Chapter 10). They are interested in the adaptations made by societies and institutions in response to socio-cultural change – for example, how some of

(18) 1952, p.190.   (19) See Ekeh 1974, pp.7–8.

24

the functions of the family are taken over by formal educational and religious institutions. With the increasing amount of information available about both historical and modern societies, these theories can be tested, but they have often seemed more satisfactory at a high level of abstraction than when attempts are made to apply them comparatively to specific societies.

Conclusion

One scientific discipline can be distinguished from another by identifying the problems which it investigates and the dependent and independent variables which it uses. What are the phenomena which it seeks to explain and what conditions or factors does it examine as possible causes of these phenomena? Sociology seeks to explain and predict variations in patterns of interpersonal behaviour. The dependent variables fall within the realm of social structure; interaction is organised in role relationships and controlled by values, norms and sanctions. Independent and intervening variables come from many sources, but attention is focused on the culture and social conditions of the society. Tracing the patterns must be the result of careful collection of data to test and, if possible, disprove hypotheses. The emphasis is on the society rather than on the individual; though data are usually collected from individuals, the sociologist studies people as part of society rather than as isolated and unique beings.[20]

There are many approaches to sociology. Those favouring different perspectives stress particular variables and methods for collecting and analysing data. No one text can attempt to cover all this material, even in relation to a single society. This book, therefore, concentrates on introducing the student to those aspects of the discipline which seem most important for analysing African societies in the post-independence period.

Chapter 2 focuses on social organisation, the structured relations between people and groups which together make up the social structure of the society. Chapter 3 shows how an individual's behaviour is shaped by the society of which he is a part. Chapter 4 is concerned with various aspects of social differentiation, the ways in which one group of people is set apart from another and the implications of this for the society as a whole. Chapters 5 to 7 discuss other institutions: family, education and religion. Two other institutions, the economy and the polity, are not dealt with separately. This is not because they are unimportant, but because they affect so many aspects of social life that it is more convenient to refer to them throughout the text.

(20) Smelser 1967, pp.4–13.

Social differentiation, for example, has many political and economic implications.

Chapter 8 is centred on the cities because so much of the social change taking place in Africa starts there. The majority of the population of most African countries lives in rural areas, but many rural families hear about the cities from kinsmen who live there; as central and regional governments are established in the towns, all of the people are affected by decisions made by urbanites. Chapter 9 ventures into applied sociology to examine problems of unemployment, housing and social control. Poverty as a social problem is reflected in all three. Chapter 10 examines the application of theories of social change and modernisation to African societies. The goal here is a better understanding of the factors involved in the acceptance and rejection of change.

Suggested reading and discussion topics
1. How would you explain to your grandmother what sociology is? How does it differ from a 'common sense' understanding of society gained by living for a long time?
2. Read some of the descriptions of social life in one of the following books, watching the way the author uses concepts such as group, institution, culture, society, role, norm and value. To what extent are these studies comparative? Gibbs (1965); Mair (1974); Middleton (1970); Ottenberg (1960); Skinner (1973) (see Bibliography).

2 Social Organisation

The social structure or organisation of a society may be seen as a network of roles involving interaction between individuals and groups which together give the society both its unique qualities and the characteristics which it shares with other societies. It includes the processes by which influence, authority and power are exerted, the interdependence of individuals and groups through segregation or integration, and the broad patterns through which social order is maintained and social solidarity promoted. This chapter will introduce several topics at a general level which will be examined in more detail in later chapters: macrosociological ways of looking at societies as a whole, the microsociological study of primary groups, patterns of leadership and authority and theories on the nature of social order.

Types of societies

Various theories have been developed to explain the differences between 'simple' and 'complex' societies. The implication of most of these theories has been evolutionary; the authors have assumed that all societies started as simple, small-scale collectivities and became increasingly complex as they developed into the society the author was most familiar with. While this change must obviously have been gradual, theorists preferred to think of a dichotomy, with all societies falling at one or the other of two extremes, because this allowed them to concentrate on the analysis of major differences. In order to make these differences clear, they developed ideal types, mental constructs which exaggerate certain traits observed in reality.[1] Ideal types allow the theorist to define precisely the concept he wishes to examine and then compare real life situations to it. It is not expected that reality will exactly reproduce the ideal type, but it provides a framework against which to explain what is found. Six dichotomous types of society have much in common:

(1) Timasheff 1955, p.177.

27

Toennies:	*gemeinschaft – gesellschaft* (community and society)
MacIver:	community – association
Redfield:	folk – urban
Maine:	status – contract
Becker:	sacred – secular
Durkheim:	mechanical solidarity – organic solidarity

Gemeinschaft, or a sense of community, is found in families, villages, neighbourhoods and friendship groups. People feel a sense of 'we' which gives the group solidarity. Each member is aware of and recognised for his role in the community and the group takes responsibility for members in need. Redfield found these characteristics in the small, non-literate, homogeneous Mexican village he studied and argued that folk culture is based on tradition, which cannot be criticised. As an ideal type, folk society stresses informal status, personal relations, emotion, religion and the family and lacks markets, money and systematic knowledge.[2]

Gesellschaft, at the other extreme, is seen as typical of the city or state, a large-scale society where people associate without knowing each other well. They are detached from their primary ties; behaviour patterns must be based on formal rules rather than accepted folkways. Maine, as a legal theorist, expressed this by saying that people exchanged status or position in a community for contractual relations (a more formal legal system); Becker pointed out that society becomes secularised as people emphasise rationality rather than a religious basis for their values and behaviour. These typologies have been strongly criticised, especially in recent years, by those who find close personal ties in cities and rationality, specialisation and impersonal relations in relatively isolated villages. Nevertheless, they continue to be used in refined form (see Chapter 8).

Durkheim's idea of mechanical and organic solidarity is in many ways similar to the others, but it develops a new aspect of the comparison. Just as every bicycle is much like every other bicycle, so a society based on mechanical solidarity consists of individuals making similar contributions. There tends to be a minimal division of labour and, more important, there is a shared collective conscience (a sense of belonging to a group more important than any individual) which strongly upholds common norms, values and institutions. It might seem that a simple society would be more 'organic' and a complex society more 'mechanical', but in this case Durkheim is using 'organic' to emphasise the interrelationships of members, with each role contributing towards the whole just as the arms, legs and eyes of the body contribute to the life of the organism. This organic solidarity is the result of

(2) The urban side of this dichotomy was of much less interest to Redfield, and was seen mainly as the opposite of a folk society. Redfield 1947.

increased interdependence (usually because of an increased division of labour in the society). This allows more scope for diversity of norms and behaviour and thus for individual liberty. This means that the relations between people must change. Whereas with mechanical solidarity social order is maintained through the collective conscience, organic solidarity means that more formal contracts and laws are needed.

A more recent formulation of these differences has been made by Parsons.[3] His theory holds that roles are defined in certain ways, which he calls pattern variables:

particularism – universalism
affectivity – affective neutrality
diffuseness – specificity
ascription – achievement (or quality – performance)
community orientation – self-orientation

Any given role may have these qualities in varying proportions, but the society characterised above as *gemeinschaft*, folk and community tends (as an ideal type) to have role patterns which are particularistic, ascriptive, diffuse, affective and more concerned with the community than with the individual. The same role can be performed in various ways because members of different societies have different expectations. For example, in a society emphasising *gesellschaft*, organic solidarity and secularism, the civil servant should have a carefully limited role (specificity) in which he treats everyone according to the same standard (universalism); be hired for his qualifications (achievement) and his feelings about the person or task should make no difference (affective neutrality) and many will be more concerned with their own needs than those of the community (self-orientation). In a society near the opposite extreme, a civil servant might be hired because he is related to an important official (ascription) and might see his role as providing a wide variety of services (diffuseness) to people who are important to him as individuals (particularism); the quality of his service will depend on whether he likes the person or the task he is asked to perform (affectivity) and its value to the community with which he identifies (community orientation).

Role performance often combines elements of both these extremes. Various roles in a society, or the values of the society as a whole, may be examined to see how they fit into this typology. Certain roles tend to one pattern regardless of the society in which they are performed (parenthood is diffuse and affective); others vary considerably between individuals and between societies. All societies have a mixture of roles and value orientations, but it is still possible to discern which end of the continuum is most valued

(3) 1951.

(and most often practised, not necessarily the same thing).

Much of the discussion of modernisation, so popular in recent years, is in terms of changing the organisation of society from one ideal type to the other. There is often the implication that both extremes exist, and even those who strongly criticise the theory find it tempting to talk in terms of ideal types because they are a shorthand way of referring to a meaningful complex. For example, there is often a longing for the 'good old days' when everyone knew everyone else and individuals in need were sure of support from the rest of the community. There is an implicit assumption here that the past as a trouble-free ideal type actually existed, and a value judgment that it was better than anything that 'progress' as an ideal type can bring. In real life, there are advantages and disadvantages on both sides.

The sociological task is to examine the implications of the ideal type for social life and to study real societies to see how these variables actually fit together. As a society approaches the 'modern', *gemeinschaft*, secular type, how does this affect people living in it? The model implies a loss of a sense of role and importance; what is one person among thousands of workers in a mine or factory? There is increased freedom for individuals to rise (ascriptive status as a slave or member of a low caste family is no longer important), but also freedom to fall without the security of family and community support. The constraints and clear norms of the collective conscience are exchanged for personal responsibility, with its advantages and disadvantages. Often certain sectors of the society benefit more from changes than others; they see as gain what others see as loss. For example, young people may welcome independence from community control whereas the elderly miss the respect and support which were formerly due to them. Communities seek to foster particularism as a means of holding the group together while the nation emphasises universalism in order to decrease nepotism and draw the allegiance of citizens to itself. Social planners need to be aware of the complex effects of any change they may introduce.

Primary groups

The overall patterns of society considered above can also be seen at a micro-level by using Cooley's distinction between primary and secondary groups. Cooley saw primary groups as having three characteristics: members associate with each other directly and continually; they have a 'we-feeling' of belonging to the group, setting boundaries between themselves and outsiders; and they have a 'common spirit' which is concerned for the good of the group. The chief example is the family, but a set of 'tight friends', residents of a small village, or a sports team might also form a primary group.

It has been suggested that the characteristics given for a primary group are necessary but not sufficient, since they can be found in groups which are not primary or in categories which are not really groups. For instance, one may interact regularly and closely with workmates without developing any sense of belonging to a primary group. Also, members of a family may not see each other face-to-face very often because one or more members has migrated, but this does not affect their feeling of belonging together. Every social (corporate) group has some sense of 'we-feeling', though most are secondary rather than primary because they are based on formal relationships and members lack a strong attachment to the group itself. Men seeking employment, for example, think of themselves as 'we' and the labour officers as 'they', but if a man finds a job he loses interest in the unemployment queue. Primary groups are essentially small, so that all the members know each other well. There is an emotional attachment and sense that the group is more important than the individual members which it is difficult to develop in a larger group.

Think of the various groups to which you belong. Some are united by ties of blood; others are the result of working together (fellow students or teachers) or similar interests (a religious sect, neighbours, a sports team or debating society). In these latter cases, there is a choice of whom one wants to associate with and whether the ties stay on a formal level or become close. Primary groups are small and spontaneous. The members share emotional bonds and identify their interests with those of the group; membership is an end in itself rather than a means (one joins a union for its benefits but joins friends just for the friendship) and the members interact in many diffuse contexts. (They may study or work in the fields together, eat together, go to a dance together; in a formal, secondary group one does the business of the meeting and goes away.)

Primary groups are seen as typical of a small-scale society, but they must exist in all societies. They give an individual a chance to relax with people who know him as he really is, but they also give him a unique identity (the best carpenter or housewife or story-teller) because the fellow members know each other as individuals. Rules can be modified to suit the needs of individual members, whereas in a formal organisation this would not be possible. Members of a primary group understand each other's difficulties and are willing to help when necessary.

Because people need primary groups, they are often present within formal organisations. For instance, in a large school there will be many small groups of friends who help each other out and who see much more of each other than they do of other students. In large, complex organisations such as factories or civil service departments, this development of primary groups is known as informal organisation. It comes from the informal relations people have with their colleagues; it brings humanity into the strict bureaucracy of formal organisations and is important for the morale of those concerned. The leaders of these primary groups may have no formal status in the organisation, but they often exert considerable influence among their followers and thus must be taken into account by management.

Informal organisation has several important functions:

1 It provides the human relations, the meaning of things, which make it possible for people to work in a large, impersonal organisation.

2 Members' cohesiveness gives them a sense of common purpose which makes formal goals worthwhile.

3 It provides a sense of human dignity and self-respect; 'someone knows that I am doing a good job'.

4 Formal communications are limited by what is considered proper, but communications in the informal organisation may be more accurate and provide vital warning that things are going wrong. This can cut 'red tape' by passing information quickly from one friend to another. Also, a good supervisor who listens when his subordinates are talking casually among themselves often has much better information on which to base his decisions than the officer who keeps himself aloof and waits for information through formal channels.

5 Informal organisation provides internal control of the group over its members and also control over outsiders. A close group of workmates can exercise social control to make sure no one works too hard and generally change work rules (at least in minor ways) to suit themselves. This means that the standard can be kept at the level where all are fairly equal. Anyone (worker or student) who seeks to excel may be seen as a threat to the group because the outstanding success of one may suggest that the others were not really trying. This internal control can be a help as well as a hindrance to the organisation, because members seek to uphold standards and ensure that no one's conduct brings the group into disrepute, just as kinsmen or migrants from the same village watch a newcomer to the city carefully so that he or she will not disgrace them.

At any given time, participation in primary groups is more important to most people than their ties to larger organisations; the state and the corporation are seen as far away and only marginally important to our daily lives, whereas the values shared with primary group members have a direct influence on behaviour. Shils[4] found that soldiers could fight well though they

(4) 1957.

had only a vague attachment to their national government and moderate patriotism; strong feelings for their fighting unit bolstered their morale. While a few people are intensely interested in either supporting their government or bringing it down, most citizens assume that the government will go on without them and take action only when things go seriously wrong or when extensive publicity assures them that it is their duty to do so, as at the time of a military coup or an election campaign. The local community, on the other hand, is something that touches their lives closely and in which they are continually concerned.

Leadership

Any large organisation, and a large-scale society composed of many organisations, must have some form of leadership which is accepted by a majority of the members. Thus, patterns of leadership are an important part of social structure. Leadership may be exercised through power, authority and influence. Bureaucratic authority is the most characteristic pattern of leadership today because it seems most suited to the needs of large-scale organisation.

Power, authority and influence

Weber[5] defined power as the ability to effect one's own will against resistance from others. Power may be exercised by using force, as when a band of marauders overcomes a guard and steals cattle or a war party takes control of a village. But it may also be used in less obvious ways, through religious or political ideology which convinces people that they must obey or through control over economic resources which people must share in order to survive. Subordinates are not necessarily aware of the power which leaders have over them; in a complex society the focus of power and its strength may be less clear than in a small-scale society. Although we tend to think of power in relation to government, it is well to remember that it is exercised in many other contexts as well: in the family, schools, hospitals and businesses, wherever it is possible to manipulate conditions so that people must obey. A prisoner, for instance, does the work assigned to him because he would be punished if he refused. He is thus reacting to power even though his obedience seems peaceful enough. People may carry out ceremonies because they fear the power of their ancestors to hurt them or prevent the crops from growing.

However, power alone ('might makes right') is usually resented and thus

(5) 1947, p.180.

is an unstable base for organisational leadership. If rulers are to continue to be obeyed, it is necessary that their power be legitimated and become authority. This is always more limited than power. Weber[6] defines authority as 'the probability that a specific command will be obeyed.' The essence of authority is voluntary obedience because one believes that the source of the command is legitimate – the person commanding has a right to do so. When we accept authority, we suspend our judgment about the order because we agree that the person in authority has a right to give it. If a farmer pays taxes because he is afraid of being sent to jail for refusing, his action is a response to the power of the state. If he pays because he believes the state has a right to tax him, his action is a response to governmental authority.

Authority exists because group members share certain beliefs; these beliefs lead to the development of group norms for accepting commands from certain sources. Obedience to these commands is then enforced by the group; anyone who wishes to remain a member of the group must accept this authority. Take the case of a child. When he is very little, his father has considerable power over him. He can make the child do what he is told to do, as far as this is within the child's ability. But gradually the child learns his role in relation to his father and other members of the family and accepts that his father has a right to command. From this time, the father exercises authority over him. The norms of the family are that children should obey their fathers. Later, when the child grows up, he may begin to question this authority; the norm about the obedience adult men owe to their fathers may be less clear than the norm about children.

A person or organisation with authority has certain rights and responsibilities, as do those under it; the authority is limited to certain aspects of life and commands outside the area of expectation would be subject to influence rather than authority. Influence is distinguished from power and authority in that one's judgment is involved. If you are persuaded by a friend to sit and talk instead of going to the library, you have made the decision of your own free will. A person who has power or authority over you may choose to persuade you instead, giving you reasons why you should act in a certain way and letting you make up your own mind. Influence is also used by individuals who need to obtain resources from others over whom they have neither power or authority. An applicant seeks to influence his prospective employer; a businessman tries to influence the Ministry to make a larger grant. Through their officers, large organisations exercise power, authority and influence over other organisations and over their members, participants and clients.

(6) 1953, p.4.

The basis on which authority is used affects the nature of the organisation and of the society of which the organisation is a part. Weber[7] distinguished three ideal types of authority: traditional, charismatic and bureaucratic. Obedience in traditional authority is based on the acceptance of custom; in charismatic authority it is given to an individual because of his personal magnetism; and in bureaucratic authority it is given to the law and positions upheld by law rather than to the individual holding the position. A fourth type of authority, professional, has been observed recently; this involves acceptance of the competence (professional qualifications) of the person giving the orders. It might be considered as a special type of bureaucratic authority.

Traditional authority is legitimated by the sanctity of tradition. Members believe that the social order was created by God and that it is man's duty to conform. This is the basis of the 'divine right of kings' and of the authority of chiefs in many societies. The chief's power is limited by tradition; he cannot extend it or change it from what it was in the past. (In practice rather than ideal type, a traditional leader's power does grow and decline.) Social change undermines traditional authority because it involves breaking away from tradition. The authority of most chiefs was grossly diminished during the colonial era because a new kind of authority gradually usurped their position; independent governments have generally continued this process because they do not want challenges to their attempts to unify the people under their authority. Few nations have gone as far as Guinea, which abolished chieftaincy, but even the highly powerful Nigerian emirs have more limited authority than they exercised in the past. Traditional authority is not limited to chieftaincy. There are many individuals in society who are able to command because subordinates customarily accept their authority. Fathers and husbands have this authority in their families, masters over their apprentices, clergy over their flocks and patrons over their clients.

Charismatic authority is based on a leader who embodies a movement and is obeyed for ideological reasons. Weber[8] defined charisma as

> a certain quality of an individual personality by virtue of which he is set apart from ordinary men and treated as endowed with supernatural, superhuman, or at least specifically exceptional powers or qualities. These . . . are not accessible to the ordinary person, but are regarded as of divine origin or as exemplary, and on the basis of them the individual concerned is treated as a leader.

Converts to a charismatic movement accept a new value system and often a

(7) 1953.   (8) 1947, p.359.

new way of life. The movement is essentially anti-organisational, a revolutionary force which is contemptuous of daily routine. This gives it strength but also contains the seeds of its downfall. If the movement is to continue and spread, some sort of organisation is necessary; people must be drawn in who are less devoted to the leader and the goals of the movement than the original members. At some point, it will be necessary to replace the leader; if no organisation has developed, this is likely to give rise to considerable conflict and continued existence may be impossible. This institutionalisation of the movement was called the 'routinisation of charisma' by Weber. It involves a change from charismatic authority to traditional or bureaucratic authority or a combination of these.

Charismatic movements tend to arise when the social order has broken down. People who feel insecure and are looking for someone who can solve their problems, as in periods of war, economic depression, or political change, seek charismatic leadership. Many religious leaders founded sects during the 1930s[9] and the independence movements in several countries provided opportunities for other charismatic leaders. Outside Africa, the career of Mao Tse Tung is a classic example.

Tiger[10] discusses the usefulness of charismatic leadership in the struggle for independence and the routinisation which must take place if the new national government is to reach its developmental goals. He focuses on Kwame Nkrumah of Ghana, who was both an organiser and a charismatic figure through most of his career. Running a national government required routinisation of charisma, a shift of emphasis from politics to administration. Tiger argues that the limited effectiveness of Nkrumah's move from charismatic to bureaucratic leadership was part of the reason for his overthrow (which came after the paper was written). When a charismatic leader makes a serious mistake or seems to be leading in the wrong direction, his followers turn to someone else.

The charismatic element has probably been over-emphasised, but it remains important in African politics because people accustomed to personal interaction within a small community prefer to identify with an individual rather than an impersonal entity and see the country as 'belonging', in a sense, to the President or Prime Minister. But as power is consolidated, it becomes necessary to run the government on the basis of rules rather than faith. Not all the promises which have been made can be fulfilled and authority must be maintained in spite of failure. Taxes must be collected and bills paid. Assistants must also have authority because the leader cannot make all the decisions himself, and provision must be made for succession to the

(9) See Barrett 1968 and Peel 1968.   (10) 1966.

leadership. Thus, to a greater or lesser extent, nations are run by bureaucracy rather than by a charismatic leader (or the army when it assumes control).

Bureaucracy

Bureaucratic leadership has developed over a long period of time because it seems to suit the needs of large-scale societies. The word is used both for the type of leadership and for the organisations in which it prevails. Blau[11] provides a sociological definition of bureaucracy which indicates its goal: 'the type of organisation designed to accomplish large-scale administrative tasks by systematically coordinating the work of many individuals'. In order to produce textiles in a factory, as opposed to weaving at home, the work of hundreds or even thousands of workers must be coordinated. Similarly, in order to run a national system of education or a Ministry of Finance, large numbers of workers must be organised so that all the necessary tasks are done well and on time. Bureaucracy involves the rationalisation of administration to achieve organisational and/or national goals.

The word rationalisation needs some explanation. In ordinary use it means 'sensible', but here it means the 'calculated use of resources for the achievement of a particular goal or set of goals in the most economical way possible'.[12] Rational action is sometimes contrasted with traditional action, the former implying a cost-benefit approach whereby there is a constant search for the best means to attain a goal and the latter a reliance on the past, the customs of the community. However, this dichotomy is difficult to see in practice. Small-scale societies on the edge of subsistence are often remarkably efficient in using whatever opportunities arise to support themselves and so-called rational bureaucracies often become very set in their ways and so inefficient in practice that the goal seems to be forgotten. The next time you have to wait in a government office, think about its goals and the means being used to realise them. How would you rationalise this organisation?

Bureaucratic organisations are characterised by specialisation, hierarchical authority, systematised rules, impersonality and a secure and meritocratic career structure.[13] Specialisation involves a division of labour whereby each participant has a certain task; there is considerable interdependence, which requires careful coordination. In a small carpenter's shop with two or three apprentices, the master can easily keep track of what each one is doing, and jobs vary from day to day. In a large furniture factory, each man produces only a small part of the finished piece; all must fit precisely and the parts must be made in exact quantities if the firm is to stay in business. Speciali-

(11) 1956, p.14.   (12) Worsley 1970, p.207.   (13) Blau 1956, p.19.

sation allows the use of less trained workers, which lowers the cost of production, but it often makes the work very boring; workers lose interest in their work. This applies to office work as well as factory employment, and partly explains the constant demands of such workers for fewer hours and more pay. (Other factors will be discussed in later chapters.)

In order to coordinate the work of specialists, there must be a clear line of authority. In a factory, this would be from the owner through the assistant managers, supervisors, foremen and charge hands, to the workers. The holder of each position should have clear rules as to what decisions he is responsible for, his rights and responsibilities. Orders are passed down the hierarchy, becoming increasingly specific as they go. Top officers are concerned with the long-term future of the organisation and its interaction with other organisations; middle level managers initiate activity within their section so that set goals may be met; and first level supervisors see that each worker carries out his particular task. Many of the difficulties of bureaucracy are due to blocked lines of communication; orders are not passed down quickly and accurately and information which might affect decisions is not passed up the hierarchy.

Ideally, the rules of the organisation are written so that participants in a bureaucratic organisation will know what is expected of them. A copy of the rules may be presented to newcomers. Individuals must conform to the rules, even in situations where acting in another way might seem more rational. It is necessary that anything which might hinder the attainment of the organisation's goals be eliminated: personal opinions, or affection, or greed, or anything but the rules. The person counts for nothing; only the office is important (not Mr Sami but the Permanent Secretary). A succession of individuals holds the post, but the job remains the same. Each office has a set of rights and obligations and candidates are selected for their technical competence, their achieved rather than ascribed characteristics. Once selected, they have the expectation of a secure post for life. Since all have been appointed on merit, promotion should be based on seniority; personal achievement within the job is unimportant.

You should have recognised by now that the characteristics of bureaucracy have been presented as an ideal type. Many of the criticisms of Weber's model of bureaucracy have ignored the fact that it was an ideal type and not intended to be a precise description of reality. Variations in bureaucratic practice are partly due to the nature of the organisation and partly to the societal expectations of what bureaucrats should be and do. Some aspects cause difficulties everywhere; others arise because of the specific cultural environment in which the bureaucracy is functioning. For example, the elimination of personal factors is considered necessary if the bureaucracy is to attain its goals. This cannot be completely accomplished in any society, but it may give rise to greater misunderstanding in countries where people are not accustomed to this type of organisation than in those where impersonality is considered normal. The proper carrying out of bureaucratic functions demands ability and interest, unselfish obedience to the impersonal discipline and sacrifice of one's own goals to those of the organisation. The goal may be the elimination of certain diseases, the provision of higher education to those who can most benefit from it, efficient tax collection, or the improvement of amenities for the largest number of people. If the objective is to be achieved, people must submit to the rules. If they resist, things will not be done which should be done. For example, guinea worm can only be eliminated from an area if all the people boil their water; if one or two housewives are 'too busy', the infection continues. If many people avoid paying their taxes, the money needed by the government for social services is not available.

The bureaucrat is expected to apply the rule impersonally, but people want to be treated as individuals. Sometimes rules need modification, but the system does not allow it. If this applicant is given a loan because he has a special need, and that child is allowed to start school because he is big for his age, someone must decide when the rule should or should not apply. To avoid such a dilemma, bureaucrats develop what Veblen called a 'trained incapacity'. Skills and responses which have been successful in the past are still used though circumstances have changed and they no longer apply. There is strong resistance to changing the rules (such as modifying the requirements for a university degree) or bringing in new techniques (computerised records, a new method of filing). Thus, a system which stresses reliability and predictability may in practice become inefficient, no longer rational for the attainment of goals. The bureaucrat may turn to ritualism (insistence on precise adherence to rules and procedures) regardless of its effect on the achievement of goals; this is the 'red tape' for which bureaucracy is notorious. For the ritualist, the rules are ends, not means to an end. Rules can be cited whenever necessary as a reason for not assisting a client. The basic problem is that while bureaucracy as an ideal type involves control by rules it must be carried out by men who decide in any given case whether or not the rules (or which rule) should be followed.[14]

The advantages and disadvantages of a bureaucratic form of leadership in developing countries have been partly discussed above, but are worth further consideration. Perhaps the most important factor is impersonality, which is difficult to accept in a society which emphasises personal relationships. Acting impersonally may improve efficiency if it results in the best candidate (on technical rather than personal grounds) being chosen for a post and a careful

(14) Merton 1957, pp.195–202.

attempt to apply the rules equally to all rather than deciding in favour of the one who can pay the largest 'dash'. But when family and other primary ties remain central to people's lives, they cannot understand why a family member should not be preferred to all others regardless of the effect this might have on the organisational goal. In dealing with civil servants, politicians and others in authority, people try to establish a personal relationship, through gifts if necessary, partly because they do not understand the rules (or even know about them) and partly because they are unused to interacting on an impersonal basis and assume (often correctly) that their chance of assistance will be improved if they are known as an individual rather than a 'case'.

The structure of an organisation and the expectations of the participants (shaped by the culture in which they live) may make strict adherence to bureaucratic principles almost impossible. For example, van den Berghe[15] describes the hiring procedures at an African university. He shows how the rules can be used by various parties in ways which are quite contrary to their intention and how in other cases the rules actually interfere with the goal of efficient running of the institution. The rules prescribe that all jobs be advertised and that a committee examine the applications and recommend who should be appointed. This process can be very time-consuming, so a majority of lower-level appointments are officially temporary at first. Temporary appointments are subject to less regulation and have fewer safeguards against nepotism, favouritism, etc. than permanent appointments made according to the rules. Since most temporary appointments are later confirmed, the complexity of the formal procedure is effectively circumvented; the attempt to maintain universalism is an inevitable casualty.

Second, the changing nature of the society must be taken into account. A strict bureaucracy may not be flexible enough to adapt to change. Members of the organisation must have some freedom of action and ability to take the initiative if goals are to be reached. Job security is helpful in that men who feel that their position is safe are less likely to resist changes. However, too much security can lead to laxity; those who cannot be sacked may see no need to work hard. Training should emphasise standards of performance rather than blind adherence to official rules. For example, if a nurse has a clear idea of good patient care, she should be allowed considerable freedom to carry out her job in the best interests of the patient and be judged only on the end result, the patient's recovery. This approach, of standardising the end but not the means by which it is achieved, should make the work more interesting and the bureaucrat more flexible. The major problem then becomes how to ensure that jobs are held by people with the technical compe-

(15) 1973, pp.95–6.

tence to do them.

The problem of alienation must also be faced. Lower-level workers in a bureaucracy are seldom allowed initiative, and their jobs are so limited by specialisation that many of the workers find them boring. The farmer or craftsman working for himself carries out a variety of tasks and can decide the order and speed of his work. The interdependence of a large-scale organisation usually makes such individual decisions impossible, but workers who have recently migrated from a village and are experiencing large-scale organisation for the first time find it very confining. Informal organisation based on personal contacts between workmates is therefore particularly welcome to them.[16]

Social order

From the very beginning of the discipline, sociologists have been concerned with the problem of order in society. How does organised social life come about and why does it persist? The other side of the question is why does social life sometimes break down and how is it restored? If one sees individuals as fundamentally self-interested, yet depending on each other for a viable society, the nature of their arrangements for holding the social system together is of prime importance. Theories of social order seek to explain how social structures and organisations are integrated and maintained.

The two main theories stress consensus and conflict. Proponents of both theories see man as basically a social animal, unable to exist outside society, but they differ in their views of the nature of that society. Their models are based on certain assumptions on the nature of social systems and social life:[17]

		Consensus or Integration Model	Conflict or Coercion Model
1	Basic elements	norms and values	interests
2	Social life involves	commitments	inducement and coercion
	is necessarily	cohesive	divisive
	and depends on or		
	generates	consensus, solidarity, reciprocity, cooperation	structured conflict, opposition, exclusion and hostility
3	Leadership through	legitimate authority	power

(16) See Peil 1972a, pp.81–92. (17) Adapted from Cohen 1968, p.167.

| 4 Social systems are | integrated | malintegrated and beset by 'contraditions' |
| and tend to | persist | change |

Theorists using the consensus model argue that most members of a society share the same values and norms; cooperation is not only necessary but rewarding and, as a result, the society is basically stable. Conflict and violence may appear from time to time, but they are contained and eventually overcome (the society returns to equilibrium) because the goals of the society can be more efficiently reached through other relationships, such as trust and cooperation, which persist even in times of conflict. They emphasise the interdependence of the various parts of a society and the necessity of working together. The society must, through its members and constituent organisations, adapt itself to its environment, attain its goals, integrate new members into the functioning whole and manage tensions as they arise. This is achieved through the activities of legitimate leaders, who provide the services required by members of the society in return for their support and obedience.

Those who use the conflict model, on the other hand, argue that values and norms are not the same for all members of the society but vary according to position and consequent interests. Many forms of social organisation provide far more benefits for some groups in the society than for others; conflict between individuals and groups is the inevitable result. Social control is not an expression of group consensus, but of oppression by the powerful. Leaders will seek to maintain the *status quo* because it supports their interests, but there is continuing pressure for change from groups which are excluded by present arrangements. They agree that society has certain functions to fulfil, but think it more important and interesting to study the way various problems are solved and the way these solutions affect groups within the society. If, for example, a nation decides to assimilate new members by providing them with education at public expense, it may be done in several ways. The government might provide all children with the same education, in years and quality, but usually some receive more than others. The consensus theorist would explain this variance as being functional for manpower needs or due to the greater ability of some children (the more intelligent) to profit from it. Conflict theorists would examine carefully who gets this extra education, with the expectation that it supports the political and economic power of the ruling class.

Differences in access to power and resources are accepted, say the consensus theorists, because the leaders' authority is considered legitimate. So long as leaders and led share the same values, there should be little political conflict;

there is agreement on the goals of the society, even though there may be disagreement as to the means by which these goals may be achieved. Government is based on the consent of the governed, and therefore people have power over the government as well as *vice versa*. Conflict theorists argue that the powerful control the social institutions of society and therefore can enforce their will regardless of what the public wants; people have no real power over government, even in a democracy. Public opinion merely represents the mass media, which are controlled by the 'power elite'; ordinary people are incapable of thinking about their situation and coming to an independent decision.[18] Radical leaders who seem likely to be successful are coopted by the rulers so they will cause no further trouble.[19]

Many authors have accepted an underlying unity for each of these models, assuming that all the sections necessarily occur together. Consensus theorists have been rather more willing to accept the presence of conflict than have conflict theorists to agree to the presence of a measure of consensus. However, consensus theorists have tended to refer to tension or strain rather than conflict, implying that this is something dysfunctional which the system will soon overcome, rather than a basic characteristic present in all societies. Conflict theorists have tended to assume that any absence of overt conflict is temporary and due to an inadequate understanding of the real situation.

However, it seems more reasonable to take these two models as emphasising certain characteristics, one or the other of which may predominate in any particular society even though both are usually present. When trying to understand the nature of society, both should be kept in mind. For example, by accepting that the two models are not mutually exclusive, the problem of change in the consensus model becomes much easier to handle. It may be easier to introduce change into a society in which there is a basic consensus as to goals than into a society in which these are the subject of considerable conflict and in which the leadership must therefore actively protect its position. Change is often inhibited by a bureaucracy which allows no disagreement about rules or methods.[20]

The view that all societies contain elements of both models and that conflict can be functional to the system and need not lead to change has been proposed by Gluckman and Coser, both following Simmel. Conflict is inevitable because individuals and groups within the society make claims on economic, prestige and power resources which cannot be simultaneously satisfied. Loosely structured groups tend to be reasonably tolerant of conflict

---

(18) There is considerable paternalism and 'we know what is good for you' implicit in conflict theory. However, it is by no means absent from consensus theory, which tends to assume that the social structures we have are the best possible ones.
(19) Worsley 1970, pp.373–89.   (20) Cohen 1968, pp.170–1.

because members do not share all the same interests and balancing one against the other promotes the stabilisation and integration of the group. Conflict with other groups often promotes integration; intragroup conflict may disappear until an external threat has been disposed of. The structure and norms of the group are gradually modified in the process of handling conflict so that it gives greater satisfaction to its members. As a result, the toleration and institutionalisation of conflict in a society may remove the need for radical changes in social structure (which does not deny that minor changes are continually being made).

Conflicts within closely knit groups (such as kin groups) are less easy to tolerate and hence more often suppressed. Members find it difficult to withdraw, so they try to maintain at least the appearance of consensus. As a result, when conflict breaks out in such a group, it is generally more intense than in loosely structured groups; it is based on accumulated grievances and hostility in which the occasion for the conflict is only the last straw. Group members are more personally involved in the conflict and its resolution is more important to them. If it cannot be resolved, one or more members may have to withdraw or be excluded from the group, but the group itself is less likely to disintegrate than a segmented group similarly beset with conflict because the 'we feeling' of its members is a powerful force for the restoration of some form of consensus.[21]

Using the Nuer of the southern Sudan as an example, Gluckman[22] sought to explain how there could be peace in the presence of feuding interest groups. He shows that conflict is a necessary part of living together. Quarrels are shaped and controlled by the customs of the society so that communal life can be maintained or re-established. They may modify the system, but they seldom destroy it and may increase social cohesion.

Societies are a tissue of conflicts and loyalties. Friends at one level may be enemies at another, or when the boundaries of conflict change from one issue to another. Loyalties to family, hometown, nation, co-workers, friends, and so on pull men in various directions. They do not prevent conflict, but they moderate it and make it less productive of change than it might otherwise be. The more opponents on one issue are allies on another, the more the society is held together by the conflicting interests of its members, the less likely it is that open conflict will occur and the more likely that a peace formula will be found.[23]

(21) Coser 1956, pp.151–7.   (22) 1955.   (23) See Hopkins 1972 for a discussion of the role of political factions in promoting unity in Kita, Mali.

Conclusion

This chapter examines some aspects of the social organisation of societies. They have often been conceptualised as either simple or complex. Societies at one extreme are seen as having social relations based on personal contact, a strong sense of community, primacy of the sacred and mechanical solidarity. Those at the other extreme are characterised by impersonal social relations, emphasis on association and secularism, and organic solidarity. There are many difficulties with this ideal type dichotomy. Research has shown that some so-called simple societies have very complex social institutions and there is strong evidence of the continuance of particularism, ascription, affectivity and community in 'complex' societies. However, it is sometimes helpful to examine the overall orientation of a society or part of a society using these ideal types as a rough guide.

Primary groups are fundamental to all societies, providing personalised support through kinship and friendship and, in bureaucratic organisations, the close contacts which enable individuals to overcome some of the limitations of this form. Although behaviour is shaped by the institutions and organisations of the society, the nature of primary groups and the level of participation in them are important factors in an individual's response to these structural constraints.

Individuals and organisations exercise power, authority and influence over others depending on their resources and needs. Authority is based on the consent of the governed and is thus less predictable than power, but leaders relying on power must continually prove that they can enforce their will. Three basic patterns of authority have been distinguished: traditional, charismatic and bureaucratic. Traditional authority emphasises immemorial custom and the symbolic meaning of the past. Charismatic authority often heralds revolutionary change, introducing new ideas through the persuasive personality of the leader. But it is not sufficiently structured to provide stable leadership and must eventually be combined with or changed into traditional or bureaucratic authority. Industrialised societies and large scale organisations are characterised by bureaucratic authority, with its stress on specialisation and rationalisation of roles, a hierarchical chain of command, the universalistic application of formal rules, impersonality and a career structure in which people are hired on merit, promoted on seniority and given security of tenure to protect them from outside pressure. While most bureaucracies are only approximations of the ideal type, these characteristics must be taken into account when examining the role of formal organisations in society.

If societies are to persist over time, their institutions and organisations must provide some form of social order. While there is general agreement that man is basically a social animal (we are human only in society, not alone) there is considerable disagreement as to the nature of the social order which holds us together. Both consensus and conflict, unity and diversity, must be accounted for. So far, no one theory satisfactorily accounts for all aspects of social organisation, but various theories can provide useful perspectives for the study of social structure.

Suggested reading and discussion topics
1. Read Fallers (1965, Chapters 6–10), Whitaker (1964) or Tiger (1966) and consider the extent to which your own national leadership is based on traditional, charismatic and bureaucratic authority. How has the situation changed since independence?
2. Take some incident which has had a prominent place in the daily newspapers within the past two months and analyse what happened from the point of view of the consensus and conflict theories of social order.

3 **Individual and Society**

This chapter focuses on the individual: the process of becoming a social being, establishing one's social position and receiving goods and services, and as the root of a social network through which contacts are made and maintained with the rest of the society. A child becomes a member of a society through socialisation. He learns, among other things, the rules of social exchange and how these are manipulated by some for their own benefit. He moves out from a small, dense kinship network to a large, extended network of friends and acquaintances, though he usually preserves a small circle of intense contacts with a strong obligation to mutual aid. This network also contributes to his adult socialisation and to changes in his self-identity as his life-cycle progresses.

Socialisation[1]

A newborn child is not yet a social being. It becomes one through socialisation – being taught all the things he or she needs to know to function as a member of a specific society. Although much of this learning takes place in the first two or three years of life, socialisation continues throughout life. When we attend school, move to a new place, or take a new job, or whenever we are called on to make changes in customs, norms, or behaviour, additional socialisation is necessary. Socialisation integrates a child into the community by teaching him the disciplines, aspirations, social roles and skills necessary for group membership. The young child is taught that obedience and respect for older people are very important. He learns to control his temper and wait for the things he wants. Gradually, these disciplines are internalised (become part of him), so that such behaviour is taken for granted.

The burden of learning discipline is made easier by the fact that aspirations as well as behaviour are socialised. Children see the prestige attached to

(1) Much of this section is based on Broom and Selznick 1963, Chapter 4.

parenthood and learn that this is a worthy aspiration; this encourages them to follow their parents' example in order to achieve the same prestige. Other aspirations are learned by watching other adults: teachers, political and religious leaders, etc. Much of children's play is imitating the social roles of adults. They learn to obey by running errands for parents and older siblings and learn to command by 'bossing' younger siblings. This socialises them into an understanding of the community hierarchy and their place within it. They also learn specific skills which they will need as adults – how to use a cutlass, herd cows, harvest crops, bargain in the market, participate in religious ceremonies, deal with government officers. In school they learn to read and write letters and how to use numbers, skills which are useful whether they stay at home or migrate for work. Later, there are occupational, marital and citizenship roles to be learned through experience. Even in old age, the socialisation process continues, as the individual learns to handle new situations which arise.

Some socialisation is deliberate, as when the parent or teacher shows the child how to do something. At other times, it is casual or even accidental. A parent or another child indicates that performance has been unsatisfactory and the child must pick up the knowledge he needs informally. Much is learned by observation; tone of voice or posture may suggest what behaviour is expected. 'Do what I say and not what I do' is often ignored; the child follows what he sees done rather than what he is told to do. This is merely distinguishing between the norms of the community (ideal behaviour) and actual behaviour. Where these two are quite different, the norms are likely to change; the child is socialised into new norms.

In addition to verbal instructions and observed behaviour, the child responds to the attitudes expressed through physical posture, tone of voice and other signs which gradually acquire meaning for him. Being carried on his mother's back or hip signals a close tie with someone who cares for him; a raised arm indicates trouble. The way people dress tells him something about their role in the society: the school uniform, the politician's suit, the farmer's cloth indicate not just what occupation the wearer has but suggest authority, income and relative prestige. Facial markings, hair style or jewellery may indicate which society a stranger belongs to. Many of these 'cues' are learned informally, through experience.

The prime source of socialisation is language. A person who cannot hear or speak has great difficulty communicating with others and is often excluded from groups. Once the child has acquired language, it can be told how to do things and, more important, why they should be done. Shades of meaning can be distinguished and the sense of the words used is amplified by the tones and gestures which accompany them. The competent speaker is particularly honoured in pre-literate societies, as he must summarise the feelings of the group as a whole and speak for the community in its dealings with outsiders. Socialisation throughout life may mean learning new languages; it will certainly involve new words and new meanings of words.

Although all members of the society are socialised, they do not all turn out the same. Each individual comes under various influences (family, friends, workmates, neighbours) and responds to them in different ways. Personality and innate capabilities are important here. While there are some theories of national character whereby attempts have been made to show that all Japanese, Americans, or some other people have basically similar personalities, there are always many exceptions. Given the same socialisation, one man may turn out to be much more independent than his brother, or more scholarly, or a better drummer. Their socialisation has not been exactly the same, because parents and other socialisers adapt their training to the child's abilities as these develop. A passive child or one who is often ill will be treated more gently than a lively trouble-maker, and a child who shows special abilities will be helped to develop these.

One aspect of socialisation which has received considerable attention is the development of a need for achievement (nAchievement). McClelland[2] and his students developed the idea that some people feel a strong need to compete against a standard of excellence, and that societies where this need is widespread will be more prosperous than other societies where people are content with more ordinary performance or emphasise either their ties with others (need for affiliation) or subordination/superordination (need for power). McClelland suggested that nAchievement is an important factor in economic growth because it is closely tied to entrepreneurial success. It can be established through the socialisation process. Parents who emphasise self-reliance and initiative, who give support but set high goals and demand high standards of performance are most likely to develop high nAchievement in their children. Fathers who are authoritarian hinder it, but domineering mothers increase it; they may be seeking achievement through their sons.

LeVine[3] has applied these ideas to Nigeria, seeking to explain personality differences between Hausa, Ibo and Yoruba as due to their socialisation. He shows the emphasis on patron-client relations in Hausa society and an individual achievement in Ibo society. The Yoruba are seen as in between, a society which rewards both independent achievement and loyal clientage. There are many difficulties with this study. The data used were reports of dreams, which many feel to be much less reliable than direct reports on attitudes or behaviour and very difficult to interpret objectively. Neverthe-

(2) 1961, 1963.   (3) 1966.

less, differences between groups of people can have important political implications, and the study poses some interesting questions which deserve further research.

The growth of self concept

The newborn child's biological needs are more obvious than his social needs, but the way these biological needs are met provide his first experience of society. A child who is fed whenever he cries learns that others are concerned about him. This feeling of security may be abruptly shattered if he is quickly weaned because another child is on the way. In many societies, an infant is indulged until it is two or three, then subject to strict discipline and expected to act in a responsible way. The world, which had seemed so reliable and satisfying, now seems harsh and capricious; the change may leave an enduring mark on the child's character, for instance making him suspicious of the intentions of others. In other societies, the weaning process is very gradual and the child is given considerable emotional support as he is being expected to take greater care of his own needs. Growing up is, for him, a less threatening experience. Because it has such a strong influence on personality, many social psychologists regard weaning as a key factor in national character.

Through socialisation the child develops, as part of its personality, a sense of itself and its relation to society. Mead saw the self as divided into 'I' and 'me'; Freud divided it into 'id', 'ego' and 'superego'. The id is the biological basis of the individual, which is not available for socialisation and may occasionally interfere with the ego and superego. Mead's 'me' and Freud's superego are ways of referring to the more social side of personality, where values of the society are internalised so that an individual acts according to societal expectations. Where this influence is strong, one gets the conventional, passive behaviour which Riesman[4] has referred to as 'other directed'. The group is seen as stronger than the individual, who must react in terms of societal norms and constantly seek the approval of others. If society rejects him, he may reject himself, identify himself as a deviant and act accordingly.

The superego, then, is an internalisation of the mores and folkways of the society, which the child has learned from its parents, so that they become part of his personality and he feels guilty if he acts against them. However, some norms are accepted less fully than others, especially those which are changing. It may not be possible to follow the prohibition against working on a certain day of the week, or a young person may decide that the pro-

(4) 1950.

hibition of sex outside marriage is 'old-fashioned'. The initial feeling of guilt may be stilled if he can convince himself that 'everybody does it'. However, those who have more fully internalised the norm usually cannot bring themselves to act against it, even though they are aware that 'times have changed'. Social control is largely due to the socialisation of members to obey the norms.[5]

The 'I' or ego is the more spontaneous and creative side of the personality. People are said to have a strong ego if they are able to think and act for themselves; they are what Riesman has called 'inner directed'. These people have also been socialised early to strive for societal goals, but they are freer than 'other directed' individuals to go about this in their own way; they feel less pressure to conform. Everyone is called on to cope with frustration, anxiety, temptation, guilt, group pressure, insecurity, etc. Those with a strong ego can handle these strains, assess the position and decide what their response ought to be; they can maintain their values and work systematically towards their goals. Individuals without these internal resources may break down under stress.

A growing child gets a progressively clearer idea of who he is by identifying with others. He sees himself as others see him (i.e., he feels guilty when his father accuses him of doing something wrong) and finds adults whom he can use as models of behaviour, taking on their identity as he becomes like them. As an adult, he takes on new identities by becoming part of organisations and accepting new values and attitudes. If you ask a person, 'Who are you?', a full answer would include a whole series of identities which give him both a place in the community and a unique individuality.

Agents of socialisation

Socialisation is carried out initially by parents and kinsmen living with the family. These primary agents of socialisation make the deepest impression on the personality because they provide the first training. Other agents (peers, teachers, employers, the mass media) must compete for attention and build on the already established framework. Socialisation which involves intense interaction over some time (as in a primary group) is likely to have more effect on the individual than less direct influence (as through the radio and newspapers). Thus, government programmes to encourage people to take up new farming methods or send their children to school are likely to be more successful if they are passed on by individuals who are known and

(5) This informal social control can be contrasted with formal social control by the police and other agents of the state. See Chapter 9.

respected than if they are only promoted over the radio; the mass media are more successful in supporting than initiating a change in values or behaviour.

The various socialising agents encountered by an individual may support each other by promoting the same goals, or they may provide contradictory advice. The child may be taught one thing at home and another at school, or his friends may urge him to do things which are forbidden by his parents. In both of these situations, the influence of the parents is weakened and the child may not fully internalise any norms because he is not sure which ones are most valuable. If he learns only to follow the norm that seems strongest in a given situation, without understanding the reasons for the expected behaviour, he is easily at a loss when faced with a new experience. Children who migrate with their parents and grow up in a community quite different from the one in which their parents were socialised often face this problem, whereas children who grow up surrounded by the culture of their ancestors get a much more consistent view of what is expected of them. Many societies have changed so much in recent years that children learn things which their parents know little about. This undermines parental authority, but the primary socialisation by the family continues to be an important source of basic training in language and behaviour because so much of this takes place when the child is too young to be aware of alternatives.

Reference groups can also be important sources of socialisation. A 'reference group' is not necessarily a group in the corporate sense. It may be a category to which one compares (refers) oneself rather than a set of people who interact frequently and pursue common goals. There are two basic types of reference groups: normative and comparative. The normative group sets standards; parents and community elders are normative reference groups for children in the village. The comparative reference group supplies a model against which to assess one's own position, as when a small trader compares his standard of living to that of his more successful neighbour.[6] Individuals in roughly similar circumstances may have different normative and comparative reference groups, and this may have an important effect on their behaviour. For example, a woman who compares herself with the wives of senior government officers may continually complain to her husband about the things he should provide, whereas another who compares her position to that of a sister who is less well off than herself may be quite satisfied.

The example also illustrates the role of reference groups in social mobility. Anticipatory socialisation (adopting the attitudes and behaviour of a group or category before one joins it) is useful in helping the upwardly mobile adapt

(6) Merton 1957, pp.283–5.

to their new position in society. If a young man learns how to behave as a member of the elite by taking them as his normative reference group while still completing his education, he is less likely to be accused of being 'bush' when he takes up a sub-elite position after graduation. Similarly, an apprentice takes master craftsmen as his reference group in anticipation of joining them and consciously imitates their behaviour when he can, as in demonstrating to a customer how competent he is. By the time he qualifies, behaving like a master craftsman seems natural to him.

The same people are often included in one's normative and comparative reference groups, but this need not be the case. A child may use adults as a norm but compare himself with his peers. Also, it is not necessary to interact with reference groups. The village teacher often compares himself with teachers in city schools, whom he has not met, rather than with the parents of his pupils; a young man may measure his progress against the elite, whom he reads about in the newspapers. On the other hand, comparative and normative reference groups may also be interaction groups, as when a mother follows the standards of and compares herself with other mothers in the village. This arrangement can be a powerful force for socialising newcomers, as group pressure is applied to enforce the norms.

The socialisation process

To give you a better idea of how socialisation works in practice, several examples will be discussed, showing the forms which socialisation takes, the agents who carry it out and the way it varies within and between societies. These studies examine the gradual move from child to adult roles in a rural community; patterns of child-rearing as they differ between patrilineal and matrilineal societies, between rural areas and the towns and between socio-economic groups within a city; and the ways in which adolescents and adults learn the values and behaviour patterns associated with urban life.

1 Growing up Ngoni and Sisala
Read[7] points out that the goal of socialisation is predictability; in a society with a clear socialisation system, it should be easy to predict the behaviour of individual members in a given situation. She shows that the Ngoni of Malaŵi have such a system, based on clear ideas of the values they wish to instill in their children and the technical and behavioural skills they will need for adult life. Adults who have not learned the proper forms of language and behaviour are as much a liability to the community as adults who have not

(7) 1959.

learned how to farm or cook. The Ngoni emphasise self-control, respect for others, obedience to elders and the law, dignity, courtesy and generosity. Orderliness, physical and moral strength and consistent hard work are also expected according to the age and sex of the individual. These virtues are taught through commands, example, stories and proverbs, and failures are greeted by verbal reproof (often with a proverb) or a beating. Example is probably the most important, as young children copy their elder brothers and sisters and adolescents gradually share the work of adults. New roles are assumed by degrees, causing a minimum of strain on those concerned.

The Ngoni do not have the initiation schools which many peoples use to teach adolescents skills and help them develop the group spirit needed to hold the community together. Instead, they spread this training out through the whole period of growing up. In place of a community-wide puberty ceremony to symbolise the importance of fertility, they have private rituals within the family as adolescents approach marriageable age. Marriage now takes place much earlier than in the past, because young men need no longer wait until they have served in the army but can marry as soon as they have earned money for the brideprice. As in most African societies, marriage establishes the man and woman as adults and full members of the community ready to bear and socialise the next generation.

Grindal[8] studied recent changes in childhood socialisation among the Sisala, a largely subsistence farming community in northern Ghana. Sisala infants are treated very indulgently. Adults watch them constantly and take considerable time to play with them. Weaning and toilet training are accomplished gradually, giving the child plenty of time to acquire the new skills. Dependence on adults and sociability are encouraged. As the child grows and acquires 'sense', he takes on responsibility for younger siblings and begins to learn adult roles. Children play at being housewives, farmers and hunters and later learn these skills from older members of the family. They also learn proper respect for elders and ancestors. Male authority is stressed by the father's role in curing illness and punishment; it is expected that 'small boys' will try to escape punishment by cleverness and lies.

Adolescents of ten to fifteen years of age gradually take on the work of adults. Boys of this age increase their solidarity with their brothers, on which the family ties of their generation will be based, and begin to be economically independent, though their success is always related to family needs. The Sisala see no need for formal puberty or initiation ceremonies. Just as the transition from infant to child, symbolised by weaning, is a gradual process suited to the child's development, so the assumption of adult status lacks

(8) 1972.

formal ceremony. When the adolescent has matured, he takes on adult roles for which he has long been preparing.

The socialisation of young Sisala has changed in recent years. Children who are sent to school are often treated more leniently than those who are not; many are not expected to become farmers like their parents. Those growing up in town often have more free time and alternatives for action, less discipline and less contact with their kinsmen than those who grow up in a village. Young people generally feel less secure than in the past. Many expect to migrate to other parts of the country, where they must compete with better educated southerners; even those who stay at home often take up new roles for which their childhood socialisation is an inadequate preparation.

2 Bete and Abure child-rearing

Comparing two peoples of southern Ivory Coast, Clignet[9] found that the time of weaning is affected by the position of the mother in the household. Women in polygynous households have more time to give to their infants and so wean them later. The more a rural woman is absorbed into her affinal group, the later she weans her children. Thus, the patrilineal Bete wives wean later than the matrilineal Abure, who maintain more economic and social autonomy from their husband's family. Urban mothers, who are often traders and who have little help from their extended family, wean their children earlier than rural mothers.

Discipline is also affected by the social structure of the society. Bete mothers have a clear line of authority from their husbands; they are more likely than Abure mothers to punish their children and to use physical punishment. The Abure child is socialised by his parents, but the ultimate responsibility for him belongs to his maternal uncle; there may be conflicting demands on him from his father and his matrilineage. Because of this, Abure mothers are less consistent disciplinarians and more likely than the Bete mothers to use the withdrawal of emotional support as punishment when children misbehave. With urbanisation, Abure mothers become harsher disciplinarians. As they are busy about the house and in various economic activities, they start training their infants earlier and use more physical punishment than rural mothers.

3 Socio-economic differences in urban child-rearing

Rearing children in town usually involves some break with the past, but this is less true for some peoples, such as the Yoruba, who have traditionally

(9) 1967.

preferred life in towns to living on their farms. Migrants to the towns who are well educated and have a good income are more likely to use new child-rearing patterns than the less well educated, who must often depend on their own experience. Several authors have focused on these differences.

Gamble[10] studied the mining town of Lunsar in Sierra Leone. He distinguishes six types of urban socialisation according to the nature of the father's occupation. Chiefly and land-owning families are large, polygynous and extended. Children are taught that they have a superior position in the community and should look down on manual work as related to slavery. They are often well educated because money is available for school fees. Marriages are arranged and initiation into secret societies enhances their political standing in the community. Children of Muslim teachers get much the same sort of training, except that their socialisation emphasises Arabic rather than Western schooling. Girls join their mothers in trading from an early age. In contrast to these two types, labourers' children get less schooling and less supervision from adults. They are freer to play in the streets, but are severely disciplined if they do anything wrong. Adults pass on their distrust of officials by threatening children that a policeman will come if they misbehave. They teach the importance of mutual aid by giving freely to kinsmen and others in need of help when their resources permit it.

Men in skilled work are more often literate in English than the three categories discussed so far. Most of them are young and monogamous. Their wives are less concerned with trading and have more time to spend with their children. Discipline is less severe, with less physical punishment and more explanation of what is expected. As the father has improved his opportunities through his own efforts, he expects his children to work hard in school and get ahead. Fathers who are clerks or teachers also place considerable emphasis on their children succeeding in school, showing respect for adults and being neat and well-behaved. They are more concerned about group activities than skilled workers and encourage their children to take part in sports, scouting, church groups and similar activities rather than just playing informally with a group of friends. Since these families are often transferred from one town to another, group activities probably make it easier for the children and their parents to adjust to a new place every few years.

The same concern with education is present when the father is a wealthy trader or on the senior staff of the mine, but there is more money available. Expensive toys are bought for the children rather than letting them play with home-made toys, but they are less free to play with other children. The

(10) 1963.

Temne tend to think that a man can only become wealthy by in some way depriving others of resources (any surplus should be given to those who have less), so the well-to-do may be accused of witchcraft or attacked by others who are envious. Therefore, children in these families are not allowed to play outside their compounds. Mothers may be so busy trading that they have little time to attend to their children and leave them to servants. Family solidarity is less important for these than for other families; children are taught that success often means moving away from one's family. Discipline is stricter than in the families of skilled or clerical workers, as the wealthy fathers are often aggressive, domineering men. Children may respond by becoming very subdued (just the opposite of their fathers) or by taking out their aggression on younger siblings, or animals, or stealing.

Two studies compare traditional and elite Yoruba parents in Ibadan.[11] Lloyd reports on the child-rearing patterns of mothers, and LeVine and his colleagues on the fathers. Mothers in Oje (the traditional area) were more concerned than elite mothers that their child was willing and prompt in running errands and obedient in other ways; they put less emphasis on intellectual achievement and self-reliance (the ability to do things for one-self). Obedience training is probably less important in elite than in less wealthy families because servants are available to run errands. Although there was no difference among fathers in the type of punishment used, Oje mothers were more likely than elite mothers to use physical punishment when the child had committed only a small offence; both samples of mothers made equal use of physical punishment for serious offences. This may indicate a gradual shift away from physical punishment or only that minor mis-behaviour causes less trouble in a small elite household than in a large compound.

Although the Oje fathers appear to maintain a greater social distance from their children than the elite fathers, they both reported spending about the same amount of time with them and were equally strict disciplinarians. The elite fathers appear to be following the practices of their own social-isation as regards discipline, though they were somewhat more permissive than Oje fathers in responding to their children's desires and in allowing their children to fight with other children. The smaller size of the elite family and its greater wealth probably make it easier to respond in this way. Elite fathers were more likely than those in Oje to discuss child-rearing with their wives and to have helped with infant care, often when they were studying abroad. New ideas of child care learned in Europe are sometimes continued, and affect the socialisation of children after the return home.[12]

(11) Le Vine *et al* 1967; Lloyd 1969.   (12) See also Oppong 1974.

4 Kinshasa adolescence

LaFontaine[13] contrasted two groups of young men in Kinshasa, those attending school and the majority who were not. The latter participated in a well-developed youth subculture which included named gangs and *Kindoubil*, their own slang. Participation in this subculture indicates that the young person concerned has learned city ways; migrants from the provinces must undergo socialisation in order to fit in. The youth subculture promotes values of personal success, especially with members of the opposite sex, and the use of drugs, especially Indian hemp. Using drugs symbolises the opposition of young people to adult authority. Children join street gangs when they are old enough; are socialised into their form of life, first as messengers, then as fighting members; and finally take their place as leaders. These street gangs, and the scholars' associations for more fortunate young people, often have a fairly short life because of conflicts over leadership or loss of interest as the members find employment and/or marry, but they are important during the transition from childhood to adult status.

In a rural area, on the other hand, young people take on adult roles at an early age and do not need an adolescent subculture to set them apart. In some societies, age sets provide well organised socialising groups for young men. In cities, this function must be filled in another way. Young people need assistance in shifting from the ascribed identity of childhood to the achieved identity of urban adulthood; the adolescent is moving out from his family into the wider society, where he must stand on his own (though kinsmen may still be helpful to him). Adolescents lack the economic and political resources to compete with adults, but they learn the principles of competition and other social skills by using their physical and mental abilities within the youth culture. Those who attend school are socialised for competition there, but for the majority, and especially for young migrants to the city, socialisation by peers is important.

5 Living in Kampala

Parkin[14] describes the socialisation of women migrants on a Kampala housing estate. The women spend much of their time near their houses gossiping with their neighbours. The more experienced wives teach newcomers their obligations towards their husbands in an urban context and give them advice on child-rearing and budgeting. Neighbourhood norms are enforced by excluding deviants; women who behave badly or are notably above or below the others in status are rejected and often find it best to move. Cultural variations between ethnic groups, which would have been seen as important

(13) 1969. (14) 1969, pp.63–71.

58

differences at home, are relatively unimportant on the estate. Instead, status differentiation is mainly on the basis of economic resources and education. Women on the estate are often acutely aware of their material position in relation to their neighbours; they aspire to furniture, radios and clothing like their neighbours' and urge their husbands to provide these things. Thus, socialisation to urban life involves changing stratification as well as behaviour patterns. Men have less time for gossiping in primary groups; their socialisation takes place primarily at work, but also in associations and other recreational activities. Ethnic and hometown associations have helped new migrants learn the ways of the town (see Chapter 8), but men are also socialised by more informal contacts with workmates and fellow tenants.

Social exchange

The view of social life as a patterned exchange between individuals and between groups has a long history. Exchange is the basis of economics (the amount of goods exchanged can be measured in money), but social goods are also exchanged as one person does another a favour and is rewarded with a smile, another favour, prestige, etc. Economic exchange with strong social implications can be seen in the brideprice. A family which gives up a daughter to another family receives from them cows, money, or other goods (and occasionally services of the groom); the goods are widely distributed among the receiving kinsmen, who often use them in further exchanges for other brides. These families, connected by marriage and the exchanges which it involves, acknowledge social, political, religious and other ties which shape their relationships with each other and with outsiders.

Mauss[15] saw the exchange of gifts as the forerunner of the money economy. He showed that people in many societies have an obligation to give and receive gifts at specific times and that gifts can be used to enlarge one's prestige in the society. For example, Cohen[16] showed how the Hausa landlords in Ibadan provide housing for a large extended family, visiting traders and other clients such as mallams and their pupils. They get a share of the profit from the business transactions of their clients, and this enables them to provide more housing for more clients. Their position in the community rests on what they are able to give as well as the wealth they have accumulated. Similarly, men who have grown wealthy through corruption often have considerable prestige if they distribute their gains widely, whereas those who keep their riches to themselves are condemned. The gifts may be in cash

(15) 1925. (16) 1969.

or in goods; in either case they symbolise the acceptance of social responsibility.

Gouldner[17] suggests that there is a universal 'norm of reciprocity', whereby people repay assistance from others in any form either by helping them in return or at least by doing nothing against their benefactors. The repayment may be of the same kind as the gift (a chicken is given and a chicken returned) or something quite different (a community votes as directed and a school is built there). What is returned is often, but not necessarily, equivalent to what is given. If reciprocity is exact, it may mean that the relationship is finished. If A borrows five plantains from B and returns five plantains, or if A buys something and pays the price which B asks, they are even and may have nothing further to do with each other; this sort of exchange is necessary among strangers. The relationship may also be terminated because reciprocity is impossible. If A is unemployed and cannot pay his debts, he is involuntarily denying the norm of reciprocity and may lose his friends in consequence. Even kinship ties suffer if benefits are never repaid.

But frequently the recipient returns either less or more than he is given as an indication of continuing social obligation. If B returns the plantains with a further gift of tomatoes, he has 'credit' with A which can be drawn on in future. Or the gift may be only partly returned, with the remaining debt constituting a moral obligation to maintain friendly relations. Thus, the social structure of a society can be seen as a network of obligations between individuals and groups based on prior services. Even relations with the ancestors can be seen as a form of exchange. They are remembered and oblations are poured partly because of their prior services to the family and partly because of the protection they can give in future; the living members of the family build up a debt which the ancestors must pay in time of need. Christians and Muslims often approach God in much the same way.

Reciprocity is not necessarily limited to an interchange between two people. Ekeh[18] distinguishes between the mutual or restricted exchange which has been discussed so far and what he calls generalised exchange (see Figure 3). In this case, individuals do not benefit each other directly, but benefits move around the group so that all profit from the whole transaction. For such a system to work, participants must be of roughly similar status and prestige, otherwise the balance of benefits will not be achieved. If one member gets ahead and starts favouring another or receiving more favours from another (thus raising his status and prestige even further), reciprocity cannot be maintained and the social exchange relationship is likely to be ended.

(17) 1960. (18) 1974, pp.48–50.

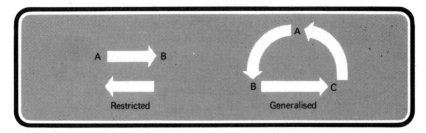

Figure 3 Types of exchange

Social exchange theorists have tended to concentrate on one or the other form. French sociologists, such as Mauss, Durkheim and Levi-Strauss, have taken the collectivist view, which emphasises generalised exchange, while British and American theorists, notably Homans and Blau, have focused on restricted exchange. The collectivists see the effects of exchange as permeating the society, a society which has an existence over and above the contributions of individual members. This is demonstrated in Mauss' 'recognition that social exchange processes yield for the larger society a moral code of behaviour which acquires an independent existence outside the social exchange situation and which informs all social, economic, and political interpersonal relationships in society.'[19] The norm of reciprocity influences the behaviour of many individuals who have not engaged in direct personal interaction because it sets the moral standards of the society. A treats B fairly and justly, even though they have not built up a relationship of mutual trust, because they both belong to a society in which a norm of trust and fair treatment has been developed from generations of reciprocal relationships between individuals. Where the moral code is based on restricted exchange, on the other hand, each individual must stand on his own. The politician grants favours to those who bribe him or have ties of kinship or other claims on his services; those who have nothing to exchange are ignored.

Durkheim's theory of organic solidarity arising from functional differentiation can be further developed by examining the role of generalised exchange in aiding social integration.[20] The social exchange processes operating in the society lead to the development of cultural communications networks based on widely accepted moral norms. These communications networks and the moral code make possible economic specialisation ('others can be trusted to do their task, so I can get on with mine'); the result is an interdependent society with an increasing degree of organic solidarity. Where

(19) *Ibid.,* p.58. (20) *Ibid.,* pp.74–5.

social exchange is restricted, these networks are missing; individuals must build up each relationship personally and social solidarity (interdependence) is minimal. This is the stage Durkheim refers to as mechanical solidarity.

Levi-Strauss' exchange theory is concerned mainly with the symbolism of exchange and its generalised nature; the important point is not what is exchanged (women, cows), but the symbolic value of the relationship and its implications for the society as a whole. Symbols are invented by humans and have an arbitrary meaning which may change over time or between one society and another. Individuals may get into difficulty if they interpret the same symbol in a different way from their partner in interaction. For example, if two men meet, one who is accustomed to greet others by shaking hands and the other by bowing, each may feel that the other is impolite because he does not give the 'proper' symbol of greeting. Symbols must be distinguished from signs, which have a universal meaning and which may be used by animals as well as by men: a sudden high wind and black clouds are signs of rain. We can learn the meaning of signs through conditioning (the sight of a pot over a fire makes us feel hungry), but there is no carry-over for signs from the individual to the society. Symbols, on the other hand, fit within a societal framework; they can be valued as part of a moral code.

Homans, reacting to Levi-Strauss' symbolism from a utilitarian, individualist point of view, focuses on the economic and psychological implications of exchange for furthering individual self-interest. Starting from the interpretation of the behaviour of individuals in groups, Homans moved to psychological reductionism – holding that all human behaviour can be understood in terms of animal psychology. He says that there is nothing separate or higher about the behaviour of humans; social phenomena can be reduced to biological responses which characterise the animal world. While there are many similarities between men and animals, most sociologists and psychologists would agree that there are also differences. Phenomenologists in particular concentrate on the meaning an activity has for an individual, which animals reacting to instinct do not have. Thus, it seems reasonable to examine social exchange between individuals by looking for both biological and social aspects (the child is attached to its mother because she provides food and emotional support, but also because the society encourages such a relationship).[21]

It is useful here to distinguish between three types of behaviour: instinctual, conditioned and symbolic. Animals act on instinct, though their behaviour may also be conditioned, as when dogs are taught to herd sheep or parrots to repeat certain words. Men's behaviour can be conditioned, as when children

(21) *Ibid.*, pp.84–99.

are taught to behave in certain ways by rewarding or punishing them. But men are also capable of symbolic behaviour, which is far more important to them than conditioned behaviour; it is what makes them uniquely human. Only humans have language and history, the ability to pass ideas on from one generation to the next. Thus, the exchange possible between humans has qualities of which animals are incapable.

Homans' work seems more meaningful when he examines economic aspects, the relationship between rewards and costs, punishment and profit.[22] For example, a new boy at school may 'invest' time and subordination in running errands and generally contributing to the prestige of an older boy in order to win security and a sense of belonging. Relationships which are rewarding are maintained; those for which the cost is too high are abandoned. (This is the same principle as reciprocity which cannot be repaid ending a relationship.)

Blau[23] put much more emphasis on economics than psychology, showing social exchange in a wide range of social contexts to be based on calculated advantage: 'What is in it for me?' Status and power are the rewards of successful social exchange relationships. Those in a position to give favours receive admiration and debts for service which can be collected when needed. Thus, the patron who can satisfy his clients receives still more clients, higher prestige and ultimately power. For Blau, power and status are 'zero-sum' qualities; there is a limited amount available and when one man gains another loses. Social exchange relationships are inherently unequal, though each participant must be satisfied if the relationship is to continue. This can be contrasted with the view that basic equality is necessary for generalised social exchange, as discussed above.

The main difference between economic and social exchange, according to Blau, is that the former is based on contractual obligation and the latter on moral obligation, a trust which is built up over a period of time. This overlooks the fact that economic exchange is also frequently based on trust and moral obligation. But it is easier to see the role of trust and societal norms from the viewpoint of the collectivist theorists, who look at generalised social exchange in a society as a whole, than from Blau's individualist point of view – seeing exchange as restricted to the two people concerned.

Kapferer carried out an extensive study of the applicability of Blau's exchange theory in a small clothing factory in Kabwe, Zambia. He provides a detailed analysis of the development of a relationships between workers over a nine-month period. Several incidents, especially two strikes, show how workers compete for power and influence and the constraints on workers in

22) 1961. (23) 1964.

various positions within the factory hierarchy. A worker can increase his influence only by decreasing that of his fellows (the zero-sum effect). It is a resource which must be used carefully: 'Power is expended in use and increased at risk.'[24] The supervisors, as 'men in the middle', are in a difficult situation. The men expect them to negotiate with the manager for increases in pay and improved conditions, whereas the manager expects them to enforce his orders and keep productivity high. The supervisors have prestige from their position, but this is lowered by their need to get compliance from the workers. Superiority over the senior tailors was especially difficult to maintain because the wages and skills of supervisors were only slightly better; thus they had few resources to exchange. The steady drain on their influence can be slowed by granting favours, leniency in enforcing regulations and teaching skills to new workers. The second strike was more successful than the first (from the workers' point of view) because the supervisors sought to improve their prestige by joining the workers against the manager; this helped them to regain the leadership they needed to do their job.

Whereas Homans and Blau treat 'elementary behaviour' as involving only one motive at a time, most people have several goals in any given situation and act to achieve as many of these as possible. Kapferer calls this a 'mixed motive game'.[25] For example, a worker in a factory has other roles which must be considered when deciding on a particular course of action. If the government has forbidden strikes and the worker is a party activist, this may make him unwilling to strike even though he feels the cause is just. A worker with large family commitments is less free to quit his job than a young man who is responsible only for himself. In predicting behaviour in a given social exchange relationship, one must assess the various motives which affect the participants. What may seem a large reward for a given course of action may be felt as unrewarding because it hinders the achievement of other goals which are less obvious to the observer but more important to the participant. For instance, a senior civil servant or big businessman may give up his position in order to return home as chief of his village. An outsider might argue that he is giving up a great deal in income, access to amenities, prestige, etc. However, the social rewards of contributing to community solidarity and leading his people are more important to him than the costs.

Social networks

The collectivist view of generalised social exchange may be seen as a network

(24) Kapferer 1972, p.326. (25) *Ibid.*, p.257.

of relationships by which a society is structured. Sociologists have long talked about the 'network of social relations', but tended to use this term in its metaphorical sense, referring to the complex interrelationships of a social system without trying to analyse the links actually existing between particular sets of individuals. However, in recent years there has been more interest in examining these links to see what information they provide to aid our understanding of the society concerned. Network analysis is more a method than a theory. By using various mathematical techniques (usually aided by computers), it is possible to show how social, economic and political networks influence the behaviour of individuals participating in them. These findings can then be applied to theories of stratification, social change, etc. Mitchell[26] has provided an extensive introduction to the study of social networks, which will be briefly summarised here, and a series of case studies based on network research carried out in Zambia.

Approaches

Networks have been studied by a variety of methods. Sociometrists, following Moreno, have been chiefly interested in friendship cliques, leadership and association for task performance. They have typically asked individuals whom they would prefer to associate with or avoid in a particular situation. This method was used by the Volta Resettlement Authority in Ghana to give villagers displaced by the Volta Dam a chance to choose which resettlement village they would go to – which families would like to continue living together.

Social psychologists have also been concerned with chains of communication. If you want to spread information through a community, whom do you contact and how is it passed on? For instance, the Liberian Government's promotion of new strains of rice was initially ineffective because extension agents contacted the men rather than the women, whereas the latter made the decision as to what type of rice should be grown. The men who got the information did not pass it on to their wives.

Another type of network study has used participant observation and detailed interviews to trace all the significant members of a chosen individual's network as an aid to explaining his behaviour. Figure 4 shows the wide variety of individuals included in the network of a successful Hausa trader. Yusuf has shown these as categories; some individuals fall into more than one category (i.e., a client who is also an affine and a disciple of the same mallam). The trader's behaviour in any given situation can be explained in terms of the

(26) 1969a.

single and multiple role relationships between himself and other participants, but the explanation may be improved by examining the links between various members of the network as well as direct links between the trader and any given individual.

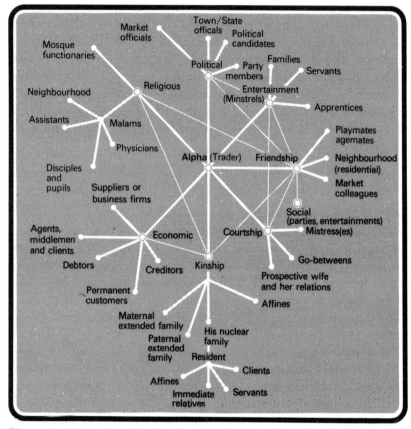

Figure 4 The network of primary and secondary relationships of an accomplished Kano entrepreneur (Source: Yusuf 1975, p.180.)

In a small community which is relatively isolated, it is possible to trace the links of every individual to all the others; in a large-scale society it is necessary to focus on partial networks. This is sometimes done by examining the relationships involved in a particular event such as a wedding or funeral, election or dispute, or one can look at relationships between individuals within a particular organisation, ignoring their ties to the outside community. This limited analysis may omit important factors; people do not segregate sectors of their life for the convenience of sociologists.

Interest in social networks has developed partly in response to the inadequacy of structural/functional theories for analysing relationships in large-scale societies. Mitchell[27] suggests that three types of social relationships must be distinguished: structural, categorical and personal. Within the structural order, behaviour is interpreted according to the position an individual holds within a corporate group: family, association, or work place. In an unstructured situation, behaviour is interpreted in terms of social stereotypes such as sex, age, or ethnicity. In a situation where we must deal with strangers without a common structure or culture, we usually interact in terms of categorical identification: not as an individual but as a type. In addition to these types, behaviour in either structured or unstructured situations may be based on personal links between individuals: ties of kinship, friendship, neighbourhood, etc. In attempting to move from social reality in particular situations to abstract generalisations about behaviour, we need to examine the structural, categoric and/or personal aspects in order to fully understand the meaning of behaviour to the individuals involved. Thus, the study of social networks (the personal order) provides an important dimension of analysis, especially in studies of social change.

Characteristics of networks

As social network analysis is a relatively recent development and has grown rapidly, a wide variety of terms is used and these are not always clearly defined. Different words are used to describe similar phenomena and the same word may have different meanings for different authors. Some of the more important terms will be discussed here to demonstrate various aspects of network research.[28] Networks can be examined for their structural and interactional characteristics. The structural characteristics are anchorage or root, reachability, density and range or span. The interactional characteristics are 'content, directedness, durability, intensity and frequency'.[29] These are used to analyse the nature of the links, what they mean to the individual concerned.

1 Anchorage or root

Network studies usually focus on a particular individual and his links to other people. This root or anchor of the network is chosen because he plays a central part in the event being analysed; he is the candidate seeking election, the leader of the work group, or the newcomer to the neighbourhood. Alpha (the trader) is the root of the network shown in Figure 4.

(27) 1966, pp.51–5.   (28) Mitchell 1969a, pp.11–29.   (29) *Ibid.*, p.12.

The root of the network is the individual whose behaviour is to be explained, and all the links which appear to influence this behaviour should be traced. For instance, the attitude of a factory worker toward his job will be influenced by his relations with his employer, supervisor and fellow workers, but perhaps also by his kinsmen (whose demands for help make his wage seem too small), his wife (who feels she would have more prestige in the neighbourhood if he were a clerk), his ties to local political leaders (urging him to uphold the government's ban on strikes), and so on. Often behaviour which seems irrational can be explained by examining the salient ties of the individual concerned. These may be primary links (direct contact between individuals) or secondary links (indirect contacts). For example, our trader in Figure 4 has primary ties to his mallam, but only secondary links to the mallam's students. Epstein[30] calls these links the effective and extended network, the latter including all the people contacted by the root individual directly or indirectly. Extended networks may be important because through them individuals are influenced by people they do not actually know. For example, a man who is looking for work asks all the people in his effective network about jobs. They ask others they know, and someone in the extended network may be able to suggest where he should apply.

2 Reachability

People in the effective network can more easily be contacted than those in the extended network; this ease of contact is measured by reachability. The researcher can count the number of steps needed to contact everyone in the network from a given anchor. If most people can be contacted within a small number of steps (as when everyone knows everyone else, see Figure 5), we

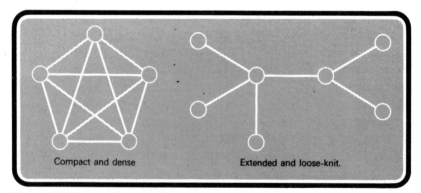

Compact and dense   Extended and loose-knit.

Figure 5 Types of networks

(30) 1961.

speak of a compact network. Norm enforcement is easier in such a network, because opinions, attitudes and information are easily spread through the group. Contacts in an extended network, with greater reachability, take longer and are less sure (links may be broken, temporarily or permanently). For example, villages with a strong hometown association are able to demand more mutual aid and contributions to village improvement than those which lack such an association, because in the first case leaders can easily reach all the members, whereas in the second case potential contributors are usually harder to reach.

3 Density

In her classic study of family networks, Bott[31], distinguished between close-knit and loose-knit networks; this is referred to as the mesh, connectedness, or density of the network. In a close-knit or dense network, all or most of the people know each other and interact. In a loose network, on the other hand, each individual has few ties and it is more difficult to mobilise support when it is needed. Kapferer[32] defines density as 'the extent to which the individuals to whom Ego is linked are linked to each other.' Whereas all possible links exist in the left network of Figure 5 (it has the highest possible density), more than half the links are missing in the right network (it has a low density). When density is low, ties are likely to be less strong and it is more difficult to exert pressure on individuals to contribute to the good of the group, inso-far as a group exists at all.

4 Range or span

An individual who has a large number of contacts may be said to have a wide-ranged network. There is as yet no evidence of the maximum size of network an individual can contact regularly; it is certainly much larger for some individuals than for others. Even yearly contact may be enough to keep a link alive. The word range may also refer to the social heterogeneity of one's contacts. The trader in Figure 4 has kinship, friendship, economic, political, religious and entertainment ties to people in a wide variety of statuses. His clients in these various sectors supply him with information (in exchange for favours) which he can use to further his interests. This wide-ranging network gives him many advantages over a young man just beginning his career in trade. Because of the diversity of educational opportunity within families and considerable social mobility, many individuals have a wide range of contacts. Some of these links are used frequently, others only in time of need. For example, if someone gets into trouble with the police, he will mobilise

(31) 1957.   (32) 1972, p.172.

any links he has with lawyers or policemen, working through his kinsmen and friends if necessary. At other times, these links may be ignored as unimportant.

Kapferer[33] uses span rather than range and has a somewhat different meaning in that he is concerned only with the range of direct or primary links. Span is the proportion of links with others in the network which are direct rather than indirect. Since his concern is mainly with mobilising resources in struggles for power, span is a useful measure of the extent to which an individual can call for aid from people with whom he is in regular contact. A leader may have direct links with almost everyone in the network (and hence a high span) even though the network is not dense (as in the left network of Figure 5); in this case, he can get support from many others but they cannot so easily get help without consulting him. If an individual has a low span, he is dependent on indirect contacts for support, and these may not be reliable.

5 Content

The interaction variables are generally more difficult to measure than the structural variables; this is especially true of content. Symbolic interactionists have been particularly concerned with the content of links, trying to analyse the meaning they have for the individuals concerned. The problem is that an observer may be completely misled because the meaning comes from prior experience or is directed toward future goals and thus is not visible to an outsider. It is particularly difficult if the observer comes from a different society (a non-African observing African interaction) or even from a different subgroup within the society (a university student who grew up in a town observing villagers) because the observer's different socialisation may lead him to misinterpret symbolic action and not even notice behaviour which is deeply meaningful to participants. In such a situation, it is best for someone who knows the society well to answer questions and explain what is happening.

The content of a link may be friendship or kinship, or it may have economic, religious, political, or other meaning. In each case, there are norms and values associated with this content and behaviour is interpreted as reflecting these norms and values. The relationship may be 'single-stranded' (based on just one content or link), or 'multi-stranded' (with several contents mixed together'. For example, if you buy oranges regularly from a certain trader but have no other contact, the content of your interaction is purely economic; if she is your mother's sister and you belong to the same church,

(33) *Ibid.*, pp.170-1.

your relationship is multi-stranded. Similarly, in a large factory run by a multi-national corporation, the relationship between workers and management is usually strictly economic, whereas in a small firm there may be many personal ties between the owner and the workers and the content of their interaction may be affected by their respective ethnic and socio-economic status, political influence, kinship, and religious ties.

The observer must try to build up an abstract picture of the content from the behaviour he sees; he may leave out strands which seem unimportant, but often recognition of multiple strands is necessary to adequately explain behaviour. Kapferer[34] explains the development of a dispute among workers in terms of their ties or 'investments' in other workers within the work group. The basic division was between younger and older workers. The younger workers could easily cope with the physical demands of the job and were accused by the older workers of being rate-busters. The older workers were, in turn, accused of threatening to use witchcraft against their younger colleagues. However, when two workers had a dispute, accusing each other of rate-busting and witchcraft, the shop steward chose to re-interpret the quarrel in terms of lack of respect for the older man. Another worker accused the young man of being drunk. Kapferer explains that the main issue of the quarrel was played down and the workers generally supported the older man because of the nature of the social networks in the group. The shop steward had multi-stranded ties with many of the workers, which he did not want to weaken on a trivial issue. The older man could mobilise support for himself through multi-stranded direct and indirect ties to most of the other workers, whereas the younger man had a much more limited network and most of his ties were single-stranded.

People with multi-stranded relationships are more tightly bound together than those with single-stranded ties and find it difficult or even impossible to withdraw from the relationship if a disagreement occurs. When people have many ties, there is considerable pressure to maintain links; this operates as a measure of social control against conflict. In a village where the mesh or density is high and where people interact in terms of kinship, neighbourhood, economic, political and social ties, efforts are made to minimise disputes between individuals because if they became serious and villagers took sides it might make it impossible to continue to live together. In a city, where links are often single-stranded and hence relatively weak, social control is also weak and open conflict may be more frequent than in villages. (But latent conflict may be prevalent in a village; the inability to quarrel openly may lead to one or both of the disputants leaving the village.)

(34) In Mitchell 1969a.

6 Directedness

In sociometric studies, where individuals may choose others with whom they would like to live or work, there is always the possibility that the choice will not be reciprocal; A may choose B but not be chosen by B. Kinship and neighbourliness are usually reciprocal, but employer–employee and patron–client relationships are not. The amount of influence one person has over another will depend on whether the relationship is reciprocal or unidirectional. For example, the foreman's job is to affect the worker's behaviour, but the workers may be able to exert little influence over their foreman if he is secure in his post. However, if the foreman gets little support from the owner, his relationship with the workers may become reciprocal; if a worker is also related to the foreman and/or is active in the same church (i.e., the relationship is multi-stranded), influence may be exerted in both directions.

7 Durability

Members of networks have rights and obligations in relation to each other because of the relationship they have built up over a period of time. Only part of a person's total network is used in any given situation, but the network is also gradually changing, with some links becoming dormant or ending while new links are taken up. In a situation such as a funeral, a person may reactivate many ties which had been dormant; when a person moves to another part of a city or from a village to a town, he will lose some ties and gain others. Multi-stranded links are more durable than single-stranded links; the individuals concerned will make greater efforts to keep in contact even though they are physically separated.

8 Intensity

We are much more closely tied to some members of our network than to others; the rights and obligations involved in some ties are much more valuable than others. Ties to kinsmen are usually intense because they are based on long-term reciprocity and moral obligation, supported by strong societal values. Outside kinship, intense ties are usually multi-stranded, because the number of links which hold people together make them more able to ask for assistance, more willing to honour calls for help and less able to back down on the relationship. An intense link to a person living some distance away may be a more important factor in a person's behaviour than less intensive links to those nearby. For example, workmates may see a good deal of each other but be more intensively linked to kinsmen at home. Although the worker may contact these kinsmen only infrequently, he would make a considerable sacrifice if they needed help. many regularly send money home even though they need it to improve their standard of living in town. Distant kinsmen are part of an individual's extended network, but those who live near enough to be reached in an emergency and who can be contacted personally are a more important part of his network in most circumstances.

9 Frequency

The last characteristic is much easier to measure than content, durability, or intensity, but it is not as useful an indicator of probable behaviour. Contacts between two people may be frequent, as they are between workmates, without much effect on behaviour or even much real interest in each other. In this case, the intensity is low. Many people never associate with workmates outside working hours, and most would not hesitate to place the request of a kinsman above that of a workmate even though they seldom saw the kinsman. While frequent contact may help to develop a multi-stranded, intense relationship and deliberate decreasing of contacts may indicate that the relationship is under stress, we should beware of judging the importance of a relationship to the participants by the frequency of their contacts.

Networks and norms

Every social situation involves implicit or explicit communication, exchange between participants and evaluation of the observance of social norms. Whether the analysis emphasises the communication, exchange, networks, or some other aspect of behaviour depends on what questions the researcher is asking. Mitchell[35] suggests that network research is particularly useful for studying normative behaviour because members of a network constantly evaluate the behaviour of other members and press them to uphold the norms of the group or community. Several reports illustrate the normative quality of networks.

Mayer[36] found that Xhosa migrants to East London, South Africa, could be divided into two types according to the nature of the networks they established in town. He called these 'Red' and 'School', referring to the red blanket which traditional Xhosa wear and the fact that most of those in the second category had attended school. The Reds establish close-knit networks of people from the same rural area, encapsulating themselves against urban influences; members are under considerable pressure to conform to traditional norms and remain essentially conservative in their approach to urban life. The School Xhosa, on the other hand, have accepted schooling and Christianity and tend to use whites as a reference group. Their networks are loose-knit

(35) In Boissevain and Mitchell 1972, p.26.   (36) 1961, 1962.

and often based on single-stranded links. This means that they are under much less pressure to conform to traditional norms than the Red migrants and more open to influences of cultural change. Some Reds become School in town; the influence of social networks is shown by the fact that their former friends say they 'got into bad company'. Information about an individual's social network is used in this case to get a better understanding of his attitudes and behaviour in a situation where he must cope with challenges to the norms and values established in his early socialisation.

Network studies have also provided useful information on the transmission and maintenance of norms through gossip. Epstein's early work in Ndola, Zambia[37] showed how news is spread in a community through the wide-ranging networks of certain individuals. The comments which accompany this news serve to uphold norms or indicate that ideas of proper behaviour may be changing. In a later study of gossip about an adulterer, Epstein[38] shows that the norms defined by the elite through their primary networks are passed on to non-elite members of the community through links in their extended networks. Attitudes toward the incident are shaped by the elite, and this helps to support the elite's sense of identity as a separate and superior group.

Jacobson[39] studied the social networks of elite men in Mbale, Uganda. An interesting feature here was the durability of many links in spite of geographical mobility. Civil servants are often transferred from one town to another, which inevitably means reshaping the network of people they interact with frequently. But former close friends who meet again after an interval of several years are usually able to reactivate their ties, which have been dormant rather than broken. Grillo[40] found the same pattern among East African railwaymen, who were also transferred from one town to another at frequent intervals but who were linked together by their work for the same organisation and the common expectations about status, income, housing and recreation which this implied.

The nature of an individual's social networks may differ according to his feeling of security in town and his intention of returning home. The migrant who feels that his income is fairly secure and who intends to stay in town indefinitely may see little need to maintain close links with his hometown, whereas the migrant who feels insecure and/or plans to return home in the near future may focus his primary network on people from home to insure that he will get help when he needs it. Parkin[41] found that there were many Kenyans in Kampala who took no part in tribal associations but were active in tenants' associations and trade unions. These were generally well estab-

(37) 1961.   (38) In Mitchell 1969a.   (39) 1973.   (40) 1973.   (41) 1969.

lished in stable employment. With Ugandan independence and growing insecurity for Kenyans, ethnic ties became increasingly important, requiring some re-alignment of social networks.

Amachree[42] reports that semiskilled factory workers in Nigeria tend to choose friends from among their workmates, whereas unskilled workers tend to prefer associating with kinsmen rather than co-workers. Workers with more than ten years' experience on the job (the most established and secure) were most likely to choose friends from among workmates rather than kinsmen, but older skilled workers who were beginning to plan a return home tended to choose kinsmen as friends, indicating a restoration of links which were less important to them earlier.

The study of social networks as resources which can be mobilised to increase one's power and influence contributes to the understanding of local politics. Harries-Jones[43] shows how a politician can recruit followers by building on hometown ties. These links involve a moral obligation to give assistance when called on; by creating a series of patron-client relationships and then utilising the extended hometown networks of his clients, a politician can develop fairly wide support.

Boswell[44] describes the social networks mobilised for three funerals in Lusaka. In the first, a mother whose daughter died in hospital was a stranger in town. A woman from her home area whom she met at the hospital helped her to contact the Anglican church and fellow Lala, who provided the assistance she needed. Thus, in a crisis social networks can be used by some-one who is not a part of them.

The second case concerned a wood-cutter who was run down by a car. He had lived alone, associating with neighbours and fellow-workers rather than with kinsmen. By the time his kinsmen had been notified of the death, the Marketing Company, in which the wood-cutter had been active, had arranged for the coffin and transport. His political party was also active; the funeral gave both groups a chance to show how well they looked after active members. The associational ties coincided with residential links and intertribal joking relationships, and so were multi-stranded and relatively intense; many members of these associations knew the deceased well and were part of his primary network.

The third funeral was of an elite woman, sister of a local politician. Many of her brother's former social and educational ties (old school friends and fellow members of the elite) were reactivated for the funeral. In both this and the previous case, extended networks were a more important source of mourners for the large funeral than the effective network with which the

(42) 1968, pp.234-5. (43) In Mitchell 1969a. (44) *Ibid.*

deceased spent his leisure time. Kinsmen were more important in the third funeral than in the other two. The study of attendance at funerals can provide as much evidence about the social networks of the living as of the dead.

Finally, Thoden Van Velzen[45] describes the conflicts of several 'interest coalitions' in a southern Tanzanian village. The central personality in these conflicts is Chomo, a rich farmer who managed to surmount the opposition of other villagers with the help of administrative staff stationed in the village. Church personnel tended to oppose Chomo but remain neutral in conflicts. Similarly, clients of Chomo would warn him of danger but stay away when he was attacked. (They objected to his methods, which were contrary to community norms, but needed his aid.) By making friends with an administrator, Chomo was able to mobilise staff networks to hs own advantage; other villagers lacked these links. Since Chomo also acquired a reputation as a sorcerer, his position seemed to be unassailable.

Conclusion

This chapter has been concerned with the socialisation of an individual into his society and the relationships he develops with other individuals through social exchange and social networks. Socialisation takes place primarily in childhood, but taking up a new role at any time of life usually requires a period of socialisation. Becoming a social being includes the ability to communicate with others through language and other symbols, such as gestures and expression; it also includes a sense of identity in relation to the society in which one is living. A community may reject individuals who do not appear to share its norms and values. Where this is due to alternative socialisation (training in other norms and values) the individual may identify with some reference group within the society or even outside it and reject characterisation as a deviant. If, however, his behaviour is merely due to inadequate socialisation, he may try to avoid or overcome rejection by taking on the qualities of his normative reference group, insofar as he can do this.

Social exchange can be seen as based on a 'norm of reciprocity'. Material and financial aid, services, prestige and respect are given in exchange for other goods, services, or sentiments. Debts are gradually built up and paid off, but some balance of benefits must be maintained if the relationship is to continue. The collectivists have emphasised generalised exchange in an interdependent society, whereas the individualists have focused on restricted exchange between individuals who are mainly concerned with furthering their self-interest. Reductionist theories that human exchange behaviour is no

(45) In Boissevain and Mitchell 1972.

different from animal behaviour can be refuted by demonstrating the symbolic quality of human behaviour: animals lack symbols. The use of the economic analogy (explaining all behaviour in terms of economic exchange) is useful for discussing relationships of inequality in contests for status and power, but it is less useful for situations in which the participants share a position of basic equality.

Everyone develops effective and extended social networks which vary in size from one individual to another and change in composition over time. Studies of the personal ties which individuals build up examine the structural and interactional characteristics of these networks for keys to the way these contacts influence the behaviour and attitudes of the people concerned, especially for their influence on the maintenance of change of social norms. These networks are important as agents of socialisation and serve as a framework for social exchange.

Suggested reading and discussion topics
1. Read something about child-rearing and early socialisation in your own area. To what extent is it a conscious 'system' with goals which are clearly evident to all parents? What are these goals? If the goals appear to change when members of the society are rearing their children away from home, what are the new goals?
2. Describe the exchange relationships between pupils and teachers in a secondary school.
3. What networks were mobilised for the last funeral you attended? Were any people who were part of the deceased's effective network absent? If so, what was the reaction of those present to this absence?

4 Social Differentiation

The last chapter examined the factors which unify members of societies and hold them together. This chapter is concerned with factors which separate individuals and groups. Various theories have been developed to account for institutionalised inequality, as seen in systems of class, status and power. Study of the role of elites and the nature of social mobility suggests ways in which stratification systems are changing. Finally, communal differentiation provides an identification which cuts across other hierarchical systems and has been a disruptive force, to a greater or lesser extent, in many societies (not only in Africa).

Differentiation tends to imply some form of social inequality, since comparisons usually contain an element of one individual or group being higher or more important than the other. Each of two parties in a relationship may consider himself better than the other, since we tend to inflate our own importance in comparisons with others. Nevertheless, an outsider can usually rank individuals or groups in a rough hierarchy, and the nature of interaction is often affected by the relative position of the participants.

No human community is completely homogeneous; even the simplest society gives some people more responsibility than others. People are differentiated from each other by many characteristics, such as sex, age, descent, race, regional or ethnic origin, physical and mental capacity, occupation, income, standard of living, etc. In each of these characteristics, there is a hierarchy of value. For example, people of greater age and more education are usually given more honour than people with less of these advantages. Societies differ in the relative importance given to each characteristic. Age, for instance, is usually much more important in a relatively stable than in a rapidly changing society. While some of these differentiating characteristics are ascribed (such as age and sex), many are open to achievement.

The stratification systems of Africa today are a mixture of traditional patterns and new developments. A man's place often depends on the context; he has certain roles at home and other roles in town. Contemporary criteria of differentiation may be quite different or fairly similar to former patterns; the possibility of rising through ability varies considerably from one society to another, as does the behaviour which is rewarded by increased prestige.

Social stratification

The basic idea of social stratification is a series of layers, rather as one bolt of cloth might be piled on top of another. It developed in European society to explain clashes between the old aristocracy of landed wealth, the new industrial capitalists and the workers over political and economic power and cultural dominance. It is less meaningful in an African context than the concept of inequality, because in a non-Western society relationships are more likely to centre on superiority and inferiority between individuals (as between patrons and clients) than in consciousness of group membership at relatively fixed levels. This permits greater flexibility than is possible in a European stratification system, at least in principle.[1] However, as African societies are often analysed as stratified systems (many of them have been stratified in the past and stratification seems to be increasing), the concept is useful providing alternatives are kept in mind.

A stratification system has both a moral or cultural and a structural base. Each culture has some view of an 'admirable man' against which individuals may measure their own and others' conduct, an ideal which people try to live up to. This may be generalised or specified as behaviour which is expected of holders of certain roles: a good chief, farmer, or mother. In addition, stratification arises from the division of labour, whereby certain roles are admired more than others. In one society, the successful farmer may receive the most honour; in another it may be the scholar or political leader. Members of the society are evaluated according to the roles they fill and also according to the way the role is carried out. In small-scale societies where most individuals have the same roles, the second factor is most important; in large-scale societies with an extensive division of labour, stratification tends to be based on distinctions between roles.[2]

In the sense that all societies value some roles more than others, stratification is universal; if, on the other hand, stratification is defined as institutionalised inequality of access to advantageous positions, some societies are not stratified. The Bushmen and Pygmies, for example, have no political leaders and role differentiation is limited to age, sex and physical capacity. Within these limitations, all members undertake the few roles available at some time in their lives and the society is equalitarian. Where more roles are available, a society can avoid stratification by giving equal prestige to all roles

(1) Fallers 1973, pp.16, 29.   (2) Fallers 1964, pp.65–7 and 1973, p.93.

or by providing equal opportunity for entering roles. There is usually more equality of opportunity than of prestige (or rewards); though modern societies tend to be equalitarian in ideology, all have a few highly valued roles and some sectors of the population always have better opportunities than others for attaining the highest places. Nevertheless, opportunities for mobility are greater in most contemporary societies than in hereditary monarchies or caste systems, where the most important roles were allocated by birth.

Much more attention is usually paid to the structural aspect of stratification (the processes for allocating people to roles and the societal structure which results) than to the cultural aspect (beliefs about how and why people are allocated and the justice or injustice of the process). Some roles are generally held to be important, but are in fact given to less able people or are poorly rewarded. Why? For example, much is said about the importance of teachers for society, but primary teachers in particular tend to have low status and the most capable young people are often warned to avoid teaching. People explain this in various ways: teachers are often not well trained; they do not make much money; the job is tedious; etc. In fact, this is a circular argument. We do not value and reward teaching highly because the most capable people do not go into it, and they avoid teaching because it does not have high status or rewards. One could work out the various beliefs about other roles and see how these differ from one society to another and over time.

The functional theory of stratification[3] holds that a society, through its members, makes certain decisions about the allocation of desirable roles. Choice is limited by the number of these roles and the number of people available to perform them. A generally agreed ideological justification of the established method of recruitment, whether this is based on merit or descent or some other system, legitimates the allocation process so that those given lower roles are satisfied with their position. The rewards attached to various roles (wealth, prestige or power) are justified by the service to society involved (especially to societal survival) and the rarity of the abilities needed to fill them. For example, the role of doctor is highly rewarded because relatively few doctors perform the important service of curing the sick. Street cleaning, on the other hand, is poorly rewarded because anyone can do it and, if necessary, the community can do without street cleaners.

There are many difficulties with the extreme functionalist position. Critics are quick to point out that there is often considerable disagreement about the relative rewards of various roles and that some roles receive far higher rewards (and others far lower) than their relative difficulty and contribution

(3) Davis and Moore 1947; Parsons 1954, 1970; Moore 1963.

would suggest. Service to society is particularly difficult to define and the allocation of rewards tends to cater more for the needs of those in power than for the society at large. Miners, for example, are only moderately rewarded for doing a dangerous and difficult job which provides considerable national wealth, whereas the political role (for which there is a great surplus of candidates and whose contribution to societal survival may be questioned) is often very well rewarded. While most would agree that rewards draw people to roles which must be performed, the functional necessity of the usual allocation of rewards and especially the large differentials between the rewards for positions at the top and at the bottom may easily be challenged.

The conflict theory of stratification draws largely on the writings of Marx, though adjustments have been necessary to adapt it to the changing nature of twentieth century capitalism.[4] Marx saw society as divided into two major groups (capitalists and proletarians or workers) who are inevitably in conflict. Critics have pointed out that most societies have far more than two groups and that they are not always in conflict. On the other hand, people who seem to have a similar position in society (or similar access to rewards) are often in conflict over their respective 'share of the cake' and find allies among people whose condition is much better or much worse than their own. For example, political leaders are often able to attract support from members of their ethnic group in their conflict with other politicians for top posts in government, even though only a minor share of the rewards allocated to the successful is shared with their followers.

In his analysis of capitalist society, Marx tended to ignore the position of peasants and the small-scale self-employed (shopkeepers and artisans) who form a large majority of the population of most African countries. They have interests of their own which prevent automatic alliances with either workers or capitalists. Even more important, Marx mistakenly believed that differences within categories (i.e., between skilled and unskilled workers) would inevitably disappear, while today we see that industrialisation has made for greater rather than smaller differences; conflicts arise within the worker category as some workers demand higher rewards than others because of the training needed, conditions endured, or necessary services performed. Thus, although conflict is evident in stratification systems and must be explained, an adequate theory must go further.

Whereas Marx was particularly concerned only with the economic or market hierarchy, which he termed class, Weber suggested that people are also stratified according to status (prestige or style of life) and power. These three hierarchies may be closely related, but this is not necessarily so. Marx

(4) Dahrendorf 1959; van den Berghe 1963.

assumed that those with a high economic position would also have power, but rich businessmen often have less power than higher civil servants on moderate salaries; clergymen and teachers usually have higher status than either wealth or power.

As a society changes, the relationship between social differentiation, the allocation of roles and ideology justifying this allocation changes and institutionalised social relations based on wealth, honour and/or power also change. As new roles come into the society, people's ideas about older roles are modified and they are given greater or lesser rewards than in the past. The result is a different system of social stratification, based on a new societal structure and culture. The rate of change depends partly on the amount of consensus or conflict in the society over the legitimacy of the old system, but other factors such as the amount of pressure for change from outside the system are also important. While we might expect that societies with considerable conflict would be most easily changed, leaders of a society where most people share basic values may find it easier to accept gradual change than leaders who feel so threatened by conflict that they make great efforts to hang on to their privileges.

Often groups which have generally consented to inequality force change when they acquire a new consciousness of their position. For example, in the early days of colonial rule most people ignored the new rulers who had taken over superordinate positions in the society. They were gradually affected, as chiefs lost their power to district officers and young men migrated from their villages to improve their economic position. Independence movements may be seen as a demand for the reallocation of elite roles and rewards to a new group within the society.

Class

Partly because of its ideological implications, there are so many definitions of social class in use that it is often difficult to tell what a particular author has in mind; the definition is often shifted to suit the argument or the findings rather than testing the data against a theory based on a clearly established concept. At one extreme, class may mean the institutionalised inequality of wealth or power in a society so that certain groups of people (whose membership is stable over time) actively pursue their own interests at the expense of other groups, with whom they are in conflict over access to societal resources. At the other extreme, class may be used as a category or type to refer to people who have something in common, usually either economic, political, or social position in the society, even though this position is highly flexible, not institutionalised, and does not result in conflict with people holding other positions; they may not be conscious of any group interest and in no sense form a corporate group. Since the implications of class vary considerably depending on what definition is being used, it is important to find out what the author has in mind.

The Marxian definition of class is a group of people who share the same relationship to the means of production and capacity to engage in political struggle. In nineteenth-century England, when Marx wrote, it was fairly easy to divide the population into industrial owners and industrial workers, with shopkeepers and the landed gentry as peripheral groups of minor importance who generally sided with the owners. Society could thus be seen as a dichotomy: the owners of the means of production and those who only owned their labour. In the twentieth century, however, ownership of industry is widely dispersed among stockholders, who may not even be citizens of the country of operation and may include the government and trade unions representing the workers. The men who run these industries are not owners but managers who sell their labour as do ordinary workmen. Many industries are owned and run by the state.[5] Industrial workers are often more privileged economically than the majority of self-employed farmers, craftsmen or traders, even though some of the latter are employers of labour.

The most significant part of this definition, then, is the idea that a person's income, and through it his relative economic position, allots him a certain place in society (Marx would say determines) which is likely to affect his attitudes and behaviour. Marx distinguishes between a 'class in itself' (a category which can be objectively determined by an outsider who observes the common position and interests) and a 'class for itself' (a social group in which members are aware of this position and take action to improve their situation by working to overthrow their oppressors). Where people of lower class position are not in conflict with the upper class, Marxists accuse them of 'false consciousness' or maintaining 'ideological/cultural residues', since conflict is seen as normal and historically inevitable. However, this is a paternalistic approach, since intellectuals are proclaiming that they know better than ordinary people where the latter's best interests lie. One cannot assume that groups in different economic positions necessarily have completely different interests; they often share many common interests such as ethnic and national pride. (Marxists treat these as false consciousness. The difficulty with such a concept is that it cannot be proved or disproved empirically.)

Weber distinguished classes as people having common life chances and

(5) *Ibid.*

economic interests based on their income opportunities and the goods they possess. These are said to be in the same market or class situation, though they may be categories rather than corporate groups and may not undertake any communal action. He followed Marx in holding that ownership or non-ownership of property is basic to a class situation, but saw no necessity for conflict between people who are differentially situated in regard to class. Furthermore, he showed that it is necessary to distinguish class (economic position) from status and party (by which he meant power); these cannot be subsumed under class as Marx assumed.[6]

Marx's emphasis on two major classes causes considerable difficulty for those making empirical studies, since a wide variety of material conditions is usually evident. Should subsistence farmers and cash crop farmers be classed together? Clerical workers and labourers? Technicians and the unskilled? Various categories have been devised, usually combining income (or estimated income) with occupation (which is easier to ascertain). Occupations such as trader/businessman and farmer cause difficulty because they are represented over the whole range of income; it may be possible to divide the population by size of farm or business, but often the objective 'class position' is evident only at the extremes of wealth or poverty.

The resulting analysis may be based on three classes (upper, middle and lower or working) or six (dividing each of these into upper upper, upper lower, etc.). The main purpose of this exercise is to study the differences in attitudes and behaviour of people in various classes. For instance, in many societies members of the lower class have more children and less interest in either education or politics than members of the middle class. If few class differences are found, it may indicate that class situation has no influence in the area of life studied or that class has little or no empirical meaning in the society. However, if there are classes, it is easier to move from one to another in a society where there are few cultural and behavioural differences between classes than in a society where such differences are clearly observable.

One method of studying classes is to ask people what class they belong to. This can be misleading if only identification is asked for and the researcher assumes that his respondents use class terms in the same way he does (as when the question asked is, 'Do you belong to the upper, middle, or working class?'). It can provide useful information if the initial question is more open and further questions are asked on the way people perceive the system and what they mean by the terms they use. Usage often differs from one sector of the society to another and subjective identification may have more to do with ideology than with economic position. The university lecturer may

(6) Weber 1946, pp.180–3.

proudly proclaim that he is working class while the factory worker may say he is middle class. An illiterate farmer will tend to identify himself with the *talakawa, mekunnu, wanachi,* or *mukopi* (commoners, ordinary men) in contrast to the 'rich' or 'big men'. This shows his dichotomous view of social structure, but we need to know further what criteria he uses for placing people in these categories, the extent to which he sees them as in basic opposition, and how rigid and stable he thinks the boundaries between them are.

Status

While some societies have no classes because rank according to economic position has not been institutionalised, status systems are found everywhere. Status refers to honour, prestige, or social privilege. It is demonstrated when we defer to superiors, accept others as equals, or derogate others as inferior to ourselves. People of common status tend to have the same consumption patterns (standard of living) but people who can afford the same material goods may be of widely different status if heredity or source of income are taken into account (the chief and the thief). Caste and slavery are part of the status rather than the class system because they affect the prestige of the individual regardless of the amount of wealth he has been able to acquire.

When people speak of 'socio-economic class' or 'social class', they are often referring to the status system. For example, class has been used to refer to the distinction between 'civilised' and 'bush' people – the degree to which an individual follows European ways in dress, food and drink, housing, etc. Fraenkel[7] divides Monrovia society into 'Elite' (senior officials and their families), 'Honorables' (other government officials and major professionals), 'Civilized' (minor officials, clerks and teachers), 'Indeterminant' (domestics') and 'Tribal or uncivilized' (labourers, fishermen and petty traders). Skilled workers fall between 'civilized' and 'indeterminant'. There is evidence that people are conscious of their position in society (especially the 'civilized' and above in relation to the 'tribal', but far more in a prestige than in an economic interest sense: 'The civilized are distinguished from the "uncivilized" less by their actual income than by what they do with it.'[8]

Mitchell[9] and Schwab[10] also found the 'civilised' distinction in Zambia and Rhodesia, though they refer to it as status rather than class. Burawoy[11] suggests that Zambians have a two-tier reference group system. High-status Zambians adopt European ways in order to demonstrate their ability to hold

(7) 1964, p.199.   (8) *Ibid.,* p. 201.   (9) 1956, p.14.   (10) In Southall 1961, p.139.
(11) 1972.

formerly white jobs. Lower-status Zambians use their high-status compatriates rather than Europeans as their comparative reference group, but this leads them also to give high prestige to European culture. A similar use of comparative reference groups was evident in Uganda during the colonial period. Gisu accepted Western education as a means of attaining the prestige of Ganda civil servants, who held authority over them. The Ganda, in turn, compared themselves with Europeans, from whom they derived their authority.[12]

Methods of measuring status have developed as a result of Warner's studies of the stratification systems of small American towns. He devised an Index of Status Characteristics for rating individuals according to their income, occupation, education, housing, life style and reputation in the community. Scores on the index were then categorised from upper class (inherited wealth and/or a managerial or professional occupation, a university degree, a large house in the best part of town) to lower lower class (unemployed, little or no education, very poor housing). While aspects of class position are included, the system as a whole has much more to do with status than with class. Many similar indexes have been used; a basic problem with the widespread acceptance of any of them has been that the criteria of status vary from one community to another. Driving a Mercedes Benz carries more prestige in Accra than in Dar es Salaam. While occupation and income are usually important (thus tying status to class), other ascriptive and consumption factors must also be taken into account, and these change over time. Identification as a Creole in Freetown had more prestige in 1940 than in 1970, and ex-detainees are generally less honoured now than they were at independence.

Grillo[13] shows that status differentiation among East African railway workers is based on occupation and grade, income and education. He divided the residents of the Nsambya railway estate in Kampala into high and low status on these criteria and found differences between them in life style, housing, possessions and the food and drink used. Friends are almost all of the same status, but the interdependence of people at different levels is recognised in that to maintain a good reputation high-status people have to be considerate superiors and fulfil their responsibilities to kinsmen and others with whom they have primordial ties.

While the various factors relating to status tend to go together (educated people have higher income and occupations), this is not always the case. One man with little education and a low-status occupation may get considerable prestige as leader of his hometown association or religious group. Another,

(12) Twaddle in Gulliver 1969, p.196.   (13) 1973.

from a low-status ethnic group, may have well-paid professional employment as a result of his university degree. Each will tend to emphasise the criteria in which they are successful and treat as unimportant those which are less rewarding.

Lenski[14] devised a means of measuring this phenomenon, which he called status crystallisation (the degree to which status variables fit together for any individual). He showed that those who suffer from status inconsistency often have different attitudes and behaviour from individuals who have a more secure place in one status or another. This concept has been used by Grillo,[15] who found that skilled workers showed the greatest status inconsistency among the railway workers he studied; they tended to be well-paid and in high grades but had relatively little education. This brought them into conflict with those clerical workers who had more education but lower income. The higher-income clerical workers and the uneducated, low-income unskilled workers showed the highest status crystallisation, and this security of position was evident in their social relationships. Well educated workers of low standing tended to have little to do with their low-status colleagues. On the other hand, skilled workers were the most active union members, using the union to improve their standing in the community.

Occupation is often used alone as a measure of status because it tends to be the most important factor in prestige (at least in industrialised countries with a complex division of labour), is easily ascertained and is relatively comparable from one country to another.[16] With a few exceptions, there is a fairly high correlation between occupation, education and income. Unfortunately, the exceptions (farming and commercial occupations) make up a large proportion of most African populations; occupation is a much better index of status in town than in rural areas. Obtaining data on occupation may also be complicated when many men have two or more occupations. Should a man who does both be recorded as a farmer or a teacher? It often proves satisfactory to use the occupation which takes up the most time or brings in the most income, but prestige in the community may come from traditional roles which take little time and bring little income or from some former occupation (e.g. the retired army master sergeant who is now farming in a small way).

Occupations tend to differ in prestige because the knowledge or training required, the wealth received and the contribution made to community welfare are potential sources of power. Occupations requiring skill and rewarded by wealth and power receive the highest positive evaluation. Although occupational prestige is basically similar in most countries (pro-

(14) 1954; 1956. (15) 1973, p.109. (16) Treiman 1975.

fessions such as medicine and the law are at the top and unskilled jobs at the bottom), there are interesting differences both between and within countries which need further study. Highly industrialised countries tend to show the greatest similarity; some of the differences between developing nations are related to the nature of the colonial regime and consequent opportunity structure. The job of policeman, for instance, may be rated quite differently if they are seen as maintaining law and order for an oppressive regime than if they are seen as protecting the public from criminals.[17]

Occupational prestige studies in Africa have generally used either secondary students or urban workers.[18] Respondents are usually asked to rate each occupation as 'very high', 'high', 'not high or low', 'low', or 'very low'. The answers are then scored from one to five and the occupations are put in order by their mean score. The answers vary because some people give more emphasis to one aspect of prestige (such as income, education, power, or service to the community) than others. If an occupation with ambiguous prestige (such as farmer) is included, responses may differ widely because some people think of highly successful cash crop farmers and others of poor subsistence farmers who barely manage to survive.

Some occupations are more honoured in some sectors of the population than in others. For example, in Ghana factory workers rated football players much lower and District Commissioners much higher than students did; middle school students and factory workers gave miners and soldiers more prestige and traditional healers less prestige than university students did. Mining and the army may be seen as stable and well-paid occupations by those with relatively little education (and soldiers also have access to power after a coup), whereas they may seem hard and unrewarding to people with more education. Some university students thought of traditional healers as upholding traditional values, whereas rural middle school students complained that healers cheat their clients.[19]

Further studies of ideas about prestige are needed to improve our understanding of the factors involved. When people are asked to rate occupations, are they answering mainly in terms of income or of deference? Are they implying that top occupations, which usually require considerable education and training, *should* be well rewarded (supporting the functionalist theory) or merely that prestige follows rewards (a more Marxian idea)? Are

(17) Hodge *et al* 1966; Mitchell in Lloyd 1966. (18) Studies have been carried out in Ghana (Foster 1965, p.272; Peil 1972a, p.118), Ethiopia (Shack 1976), Ivory Coast (Clignet and Foster 1966, p.147), Nigeria (Morgan 1965; Armer 1968), Rhodesia (Mitchell in Lloyd 1966, pp.260–1), Sierra Leone (Gamble 1966), Zaire (Xydias in UNESCO 1956b, pp.460–1) and Zambia (Mitchell and Epstein 1959). (19) Peil 1972a, p.118.

they answering in terms of what they themselves think of people with these occupations, or giving their impression of the general public's attitude? (University students might think that ordinary people honour politicians when in fact they do not.) How reliably can one place an individual by knowing only his occupation (or only his education, or income) and in what circumstances is such placement likely to be seriously wrong?

Differentiation, past and present

Having discussed the theories of class and status as they were developed in response to conditions in Europe and America, we can now examine the evidence from African societies as to the extent of institutionalised social inequality and differentiation. Some of the precolonial patterns will be discussed first, because people's perceptions of their society today are often based on criteria that were established long ago. Second, arguments for and against the presence of classes in the Marxian sense will be investigated. To what extent has there been an uncritical use of terminology which is not particularly relevant to the African situation and to what extent is a small group of people in each country allocating to itself a major share of national economic resources and, conscious of its position, keeping others from access to power and wealth? Third, the elites will be studied as a category and a reference group rather than for their potential as a social class. What are the criteria of elite membership and what is their role in society?

Precolonial stratification systems[20]

African societies in the precolonial period demonstrate the full range of social inequality from hereditary slavery, castes and monarchies to highly equalitarian societies and those open to achieved mobility. Many societies in all parts of Africa had slavery, (defined as 'the legal institutionalisation of persons as property')[21] though it was usually domestic rather than chattel slavery, as practised in America. Slavery in Africa lacked the racialist overtones and much of the ideology of innate inferiority which characterised the system in other parts of the world. Slaves were recruited in wars and through the capture of strangers, purchase of debtors, or punishment for crime. Some were resold abroad, notably from the West African coast and by Arabs in East Africa, but those who remained within the society usually had a standard

(20) For references to the large number of studies of stratification in African societies, see Smith 1966 and Southall 1970.   (21) Tuden and Plotnicov 1970, p.11

of living which differed little from that of their masters; they were often integrated as members of the society within a generation or two. The status of slave was often indistinguishable from that of pawn, serf, or member of a subject population.

As most societies were organised around kinship and had no institutionalised role for outsiders, incorporation of slaves was accomplished through marriage (making children full members of their father's family) or some form of adoption or fictive kinship. The family may remember which lines come from free or slave origin, but after several generations this may not be evident to outsiders. (In some rural areas where slaves were freed by law and not incorporated into the local kinship structure, the stigma remains.) An exception to the possibility of integration is the Osu system of the Ibo; slaves dedicated to this religious cult remained a separate and despised group at the bottom of the society and could marry only other Osu.[22]

There are various definitions of caste, some of which limit the phenomenon to India. In its broader version, caste is a stratification system based on ascription and endogamy and emphasising ritual purity. Interaction between castes is limited because it is considered polluting; the higher the caste, the greater the purity. Each caste is endogamous (members must marry within the group) and specialises in one or more occupations which are not carried on by members of other castes. Ideally, there is no social mobility in a caste society, though occasionally it does take place. Castes or subcastes may change their relative position by following purification rules more closely and refusing contacts which were formerly permitted. Individuals may make an inter-caste marriage, but this attracts considerable community disapproval.

The clearest example of a caste system in Africa is in Rwanda.[23] The Tutsi king and pastoral aristocracy (about 15-20% of the population) ruled over the Hutu farmers by right of conquest. Twa potters and servants (only 1-2% of the population) were at the bottom. Each group had a recognisable physical type (Tutsi very tall, Twa very short and Hutu of medium build) and cultural differences also helped to make caste membership obvious. Although many neighbouring peoples had similar differences between high-status pastoralists and low-status agriculturalists, boundaries were especially strongly maintained among the Rwanda and Rundi; this led to communal violence when the system broke down on independence. Until then, conflict was mediated by patron/client relationships between Tutsi and Hutu; the latter looked after Tutsi cows and provided gifts and services in return for the milk and, more important, protection from the demands of other Tutsi. Both also

(22) Achebe 1960; Uchendu 1965, p.89.   (23) Maquet in Tuden and Plotnicov 1970; see also Lemarchand 1966.

belonged to the Ryamgombe cult, though they held separate ceremonies. Caste segregation was also maintained in that interaction was kept to service relationships; Tutsi and Hutu never ate or socialised together. In the rare cases of intercaste marriage, the children's caste depended on whether the Hutu spouse was being promoted (a beautiful woman) or the Tutsi spouse demoted (a man who lost his cattle and the king's trust or a girl who lost her virginity).

Blacksmiths have often been looked on as a caste in the Western Sudan, even in societies which have no other castes. Working in iron is considered polluting and also dangerous (supervised by special gods and providing blacksmiths with access to special power), so blacksmith families are kept separate from the rest of the society. However, their position is often merely different rather than inferior to everyone else, as they fill a vital role in providing farming tools.[24]

Another common pattern is the division of society into nobles and commoners (or nobles, commoners and slaves). Nobles may come from a different ethnic stock, having conquered the local people at some time in the past, and emphasise their cultural and lineal distinctiveness by refusing to marry commoners or do the work allocated to commoners. While the occupational aspect of caste has tended to disappear with the expansion of opportunities in recent years, caste membership may continue to be important for marriage and success in politics. There is still considerable opposition to intermarriage between the offspring of noble, casted and slave families in Senegambia, even when both fathers have a similar economic position, and higher political offices are usually held by nobles.[25]

In other societies, the presence of a monarchy has not led to rigid divisions between nobles and the rest of the population. Unsuccessful claimants to the throne were sometimes killed, exiled, or changed to commoner status. Intermarriage with commoners was fairly common in some societies and required in others. Some monarchs promoted commoners rather than giving posts to kinsmen because this gave them greater security; they were surrounded by advisers who owed their positions to the king rather than to birth and were not candidates to succeed him.

Societies with more open stratification systems varied in their emphasis on hierarchy or equality and on the characteristics considered important for high status. Political leadership was often crucial; this could be obtained through heredity, charisma, or skill in valued activities such as war. Societies which lacked institutionalised political leaders (acephalus societies) usually gave

(24) See Vaughan's paper on the Marghi in Tuden and Plotnicov 1970.
(25) Meillassoux 1970, p.101.

prominence to ritual roles such as diviner, prophet, or rain-maker. Many were unstratified in that the only positions of differential advantage were based on biological and kinship differences (sex, mother/child) and/or were open to all in turn (age sets).[26]

In other societies, ritual roles provided an alternative to political roles as a means of reaching high status; ritual leaders of a conquered people might maintain authority through their influence with the spirits of the land even though political leaders of the invading people took over political roles. Age was also important in that it implied the acquisition of valued experience, and this was enhanced by having a large family of wives, children and grand-children over whom to exercise authority. Descent was particularly impor-tant for nobles, but most men valued an opportunity to gain status from the remembered feats of their ancestors. Occupations also provided possibilities for differentiation, though these were relatively unimportant because most men spent much of their time on subsistence activities.[27]

Economic differentiation, which is such an important factor in strati-fication in contemporary societies, was less important in precolonial societies. Opportunities were available to increase one's status through economic success as a farmer or warrior, but religion, marital patterns and technology interfered with the institutionalisation of positions of economic advantage. Through the practice of their religion, the society was linked with a system of tribal gods, the founding father, ancestral spirits and the earth; this was a powerful unifying force. Chiefs, elders, or specialised ritual leaders made sacrifices for the whole people, and they shared the good or ill fortune which resulted. The practice of Islam, which unites peoples in many areas, empha-sises that the faith is much more important than economic position; marriages between a patron's son and a client's daughter are often favoured and the prescription to give alms raises the status of beggars. Marriage is a matter for kinship groups, and there has been considerable intermarriage of people at different economic and prestige levels, especially where polygyny is wide-spread. Polygyny also meant that surplus was invested in an enlarged family; this contributed to farming success of one generation but lessened the material inheritance of each child.[28]

The low level of technology prevented the development of significant economic inequality in most societies; everyone lived at much the same economic level. Goody[29] argues that this economic homogeneity encouraged intermarriage because leaders were not concerned to maximise inheritance for their children, as in much of Europe and Asia. Few parts of Africa experienced

(26) Smith 1966, pp.148–51.   (27) Mitchell in Tuden and Plotnicov1970; Southall 1970.   (28) Hill 1972.(29) J. Goody 1971.

land shortage until recently. Communal land was not inherited (and so could not contribute to economic differentiation), but was available to each individual as needed. Economic advantage came through an individual's success as a farmer (or trader or warrior) rather than through family advantages, and each individual had to start afresh. This was less true of pastoral peoples, but limited water and grazing land and the incidence of disease tended to keep herds small. Limited technology also made it difficult to store surplus, so this was usually used up in celebrations. Monarchs and chiefs received tribute, but were expected to redistribute it in hospitality, so their standard of living tended to be similar to their people's.

Such differences in wealth as occurred could be translated into differences in power, because the wealthy could support more followers and a large following gave prestige. A successful trader or warrior could start his own village, passing on to his son the position of chief. But if the son were not equally successful, villagers could move elsewhere. Because travel was difficult and often dangerous, societies were usually culturally homogeneous. Cultural differences between rulers and commoners were limited, unless the former were conquerers from another group. Slaves often differed from the rest of the population in ethnicity as well as in status and economic position the degree of difference affected their chances of eventual incorporation.

Four examples of systems of stratification provide an indication of the wide variety found in precolonial societies. Hierarchies were important to the Hausa/Fulani and the Ganda, but the Hausa/Fulani system was more closed to achievement than the Ganda. The Ibo and Tiv systems were more equalitarian than either, but the Ibo provided more opportunities for achieved mobility than the Tiv.

The Hausa/Fulani had a steep hierarchy, with only limited opportunities for changing one's position. Status was a combination of ethnicity, descent, age, occupation, place in the official system and friendship or client relationship with others in the society. The Fulani conquered the Hausa kingdoms in the early nineteenth century and Fulani were generally accorded more prestige than Hausa, though there were some Hausa rulers and some Fulani subjects. Slavery affected status, but slaves were found at all socio-economic levels, they could hold important office and thus have power over free men. Status could not be based on kinship, because this was counted on both father's and mother's side. Children had their father's status, but wives' status was separate from their husbands and based on ability to trade or carry on a successful business. Primogeniture meant that younger sons could not inherit their father's status but had to make their own way. (They could be helped by their father's connections.) Age might be relevant in certain contexts, but slave or free status and political and economic position were more important. People at all status levels could hold office; an office-holder's status depended on whether he was royal or commoner, slave or free, and the position of his superior or patron.

Most occupations were hereditary. They can be divided into three or four categories. Higher officials and chiefs were at the top, with mallams and wealthy merchants either in the same strata or just below. Musicians, butchers, servants, porters and the poorest farmers were at the bottom of the society; the rest of the population fitted into the middle. However, many people had more than one occupation and their status depended on the combination of roles and the contacts they were able to maintain with important patrons. Thus, there might be complete status crystallisation for many people (all of their roles placed them clearly in the same sector of society) and a lack of crystallisation for others (a noble with a low-status occupation, a poor man with an important patron). In such circumstances, status might vary with the situation, depending on which role was most evident at the moment. The multiplicity of officials at all levels and the importance of patron/client relationships provided opportunities for achievement within this largely ascriptive system. Trading and Koranic scholarship also provided openings for boys from otherwise undistinguished families.[30]

Ganda stratification also featured a strong hierarchy, but it provided for more mobility than the Hausa/Fulani system. Fallers[31] holds that the Ganda had little or no idea of strata or status groups having common interests. Rather, the emphasis was on superiority and inferiority between two individuals in which the patron helps the client to succeed. Almost all positions of authority and prestige were open to achievement. The gradual centralisation of power meant that eventually chiefs at all levels were appointed by the Kabaka; although palace and other official positions (such as tax collector) were sometimes hereditary, lucrative tasks were often assigned to favourites. Clan and lineage headship was hereditary, but successors were chosen from among many eligible candidates.

Humble birth was not considered a handicap to a man who could show his obedience, loyalty and cleverness, especially in battle. Since a large proportion of the men took part in wars, there were likely to be several opportunities for demonstrating one's ability or, at least, for improving one's economic position through the taking of booty. Young men who were educated as pages in the court of the Kabaka or of chiefs had the best chance of attracting attention. These tended to be sons of important men, but promising sons of ordinary men were occasionally sent. Downward mobility

(30) Smith 1959.   (31) 1964, pp.70, 74.

was also evident. Royals not eligible to be Kabaka lived as ordinary men and were not selected for other offices. Chiefs who incurred the Kabaka's displeasure were quickly demoted and sometimes killed. Sons of important men who failed to find favour reverted to the status of ordinary peasant. The fluidity of the system generated widespread aspirations for upward mobility and fierce competition for positions at all levels. This gave the Ganda considerable advantage during the colonial period.[32]

The Ibo and the Tiv both lacked centralised authority. In most Ibo groups, authority stemmed from lineage heads and village councils. However, upward mobility within Ibo society was possible through rising in a title society. (These are also found among neighbouring peoples.) Initiation into the society may be open or limited to one member of each lineage. Members may purchase successively higher titles as they become available, and are rewarded by higher prestige and power in the community. Women had separate title societies, which were less important than those of the men. Each provided a prestige hierarchy open to those who could find the necessary economic resources. Thus, access to wealth, power and prestige in the Ibo community is open to achievement through hard work and careful planning.[33]

Finally, the Tiv provide an example of a society which places a very high value on equality. They had no institutionalised authority beyond the elder who headed each compound, and any man who lived long enough could look forward to taking this role. Hierarchical social relations were limited to older and younger kinsmen; social differentiation was by lineage rather than wealth or power. Nevertheless, some people were admired and/or feared for their evident worldly success. They were held to have *tsav*, a spiritual power which could be used for good or ill – to bring a good harvest or make an enemy ill. Elders were held to gain more power by 'eating' the spirits of neighbours, who would then die. Since power demanded more power, it was every Tiv's duty to keep everyone as equal as possible.[34] Thus, stratification was prevented by emphasising the dangers powerful men posed to the community. More successful farmers were strongly encouraged to share with their kinsmen, because otherwise they would be accused of spiritually taking their kinsmen's share of luck; this made it difficult to translate economic differences into increased power or status.

The clearest differentiating principle in precolonial societies was power, with higher status going to those holding authority roles and the clearest hierarchical principles being found in caste societies and centralised kingdoms. Economic differentiation was more limited than it is today, and other

(32) Fallers 1964; Perlman in Tuden and Plotnicov 1970.   (33) Morrill 1963; Uchendu 1965, p.82; LeVine 1966, p.34; Henderson 1966.   (34) Bohannan in Gibbs 1965.

sources of differentiation were also minimised by the relative homogeneity of these societies.

Class in Africa?

Anyone trying to answer the question, 'Are there classes in Africa today?' is caught immediately in the problems of terminology and viewpoint. Part of the difficulty is that most analysts are committed ideologically but lack data to support their claims. Those who fail to find classes point to examples of exploitation and inequality of wealth and power as certain indications that classes are developing. From an observer's point of view, it is possible to say that categoric groups having differing access to economic and political resources can be found in these societies. The participant's view is less certain; the concept of inequality is universal, but the idea that this has been institutionalised into a social structure of corporate interest groups is much more limited among the general population than among observers. From both points of view, if the presence of classes means stable, unified and homogeneous groups of people conscious of their economic interests and working to promote them at the expense of other groups, the answer seems to be, 'not yet'. (The question of political classes is somewhat less certain, but so far these have not been stable and boundaries have generally been perceived as permeable.) In addition to the cultural factors (an ideology of equality inherited from the past and/or promoted by national governments), class consciousness is inhibited by the low level of specialisation and the multitude of inter-class ties which are often more important than economic interests. However, it is beginning to develop due to the expanding power of bureaucrats, the growing privileges of elites and the increasing proportion of the population working for wages in urban areas.

1 Low occupational specialisation

It is quite possible for one man to be, in the course of a single year, a farmer employing labourers, wage labourer, skilled worker (house builder), professional (traditional healer) and trader. In what class would you put such a man? Is he exploiting or exploited? He is probably a little of both, but his economic interests are by no means clearly defined. Less extreme but more common cases are cited by Hart,[35] who shows how easily the urban poor shift from wage labour to self employment, including crime. Skilled workers often combine wage labour with a business of their own, in which they employ apprentices.[36] A wage employee often has a much larger yearly income

(35) 1973.   (36) Peil 1969, 1970.

than a farmer, even though the latter hires several labourers. It might be argued that, in spite of their varying relationship to the means of production, all these people can be relegated to the working class because of their low income. This course would be opposed by some Marxists,[37] but applauded by others who see only a division between 'haves' and 'have nots'.[38]

However, it is by no means easy to draw a clear line between 'haves' and 'have nots'. Among wage employees, farmers and traders, income may vary considerably from one year (or part of a year) to another and a continuum is much more apparent than any clear division into two or three categories. Any boundary must be an arbitrary one established by the observer rather than one recognised by the participants. A trader may corner the market in a time of shortage or bring off a large smuggling job and be well off. Six months later, he may make a wrong decision and lose all or most of his capital. Farmers, traders and wage employees are found at all income levels, and the ill-paid are as likely to share interests with the better paid in a similar occupation ('my turn will come') than with others having similar economic problems.

Another aspect of low specialisation is the expectation of many workers that they will be able to move from their present occupation into something more profitable, if not this year then perhaps next. Skilled workers save for equipment for self-employment; others look forward to trading or a small business which will (of course) prosper. Lloyd[39] shows that the typical urban Yoruba lacks class-consciousness because 'he sees his own attainment of an enhanced status lying in his own efforts rather than in collective action.' Peace[40] found that many Lagos factory workers see their future in successful trading and therefore do not resent the success of wealthy traders.

2 Inter-class ties
It has often been pointed out that there are many relationships in African societies which cut across economic interests. Of these, kinship and ethnic relationships are particularly important. Families and villages are quite properly proud of members who have made good and profit by this success in the form of remittances, school fees paid, migrants to town supported until a job has been found, amenities provided, etc. Hart[41] found that most Frafra entrepreneurs in Accra send or give substantial sums to their kinsmen. While there are some complaints on the amount shared, the Frafra have no objection to wealth if it is gained at the expense of outsiders. Aronson[42] shows that the ties between rural and urban Ijebu Yoruba are so close that they can only be seen as members of a single system, 'a finely-woven net of mutual

(37) Allen 1972, p.187.   (38) Williams 1974, p.109.   (39) 1974, p.219.
(40) In Sandbrook and Cohen 1975.   (41) In Goody 1975.   (42) 1971, p.279.

interests, attachments, and influences.' Pfeffermann[43] found that, far from being a 'privileged aristocracy' (as factory workers have sometimes been called), Dakar workers either sent home money or supported kinsmen in town at a rate which effectively equalised rural and urban incomes; those who sent little were likely to be visited by kinsmen whose expenses were about the same as what might otherwise have been sent.

While the amount of assistance given to family, kinsmen and hometown varies from one individual or ethnic group to another, sharing is certainly considerable and is an important factor in lessening economic differentiation. Those who do not share, or who share too little, lose considerable prestige and the community support which might be invaluable should their fortune desert them. The strong public condemnation of former 'big men' after a coup is generally because they were selfish rather than because they were either successful or corrupt. This serves as a warning, and the proportion of the elite who cut their ties to kinsmen is probably small. The manipulation of kinship and patron/client ties moderates inequality by allowing those below a small share in the wealth, status and power of those above. It also leads to an emphasis on personal ties rather than group membership, hindering the development of class-consciousness.

Ethnic interests cut across class interests throughout the society, and when these are in conflict ethnic interests are likely to be considered more important by most of the participants. As an example, the Nigerian trade unions held a successful general strike in 1964. Their complaints about corruption and self-interest in national and regional governments brought them widespread support from members of the public who would be expected to share working class interests. The government had to give in or face the possibility of being deposed by public revolt. Labour leaders assumed that they had a force which could be moulded into a successful labour party, but this unity disappeared at the elections a few months later because voting was in terms of ethnic or sub-ethnic interests, not class interests.[44]

Similarly, ethnic as well as kinship interests are expected to operate in supplying employment, helping to cope with bureaucratic regulations, providing political protection and amenities, etc. This again gives people at different economic levels the idea that they have much in common and encourages intra-group conflict when the economic interests of two people at the same level cannot both be satisfied. Ethnic differentiation will be discussed later in this chapter.

The primacy of ethnicity over economics is also evident in marriage patterns. It was pointed out earlier that there was considerable marriage

(43) 1968, p.223. See Elkan 1976 for comparable evidence from Nairobi.
(44) Wolpe 1974, p.193.

between people of varying strata in traditional society; this seems to be continuing, though the lack of data from both past and present make it impossible to say whether it is increasing or decreasing. While some educated young people meet their spouses at school, men usually prefer wives with less education than themselves; many men with completed secondary or even university education still marry women with primary or no education, usually from their village and chosen by, or at least with the approval of, their parents. Most members of the elite are first generation in this status, so their marriage patterns have been more influenced by their origins than by their present position. It must also be remembered that marriages of the well educated are a small minority of the total. Marriage is still mainly a joining of lineages, in which wealth is less important than character and origin or ancestry.

Other aspects of marriage which inhibit class formation are polygyny and the widespread employment of women, whose economic and social position derives more from their own efforts than for their husband's position. European ideas of class assume that a man has only one wife and that they share the same class and status. But a polygynist often chooses wives of differing background (in the cities, even of different ethnicity), and each wife, at least in West Africa, is often expected to establish her own position in society. If a chief or big businessman has one wife who is a primary teacher and others who are traders (one more successful than the others) or farmers, what 'class interests' exist within this family? Where male migrants to the towns leave their wives behind to run the farm, can they be said to share the 'class interests' of their spouses?[45] What about the low-income craftsman who is married to a very successful woman trader? While class conflict might be seen as causing the breakdown of some marriages, generally there is some sharing and a willingness to grant autonomy which is inimical to the development of class consciousness.

Finally, most urban neighbourhoods are sufficiently heterogeneous economically that residents have many opportunities for mixing with people whose 'class' position is different from their own. A wealthy trader often shares his house with less fortunate kinsmen; resident landlords get to know their tenants well; patron/client relationships develop between neighbourhood businessmen, politicians and other residents with aspirations to improve their position. The life histories of the successful are well known and provide a reference group for new migrants. As success often has an element of chance as well as family support and careful planning, aspirants to upward mobility are more likely to look for individual opportunities and

(45) Schwab in Southall 1961, p.143.

seek appropriate relationships rather than to join in class actions.

Studies of the Yoruba reported by Lloyd[46] show how a pervasive atmosphere of individual achievement gives a meaning to class terminology quite different from the Marxian. Factory workers do not see themselves as an oppressed majority, exploited by management (except when they are striking for higher wages), but rather as potential businessmen and employers who have not yet saved enough or found the right patron to get started on the route to success. Differences in income are accepted as just providing that the 'big man' has 'suffered' to attain his position. This 'suffering' may mean long hours of work or struggling over school books, so success through education is just as legitimate as success through entrepreneurship. The senior civil servant who spends extra hours at the office is considered as much 'working class' as the craftsman who has similarly long hours. 'Lower class' has a moral rather than an economic meaning, implying that beggars and criminals are not making a proper contribution to society. 'Upper class', on the other hand, is used approvingly of the wealthy, but it is expected that such people will share with the workers and provide useful connections and patronage for them. Such people acquire the following necessary for political leadership (open or behind the scenes). So long as they perform their service role adequately, ordinary people see no reason to oppose them. Thus, inequality is often seen as legitimate and 'class' implies status differences rather than group conflict.

3 Bureaucratic power

Insofar as a feeling of 'we' and 'they' is developing, it is more often in relation to the bureaucracy than to indigenous businessmen. Middle and upper level civil servants make decisions which affect the whole society, but are much less under the society's control than precolonial leaders were. They are a parasitical group in that government employees (including the army) take up to 80% of the national budget to provide services often of more benefit to themselves than to the population of which they are only a small part. Free secondary schooling benefits their children most, as they are likely to do well on entrance examinations to the best schools; they have easy access to agricultural extension advice for improving their farms; they can organise contracts for their trading wives and jobs for their duller children; they get subsidised housing and car allowances and secure pensions, yet they pay relatively low taxes. In return, they are often slow to respond to public demands and concerned largely with furthering their own interests and the *status quo*; the state as established at independence suits their purpose very well.[47]

(46) 1974.   (47) Cohen 1972, p.249.

Meillassoux[48] shows how the Malian socialist ideology benefited the bureaucracy far more than the people. The position of chiefs (the traditional aristrocracy) was downgraded, though they maintained considerable prestige and some broker functions in the rural areas. Attempts to control traders by bringing all trade under a state corporation were unsuccessful because those who operated internationally took their business to nearby countries and others dealt in local foodstuffs, which could not be controlled by the government. The bureaucrats found that they had power but not status; their low social origins were remembered and held against them by a people whose ideas about society had changed little during the colonial period. From an outsider's point of view, the people are still exploited, though the personnel in power have changed. The bureaucracy has not attained as much power in most countries as in Mali because there have been other emergent groups to counter it, but the spread of military rule has generally given it more power than was possible when politicians were in control. Only in Tanzania have strong efforts been made to control the acquisitiveness of political and civil leaders.

4 Elite privileges

The elite are sometimes referred to as an 'incipient class', a 'political class', or a 'ruling class' in comparison to the bureaucratic 'administrative class'. This implies a definition of class based on institutionalised access to power rather than wealth, though they are frequently found together because power is used to obtain wealth. The corruption and self-seeking of the new rulers has led to their overthrow by popular coups, especially in West Africa, though this has not necessarily ended their opportunities to gain a large share of the profits of development for themselves. In societies where personal relationships are more important than bureaucratic standards of merit and efficiency, the successful have many chances to use their position to increase their wealth and power. This was balanced in traditional society by the norms of reciprocity and hospitality through which the successful gained status in exchange for sharing their material goods widely.

To the extent that this system has broken down and the elite have separated themselves from the ordinary people to form a group with interests of their own to protect, they are becoming a class. So far, elite interests are diverse and often conflicting (best exemplified by the inter-ethnic competition for occupational preferment and power), but occasionally this mutual interest appears, as in pressure for low taxes on personal income and imported consumer goods such as cars or for laws against small foreign businessmen.

(48) 1970.

(Multi-national corporations can be tapped by the elite either for employment or for cuts on contracts, so they attract less disfavour than small businessmen, who compete directly with local entrepreneurs.)

Consciousness of a collective position which must be defended is generally limited, however, by the insecurity of power and the ties which elite members find it useful to maintain with other sectors of the population, both for economic advantage and for prestige. Clients are invaluable sources of information and protection in a highly competitive situation. Until government and business become more stable and predictable than they are at present, it seems unlikely that a majority of the elite will find it expedient to think of themselves as a class apart.

5 Industrial workers

The clearest evidence of 'class action' is the development of trade unions demanding higher wages and better conditions for their members. These activities have a long history, since before the turn of the century.[49] They have sometimes acted in support of the elites (in independence movements) and sometimes against them (in major strikes since independence). Although Sandbrook and Cohen [50] found several cases where 'there does appear to be a growth of a reasonably homogeneous, corporate identity which approximates a class consciousness', this has generally been limited to a specific group (such as railway or dock workers) or has been unstable, appearing in times of overt conflict (such as a strike) and later subsiding into latency. In most if not all countries of Africa, a working class remains more of an occasional manifestation than an established social group. Obligations to kinsmen, ethnic group or subgroup, and to political and economic patrons are generally more important than class identity, for reasons given above.

Peace[51] shows how class consciousness arises and is expressed in times of overt conflict, but once the conflict has been resolved all but a few leaders revert to their own interests, which cut across those of class. Workers can be categorised as populist militants in that they draw considerable support from low-income self-employed urban residents because of their greater ability to organise and demand a greater share of economic resources. They also see similarities between their position and that of farmers, who are often heavily taxed by the government, but the strong feelings which arise in particular circumstances are not yet manifest in a stable working class identity.

It thus seems reasonable to suggest that research on class in Africa be severed from European assumptions of permanence and be focused instead on incidents exemplifying the development of class consciousness and class action. This would include the rhetoric and symbolism of strikes (slogans

(49) Hopkins 1966.   (50) 1975, p.312   (51) 1974.

and placards emphasising class antagonism), tax riots such as the Agbekoya Rebellion in Yorubaland,[52] demands made by various groups for more or better schools or jobs, lobbying for laws favouring certain sectors of the society, etc. Some of these will represent small groups who might be considered part of a class; the support and condemnation they receive will suggest whether larger groups are in the process of formation.

Elites

Much of the early study of contemporary stratification in Africa concentrated on the elites[53] because they have a high visibility, are considered politically important and are closer to scholars in culture and standard of living than the rest of the population. Elites are conveniently defined in terms of Nadel's criteria: (1) a definable, corporate group which is exclusive and aware of its high status and group character, but is not necessarily fully organised or closed to new members; (2) having a general superiority resting on special skills or talents (acquired or inherited) which is rewarded by deference and can be at least partly imitated.[54]

If a set of people has only specific possessions (an art collection) or competence in some field of little concern to the wider community (ancient Greek literature), it would be only a privileged, isolated interest group, not an elite. The elites are reference groups which set standards for the rest of the society. Ordinary people may not be able to imitate the wealth of the rich or the education of the intelligentsia, but they can copy, in some measure, their interests, manners and way of life, especially their ideals and values. In fact, it is precisely because elites embody the values of the society that they maintain their elite status.

This has both advantages and disadvantages. Elites tend to support the *status quo*, because society as it is generally gives them considerable power, but they must lead the way in change or they will be overthrown by new leaders. On the other hand, if they change too quickly people may cease to want to imitate them, since they no longer embody societal norms and values. The Malian bureaucrats, for example, have had to make concessions to traditional leaders and community expectations of behaviour in order to maintain their authority over the people.[55] A conquering power may not be an elite at all if it does not embody the norms of the society and is not imitated. This was the case with colonial rulers in many areas. Later, they gradually became elites to those who attended schools, became Christians, took up civil service occupations and began to imitate European styles of

(52) Williams 1974.   (53) UNESCO 1956a; Lloyd 1966.   (54) UNESCO 1956a, pp.415-7.   (55) Meillassoux 1970, p.107.

living. New elites also come from the ranks of deprived or aspiring elites. While the former may consist of opposition party supporters, the latter are often young people who have yet to make their mark. New graduates and men working their way up the civil service often see themselves as future elites and act accordingly. Labour leaders may also develop their contacts in the interests of joining the national leadership.

Elites are usually spoken of in the plural. There are political, intellectual, artistic, religious, and military elites. These tend to be more unified in a small scale society than in a large and highly diversified industrial society. In Gambia or Liberia, for example, the elites all know each other well and many are kinsmen. The Nigerian elites are more diverse in background and interests and do not all know each other personally.

Elites have often been classified as traditional or modern (or 'new'), but this dichotomy is not as useful as it appears to be. There are some elites whose influence is drawn almost completely from traditional sources, from customary roles which provide considerable prestige to the holders. Some paramount chiefs and the emirs of northern Nigeria have maintained considerable power and prestige in spite of governmental changes,[56] but they must now be seen as operating within a contemporary political framework rather than relying solely on inherited values. In Ethiopia, the colonial period was very brief and the nobility maintained its traditional power through the patronage of the Emperor until the coup of 1974, but it had to share with new military and Europeanised elites and thus adapt to new societal conditions.[57] Other elites draw most of their influence from their Western education and the occupational roles which it allows them to fulfil, but many of these (especially politicians) also seek longer-established bases for status, as when a Member of Parliament or a businessman takes a chieftaincy title. Recognition of elite status is most easily given to those who can demonstrate that they represent the norms of both the past and the present and thus are not seen by the general public as either wholly 'traditional' or 'modern'.

The common use of the term treats elites as a category rather than as a corporate group. They have influence (and often authority and power) and are imitable, but they may have no consciousness of special group membership or common interests such as is assumed for an upper class. In countries where there is an upper class, not all of its members necessarily belong to the elites, and not all elites belong to the upper class. Elites often have some idea of their mutual interests compared to those of other people in the society, but various elites also have interests which are in conflict (i.e., politicians and the

(56) Whitaker 1964, 1970.   (57) Levine 1965 and in Lloyd 1966.

military, or businessmen and government leaders who favour socialism). Some members of the elites do not have the economic position to qualify for membership in an upper class. Lastly, they tend to lack unity because individualism is strong among them; most have reached their position through their own efforts. They generally work for individual (or family) rather than group interests. Thus, what may seem a powerful monopoly of privilege to the outsider who is unacquainted with the system may be quite easy to penetrate. Ability to acquire followers is still an important aspect of prestige, and an elite which became an upper class (in conflict with those below) would cut itself off from clients and thus lose both prestige and the influence which is essential to the maintenance of elite status.

It is assumed by definition that the elites form a normative reference group for the society as a whole. They innovate new ideas and values which gradually filter down through the society in what Fallers[58] calls the 'trickle effect'. Epstein[59] demonstrates how this works as gossip and fads are passed on from one member of a social network to another. The frequent contacts which African elites have with non-elite kinsmen means that ideas and new norms of behaviour are easily passed on. Oppong[60] describes the complex relationships between the Akan elite in Accra and their kinsmen in town and at home. A few break their ties with rural kin, but most accept the prestigious if expensive position of provider and send home money frequently, pay school fees, accommodate visitors to town, etc. Ross[61] found in Nairobi that 'the higher the socioeconomic status of an individual the greater the intensity of his contact with rural areas.' Broken ties usually meant a lack of economic resources rather than a class-conscious rejection of poorer kinsmen.

Luckham[62] reports that Nigerian army officers are also easily accessible to non-elites:

> There is a constant stream of 'brothers', kinsmen, acquaintances from the same village or town-ward or the same ethnic group who come to pay their respects at an officer's house and to drink his beer and Fanta orange. They may be there for advice on recruitment into the army, to raise a contribution for a funeral or some other common function, to bring messages from family and friends, to pay homage, to listen to the radiogram or watch television, or merely to seek company. . . . It is impracticable to impose status barriers . . . which cut across the accepted norms of sociability.

Officers make similar contacts whenever they go out. This makes the military elite far more responsive than they would otherwise be to social and political

(58) 1954. (59) In Mitchell 1969a. (60) 1974. (61) Ross 1975, p.48. (62) 1971, pp.112-3.

changes in the society; they do not remain an isolated group as so often happens in industrialised nations.

Although most members of the elites have achieved their position, there are some long-established coastal elite families in Sierra Leone, Liberia, Ghana, Benin and Nigeria. They have often been known as Creoles or Brazilians because they settled as freed slaves and had relatively little to do with the indigenous population until near the end of the colonial period. Priestly[63] reports on another type of elite family, descendants of an Irish trader and his Fante wife. The description of positions held by Brew family members over a two hundred-year period provides interesting insights into the development of the educated elite in Ghana.

The combination of a largely first-generation elite, regular contacts with non-elite people and the ideology of independence has inhibited the development of a separate elite subculture, though members of the elites tend to have a common educational background and meet frequently on social and official occasions. They tend to be more Westernised than the rest of the population, but are under pressure not to depart too far from customary values. Soyinka's *The Interpreters* graphically describes the conflict between those who feel that their position requires that they follow Europeans in all things and those who think that the old ways, suitably modified for modern conditions, are best. Countries with a socialist ideology tend to emphasise the need for the educated young to maintain their links with the people, but the nature of primary socialisation, the realities of daily life and the need to maintain a sense of personal identity mean that few members of the elites are able or willing to isolate themselves from the rest of the population. They may have fewer contacts with kinsmen than their non-elite siblings, but this is partly because they must maintain elite networks to keep their position in the community.

The elites tend to live in the capital and hold important national positions, but in nations which are culturally or structurally divided each local community or region must be considered to have an elite of its own, at least during the transitional period, which is unlikely to be absorbed into the national elites. One might speak of a northern elite, or an Asante elite. There are also people who fill the functions of elites in local communities. They are seldom of consequence on a national level, but they serve as intermediaries between people of the countryside or small town and the national elites.[64] These are the 'locals' as compared to the 'cosmopolitans', to use Merton's terms. In a large-scale society, we would probably not refer to the locals as elites except in a very restricted sense, but they may be very influential in

(63) In Lloyd 1966.   (64) Hanna and Hanna 1967.

the process of development and certainly exercise considerable local influence. When communications systems are poor, it is difficult for national elites to extend their influence outside the capital except for occasional visits to their hometowns. Therefore, local and regional leaders continue to be important. Local leaders may manipulate traditional models (consciously or unconsciously) for political purposes in order to maintain their position in the community. They help to redefine norms, keeping touch with the past but helping the community adjust to changing conditions.

Identifying members of the elite is not necessarily an easy task. The most central characteristic of elites is their ability to exert influence on each other and on the rest of the community. However, influence is difficult to measure; people may be unaware that they have been influenced or unable to identify the sources of their ideas. Therefore, the elites are usually identified indirectly; it is assumed that people in certain occupations, with a certain level of education and/or income, are most likely to be influential. This is risky, because people in positions of power and authority do not necessarily have much influence on the society at large; religious leaders may be known only to their followers, businessmen only to their employees, etc. However, in Africa most 'big men' are drawn directly or indirectly into politics and are often called on to sponsor local projects, speak at speech days and generally take on leadership roles. Their activities and often their words are reported in the newspapers, and thus they become more widely known. This simplifies the task of identifying community influentials.

Attempts to specify the qualities characterising contemporary elites have not been particularly successful except in establishing boundaries below which there is not much point in looking. The income and educational qualifications listed by Lloyd[65] are an example of how quickly such a project becomes out of date and the great differences between one country and another, especially between countries with a long educational history and liberal colonial rule and those where education started late and opportunities for advancement were severely limited. The new generation of elite aspirants tend to have a university degree, though less education may be a better base for political leadership. (Voters tend to favour candidates with secondary rather than university education because the former are thought to have a better understanding of the needs of ordinary citizens.)[66]

Occupational qualifications for elite status can be divided into eight categories. Some have lost prominence in recent years, while others have gained; some are far more important at the local than at the national level. Many categories can be graded, with only the top members actually part of

(65) 1966, pp.4–6.   (66) Peil 1976b, p.133.

the elites and others sub-elites or incipient elites.

1 Governmental

The most obvious are the ruling elites: parliamentarians, professional politicians, higher civil servants, military officers and traditional rulers who have maintained a measure of authority. The top civil servants may be the most important part of the elite, since their job is the establishment and consolidation of governmental institutions, including regulations which affect behaviour at all levels of the society. If the country is under military rule, top officers are the ultimate decision makers and thus have an opportunity to exert considerable influence on the direction of societal change. Their activities are widely reported and they are in a classical elite position. If the country has not yet had a military coup, army officers tend to be largely hidden from public view and exert influence only on their subordinates; politicians and parliamentarians then form the most widely known comparative reference group. Major traditional rulers may also play an important part in the national elites, sometimes including appointment to official political roles, but most have more status and influence than power. Generally, they are more important at the regional or local than at the national level.

2 Judiciary and lawyers

These are, in a sense, formal custodians of the central value system of the society. Because it is fairly easy to become a lawyer and is likely to be lucrative (especially where inheritance and land laws are complex and people have a tradition of litigation), lawyers are usually in better supply than other professionals. Where there is an oversupply of lawyers, the inferior ones tend to be grossly underemployed and only the better ones belong to the elite. Many lawyers find politics attractive and make their way into the governing elite.

3 Doctors

Like lawyers, doctors are among the elite of a developing country, though most of them would not have this role in an industrialised country. Because their training is expensive and standards are high, doctors are always in shorter supply than lawyers; they are often too busy for the active social and political life of lawyers. But the doctor is more often seen by the poor than the lawyer, and his profession of service provides a role model which many parents would like their children to follow. Other semi-professionals in the health field, such as nurses and pharmacists, are not among the elite (with the possible exception of the matron of a large hospital), but they may exert influence as local leaders. Many nurses participate in elite society through their husbands.

4 Teachers

All types of teachers are important sources of influence because they contribute to the fundamental development of opinion, the introduction of new ideas and the formation of a world view. Only university staff would now be considered part of the national elite, though secondary teachers may belong to the local elite as primary teachers did in the past. With improved communications and increasing education and migration, teachers no longer have a monopoly of outside contacts, and their influence in villages has declined considerably. University lecturers, on the other hand, are now likely to be indigenous to the country and, as such, to be invited to advise the government on its programmes. Their pronouncements on future development are reported in the newspapers and they belong to elite social networks.

5 Businessmen

A few really successful businessmen may be among the elites, but more because of their willingness to finance elections and influence government officials than because of their occupational position. Businessmen are more likely to be among the elites of an advanced country (where they command larger enterprises) than in Africa, where the largest private businesses are run by expatriates who have little influence (and often little contact) with local society. Managers of state enterprises may have more influence than private businessmen if they are political appointees. Middle managers of large state and foreign firms may be considered marginal elites or incipient elites; many are on their way to more important positions and follow an elite style of life as far as possible. A few outstanding businesswomen have exercised considerable political influence in Ghana and Nigeria.[67]

6 Landowners and landlords

Large scale landowners were among the Ganda elite of the colonial period,[68] but today landowners and landlords are likely to be local rather than national elites. Like the businessmen and women, they tend to have relatively little education and to be more traditional in their way of life than other elites. Nevertheless, they exercise important local leadership in showing the mass of the population how to adapt to changing conditions. Wealthy cocoa farmers, for example, have provided higher education for their children, improved the amenities of their town houses and continually reminded the

(67) Peil 1975a. (68) Fallers 1964.

government that the farmer is an important part of society and must not be neglected. Landlords often play an important leadership role in migrant communities, setting a standard of success toward which newcomers may aspire (see Chapter 9). Cohen[69] shows how ownership of houses is a pre-requisite for leadership among the Hausa community in Ibadan. The rest of the community depends on the patronage of the landlords and they are responsible for decisions affecting the entire community.

7 Clergy

Bishops, the chief imam, and equivalent religious leaders are among the elite, at least the local elite, of any society; in a developing country, they are among the national elite and their pronouncements may have considerable impact. The Catholic archbishop and the Asantehene (the highest traditional ruler in the country) were both on the advisory council set up under Ghana's second constitution. Pastors and mallams can be considered local elite in religion-centred communities; they have an important role as prime arbiters of behaviour, though they may now be more active in maintaining the *status quo* than in pressure for change. If this is so, they can be expected to gradually lose influence, expecially among the young.

8 Others

Several categories exist only in small numbers, including scientists and engineers, authors and journalists. Scientists and engineers stand high as symbols of the new society and, like university lecturers, are important as government advisers. However, scientists often have rather limited contacts and few people understand the contribution they are trying to make. Journalists are at best a sub-elite because their standard and pay tends to be low, but they exert influence through their participation in politics. Authors are more likely to be among the elite than in an industrialised country because they are generally well educated and are able to mould public opinion by expressing the continuity of past and future. They are thus useful to politicians. Both authors and academics gain local prestige through the respect they earn abroad.

Social mobility

Social mobility involves movement up or down within the stratification system (in class, status or power). It exists to the extent that the system is open

(69) 1969.

to achievement within the life of an individual (intra-generational mobility) and/or from one generation to the next (inter-generational mobility). If everyone remains in the position in which he was born (as in a caste system), social mobility is impossible. Research on social mobility has often focused on movement into the elites. This process has been particularly important in African societies during the period immediately before and after independence, when new leaders often came from very humble backgrounds.

However, this long distance mobility is only a small part of the mobility which takes place and has probably declined in recent years. Most mobility is short distance: from employee to small-scale employer, from ordinary citizen to local councillor, from a father who farms one acre to a son who farms five acres. Not all mobility is upward; a man who starts as a clerk sometimes ends as a labourer, and a son may be a less successful farmer than his father. The social mobility of women has generally been ignored, on the assumption that women are mainly mobile through marriage and share the position of their husbands. Insofar as women have an autonomous position, studies of their mobility should be made to find out to what extent female mobility is similar to, or different from, male mobility.

The individual moves which take place may in time affect the whole shape of the system. If as many people move into each stratum as move out (or if there is almost no mobility at all), the system will remain the same; but if more people move up than move down (as tends to be the case in contemporary societies), the size of various strata will change, with some becoming

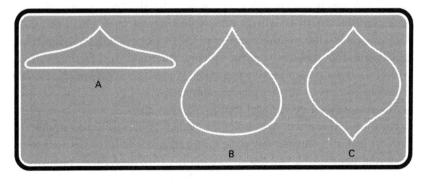

Figure 6 The shape of stratification systems

larger and others smaller. A precolonial society might be visualised as a flat pyramid (see Figure 6), with most people at a fairly similar standard of living and a few chiefs or traders somewhat better off and/or higher in prestige. With more opportunities for trade, industry and the professions, the society may come to resemble B. There are now more people above the bottom, and difference between the top and the bottom is greater. Another possibility is

C, where most of the people are in the middle and there are small numbers at both the top and the bottom: the elites and those who are barely able to support themselves or are very low in status or power.

Studies of social mobility are concerned with

1 the rate (What is the probability of a son changing from the position of his father or of his first job?)

2 the amount (To what extent does a man's position depend on the initial position inherited from his father or achieved in his first job?)

3 the distance (What are the relative proportions of large and small moves?)

4 the pattern (Which occupations feed other occupations and which are largely hereditary?) and

5 the process (What variables affect occupational change or stability, increasing or decreasing the correlation between father's and son's position or between first job and eventual position?)[70]

African mobility studies have generally concentrated on education as the chief intervening variable in the mobility process rather than attempting to measure mobility directly. The relationship between education and social mobility is discussed in Chapter 6.

Social mobility may be measured using any or all of the status variables. (Changes in income, occupation, age, power, etc. can result in a new prestige or socio-economic position and therefore in social mobility.) While the use of several measures would give a more accurate assessment of the mobility of any particular individual than relying on one indicator, the increased accuracy is usually not enough to compensate for the difficulty in collecting such complex data from a large sample and various factors tend to cancel each other out when the study applies to the society as a whole; so it is more convenient and almost as reliable to concentrate on one variable. Occupation is usually chosen because it is easier to measure and more comparable from one country to another than the alternatives.

There are as yet no national studies of either inter- or intra-generational occupational mobility in Africa, but the evidence available[71] suggests that the rate has increased considerably since independence because of the many new opportunities available and the decline in the size of the farming population. Although education is important for placement on the first job, many urban workers experience considerable career mobility because there are still many occupations open to people of little or no education. The top positions in the civil service usually require a university degree, but school leavers of lesser attainment may move from primary teaching or minor clerical posts into factory work or skills such as radio-repairing. There is con-

(70) Treiman 1975, p.185. (71) Peil 1972a, p.50.

siderable movement between wage and self-employment and from one sector of the labour force to another. Ex-farmers who find labouring jobs may later move up to skilled work through an apprenticeship. Many employees aspire to move into trading where, if successful, they can achieve considerable income, prestige and even power. Many men return to farming at the end of their career, though their status as a returned migrant depends more on their success abroad than on the nature of their activity after 'retiring' to their home. This flexibility during a career makes it difficult to measure the rate and amount of mobility, because much depends on when the measurement is taken.

Another problem in comparing occupational mobility of various nations is that the rate and amount of mobility reported depend on the number of divisions used. If a society is divided only into manual and non-manual workers[72] (as has often been done), the move from primary teacher to factory worker counts but the move from labourer to skilled worker (which may involve a greater difference in income and status) does not. The manual/non-manual dichotomy has lost popularity in recent years because there are now manual occupations which provide more income and/or prestige than some non-manual occupations. For example, Ghanaian factory workers rated miners and lorry drivers above typists and Zambian students gave the same mean rank to carpenters and primary teachers.[73]

The division of occupations into more categories provides more useful results, since occupational prestige studies show a consistent hierarchy of categories even though individual occupations may get out of order. Peil and Lucas [74] suggest eight categories for occupations found in West Africa: farmer, unskilled, semi-skilled, skilled, commerce, clerical, semi-professional and professional. Although these categories are in hierarchical order, some of the occupations could be moved up or down to reflect their prestige level more accurately.[75] Wallace and Weeks[76] divided the occupations found in Uganda into five levels; farmers are at three levels according to the number of acres farmed. If the information is available, social mobility studies should subdivide the farming category and compare the proportions of sons leaving farming of (1) fathers doing subsistence and cash crop farming and (2) fathers with varying levels of income and education. It would also be useful to measure the amount of education fathers in these categories give their sons, since this would facilitate or hinder mobility into urban occupations.

(72) These are referred to as blue collar and white collar workers because manual workers in America used to wear blue shirts and clerical workers wore white shirts. (73) Peil 1972a, p.118; Mitchell and Epstein 1959, p.24. (74) 1972, p.55. (75) See Treiman 1975 for a comprehensive set of codes based on international studies of occupational prestige. Most occupations found in Africa are included in this list. (76) 1974, p.13.

Movement from farming to a non-farming occupation may be upward mobility as far as income is concerned but downward status mobility. A man who leaves a respected place in his community as an independent farmer to become an urban labourer is downwardly mobile in status, though he hopes to improve his economic position (and eventually the size of his farm) by the move. The son of a rich farmer may also have to settle for a low-status urban job unless he has at least completed secondary school. Although most occupational mobility studies have focused on movement out of farming and within the urban job hierarchy, it is as well to remember that in any society where a high proportion of the population remain in farming the rate of mobility will be low (i.e., the occupationally mobile will be in the minority). Nevertheless, social mobility is found throughout the society because there tends to be considerable inequality within the farming population, at least where cash crops are grown, and many farmers do better or worse than their fathers or than their own performance at another stage of their careers.[77] One man inherits little land, and by diligence (and sometimes luck) builds up a large farm; another has many sons who help him farm an increased acreage; a third gradually declines into poverty because he is a poor planner or a drunkard; a fourth gets into debt because locusts or drought destroy his crop and never manages to return to his former position. Thus, personal qualities, fertility and the weather are agents of social mobility among the farming population.

Some farmers also improve their position through non-farming activities such as trading, divining and traditional leadership roles. The first provides additional cash which can be invested in land, equipment such as tractors (which can be rented out to other farmers), wives, labourers (making it possible to increase acreage), etc. Other roles provide status independent of the size of one's farm (assuming that one is not a completely unsuccessful farmer), but leadership roles are likely to go to those who have already demonstrated their ability in farming and/or interpersonal relations.

There is considerable difference between ethnic groups in attitude toward social mobility. Some, like the Ibo and Yoruba, emphasise competition and achievement; others, like the Frafra, stress equality to an extent that makes it difficult for individuals to improve their position. For example, prestige among the Ibo is tied to occupational skill, but also to individual enterprise and initiative. Each man is expected to make his own way, though he should help his kinsmen if he is able to do so.[78] Frafra put far more emphasis on membership in the community. Migrants are expected to share whatever they have with their fellows, and this effectively prevents one man from

(77) Hill 1968, 1972. (78) LeVine 1966, pp.34–5.

rising above the others. As saving is considered anti-social, material goods can only be acquired by isolation from the community and consequent loss of respect, both in town and at home.[79]

This is a widespread dilemma for men who aspire to upward mobility. Their socialisation has taught them to share their good fortune with kinsmen and friends, yet there is not much point in working very hard if all personal reward disappears in hospitality.[80] Given the insecurity of urban life and the strong desire to return home eventually, most migrants settle for generosity rather than upward mobility. Some find a level of distribution which enables them to keep a 'reasonable' share of the rewards for themselves. This is easier for traders (who can hide their income) than for civil servants (whose salary scale is common knowledge), and for the young than for older people, who are frequently solicited to take leadership roles. Very few opt for isolation, and these tend to have a high, secure income and the expectation of an adequate pension on which to retire. Even among these, most find as they grow older that increasing prestige at home can be an attractive exchange for their benefactions.

Rapid social mobility for large numbers of people (as at independence) can have considerable effect on the individuals concerned and on the society. Hurried localisation of posts in many countries has meant that the new holders are often young and not sufficiently experienced for their roles. Their youth poses serious problems for the cohort coming after them. If the Principal Secretary, General or Professor is only thirty-seven, it is likely to be a long time before there is an opening for the (perhaps better qualified) man of thirty. The first men to reach the top faced little competition and spent little time in intermediate positions; they often hold minimum qualifications and find it difficult to cope with a position for which they are not well prepared. They feel the envy of those under them, and see the improved training of these newcomers as a threat.[81] Some departments have refused to hire university graduates because those in control see this as the best way to maintain their authority.

Second, many of the new elite, especially in countries where a colour bar severely limited opportunities before independence, feel anomic (that is, unsure of what values they ought to uphold or norms they ought to follow) because there is 'no pre-existing social class whose norms would regulate his aspirations, . . . behaviour, etc.'[82] They may neglect their work (perhaps leaving it to a behind-the-scenes expatriate) or decide to make the most of their opportunities, engaging in corruption, nepotism and abuse of power in the interests of themselves and/or their kinsmen and followers. The periodic

(79) Hart 1971. (80) Mboya in Gulliver 1969, pp.94–5. (81) See Burawoy 1972b, pp.42–48. (82) *Ibid.*, p.68.

sacking of civil servants and political appointees (as in Ghana and Nigeria) has so far had little effect on this syndrome, because the norms remain unclear and new incumbents seem to suffer from the same disabilities as those they replace (see Chapter 9). As social mobility slows down, allowing larger numbers of competent people to build up experience over a longer period, promotion to the top should pose less of a strain.

Ethnocentrism

Differentiation according to origin is found in every society. Often a people's name for themselves means 'the people'; everyone else is somehow less human. This justifies ethnocentrism – looking down on others and discriminating against them. Killing a member of one's own society is severely sanctioned as murder; killing an outsider or stranger may be rewarded as a valiant deed. The increasing interdependence of peoples has modified these attitudes somewhat, but the tendency to glorify one's own origins and denigrate those of others remains. Four aspects of this phenomenon will be discussed: prejudice, attitudes towards strangers, racism and tribalism (ethnic communalism and conflict).

Prejudice

Prejudice combines affective and cognitive factors – hostile feelings toward members of another group and beliefs (often inaccurate generalisations) about them. It tends to be acquired as part of primary socialisation and, because of the emotional element, it is difficult to change. Through jokes, stories and solemn warnings, the child learns the boundaries of his own group and the common stereotypes for other people: the As are dirty (they take only one bath a day), the Bs are immoral (they allow easy divorce); the Cs are ignorant (few of the children go to school); the Ds are lazy (they do not grow cash crops); the Es are grasping (they are successful traders). So it goes. Partly through personality and partly through experience, some people acquire less prejudice than others. Ideas are sometimes modified through interaction with 'strangers' at school, on the job, or as neighbours, but it is more difficult to unlearn prejudice than to acquire it.

The other side of prejudice is group solidarity, which may have as positive functions as prejudice has negative functions. Group solidarity provides security in situations of potential conflict and informal support when official agencies cannot or will not help. It gives an identity and self-respect to people whose status might otherwise be very low. But it also turns prejudice

116

(which is basically an attitude) into discrimination (which involves behaviour). There may be strong pressure to exclude outsiders, especially during political campaigns and in job competition. Each group builds up vested interests and legitimates discriminatory behaviour towards other groups in order to maintain their own advantages. This operates at all levels. The first people to get European education (Creole, Ganda, Yoruba) assumed that they would get priority as new opportunities opened up. At the other extreme, night watchmen, bottle collectors and other specialists at the lower end of the occupational hierarchy do their best to maintain a monopoly in their 'trade' for migrants from their own area.

Prejudice and discrimination are often related to conflict over the stratification system. Partial closure of the system, so that members of the society have unequal opportunities for advancement, often involves discrimination of some sort. Only certain children are allowed into the better schools or only those of the 'right background' are considered for the top jobs. This may be economic rather than ethnic or racial discrimination (as in schools with high fees), but the effect is the same if, as sometimes happens, origin and economic position are highly correlated. (In this case, race or ethnic identity may be almost identical with class position; see below.) The explanation is often in social or cultural terms (those excluded would not 'fit in' or 'get along'), but this is usually an assumption based on prejudice rather than evidence. Members of the conflicting groups often get along quite well when they get to know each other as individuals rather than as categories.

To the extent that equality of opportunity for all members of the society is stressed, pressure will be applied to avoid discrimination, at least in its more open aspects. This, in turn, discourages the expression of prejudice and may, in time, help to overcome it. Prejudice can be a result of the cultural or colonial heritage; it is often fostered by the political and economic structure of the society. A legacy of racial or ethnic conflict can be very difficult to overcome, and conflict is often increased by a 'winner take all' political system and/or a severe shortage of employment opportunities or land for expanding agriculture. National leadership then becomes a crucial factor in the increase or decrease of prejudice.

Strangers

The sociology of the stranger derives from a short essay by Simmel.[83] Strangers, according to Simmel, are individuals who come to a place and live there without ever settling down, who are in the community but not of it,

(83) 1950.

and thus remain more objective than full members can be. More recent studies have demonstrated that there are other types of strangers: the guest or tourist who comes for a short visit, the newcomer or migrant who intends to become a full member of the community and the marginal man who does not 'fit in' though he is committed to permanent residence. The community may welcome outsiders, or it may treat visitors as intruders and make it impossible for migrants to ever be accepted as citizens. Some people who attempt to join a community become marginal men because they no longer fit into their old culture but are not accepted into the new culture either. This marginality occurred in the colonial situation, when individuals with extensive European schooling were alienated from their own society but not accepted into European society. They became strangers at home.[84]

People who share cultural attributes of two or more groups, either because of mixed parentage or from a desire to become identified with a higher status reference group, often have an ambiguous status in the society and limit their social contacts to others in the same position. They may be distrusted and/or looked down on by those with a secure place in one culture or the other, but at times they exercise considerable influence because of their intermediate position.

The position of sojourners (strangers in Simmel's sense) is particularly difficult in present-day Africa. Whether they are Asians or Lebanese, Luo in Uganda, Dahomeans in Ivory Coast, or Yoruba in Ghana or Zaire, they have found that they are much less welcome than in the past. There are social, economic and political reasons for the hostility of the host populations; as these seem to be intrinsic to sojourner status, these strangers may find that they must either become assimilated or leave.

They have generally been 'middlemen minorities',[85] in occupations such as trading where a small amount of capital can be built up through hard work and saving. Others have had skills that the local population lacked: carpenters or tailors or (as the Dahomeans and Ganda) enough education to act as clerks for the colonial rulers. While some remain poor, most are in the middle of the economic hierarchy and some have become wealthy. Savings are reinvested in the business or sent to kinsmen at home rather than being spent on a high standard of living. This often gives them a reputation for penny-pinching, being unwilling to make loans, and draining away the resources of their country of residence. Their success makes them resented by the local people, who are sure that they are being exploited but often cannot compete because their kinsmen do not understand the need for strict business practices. The stranger is isolated from kinsmen (except for those who either

(84) See chapters by Levine and Skinner in Skinner and Shack 1977.
(85) Bonacich 1973.

work for him or are also in business) and therefore is not subject to the same demands for free goods or a share of the proceeds as the local businessman. This makes it much easier for him to succeed.[86]

In addition, group solidarity is fostered by their position as strangers. They remain more interested in their homes than in the locality where they are living and they prefer friends of their own group to local people. They resist assimilation, maintaining their own norms, customs and religion rather than adopting local ways. They form their own networks and associations[87] to help each other in business, hiring and training only members of their own group so that they effectively exclude potential local entrepreneurs. This does not mean that there are no internal divisions within the stranger community; Indian divisions by caste, religion and language are a notable example of the formation of sub-communities.[88] But these divisions are brought from home and do not affect the more important boundary between locals and strangers.

Independence brought many political and social problems for alien strangers.[89] Citizenship and the right to vote set them apart from local people. While countries formerly under French rule have been very liberal in granting citizenship (perhaps because of the assimilationist policy of the French), nations with an English legal tradition have generally made it very difficult for anyone not belonging to a local ethnic group to obtain citizenship. The problem was most severe for the Asians of East Africa. Most were settlers rather than sojourners in the sense that they had no intention of returning to India or Pakistan, but many felt that citizenship would not give them full rights because of prevalent racial feelings and most were not sufficiently committed to want to become full members of the community; the stranger habit of separation was too strong.

Aliens in West Africa have generally not been as long-established as Asian communities in East Africa, but there are Nigerian and Voltaic communities in Ghana,[90] Ghanaian communities in Liberia and a Kru community in Sierra Leone. African immigrants were primarily identified by ethnic group and saw citizenship as an extension of ethnicity regardless of their place of birth or residence. Thus, official regulations conformed to local perceptions. But the role of second or third generation immigrants became a problem when political parties began canvassing for votes and later when governments had trouble balancing the budget. Losers could claim that any support aliens gave the winning party was unfair, but they could be considered disloyal for either supporting the losers or taking no part in the nation's political enthusiasm. Their economic activities are a challenge to

(86) Garlick 1971; Marris and Somerset 1971.   (87) Morrill 1963.   (88) Bharati 1965.   (89) Skinner 1963; Peil 1971.   (90) Schildkrout 1970, 1974.

local entrepreneurship (more so than multi-national corporations because their capital investment is much lower) and the jobs, housing and school places they take up are considered unnecessary expenses for the local tax-payer. (Their economic contribution in providing employment and paying taxes is often overlooked.) Thus, several governments under pressure have found it convenient to expel aliens, concentrating on the 'middleman minorities'. The most notable have been Ghana and Uganda.

A great deal of research remains to be done on the changing role of strangers in African societies, and it must be remembered that by no means all strangers are aliens. The indigenes of a town may consider even members of their own ethnic group from another town as strangers. Migrants from other ethnic groups tend to remain outsiders, even though they learn the local language, because they maintain their customs and ties with home, have their own associations and seldom intermarry with the indigenes. Conflict in local politics, especially in Nigeria, often centres on the divergent interests of indigenes and migrants; it is aggravated when most elite positions are held by strangers and local people are mostly relegated to the bottom of the social system.[91]

Strangers are generally welcomed or at least tolerated when the host community feels secure and the strangers are a relatively small group which does not challenge the prevailing norms or hierarchy. They are less welcome and may be treated with hostility or even expelled when their numbers or position are seen as a threat by their hosts. They may be made scapegoats in a time of political, economic, or social insecurity, as when the government is trying to cope with problems of national identity, economic independence and development, or is unpopular and needs to increase its public support. However, action against aliens may highlight divisions within the national community which cannot be solved in the same way. Mass expulsions have relatively little economic effect from the viewpoint of the common man if the more successful middlemen either do not go or are quickly replaced by wealthy local people who are just as exploitative. A more positive approach would be to find some means of integrating the strangers into the society by promoting national consciousness and working together for national needs.

Racism

Hostility to strangers is greatest when it is based on differences of race, because this makes the outsider seem most unlike ourselves and therefore a greater threat. Race is a biological concept whereby people are classified by inherited characteristics such as colour of hair and skin, shape of head, body

(91) Baker 1974; Peil 1976b.

build, etc. This would have no particular importance if people were content to be physically different but socially equal. However, there has been a tendency throughout history to see race as a determinant of social and cultural variation – to assume that race influences morality, form of government, attitudes and behaviour. If a society is less developed technologically, or has religious beliefs or marriage customs of which one disapproves, the idea that its members are inevitably inferior is strengthened if they are also physically different from oneself. Such beliefs legitimate conquest and the denial of opportunity for advancement, because it is assumed that what is inherited cannot be overcome.

Race is like caste in that it is basically ascriptive. Because races differ on easily seen physical characteristics, assimilation into another racial group is even more difficult (unless one has mixed characteristics) than assimilation into another caste. Therefore, societies where social differentiation is mainly based on race and where class, status and power positions correspond to racial identity are more sharply divided than other societies.

The lack of evidence for a connection between physical and social characteristics has never proved a hindrance to racism. There are a few diseases, such as sickle cell anaemia, which are racially linked, but the wide variety of cultures found within each race and the considerable overlap in physical types between races demonstrate conclusively to anyone open to objective evidence that racial determinism is false. Attitudes and behaviour, measured intelligence and even physical performance are largely shaped by social and cultural background (transmitted through socialisation) rather than by inherited racial characteristics. If a certain people does less well than others on intelligence tests or consistently fails to win athletic contests, it is probably because their socialisation does not provide them with the information needed for the tests and because they have not had an adequate diet or an equal amount of training in athletics.

Colonial rule provided fertile ground for the development of racism. Early contacts between black rulers and white traders were often on a fairly equal basis and Africans held important positions in several areas at the beginning of colonial rule. But as more Europeans were sent out (missionaries and merchants as well as administrators) the aid of Africans became less necessary and the idea spread that it was also not possible; the 'white man's burden' was to rule and the African's duty was to obey. Europeans needed to believe that they were innately superior to Africans in order to legitimate their continued rule over them, and where they have continued to rule the myth of racial superiority is still strongly supported.[92] Open racism tended

(92) Mitchell in Tuden and Plotnicov 1970, p.314.

to be in direct proportion to the number of whites resident in the colony. It was greatest in South Africa, Rhodesia and Kenya and least in West Africa.

In addition to laws enforcing segregation and reservation of jobs to whites, denigration of Africans can be seen in many plans and regulations which were not officially viewed as discrimination. For example, programmes of formal education often emphasised manual or agricultural training and aimed at only a low level of literacy, because it was assumed this would best fit Africans for their place in society. Such programmes were rejected by Africans, who wanted to equip themselves for the highest rather than the lowest places.

The concept of pluralism has been a popular but not particularly fruitful way of explaining sociologically the interaction of races in society, especially in colonial situations.[93] Furnival, who first developed this concept, held that, as a result of rule by aliens, some societies are composed of separate ethnic sections which share only political and economic institutions and interact only in the marketplace. Each section has its own culture, norms and values; there is no societal consensus but rather subordination of the majority to a minority and the social institutions of this minority. This model of society has been used by conflict theorists to attack Parsonian functionalist theory of a society based on consensus and common values. However, careful study of plural societies shows that considerable conflict over power and resources is often accompanied by at least some basic agreement on values. If the cultural sections were completely separate (ignoring each other and institutionally autonomous), there would be no society at all. Insofar as they co-operate (forming a common society), they have at least some common goals; conflict is in fact often based on the desire of both sides for the same limited resources. Burawoy reports[94] that the norms of segregation in Northern Rhodesia 'were widely accepted even though they imposed severe constraints on the behaviour of each race.'

Economic and cultural similarities across racial boundaries are not accounted for by the pluralist model. The stratification system tends to place members of different races in an hierarchical order, but economic distinctions are never complete (see Figure 7). Some members of the lower and middle races are highly successful and thus qualify economically for membership in the upper category. A few members of the upper race are so unsuccessful that they fall into the lower or at least the middle category. There were, for instance, *petit blanc* Frenchmen in West Africa doing very menial jobs and wealthy African merchants (and later politicians) whose standard of living was equal to that of the French rulers. Although the overlap in income

(93) Kuper and Smith 1969; Benedict in Plotnicov and Tuden 1970.
(94) 1972b, p.67.

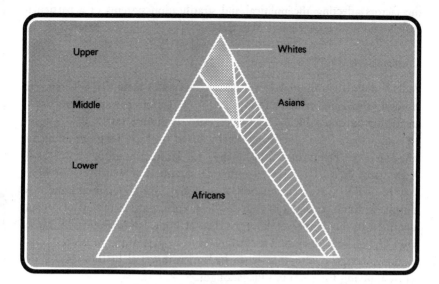

Figure 7 A multiracial stratification system

between racial groups in Jinja, Uganda was small, Sofer and Sofer[95] found that relatively wide differences in income and occupation within the European community decreased its social solidarity; low-status Europeans could not afford the same style of life as the rest and felt excluded. The Asian community was likewise divided; some had about the same income and standard of living as the better paid Africans (the study was made ten years before independence) and some were on a par with Europeans. Caste and religious distinctions among the Asians seemed to be gradually giving way to political and economic differentiation.

The close copying of European ways by the Creole of Freetown, the Americo-Liberians of Monrovia and the Saro of Lagos supports the theory that it is inaccurate to assume that there is necessarily conflict over values whenever a society includes more than one race (or more than one ethnic group, since ethnic pluralism may be analysed in the same way as racial pluralism; both can involve varying amounts of cultural difference and superordination/subordination). Racist attitudes may even be taken over by members of the subordinate race. For example, Burawoy[96] reports that Zambian government and mining officials often repeat white criticisms that African miners are lazy and undisciplined, though the evidence suggests that they are as diligent as miners elsewhere. Rather than relying solely on a pluralist model based on cultural conflict, it seems more useful to study all of

(95) 1955, pp.52–3.   (96) 1972a, p.248.

the factors affecting the political and stratification systems of a particular society and how these change over time.

Communalism

Paden[97] defines communalism as 'ascriptive types of identities, adherence to cultural norms and values, and loyalties or obligations towards members of an identity group which tend to be relatively diffuse rather than specific or contractual.' This identity is usually based on race, religion, ethnicity, language, or primordial attachments to kinsmen and/or hometown. Individuals often have several communal identities, of which one or more may be used in any given situation. A man may be a Nigerian in London, a Yoruba in Kano, an Egba in Lagos (where Yoruba are in the majority) and identified by his family or lineage when at home in Abeokuta. A Moshi from Upper Volta may find it convenient to be part of the Muslim, Hausa-speaking Zongo community when in Kumasi but use his hometown ties when applying for a job in Ouagadougou.[98]

Where interaction is impersonal but particularistic, the relationship is often categoric.[99] When we don't know someone, it is easy to put him into a category and treat him as 'typical' or 'people like that'. This categorisation may be based on any factor which is known: sex, age, ethnicity, etc. In towns, where categoric relationships are most necessary, race or ethnicity is often used because this makes it possible to divide up the whole population into a manageable number of categories and to keep in mind what sort of behaviour is expected between 'us' and each of 'them'. We can expect friendship from some groups, joking from others and conflict or avoidance from still others. Each group is stereotyped as aggressive or lazy, intelligent or ignorant, wily or naive. Even though most of its members do not fit the model, there is often some basis of truth which helps to prolong it. Personal relationships break through this categorisation and make it possible to treat people as individuals. While it is impossible to know everyone at work, in the street, or in the market, Africans generally prefer to personalise a relationship whenever possible, to get behind categories and structures to the individual. This is easiest to do when there is a shared communal identity.

There are two sides of communalism which make it such an important factor in behaviour: the need to categorise outsiders with whom one has no close personal relations and the need for identity and a secure source of sup-

---

(97) In Melson and Wolpe 1971, p.114. (98) Schildkrout 1974; Skinner 1974, p.85.
(99) Mitchell 1966, pp.52-4.

port, especially in competing for scarce resources.[100] Communalism provides we/they boundaries which vary from one situation to another but which become increasingly important as societies become larger in scale and more interdependent. Ethnicity has become a focus of conflict in towns because it enhances symbolic and behavioural differences which can then be used to promote or defend the political, economic, or social interests of the communities concerned.[101] In most independent African countries, ethnicity is a more important factor in communal differentiation than race, and the use of ethnic boundaries, especially in politics, is considered a serious problem in many.

There are many definitions of the word tribe,[102] none of them particularly useful for describing the patterned ethnic relationships which characterise present-day African society. The preference for a word of their own (ethnic group) rather than using the word in common use (tribe) is not just perverseness on the part of social scientists. 'Ethnic group' has much the same meaning as tribe, but it avoids the pejorative implications of this term and also can be used more inclusively to describe large societies which some of their members prefer to call nations and also small groups which might otherwise be called sub-tribes or communities but which establish cultural boundaries between themselves and other people. The outside observer of social structure, concerned with analysing similarities of behaviour in groups of varying size, finds it useful to have a single term to refer to this type of interaction.

The basic characteristics of ethnicity are group identification (by members and non-members) based on a common name, descent and culture. There is usually a common language, though this may have local variants and be shared with neighbouring groups. Some peoples were politically unified in the precolonial period, but others had no centralised leadership; in either case, there is usually some territory designated as (at least originally) belonging to the group. The most important social factor is the boundary which the group establishes.[103] Schildkrout[104] points out that ethnic boundaries may in time lose much of their cultural content as the wider society becomes more integrated. When this happens, members of ethnic groups who wish to maintain a separate identity develop new symbols (such as clothing, associations, or religious separatism); ethnicity becomes a means of social rather than a cultural categorisation, useful chiefly for status and political purposes. While ethnic identity continues to be important, the idea that there are

(100) These have been distinguished by Luckham (1971, p.193) as primordialism of projection and of identity. Attitudes of aggression or alliance are projected on others when we see them as acting in a unified way in relation to our own group. Primordialism of identity produces the 'we' feeling which holds a group together.
(101) Parkin in Gulliver 1969, p.295; A. Cohen 1974; p.xxi.   (102) Gulliver 1969, pp.8–25; Gutkind 1970.   (103) Barth 1969.   (104) 1974, p.192.

autonomous tribes which have ascribed membership and clear boundaries between themselves and outsiders no longer conforms to reality, if it ever did. Many 'tribes' (such as the Luhya, Nyasa and Yoruba) only acquired a communal identity during the colonial period, when bureaucrats, missionaries or politicians began to treat certain peoples as a unit.

There has always been considerable flexibility of boundaries, both for groups and for individuals. For example, the LoDegaa people of northern Ghana identify with their neighbours for a few miles on each side of the family compound but not with people of similar culture who live further away. Their idea of 'our people', therefore, depends on the location of the speaker. Peoples who share territory with others of a different cultural tradition or who live near others having a different culture or political allegiance often have customs and language which show the influence of both groups. There is usually some shifting of family identity over time from the group with less power and prestige to the group with more. Salamone [105] shows how new ethnic groups arise where a people move from their home area and take up a new occupation.

Individual identity can also be shifted from one ethnic group to another and in the level of identification. Children of mixed parentage may identify with either their father's or their mother's people depending on where they are brought up and in which society they feel most at home. When looking for a job or votes, identification is pragmatically manipulated to yield the best results; region, home town, or extended kinship may be more useful than ethnicity. Immigrants who choose to assimilate rather than remaining strangers can adapt the clothing and language of their hosts and fade into the local community, at least in towns. This is more difficult in rural areas (because usually only local people have access to land and without land one remains an outsider), but the Tonga and Ganda incorporated large numbers of strangers in the past. This is less common now, perhaps because of pressure on land or the greater salience of ethnic boundaries.[106]

Mitchell[107] showed how various communal identities were manipulated on the Copperbelt. Members of a dancing team, all from the same ethnic group, sang derogatory songs about other groups. These were taken in the sense of joking relationships (in which hostility can be expressed between members of two groups because of the basic friendship between them) and thus served as entertainment rather than precipitating conflict. This was one of the few expressions of ethnic communalism on the Copperbelt before independence; all groups generally ignored ethnic differences because racial differences were so much more important. Even in this case, the dancers were

(105) 1975b.   (106) Richards 1954, pp.161–88; Colson 1970, pp.39, 51–2; Horowitz 1975, p.117.   (107) 1956.

dressed in European style and used the *lingua franca* rather than their own language, so emphasis was on a wider community than their own.

Ethnic groups vary considerably in the amount of corporate feeling and the use to which this is put. The Hausa of Ibadan maintain religious, economic and residential exclusiveness in order to ensure participation in a tightly knit corporate group.[108] At the other extreme are peoples such as the Temne of Freetown described by Banton,[109] who had not found it necessary to develop corporate group structures to defend their interests though they were aware of the culture they had in common; Parkin[110] suggests that they should be considered a category rather than a group. Most peoples are somewhere in between, but the possibilities of ethnic politics since independence have increased the tendency toward corporate structures. The Kru of Liberia and the Luo of Kenya both started with highly autonomous and competing subgroups; in the cities these have become more united, through the Kru Committee and the Luo Union, as corporate interests have developed.

Since independence, many nations have experienced an increase in interethnic conflict. The antagonism toward colonial rulers which held peoples of diverse cultures together in a common cause has not yet been replaced by allegiance to a national community. Rather, various communal groups have begun to pay more attention to their relative position. Cohen[111] suggests that ethnic stratification is an important factor in power and class relationships. Some groups find it easier than others to assume superordinate positions because of their size (providing large numbers of voters), natural resources (more money to spend on education and improved communications), geographical location (better access to urban jobs and amenities) and previous political control (experience in administration and well-developed contacts). Those groups which got a late start are often looked down on as 'bush' and their members meet intense competition from more established groups when they attempt to move up. This conflict is often called tribalism, though it has little to do with the cultural origins of the contestants and it exists in ethnically unified countries such as Somalia as well as in heterogeneous ones.[112]

However, cultural differences can aggravate conflict which is basically economic or political. It is now fairly easy to move from one part of the country to another and this brings peoples of varying cultures into contact with each other. Salamone[113] points out that northern Nigerians shared fishing grounds with little difficulty because they observed a common code of courtesy; southern fishermen were considered a threat because they ignored these norms. Their adherence to Christianity in an Islamic society enhanced

(108) Cohen 1969.   (109) 1957.   (110) In A. Cohen 1974.   (111) 1972, pp.244-5.
(112) Lloyd 1967, Chap. 12; Peil 1976b, Chap. 4.   (113) 1975b, pp.94-5.

their position as outsiders.

Ethnic ties, as they exist today, are an expression of communal attachment in a specific situation; individuals or groups which willingly join together in certain causes find themselves on opposite sides in other contests. This is most evident in Nigeria, where the potential for factionalism seems to be infinite. Van den Berghe[114] shows how various groups and subgroups competed for power at 'Ilosho University', with the lines of conflict shifting according to the personal and departmental as well as ethnic interests involved. This also illustrates another problem of ethnic conflict. Outsiders often see ethnicity as an independent variable when other factors are more important. Political contests over scarce resources are phrased in ethnic terms because this is the easiest way to draw the large number of followers needed for success. Melson and Wolpe[115] provide many examples of the use of communal attachments for political ends in Nigeria; the same sort of actions can be found in other countries.

Communalism is often a defence reaction of a group which feels itself threatened; it arises in situations of inequality and is fostered by suspicion that others have or may gain opportunities which members of one's own group are denied. It may find expression in ethnic conflict, but may equally arise when national, regional or local interests are seen as being ignored or rejected by more powerful groups. People of one state or district or area complain that more government funds are spent on the education of other children or for the provision of amenities in other places than on their own; this gives them a sense of common purpose which they may previously have lacked.

While the communal attachment may be strongest among ordinary people, its expression and manipulation are more frequent among the leaders, who stand to gain or lose more from the conflict than their followers. The politicians get places in government; the educated get well-paid jobs. Thus, although one might expect the elites to be more universalistic and nationalistic than the masses, this tends not to be the case. They see how the 'national cake' is being divided, and mobilise support in order to get at least their share. Threatening followers with dominance by others and the deprivation of amenities which often accompanies allegiance to the opposition has proved a sure means to success at the polls.

The communal ties of ordinary people are most evident in marriage. Parents assume that a marriage is most likely to be successful if the prospective spouses share the same culture, language and religion; they oppose marriage to a 'stranger' because the lack of a shared culture puts extra strain

(114) 1973, p.263.   (115) 1971; see also Wolpe 1969.

on the couple. The incidence of interethnic marriage is, therefore, low. It tends to be greater in cities, where people of many different backgrounds meet and where migrants may have difficulty finding a spouse from their own group. It is also higher among people who are least subject to the control of kinsmen and their home community, the better educated who have relatively secure employment, migrants far from home and members of ethnic groups which place less emphasis on lineage. Muslims usually stress religion rather than ethnicity of spouses, though cultural factors are relevant to the extent that marriages among Muslims as among others tend to be between people who are members of culturally related groups.[116]

Other types of mixing are much more acceptable and usual than marriage. Urban residents amicably work together and share housing with members of other groups, some of whom might be enemies at home. Nevertheless, there are generally some peoples who are preferred to others. These preferences can be measured by social distance scales.[117] There is generally a hierarchy of acceptance, which can be expressed in terms of distance: one would intermarry with few or no other peoples, share housing or live near more, eat and/or work with still more, and prefer to have no contacts at all with certain others. Some individuals and members of some groups are very open in their acceptance, discriminating against no one; others prefer to limit interaction to their own group and maintain as much distance as possible from all others.

Mitchell[118] found that some Zambian peoples such as the Ngoni, Ndebele and Bemba had a high rank with most other groups (were preferred associates) because of their military reputation; others such as the Luvale had a low rank (were avoided) because they were stereotyped as night soil men. In between, people preferred to associate with groups they knew (that lived near them at home) and, secondarily, with peoples of similar culture (i.e., that were also matrilineal). They felt most distant from peoples who were both geographically and culturally separate from themselves. Peil reports that social distance ratings in Nigeria vary with the location and ethnic heterogeneity of the town, the prestige and economic/political control exercised by the group, and the sex, education and ethnicity of the individual doing the rating. Respondents in four towns showed different patterns of preference and avoidance, which suggests the need for large-scale studies before any reliable conclusions can be drawn about ethnic stratification on a national level or on the factors which reduce prejudice and discrimination in the society as a whole.

(116) Busia 1950, p.29; Mitchell 1957; Parkin 1966a; Peil 1972a, p.192 and 1975b, pp. 118–9; Schildkraut 1974, p.210.   (117) Mitchell 1956 and in A. Cohen 1974; Peil 1975b.   (118) 1956.

As social distance scales are measures of attitudes, their relevance to actual behaviour is often questioned. Individuals marry even though their societies are at war, and it is easier to proclaim one's tolerance than to treat all people equally. However, both Mitchell and Peil found considerable agreement between the statements people made about their attitudes and behaviour measured by housing and friendship choices.

Lest it seem that communalism has only negative features, it is important to remember that it also provides social security far beyond what the state can provide and that in cutting across interests of class, status and power it serves as an equalising influence, lessening conflicts which might otherwise arise on these bases. Individuals feel a share in the success of others in the community, and the successful are under considerable pressure to share some of their resources with less fortunate members of the community. Communalism is theoretically irrelevant to a modern, universalistic social system, yet it persists everywhere because its very real benefits outweigh its disadvantages.[119]

Conclusion

Social differentiation is pervasive in every society. People measure others against themselves and construct hierarchies on whatever variables appear to be relevant to the situation: income, occupation, education, power, ethnicity, race, etc. Those who are rated highly are rewarded with prestige and deference; those with a low rating are looked down on by the rest.

African societies differ considerably in their precolonial stratification systems, in the way these were shaped by the colonial period, and in the level of social differentiation which has developed in the post-independence period. All have both customary and new elites, but some are far more exploitative than others. So far, these elites have not become a clearly identifiable upper class, but there is evidence of change in this direction. Economic inequality has increased, but data on social inequality are not as clear and social mobility appears to be open to anyone who can acquire a good education or demonstrate superior capability in business or politics. Class-consciousness is at most intermittent and subject to conflicting ties of kinship and ethnicity.

The important factor in social differentiation appears to be the extent to which class, status, power and ethnicity coincide or cut across the population. Where some groups are low on all criteria of ranking and others are high, community conflict (or at least the potential for conflict) tends to be much

(119) Marris 1967, pp.13–14.

greater than where crystallisation is lower and individuals have cross-cutting ties to various statuses. If everyone in the community fits neatly into either Category A or Z, any issue which divides A and Z will be very difficult to solve because no one will be able to mediate between them. If, on the other hand, some individuals belong to both factions (they have an A occupation but Z ethnicity), they are pulled in both directions and it will be in their best interests to arrange a compromise before the conflict gets too serious. The more people there are in this intercalary position, the greater the chance that the community will avoid overt conflict.

In South Africa, for example, income, status and power are all closely tied to race and opportunities for social mobility are consequently limited; cross-cutting ties (marriage, shared neighbourhoods, or union membership) are forbidden by law and conflict is contained only by the threat of massive force. At another level, we have nations such as Nigeria and Uganda where one ethnic group got a considerable start over the others in education and participation in modern occupations, which helped its members to powerful positions in the civil service at independence. Inevitably, there has been conflict as other groups have claimed their share of elite positions. As a third type, Banton suggests[120] that 'ethnic differences did not get built into the economic structure' in Sierra Leone because the Europeans and Creoles, who held the important positions before independence, ignored them. Mende did do somewhat better than Temne occupationally because they got a head start in Western education, but politics, religion and occupation have not generally crystallised to give one ethnic group an overwhelming advantage over the others. This may be one factor in Sierra Leone's ability to return from military to civilian rule.

Cultural differences are becoming progressively less important throughout Africa. Nevertheless, ethnicity and other forms of communal boundaries continue to be relevant because they are an assumed part of self-identity (everyone is expected to have a tribe just as they have a family) and, more important, because they have become factors in status ranking within the society. Because ethnic stereotyping has some basis in historical differences in access to education, cash crop income and other opportunities, some ethnic groups are ranked higher than others by the society as a whole. This, in turn, encourages members of the disadvantaged groups to join together in improving their position rather than concentrating on individual or family mobility and encourages poorer and lower-status members of advantaged groups to identify with their more successful members rather than initiating class conflict.

(120) In Kuper 1965, p.139.

Suggested reading and discussion topics

1. Read the chapter by Boswell in A. Cohen (1974). Discuss the positive and negative effects of social mobility.
2. List the major ethnic groups in your country and the common stereotypes people have for each of them. On what evidence are these stereotypes based?
3. Describe the system(s) of social differentiation in the town you know best. What criteria are most important? To what extent do people in one position have ties to people who are higher or lower than themselves? Do most people have more than one position according to which system is used, or are most people easily placed in a single position? What evidence can you give to support your answer?

5 The Family

Family institutions (sex, marriage, parenthood, kinship) are basic to society because they provide and cherish new members without which the society would disappear. Everyone assumes, as a result of his primary socialisation, that he knows what the family is, but the more one studies families in different societies the more one finds differences from what is commonly accepted at home. The bundle of relationships which have come to be identified with the family vary within as well as between societies. The chief, 'big man' or member of the elite often has different types of family relationships and a larger family network than the ordinary farmer or labourer, and family life in pastoral societies or matrilineal societies is based on different sorts of assumptions and relationships than family life in settled agricultural or industrial societies or those with patrilineal inheritance. Systematic study of the family in various societies provides important clues to social structure and helps us to a better understanding of the role of the family in our own society. This chapter will examine some of the different types of family systems and the changes which are taking place as a result of increasing migration and urbanisation.

Kinship

Social anthropologists concerned with how societies function have made careful studies of kinship systems, since these form the core of small-scale societies; the political, religious and economic systems are closely tied to kinship if not an integral part of it. As a basic principle of social organisation, kinship gives a person his place in society; he is the son of X and the grandson of Y. This basic ascription is less important in more developed societies, but it is still significant, especially for women and children and among the wealthy, where inheritance provides considerable advantages.

Kinship implies ties of blood (biological kinship), descent (jural or legal kinship) and marriage (affiliation). People descended from a common ancestor are referred to as cognatic kin or cognates; those who become kin through marriage are affinal kin or affines. Kinship terminology reflects the relative importance of various social relationships within a society; study of the names given to kinsmen tells us a good deal about the structure of the society concerned. The terminology may be either descriptive (MB, FZS)[1] or classificatory (any male on the father's side is called father). A descriptive system is more precise, but if it is used beyond a narrow range it becomes very cumbersome; therefore, some system of classification is used for distant kinsmen. Classification is useful for an outsider because it indicates the nature of the relationship, the rights and responsibilities which are likely to exist between two individuals. In a wide sense, this is demonstrated by the use of the term brother for many people of roughly the same age with whom we feel a close bond, even though they are not kinsmen at all. This is the same use as 'brethren' in the Bible.

People who claim to be cognatic kinsmen may trace their common descent in one of several ways.[2] (see Figure 8). In patrilineal or agnatic descent, links are traced and rights and duties follow the male line; in matrilineal or uterine

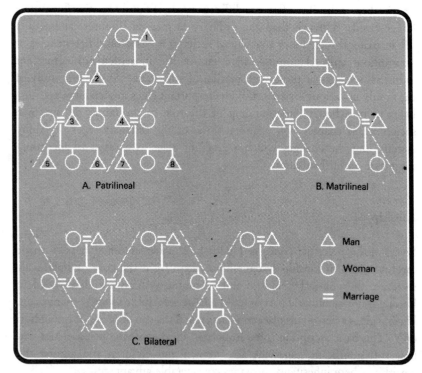

A. Patrilineal

B. Matrilineal

C. Bilateral

△ Man

○ Woman

= Marriage

Figure 8 Forms of descent

(1) F=father; M=mother; B=brother; Z=sister; S=son; D=daughter.
(2) Fortes 1953.

descent, they follow the female line. Bilateral descent, where both the mother's and the father's lines are traced, is more common in Europe than in Africa. This method poses difficulties which are not present with unilineal descent. The number of ancestors, or of descendants, soon becomes too great to be remembered and the lack of boundaries makes it hard to define and perpetuate a corporate kinship group. (Whereas group membership and allegiance are clear in a patrilineal society, individuals in a society with bilateral kinship rules can often describe their relationship to others in various ways and find it difficult to draw a clear line between kin and non-kin.) Double descent is practised in some societies; some rights and duties are transmitted through the male line and others through the female line. For example, land or cattle are passed down from father to son and ritual status goes from a man to his sister's son.[3]

The situation may not be as clear as these definitions make it seem. Although lineage ties are held to be very important, people may claim to be related who cannot trace all the links between them to a common ancestor and, as the record is seldom written down, less important ancestors are likely to be dropped from the list. The Tiv, for example, all claim to be descended from an ancestor called Tiv, but many of the intervening ancestors have been forgotten. In some societies, subgroups differ in their rules, so that part of the society follows patrilineal norms and another part matrilineal norms. This may indicate that a changeover from one system to another is taking place, or that what is at present considered a single ethnic group was in the past two or more separate societies. (This is part of the flexibility of boundaries discussed in the last chapter.)

A society with unilineal descent may trace rights and duties in one line and inheritance in some other way. For example, in a patrilineal society women may have some inheritance from their mothers and in a basically matrilineal society children may inherit some goods or positions from their fathers. In other words, many supposedly unilineal systems have some double descent aspects. In addition, titles and honours may not be inherited in the same way as material objects. They may go to the eldest son (primogeniture), or the eldest member of various lineages in turn, or to all the brothers before moving down a generation to the son of the eldest brother, or to any member of a particular lineage who is considered most worthy by the group. Thus, although some lineage connection is usually necessary it may not be sufficient to predict the next holder of a position. Most important, actual behaviour may not follow the norms, so that careful recording of who inherits from whom or the way rights and responsibilities are recognised often

(3) Forde in Radcliffe-Brown and Forde 1950.

shows a quite different pattern than is said to characterise a society. The ideal is always subject to change to suit particular circumstances.

Lineages can be linked together into systems. This makes it possible for any member of the society to establish his position in relation to anyone else by tracing the geneological links between them. Two basic principles can be followed, segmental opposition or 'spinal cord'.[4] Segmental opposition is found among many peoples who have few or no leadership roles outside the family, such as the Nuer, Tiv and Tallensi. The basic principle is that conflict is carried to the level at which the parties have a common ancestor. If, in Figure 8A, 5 and 6 have a quarrel, it need involve no one else, since 3 is the father of both of them. If, however, 5 quarrels with 7, he will be supported by 6 and 7 will be supported by 8. Each segment is thus opposed to all others at the same level, but joins with nearer kinsmen against more distant kinsmen. Such a system can affect support for modern political parties, as members of a lineage feel they must oppose any candidate sponsored by a rival lineage.

The 'spinal cord' form of organisation emphasises control over a specific position or piece of property and is more common in societies with centralised leadership. Where there is a line of inheritance for a kingdom, for example (or stool, skin, emirship, etc.), lineages which do not inherit the position are 'sloughed off' at various levels and become more and more distant from the royal line. If, in Figure 8A, a position passes from 1 to 2 to 3 to 5, the descendants of 4 are pushed out, and the descendants of 6 will be slightly closer than the descendants of 7 and 8 because their branch is one step lower. If the male line fails to produce an heir, the next nearest line is substituted. Theoretically, every lineage in the society can be ordered by its closeness to the central line or 'cord'.

Regardless of its method of organisation, the kinship system constitutes a hierarchy in which everyone has a place. This network of roles has much in common with the societal differentiation systems described in the last chapter, and may be an important part of them if social relations are based on ascription. Roles in the kinship system change over time, as the son-nephew-brother becomes father-uncle-brother-husband-affine.

Institutionalised kinship patterns provide ways of preventing and handling conflict which might easily arise from close interaction or particular situations such as inheritance, which may be a considerable source of strain if the norms are not clear. The most straightforward system is primogeniture, in which the eldest son (or the eldest sister's son in a matrilineal system) takes everything. Besides eliminating conflict as to who should inherit or how the

(4) Bohannan 1969, pp.137–9.

136

goods should be divided, such a system prevents land division and so is used in some agricultural societies where land is in short supply. Nevertheless, it is generally unpopular because all the other children are disinherited unless the heir chooses to give them something. There may be partial primogeniture, in that ritual or political office goes to the eldest whereas property is shared, or the heir may get control over family property (seen as belonging to the ancestors) but be obliged to use it to provide for younger siblings.

It is more common for all the children (or the children of each wife, or all the males) to inherit equally. Such a system has many advantages in giving members of each generation a fairly equal start in life. Since polygyny allows rich men to have more wives and children than poor men, the former's property is widely distributed whereas the latter usually has only a few heirs.[5] However, difficulties arise if the property is indivisible, such as a house. The heirs may each get an interest in one room of the house (to live in or rent), but it is more difficult in the next generation, and sales become very complicated. It is hard to obtain clear title to urban land in some countries because every one of the heirs must give permission for the sale. When the Lagos government bought land for redevelopment, the money was so widely dispersed that very few families could keep enough to rebuild their houses.[6]

Prescriptions for relationships between generations also help to avoid conflict. Children are expected to show great respect for their parents and, by extension, all those of their parents' generation. Certain people may be directed to avoid each other entirely. For example, when a man marries, he takes over responsibility for his mother-in-law's daughter. Since they may easily disagree on certain matters, conflict is avoided if they do not interact. Similarly, a man and his heir often avoid each other or maintain only very formal relations. There is always the possibility that the heir may want to profit from a man's death, so it is better to be careful. On the other hand, relations between children and their grandparents are usually very cordial. They can be friendly because the relationship involves little or no responsibility on the grandparents' part. Relations with siblings of one's parents are often friendly if inheritance is not involved; the parties concerned can decide how close they want the relationship to be. They may have a 'joking relationship', whereby the two parties abuse each other freely in a friendly way, saying things which might lead to conflict if the special relationship did not exist.[7] This sort of relationship may also exist between ethnic groups, as mentioned in the last chapter; it is a way of distinguishing 'friends' from 'strangers' and implies that some distant kinship relationship

(5) Hill 1972.   (6) Marris 1961.   (7) Radcliffe-Brown 1952.

exists, at least symbolically.

Fictive kinship is a convenient way of establishing norms of social inter-action in ambiguous situations. If the two parties agree to treat each other as brothers, or as father and son, they have a clear idea of their rights and obligations. It also provides substitutes for missing kinsmen, so that necessary duties can be carried out. Thus, in towns migrants from the same hometown, clan, district, or ethnic group may call each other 'brother' and act as if they were brothers. When the migrant has few biological kinsmen in the same town, he can turn relationships with his landlord, cotenants, workmates, patrons, or other friends into fictive kinship and thereby get the help he needs. In turn, he will be expected to loan money, provide services, and carry out other duties within the framework of this kinship norm. While it might be expected that kinship would become less important in towns because social networks are based on other links, at least some of these links become symbolic kinship ties and thus the norms of kinship remain strong.[8]

Marriage

Until the twentieth century (and in many respects even today), it was relatively rare for adults to go through life without marrying. Marriage is still taken for granted to the extent that most people assume that anyone over thirty years of age is married. Adult women are customarily called 'Mrs' in European societies even though as much as a quarter of all women never marry. In a polygynous society, women usually marry early and men must often wait until they are twenty-five or thirty because only in this way are there enough women for some men to have more than one wife at a time. At any given time, there will be many men and women who are widowed or divorced, but it is expected that most of the younger ones will soon find another spouse. There may be no role for an unattached adult woman except prostitute. In a farming community, women must live under the care of a man because some of the work is too heavy for them. Adults who do not marry and (more important) have children, are seen as denying their responsibility to provide for the future of their group.

Basically, marriage is a publicly recognised, more or less permanent alliance between a man and a woman (the conjugal unit). In most societies, the families of the partners have a role in establishing the relationship (often choosing the mate and at least manifesting their approval of the choice) and participate in the rite of passage which constitutes the formal marriage. The

(8) Schildkrout 1973.

marriage legitimises sexual access and the children which result, giving them an ascriptive place in the society as members of a particular lineage and family. They have rights and responsibilities to their kinsmen because of their parents' union.

Types

The practice of bridewealth is tied, at least in principle, to the transfer of sexual rights, and therefore rights in children who will be born of the marriage. Sexual rights vary between societies and sometimes according to the type of marriage within the society. These may be uxorial rights (to domestic and sexual services) or genetricial rights (to the woman as a mother, giving ownership of all children born to her). With genetricial rights, a man is socially the father of all children born to his wife even though he may not be their biological father; he is the *pater* even though he may not be the *genitor*. The Asante summarise this by the proverb, 'A thief has no child.' In some societies, any children born before the full bridewealth has been paid belong to the mother's family rather than to the father's; he has only uxorial rights until the account is settled.

Three kinds of marriage are recognised in most African countries: customary, religious and civil. Muslim marriages may be classified as both customary and religious, as in Muslim areas this form has largely replaced other customary forms. Customary marriages are arranged by the families concerned and usually involve some form of brideprice or bride-service through which the husband's family compensates the bride's family for the loss of a member. In matrilineal societies, where the children will belong to the bride's lineage, this payment is usually very low.

Although survival is less of a problem with the declining infant death rates of today than it was in the past, lineage members still look on marriage as vital to the continuance of their group. The exchange of goods and services for a member of the group enables the lineage to replace those who marry out. For example, a woman is given in exchange for cows (or salt, or money) and the cows are given to obtain a wife for one of the men. This exchange ties the two lineages together, so that many people are interested in the success of the marriage. The ceremonies and payments associated with customary marriage often take place over a considerable period, symbolising the importance which the kin groups give to this alliance and their support for it.

Christian marriage, as introduced by the missionaries, has tended to emphasise legalistic and prestige factors at the expense of the societal integration aspects. A church marriage is supposed to be monogamous and for life. Additional wives are considered illegitimate and the marriage can be formally ended only by divorce. Although customary marriages are often celebrated by expensive entertaining, church marriages have become associated with far greater expense, to the extent that couples who would like a church marriage often put it off for many years because they cannot afford the conspicuous consumption which is expected. Many churches require that customary ceremonies, including the payment of brideprice, be fulfilled before the church ceremony because this is likely to give greater stability to the marriage; breakdown is more likely when the respective families have not been consulted and customary duties have not been carried out.

The proportion of Christians who marry in church varies considerably from one area to another, but is generally far lower than church leaders would like. Hastings[9] found high rates in some areas of Malawi and particularly low rates in some parts of Uganda. There are Catholic churches in Ghana which have never had a church marriage and others in Nigeria which have many. The strength of local attitudes toward polygyny, the level of marital breakdown, relations between the clergy and the faithful and the effectiveness of teaching on various aspects of Christianity (including marriage) are important factors. Insofar as a high rate of church marriage has been fostered by close pastoral supervision and relative isolation, the development of communications and opportunities for migration and the more rapid growth of the Christian community than of the clergy seem likely to lead to a decline.

Civil marriage takes place in a register office rather than a church, but otherwise involves the same obligations and usually the same expense as a church marriage. It often gives the wife and children stronger inheritance rights than they have with a customary marriage, an important factor in a matrilineal society. Civil marriage is usually limited to the elite, though some northern Ghanaians use civil marriage because it is cheaper than the brideprice of several cows which is required for customary marriage.

Choice of spouse

The development of a cash economy has given prospective marriage partners considerably more freedom of choice than was possible in a subsistence economy. Actually, many young people had a say, at least a veto, in their marriage partner in the past, but they are now less dependent on family approval and backing than before. Those who want to make an independent

(9) 1973.

choice and can pay their own way can carry on even if their family strongly disapproves, but the majority still seek family consent for their choice. Women with their own source of income can also break off a marriage they dislike because they can pay back the brideprice themselves; others get the prospective new husband to pay.

Although the choice of a spouse may give rise to conflict, most young people still consult their parents about it. Omari[10] asked a group of Ghanaian training college students what they would do if their parents objected to their choice of a spouse. While 41% of the students (more of the women than the men) said they would give up their choice if their parents disapproved, 14% said they would marry anyway and 35% were undecided. Those who were courting at the time were more likely to say they would be obedient, so there are probably many who talk about independence but at the crucial moment follow their parents' advice. This goes back to the strong feeling that marriage is at least as much a family as an individual affair; the support of the family for the ceremony and during married life (and, for women especially, should the marriage break down) makes it important that their approval be gained.

Societies usually have definite norms about mate selection, defining who is and who is not an eligible spouse. These are institutionalised as rules of exogamy (marriage outside the group) and endogamy (marriage within the group). The strongest and most widespread rule of exogamy is the incest prohibition; marriage between two people who are closely related, or even sexual relations between them, is abhored. But societies vary in the relationships which are considered incest. In some, it may be limited to the nuclear family; father/daughter (F/D) mother/son (M/S) or brother/sister (B/Z). In others, a wide variety of kinsmen are included, even kinsmen who are preferred partners elsewhere. For example, cross-cousin marriages (between children of siblings of the opposite sex, MBD/FZS or MBS/FZD) are preferred in some societies and prohibited in others. Most societies forbid the marriage of parallel cousins (between children of siblings of the same sex, FBS or MZD), but this is approved among Muslim peoples.

The most important reason for the incest prohibition is biological; marriage between close kinsmen increases the likelihood that the children will inherit negative physical characteristics. A sociological explanation would be that children of such parents would have an ambiguous position in the descent group; a child of a F/D incest would be a sibling of its mother. In addition, since incest is usually extra-marital, it conflicts with societal rules on premarital chastity and adultery. Levi-Strauss[11] argues that the incest

(10) 1963, p.151.   (11) 1956.

prohibition forces potentially isolated and hostile families into marital affiliation and therefore into social relations.

Marriages with certain other kinsmen may be preferred because of the economic advantages of keeping property within the family. For example, in a matrilineal society the father's sister's son (FZS) will inherit the property. If the father marries his daughter to this nephew, she can share in her father's inheritance. Other marriages with kinsmen (usually exogamous to the lineage) are seen as reinforcing a relationship between families which has worked well in the past. These forms of preferential marriage to kinsmen seem to be declining as young people have a wider and freer choice of partners.

Two other characteristics of potential spouses are significant to the families concerned, ethnicity and socio-economic status. When a young man comes to tell his parents about his lady-love, they are likely to ask, 'Who is she?', meaning who and what is her family? Where choice is within a village or a group of neighbouring villages, they can easily ascertain whether she comes from a good lineage from the fertility, personality and family point of view; where the son wishes to marry a girl from further away, it is more difficult for his parents to get this information. Parents everywhere prefer that their children marry 'one of us', but the limits of this endogamous orientation vary. They may prefer someone from a lineage with which their lineage has regularly exchanged spouses but approve of someone belonging to the same subgroup or even ethnic group. They often object if the prospective partner speaks another language and follows different customs, feeling that he or she cannot fit into the family as they should. Similarly, they may prefer that their child find a wealthy or potentially prominent spouse, approve of marriage to someone at the same level as themselves and try to stop marriage to someone of a lower caste or discriminated group within the society. (Achebe's *No Longer at Ease* describes such a situation.)

The amount of marriage between two groups may be a measure of prejudice between them, or it may be merely a reflection of the level of opportunity. Some peoples who are basically very tolerant of others have strong views on endogamous marriage. Others might have no objection to marriage to a member of a relatively unknown group but would disapprove of marriage to someone from a nearby group with whom they are traditionally at enmity. However, individuals belonging to warring groups do intermarry, and families are sometimes willing to approve the choice of a particular individual even though they prefer to have nothing to do with members of the individual's group.

Although migration to heterogeneous cities provides an opportunity for meeting a wide variety of potential spouses, the majority of migrants still marry within their own group. Cultural factors are important; one wants a wife with whom one can communicate easily, who cooks the food one is used to and shares the same views on marriage and family life as oneself. But, apart from personal attraction, choice may depend on whether one intends to stay in the town and the number of single women in the migrant stream. Where there are far fewer migrant women than men, the young men may marry indigenous women rather than sending home for a wife, especially if their home is a long way off. Permanent migrants may also marry local women, as they are more committed to the town and see no need for an alliance with a lineage at home. But there will not be enough women for all; many will have to find a wife at home if they are to marry at all.

Mitchell[12] found that mixed marriages on the Copperbelt tended to be between people coming from the same geographical and cultural area, i.e., those who could not find a spouse of their own group married someone from a neighbouring and culturally similar group. In Nigeria, mixed marriages are few and propinquity, education and personality seem to be more important than cultural similarity.[13] Spouses from different ethnic groups had often both grown up in the town, becoming accustomed to contacts with people of differing ethnic groups. Schildkrout[14] found that second generation Mossi in Kumasi were more often interethnically married than men who had migrated themselves.

There appear to have been more ethnically mixed marriages in Takoradi, Ghana, when the sex ratio was high than later, when it became more balanced; men married out when they could not find a wife belonging to their own group, but when women of their own group were available they chose these.[15] The same principle appears to be operating with education. This initially raises the incidence of interethnic marriage because it provides a common language and socialisation for the spouses, because well-educated men often have to look outside their own group for educated women and because educated people tend to interact both at work and during their leisure time with members of many other groups. However, there is some evidence from Nigeria that, with increasing education for girls within a group, the level of endogamous marriage among the well-educated tends to rise again.

Goody[16] has shown that socio-economic position has been relatively less important as a basis for choice of spouse in Africa than in Eurasia. Pre-colonial African societies tended to be relatively economically homogeneous, with minor differences between the inheritable wealth of chiefs and people. Rules of exogamy meant that members of chiefly families usually married

(12) 1957.   (13) Peil 1975b, p.118.   (14) 1974, p.210.   (15) Busia 1950, p.29; Peil 1972a, p.194. (16) J. Goody 1971.

commoners. Systems of rotation of the chiefly role between lineages or of election by 'kingmakers' with the relegation of all other members of the chief's family to the status of commoners meant that status could not be permanently maintained by limiting marriage to members of a high status group. Therefore, there has generally been more intermarriage between socio-economic levels in Africa than in Eurasia. Although in recent years education may have cut down somewhat the amount of marriage between people at different economic levels, so far there is still considerable mixing, and ethnicity or community membership continue to be more important than socio-economic status in the choice of a partner.

Residential units

The census definition of a household is a group of people who share a dwelling place and their main meals. While this is clear when parents and children live, eat and sleep together in a compound or room, difficulties arise when some members of the family eat or sleep elsewhere even though they think of themselves as forming a united group. A man may have wives living in several houses or even different villages and sleep with each in turn. To which household does he belong? Residents of a single dwelling or room may make separate arrangements for meals, or meals may be shared among residents of more than one dwelling. Thus, people's idea of their household group may not conform to the census definition.

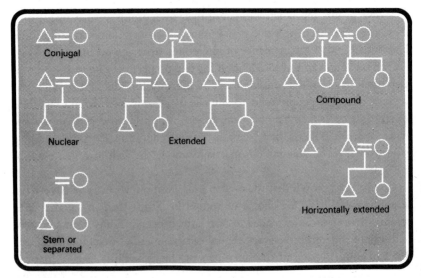

Figure 9 Types of residential units

Various types of family may be distinguished according to the location and inclusiveness of accommodation. When the couple live with the husband's kinsmen, residence is said to be virilocal; when they live with the wife's people, it is called uxorilocal; when they establish their own residence, it is called neolocal.

The man and wife are known as a conjugal unit. With their children in a neolocal residence, they become a nuclear family. The children may be the product of the marriage, or of a previous marriage of either husband or wife, or they may be fostered or adopted by the couple (see below). Virilocal and uxorilocal residence often include an extended family (two or more generations living together under the authority of a head). Where virilocal residence is customary, sons settle with their wives in the household of their father; in uxorilocal residences the daughters bring their husbands to their mother's household. The former is much more common and generally more satisfactory than the latter, because a group of brothers find it easier to cooperate in farming under their father's authority than a group of unrelated men working under the authority of their wife's father. Both of these arrangements have become less common in recent years because the attractions of migration draw young men away from cooperative family farming.

An extended family may include more than three generations, but this has been rare even in societies which favour it because most adults have not lived to see their great-grandchildren. When the head of the extended family dies, the residence usually breaks up; members of the next generation become family heads in their turn. If there is enough land, they often settle near each other so that family ties can be maintained.

Horizontally extended families are common in towns. A migrant moves in with a brother or sister until he gets a job and can afford a room of his own or, if a woman, until she marries. These households may include two generations, as when a nephew is sent to town for schooling or an apprenticeship. While some urban families are quite willing to accommodate their kinsmen, others find it a burden, especially if they are already seriously overcrowded. Ohadike[17] found that extended family households were more common in Lusaka than in the Zambian villages he studied; they were also more common in urban households of high than of low socio-economic status. The better-off households were accommodating more kinsmen than the poorer ones. Oppong[18] reports that Akan senior civil servants must often accommodate kinsmen who would live separately at home. This leads to modifications in customary relationships (of respect and hostility) between kinsmen.

(17) 1971, p.196. (18) 1974, p.84.

The compound family is based on polygynous marriage. The case shown in Figure 9 has two nuclear sections. Each of these could be extended, vertically or horizontally, or may live separately as a stem or separated household. This often occurs when the husband migrates to town, leaving his wife and children at home. He may live in a nuclear family in town if he takes another wife, and his rural wife often lives as part of an extended family under the supervision of her father and mother-in-law. Ga and Yoruba wives sometimes go to town to trade, leaving their husbands on the farm; they may take the children with them or leave them with another wife. Some women also choose to remain in town with their children after their husband retires to his hometown. In this case, the mother usually forms an extended family with her children and grandchildren. In some societies, such as the Ga and Akan, spouses live separately, with the wives sending food to their husband and visiting him in turn at night. Boys go to live with their fathers when they are old enough to have 'sense'; girls continue to live with their mothers (and grandmothers). This arrangement could be considered as two extended stem families or merely a nuclear or extended family which only partly shares residential accommodation.

Complications of residence are less important than the social relations which accompany them; definitions based on the use made of kinship links explain more than those based exclusively on residence. Increased migration and urbanisation interfere with common residence, but if the links continue to be relevant it is meaningful to talk of extended families. Many couples live as a nuclear family in town, or as a horizontally extended family (with the addition of one or two kinsmen), but think of themselves as part of extended families and maintain regular relations (through messages and visits) with these extended families. Members of compound families often live separately in town because the husband finds rooms in different houses for each of his wives. In the case of the separated or stem family, the village spouse may visit the town from time to time. Meaningful ties are more important than permanently shared residence.

Nevertheless, the nature of these ties is affected by the residential pattern. Children growing up in an extended family household get to know their kinsmen much better than would be possible if they lived some distance away, but they usually know their parents less well because attention is shared among several adults. A child in such a household may have closer ties to an aunt or grandmother than to his own mother, especially if he has many siblings and/or his mother is busy trading. The father may be an even more distant figure for the young child. Not only is it important for a father to maintain his dignity and demand the respect due to him; a polygynous father also avoids conflict by treating his children equally and, as he usually has many, he cannot devote much time to each one. A child growing up in a nuclear household, on the other hand, usually develops close ties to his parents since, being relatively isolated, they are more dependent on each other. Also, because the group is small, more emphasis can be put on individual rather than communal ties.[19]

The nuclear family often has kinsmen nearby who can be called on in emergencies, but special arrangements may be necessary because the relative who is needed in a specific situation is not available. For instance, it may be customary for the mother's brother to officiate at the outdooring of a baby. If the father's brother is the only kinsman available, he must be called upon. Thus, the presence of only part of the extended family in town often means that kinship roles become less specific; the fact of being a kinsman is more important than the precise relationship.

Polygyny

Polygyny is an aspect of African marriage which attracts considerable interest from foreigners. It used to be practised in Asia and is still common in some Islamic countries outside Africa. The opposite, polyandry (one woman having more than one husband) was formerly practised in Tibet. Africans often take polygyny so much for granted that their ideas of monogamy are not too clear. An article in the Lagos Morning Post[20] on the U.A.M. referred to it as 'the only African Church founded as a result of the insistence on monogamy (the idea of having only one wife and not even having a girl friend outside your home to bear a child)'.

This makes clear a fundamental reason for the existence of pologyny, the desire for a large number of children. When few babies survived into adulthood, parents needed many children to be sure of an heir. Marriage to a barren woman would be broken up by kinsmen, but it might be allowed to continue if the husband could marry another woman and have children by her. Wives had considerable responsibilities on the farm as well as in the house and were often glad of additional help. In societies with relatively few consumer goods, wives are also a form of conspicuous consumption; the Arabian potentate who had many wives, none of whom did any work, had a deserved reputation for opulence which can now be expended on Mercedes Benz cars, air-conditioned palaces, private aeroplanes and so on. Nevertheless, paying the brideprice for, and supporting, several wives still demonstrates that a man has been successful and reinforces his status in society. This inevitably lends support to polygyny; if a man is successful,

(19) B. Lloyd in Lloyd 1966.   (20) 27 September 1971.

147

people expect him to take another wife.

This societal expectation has caused considerable difficulty for the Christian churches, which have generally condemned polygyny (often at least partly on the ethnocentric grounds that it is not practised in Europe), but whose members have often been materially successful and followed the societal norm. Vanden Driesen[21] found that Christians in Ife Division of western Nigeria were more often polygynous than Muslims and reports from Ghana, Uganda and Zambia[22] indicate that Christians there have rates of polygyny which are not much lower than those of non-Christians, even though this means that they cease participating in Christian sacraments. The 1960 Ghanaian census showed that members of Christian sects had a higher rate of polygyny than members of the major mission churches and both Muslims and those adhering to traditional religions were more often polygynous than Christians, but the differences were rather small and certainly indicate that long years of preaching against polygyny have been unsuccessful in devaluing it.

The rate of polygyny has often been estimated as much higher than is demographically possible. Casual observers generally overestimate polygyny, just as they overestimate unemployment and other obvious conditions, where a few cases can be mistaken for a general norm. While many men are polygynous at some time in their lives, the numerical equality of men and women means that polygyny at any given time is limited. It is usually confined to older men and is achieved largely by women marrying as soon as they are nubile while men must wait many years for a wife. If, for example, the population is growing at 2% per year, there will be 10% more women aged fifteen than men aged twenty-five; if the average female marries at fourteen and the average male waits until he is thirty, even a population growth rate of 1% per year will provide 16% more women available for polygyny.

Dorjahn[23] estimates that the mean rate of polygyny for sub-Saharan Africa in the early 1950s was 35%; it was highest on the relatively affluent Guinea Coast (43%) and lowest among the Bushmen and East African cattle peoples (25%), who are generally living much closer to bare subsistence. The 1960 Ghana census showed that 26% of married men (16% of all adult men) had two or more wives; only 6% had three or more. The rate for Ivory Coast in the early 1960s was 29% in rural areas and 14% in Abidjan.[24] This suggests that the rate will drop as countries become more urbanised. Polygyny is relatively more expensive in town, where housing and food must be paid for, than in the countryside, where extra wives and children are often self-supporting.

(21) 1972, p.51.   (22) Aryee 1967; Hastings 1973.   (23) In Bascom and Herskovits 1959, p.102.   (24) Clignet and Sween 1969, p.134.

However, it may only seem to be lower in towns because such a large proportion of the urban population is young and it is usually older men who can afford another wife. Ohadike[25] found only 5% polygyny in Lusaka (where husbands averaged thirty-four years of age) and 15% in rural households (age not specified). Only 8% of a large sample of Ghanaian factory workers were polygynous, but the rate was 22% for those over forty years of age.[26] Similarly, only 7% of the men in Abidjan under thirty were polygynous, compared with nearly a quarter of those aged forty or over.[27] Parkin[28] found that polygyny increased from 11% of the men in their twenties to 41% of the men in their fifties and varied from 33% of the Luo to 7% of the Kikuyu in his Nairobi sample.

Unless respondents are asked to specify the whereabouts of all their wives, some polygyny is likely to be missed because wives live in different places. Vanden Driesen[29] reports that the rate of polygyny of small farmers in Ife Division was highly correlated with the spread of their farm plots; 89% of those whose plots were outside a twenty-mile radius were polygynous, whereas 78% of those whose plots were closer together were monogamous. It is difficult to look after widely scattered farms oneself, so extra wives are an important asset. (Men with scattered plots may also be wealthier than those with only a plot or two; over 90% of men with more than 7½ acres had additional wives.)

Men who migrate to town also find it useful to have someone to look after their needs as well as a wife at home to maintain the farm. The urban arrangement may at first be casual, but if they get on well together they may consider themselves married. Many do not pay a brideprice or go through any ceremony, but let their families know that a more enduring relationship has been established. However, wives of long-term migrants generally try to join their husbands in town if this is possible. Where there is more than one wife at home, the first wife usually moves to town, leaving a younger wife to uphold the migrants' right to land.

Various reasons are given as to why the rate of polygyny is expected to decline, especially in urban areas:

1 Polygyny flourishes where extended families exert close control over their members, but migration fosters individualism.
2 New values acquired through education and occupational mobility should lead to a decline in traditional values such as polygyny.
3 Large families are dysfunctional in town, especially when there are few economic opportunities for married women.
4 Polygyny hinders the adoption of new types of family interaction and

(25) 1971, p.202.   (26) Peil 1972a, p.191.   (27) Clignet and Sween1969, p.135.
(28) In A. Cohen 1974, p.152.   (29) 1972, p.53.

often increases tension within the marriage.[30]
5 Women who object to it are gaining social and political power. Two studies of educated people indicate general condemnation at this level, but a third suggests that opportunity and the strength of customary values are important factors.

Omari[31] reports that 61% of the men and 86% of the women he interviewed in a Ghanaian training college felt that polygyny was a backward practice. Caldwell[32] found that only 21% of the women and 31% of the men in an elite Ghanaian sample thought polygyny was a good thing. Their reasons are shown in Table 1.

Table 1 Reasons for Approving or Disapproving of Polygyny (Percentages)

Reason	Females	Males
Yes, a good thing		
Economic advantages (often referring to a village)	6	13
Ensures marriage of all women	7	6
Accommodates greater sexual strength of men	1	4
Solves problem of barren wife	2	2
No specific reason	8	6
No, not a good thing		
Emotional problems, especially for wives	54	37
Financial problems of extra dependants	15	19
Divides family, especially children	6	4
Religious or moral objections	4	8
Qualified or no response	3	3
Total[a]	106	102
N	331	296

Source: Caldwell, 1968b, p. 55 (adapted).
[a]Totals are over 100% because of multiple responses.

The majority of answers stress the difficulties which wives experience when they must share their husband and the expense of a large family, especially in towns where housing, food and clothing are more expensive

(30) Clignet and Sween 1969, pp.123-4. (31) 1960, p.203. (32) 1968b, p.55.

than in the village and where children must be supported through schooling rather than contributing through farming activities. It is notable that the rate of urban polygyny is higher among the Yoruba, most of whose wives support themselves as traders, than among other peoples whose wives are less economically active. The low proportion objecting on moral grounds (4% of the women and 8% of the men) indicates the relative unimportance of Christian teaching in this respect (all of the respondents were Christian).

LeVine's comparative study in Ibadan[33] found that the elite fathers generally rejected polygyny as expensive and conducive to family quarrels, though they did not necessarily disapprove of having 'outside wives'; their legal wives disapproved strongly of both practices. The fathers interviewed in a traditional area (half of whom were polygynous) felt that it produced a large, happy family of which they could be proud. Unfortunately, their wives were not questioned, but successful Yoruba women traders often prefer either polygyny (so that another wife can take care of the cooking and housework) or to 'retire from marriage' altogether in order to pursue their business.

Clignet and Sween[34] suggest that there are two possibilities for the relationship between participation in the urban economy and level of polygyny, linear and curvilinear (see Figure 10). If the relationship is linear, we would expect that polygyny would decline with increased education,

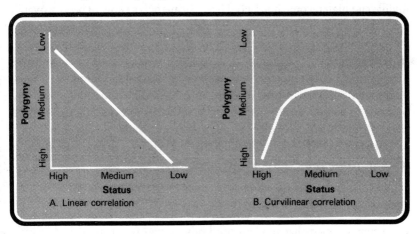

Figure 10 The relationship between socio-economic participation and polygyny

wealth and participation in high status occupations; it would be most widespread among illiterates and labourers and least among the elites. However,

(33) In Miner 1967, p.239.   (34) 1969.

if the relationship is curvilinear, we would find a fairly high level of polygyny both at the bottom and the top of the society and less in the middle (or a high rate in the middle and low rate at the ends). The Ivory Coast census data suggest that farmers and traders still find polygyny useful, so if they can afford to be polygynous, they are. Urban wage-earners can seldom afford it, but those who are more successful often choose (at least in Ivory Coast) to continue this traditional family style. Thus, while polygyny may be declining for economic reasons, it remains a high social value and may increase again as the urban standard of living improves. Modern means (cash income from a good job) are being used for a traditional end (an extra wife).

Clignet and Sween also found that the relative decline in polygyny varies according to its customary importance to each ethnic group. Incidence varied more from one part of the country to another than by size of city, indicating that ethnicity is more important than urbanisation; there may also be more opportunities for earning enough to support extra wives in larger than in smaller cities. In societies where polygyny was prevalent, it continues to be highly valued (and success in the modern sector is seen as a means to achieve it); in other societies, where it has never been important, it seems to be dying away completely; material success is used for other goals.

These hypotheses need to be tested in other places. For example, Ohadike[35] found a linear relationship in Lusaka, with 5% of low income and 2% of middle and high income household heads being polygynous. The low overall rate suggests that polygyny is not highly valued in the societies from which the migrants come. A somewhat more stable and older urban population may be responsible for the rise in the polygyny rate from 1% in the 1950s to 5% in 1968/9, but increased prosperity may also mean that more of those who prefer polygyny can now afford it. It seems likely that polygyny will continue to be important in Africa for many years to come, though various factors of social change will probably lower its incidence. The substitution of 'outside wives' is a more symbolic than real change, and probably lowers rather than raises women's position in the society.[36]

Divorce

It is often assumed that modern life leads to increased marital instability – that marriage in traditional societies was practically permanent, broken only

(35) 1971, p.202.   (36) Harrell-Bond (1975) found that it is common for elite men in Sierra Leone to have 'outside wives'. Creole society has a strong norm of monogamy and 'outside children' are often stigmatised as illegitimate, but men tend to see this as a way of producing a large number of children and thus enhancing their prestige.

by the death of one of the partners. However, empirical comparisons are difficult to make because we have few statistics on marriages in the past and, for that matter, few on the present situation. Part of the difficulty is the problem of deciding when a marriage is finished. If the couple are married under the Marriage Ordinance, a legal divorce is necessary. If not, separation may or may not signal the end of the marriage.

At least in certain societies, it seems that divorce was more common than it is among today's townspeople, regardless of the temptations they supposedly undergo. Mitchell[73] suggests that marriages on the Copperbelt are no more likely than those in the rural areas to be dissolved. The proportion of breakdowns for various ethnic groups in Zambia varied from 37% to 61%, which contradicts the idea of rural stability. The 1960 Ghana census found the following rates for the country as a whole:

Table 2 Marital Status by Sex and Place of Residence, Ghana 1960 (Percentages)

Sex and Residence	Never Married	Married	Divorced	Widowed	Total	N
Males						
Urban	39·7	54·9	4·2	1·2	100·0	472 660
Rural	31·3	61·0	5·6	2·1	100·0	1 353 860
Females						
Urban	12·3	71·5	7·9	8·3	100·0	426 960
Rural	7·3	76·2	7·0	9·5	100·0	1 402 880

Source: *1960 Census of Ghana*, Vol. VI, Table C1.

The proportion who were divorced at the time of the census was higher among rural men than among urban men and slightly lower among rural women than among urban women; it was higher among women than among men, as was widowhood. Note that there are only 3 320 more women than men, but that females of fifteen or older are more likely to be married than males. These rates seem very low compared to those quoted for Zambia, but they refer to marital status at one point in time; most divorced people soon

(37) 1957, p.10.

153

remarry. Divorce is particularly prevalent in central Ghana and among the peoples studied by Mitchell because of their matrilineal system. Women remain strongly attached to their own lineage, children belong to their matrilineage, and the husbands remain outsiders. If the marriage breaks down, the mother retains control over her children, which she could not do in a patrilineal society. The idea of marriage based on love and/or mutual attraction has long been established in Asante society, and where this attraction fades, the marriage tends to dissolve. Thus, over 11% of the rural women in Ashanti Region were divorced at the time of the census, compared to 7% for the country as a whole.

Goody's study[38] of divorce among the Gonja of northern Ghana shows a different type of customary pattern. The brideprice is low (as is usual where breakdown is frequent, see below). Marriage confers only uxorial rights (sexual access). The biological father is accepted as father regardless of whether the child was conceived before or within marriage or through adultery. So long as a child is recognised by its true father, it gets full rights in its paternal lineage. Marriage may be ended by the husband saying, 'I refuse you, you are no longer my wife', which is similar to the Muslim divorce ritual except that it is subject to negotiation. In practice, a husband seldom puts his wife out, but may indicate by his behaviour that he would like to. More often, the marriage is ended with the wife going home, refusing to return and then marrying someone else.

As in many societies, divorce is frequent in the early phase when the partners are testing each other for compatibility, but among the Gonja it is also frequent during child-rearing and especially in old age. Younger women usually remarry within a year or two of leaving their husbands, but women over fifty prefer to 'retire' from marriage and return to their patrilineal home. (Some Yoruba women do this as well.) An older woman may decide to end her marriage:

1 because she has been accused of witchcraft, a sign that she is not getting on with her husband's kinsmen.

2 if she or her husband become ill. If her husband's remedy does not work, she goes to her own kinsmen, who are expected to give her better care than her husband's kinsmen. If he is old and ill, she leaves because his kinsmen will not support her and will only care for him if she leaves. By the same token, she returns home if her husband dies.

3 if her husband takes another wife after a stable monogamous marriage, the wife who is unwilling to share her prerogatives leaves. Thus, intended polygyny is responsible for considerable marital breakdown.

(38) 1962.

Various theories have been developed to account for marital instability. Gluckman[39] suggested that marriage is more stable in patrilineal societies, less stable in bilateral societies and least stable in matrilineal societies. This is supported by the high instability of marriage among matrilineal societies in both Central and West Africa. Stability is also related to the level of payment; low brideprice is often associated with low stability and high brideprice with high stability, though it may be questioned to what extent a low payment is a recognition that the marriage is likely to fail. Fallers [40] challenged this explanation by pointing out that the Soga of Uganda (a patrilineal society) have very unstable marriages but a high brideprice. He suggested that the important factor was whether the bride's loyalty is transferred from her own kin to that of her husband. Where she maintains strong ties to her own kin group, because it offers her greater security than her husband's group, the marriage tends to break down.

Brain[41] found that among the matrilineal Guru of southern Tanzania, couples living in more fertile areas with a denser population had more stable marriages than those in more isolated mountain villages. In the former, the wife was less cut off from her own lineage by virilocal residence than in the latter. However, he confirms Mitchell's report that matrilineal marriages are frequently ended when the children are old enough to return to their matrilineal home and support their mother there. Christianity seems to make little difference to the pattern of marital instability. The Ijaw and Weppa-Wano of southeastern and midwestern Nigeria have two kinds of marriage. One form involves a high brideprice, genetricial rights, and incorporation of the bride into the husband's lineage, from which her children will inherit. The low brideprice form confers only uxorial rights; the wife remains attached to her own lineage and the children inherit from a male of their mother's lineage. This form is much less stable than the high brideprice form.

The importance of personality and economic factors in divorce is demonstrated by Lloyd's study of Yoruba divorce.[42] The lack of sex role identity (both men and women trade) and relative economic success of Yoruba women contribute to marital tension because men feel that they are not given the respect due to them. Each spouse tends to be economically autonomous and divorce proceedings can be initiated by women because they can afford to repay the brideprice themselves. Many Yoruba women were already living with a lover at the time their case came to court. Divorcees tend to marry other divorcees or polygynists, so a high divorce rate may mean that relatively few people are making several marriages while the

(39) In Radcliffe-Brown and Forde 1950.   (40) 1957.   (41) 1969.   (42) 1968.

majority remain in stable marriages.

Data are lacking as to whether elite marriages are more stable than those of ordinary members of the public, but Oppong[43] suggests that elite women have more to lose by divorce. Their salaries are seldom sufficient to provide the standard of living to which they are accustomed, their kinsmen are usually unable to help them maintain this standard and it is difficult to find another member of the elite to marry, so marital breakdown is likely to mean downward mobility for them. At the same time, elite couples often quarrel over the amount of time and/or money being given to kinsmen and husbands often establish 'outside wives' if Ordinance or church marriage prevents polygyny. There are also conflicts over differential expectations of married life. The wife often wants the sort of companionate marriage she has seen abroad or read about in women's magazines whereas the husband expects to maintain his customary authority. Caldwell[44] found that 13% of the women and 19% of the men in his Ghanaian elite samples had been married before; 12% of the women and 8% of the men thought that variety in marriage was a good thing and that spouses should be able to escape if they found the attractions of marriage too slight or the responsibilities too burdensome.

Marital roles

Within marriage, men and women have sexual, economic, domestic and power relationships with each other. Certain roles are seen as properly belonging to the husband or the wife; other roles are shared between them. These are known respectively as segregated and joint roles. Sometimes roles, activities, or decisions are carried out by the conjugal couple; others are shared with kinsmen or outsiders. The first system is referred to as closed (shut to outsiders) and the second is open.[45] Although ordinary marriages tend to demonstrate open/segregated roles and the closed/joint pattern is more often found in elite marriages, the system followed may vary from one role to another. Sexual roles are always joint, though they may be more open on the husband's part than on the wife's. Child-rearing roles are often open and at least partly joint; economic roles are usually segregated. There may be conflict over the right to exercise authority in the household, or it may be segregated so that each spouse has a proper share of authority; in some households it is monopolised by the husband. Partners in a marriage gradually work out a pattern of rights and duties which suits them; conflict over roles

(43) 1974.   (44) 1968b, p.36.   (45) Oppong 1974, p.24.

can be a prime cause of divorce.

Parenthood

Every society has rules governing sexual relationships designed to produce new members of the society. These set the norms for establishing and dissolving a marriage and the rights and obligations of the partners. Although a society may recognise an enduring sexual relationship without defining it as marriage (concubinage and the 'outside wife') and accept as marriages relationships which do not produce children, marriage is usually assumed to include parenthood. Because the reproduction, sustenance, socialisation and social placement of children are considered the family's major social functions, societies rarely approve of children being born outside marriage. Where such children are born, the society usually has some provision for incorporating them, either through the mother's marriage or by adoption.

Some societies distinguish between the *genitor* and the *pater* of the child, separating the biological and social functions of parenthood. Sexual rights may not be accompanied by social rights, as when the child belongs to its mother's husband regardless of who its physical father is. Acceptance of this distinction makes it possible to produce descendants for a man who dies childless or a woman who is barren. A brother of the dead man may marry his widow (levirate marriage) or another woman in his name, so that the dead man is considered *pater* of the children even though the brother is their *genitor*. A wealthy but barren woman may officially marry another woman, paying the brideprice herself; she then arranges for her 'wife' to bear children, of whom she is considered the *pater*. They take their social position and inheritance from her.

Child-rearing was discussed in Chapter 3. Although a child has a mother and father at birth, it may be reared by one, both, or neither of these parents. Although rearing by both parents is the most usual, this pattern is often broken by death, marital breakdown, customs of separate residence of spouses, or fostering. The life span is gradually lengthening, but many children still lose one or both parents before they reach adulthood. Divorce is also prevalent in many societies, with the children usually going to their father in patrilineal societies and their mother in matrilineal societies (unlike the situation in Britain and America, where children are usually kept by their mother though inheritance is mainly through the father). When a marriage breaks down through death or divorce, it may be considered better to foster the children with kinsmen rather than allowing them to live with a stepparent who might not treat them kindly. This is known as crisis fostering.

Voluntary fostering is also common in some societies; over a fifth of all children may be fostered. Fostering is the assumption of the rights and duties of parenthood by adults who are not the child's natural parents without the latter surrendering their full rights (as they would in adoption).[46] The kinsman (or occasionally non-kinsman) feeds, houses, clothes and disciplines the child, often until marriage. The child, in turn, looks to this foster parent rather than to his biological parents for assistance and gives him the obedience and services which are expected of a child. Customarily, fostering is based on a balance between the rights and obligations of kinsmen sharing responsibility for rearing each other's children and between the advantages and disadvantages of additional children in the household. The parents delegate rights to others as a means of unifying the kin group which has become separated in space and to provide childhood help in households which would otherwise have no children.

Children are sent to live with a grandparent so that they can provide help around the house, or to a sibling of their mother or father so they can be taught a trade or disciplined more carefully than they might be at home. For example, the Gonja believe that a chief's son should not grow up in his father's court, as he might become proud. Yoruba women traders sometimes foster their children with older women so that they will have freedom to trade; Mossi women in Kumasi foster children to have assistance in their trading. Hausa women who are not allowed to leave the house must get a foster child to run errands if they have none of their own. Migrants may foster their children at home because they cannot find a place for them in a town school or because they want them to know their kinsmen and language. Other children are sent from the village to be fostered in town because opportunities for education are better there and their parents want them to learn city ways. Fostering is thus used to cement kinship ties and aid social mobility as well as in response to emergencies.[47]

The child who is fostered according to this customary system has considerable security; he has added parents rather than losing any. The foster parents have usually requested the arrangement; his biological parents keep track of his progress and would call him back if he were mistreated. Economic and social changes have brought new models of fostering which provide less security for the child. Fostering by non-kinsmen may be according to the customary model (with foster parents acting as fictive kinsmen), or children may become apprentices or servants, new models over which the parents have less control.

The apprentice is sent to learn a specific trade. There is often a signed contract covering the number of years of apprenticeship and the amount to

(46) Schildkrout 1973, p.51.   (47) Goody 1966, 1970, 1971; Hill 1969; Schildkrout 1973.

be paid at the start and end of the training. The apprentice may be taken into the master's family, but he may remain an ill-fed and ill-treated outsider, expected to provide services for the master's wife after long working hours and to guard the workroom by sleeping there.[48]

Girls who become housemaids may receive even worse treatment. Sometimes their parents have sent them to a wealthy kinswoman in the hope that they will go to school or learn to trade; at other times there is an arrangement that a small sum will be paid to the parents as wages. But the parents are often far away and have little control over the treatment their daughter receives. As more children remain at home for some years to attend school, apprentices and servants are likely to be older and better able to take care of themselves; this should help to overcome some of the problems of the system.

Domestic and economic roles

Domestic roles are generally segregated by sex and age. In a large, extended family compound, the oldest man and woman have considerable authority to supervise the others and resolve the inevitable conflicts which arise when people of different interests live closely together. The other men do their work in a corner of the compound (usually separated from the area where young children play), or go out to farm and return for relaxation. The women take turns cooking, cleaning and washing. Older women help to look after the children; the latter go for water and wood, run errands, etc. If, on the other hand, the household is limited to a nuclear family, roles are more likely to be joint. The father may help to care for the children while the wife is cooking; he may even cook and clean when his wife is ill. The wife may have to take the children with her when she is trading because there is no grandmother to leave them with. In wealthy households, servants take over domestic duties which were previously shared among kinswomen. Each of these patterns of domestic relationships provides children with a different view of family and kinship which they carry with them into their own marriages.

The economic support of the household is primarily a male responsibility, but women also have economic duties in most farming communities and in many towns, especially on the Guinea Coast. These roles are generally segregated; even where both the man and wife farm there is usually a division of labour into male and female tasks. Men prepare the soil and plant the crop, women weed and help with the harvest; or the men grow cash crops and the

(48) Callaway 1964; Peil 1970; King in Court and Ghai 1974.

women food crops.

Whether women are farmers or traders or have wage employment in town, their economic role is an important part of their self-image; they are not just wives and mothers but also engaged in specific economic activities which give them security and autonomy which they would otherwise lack. Economic change over the past fifty years has opened up new economic opportunities for women, but in some areas their lot has become harder rather than easier. Ottenberg[49] shows how the enforced peace of colonial rule made it easier for Ibo women to become successful traders and how the introduction of cassava (rejected by the yam-farming men as beneath their dignity) gave women farmers a crop of their own and a source of food during the hungry season. On the other hand, LeVine[50] reports that Gusii women had to take over all farming operations when their husbands migrated and thus found themselves grossly overworked and unable to look after their children properly. Where new cash crops have been monopolised by the men, women who formerly had fairly equal standing in their society as contributors to economic production may lose prestige because almost all of the family income now comes from their husbands.[51]

Female participation in the labour force varies considerably between nations and ethnic groups; women appear to have higher prestige in societies where they participate most fully. Women in the coastal and forest-belt towns from southern Ghana to southern Cameroon generally have a rate of economic activity which is very high by world standards and have considerably more power and prestige than urban women of East and Central Africa, who have generally been less active; often the latter's opportunities have been limited to beer-brewing and prostitution. Akan, Ga and Yoruba societies customarily gave women considerable prestige and expected active economic and political participation from them; other women, who have been used to greater subservience to men, find it harder to adjust to autonomous economic roles in town.[52]

The separation of economic activities from the home which is typical in towns makes it more difficult for children to learn from their parents. In the rural areas, they would go out to farm as a family, and young boys and girls would learn other productive tasks by watching and helping their parents. This pattern continues in town if the parents are self-employed (girls start early helping their mothers trade and boys learn skills from their artisan fathers), but they lose this opportunity if the parent is in wage employment. This makes the transfer to adulthood more abrupt and increases the need for special training for adult tasks.

(49) In Bascom and Herskovits 1959.   (50) In Middleton 1970.   (51) Boserup 1970.
(52) Peil 1975a.

Women have generally been subservient to men, largely because their reproductive contribution left them less time and energy for subsistence and defence. Men have therefore been able to accumulate the resources necessary to ensure high prestige and power in the society.[53] The situation has gradually been changing as women have fewer children (allowing them more time for other activities) and technological improvements have placed less premium on physical strength. This has enabled women to take a more equal part in the labour force and they have often moved toward greater equality in other areas, within the family and in political, religious and economic institutions. Independence has often improved women's political position because all adults could vote, but women were denied this right in Zaire until 1970 and in northern Nigeria until 1976.

Marriages may be characterised by the nature of authority and decision making which predominate. Two typologies are commonly used: 1 patriarchal, matriarchal and companionate or equalitarian democratic, and 2 autocratic, autonomous and syncratic. In the patriarchal family, the father or grandfather has all the power and makes decisions for the whole household. In a matriarchal family (rare as a norm but less rare in practice) the mother or grandmother or chief wife makes the decisions. In companionate marriage the couple make important decisions together. Few households are run strictly on any of these ideal types, though the general pattern is usually evident. In this, as in so many areas of human relations, it is important to distinguish between the ideal and what happens in practice. African families are usually said to feature patriarchal authority, but if one investigates closely there may be a female 'power behind the throne'. Part of the difficulty with marriages today, especially between educated spouses, is a difference in expectations. The husband assumes that he should have customary authority and respect, whereas his wife wants a companionate marriage, in which she is treated as an equal.

Oppong[54] shows how families can be distinguished as autocratic (one spouse makes all the decisions), autonomic (each spouse makes decisions separately in specific fields, i.e., the wife is responsible for food and servants and the husband for housing and school decisions), or syncratic (spouses make major decisions jointly). Rural households are likely to be autocratic (at least in principle), with the husband or patriarch in a firm position of dominance. In coastal West African societies, wives trade and hence make a considerable economic contribution to the household; they generally have

(53) Sanday 1973. (54) 1970.

considerable independence and decision-making tends to be autonomic. The ideal Euro-American pattern is syncratic marriage with shared decisions, but this is much better established in some countries than in others and may not be followed in practice even where it is symbolically most accepted.

On the basis of studies of senior civil servants in Accra, Oppong found that sharing of rights and duties varies from one area of interest to another. Economic resources, child-rearing, schooling and household chores may each be divided differently. For example, the couple might decide together about sending the children to school, but make autonomous decisions about spending money they earn and keep separate bank accounts. Still, when couples are divided according to how the main decisions are taken, it is possible to show some of the factors which affect the pattern chosen. Couples with syncratic marriages are likely to be similar in age and education and the wife usually makes a substantial contribution to household expenses. Couples with a low educational level are most likely to have the customary autonomic pattern, whereas men whose wives make little or no contribution to household expenses usually make decisions autocratically. This can be explained by exchange theory; those who contribute resources or have alternative sources of the things they need can be independent whereas those who are dependent on others for benefits and/or services must be subservient to their power.

There is additional evidence that economic contribution is an important factor in household decision-making. Lucas[55] found that Midwestern Ibo women who had migrated to Lagos were more likely to share major decisions if they were working and able to contribute to household expenses. Barnard[56] suggests that the wives of teachers in Kinshasa make no economic contribution and thus must put up with their husband's authoritarianism. Here, as in Ghana, the wife of a member of the elite usually has a low income compared with her husband even if she is employed as a teacher or nurse, and this means that she has much more to lose than the ordinary woman if the marriage breaks down. She is thus often caught in an autocratic marriage even though she prefers a syncratic one. Ordinary women, who can earn as much or more than their husbands if they are successful traders, tend to settle for an autonomic marriage, where each partner goes his or her own way making decisions in his or her own sphere.

Custom also affects decision-making, allowing more autonomy in some areas than in others. In some societies women are expected to make independent decisions on any economic resources over which they gain control. Reports from Ivory Coast, Liberia and Nigeria[57] indicate that women often

(55) 1973.   (56) 1968, p.157.   (57) Clignet 1970, p.142; Fraenkel 1965, p.131; Peil 1975a, p.83.

have autonomous control over household budgeting and their own income even if they remain housewives. At the same time, women who are autonomous in economic decisions usually call on their husbands for other decisions which are seen as part of the male role, such as where the couple should live; it is usually the husband who decides whether he alone or the whole family should migrate to town and when the time has come for retirement to the village. If the wife does not agree, the marriage may be terminated.

Patterns of family change

Because our ideas of the family are shaped as part of our primary socialisation and because it is so fundamental to the continuance of society, family institutions are highly resistant to change. Nevertheless, they do undergo gradual change as a result of other social, economic and political changes in the society. Two types of change will be examined here, the increasing importance of the nuclear family and the implications of rapid population growth.

The Goode hypothesis

In an extended comparative study of the family in various parts of the world, Goode proposes that family patterns are gradually changing from an extended to a conjugal pattern; ties with distant kinsmen are loosened and more emphasis is put on the nuclear family. Lest this seem too sweeping a generalisation, several points must be taken into account:

1 The family as a social institution varies greatly from one society to another, so that the present tendency to convergence comes about in different ways. For one society, it may mean that the husband and wife live together rather than separately; in another, children are more closely tied to their biological parents.

2 As in other aspects of social change, adjustments within the system are not likely to be smooth and coordinated. Aspects of the traditional system which caused conflict may be subject to more rapid change than aspects which made for more harmonious relations. Changes in residence may be easier to accomplish than changes in inheritance patterns.

3 It is often said that family change is due to industrialisation and urbanisation, but we are not very clear on the factors involved or how they operate. Industrialisation and urbanisation may be causes of family change or merely intervening variables.

4 Generalisations about family change may be based on inadequate or even

false information. Ideas about the traditional family system must be con-continually revised in the light of new data, and care must be taken to distinguish between the 'ideal' system and the behaviour and values of the average family in a particular society.[58]

Early ideas of family change came from the evolutionists, who said that families had developed or 'progressed' from sexual promiscuity through group marriage, matriarchy and polygamy to monogamy. Their ideas of the past came from stone age societies then in existance. We now know enough about such small-scale societies to be aware of the differences between them. In addition, since societies now in existence are all roughly equal in age, it is impossible to prove that certain patterns are 'earlier' than others; the evolutionists were merely expressing their prejudices. Family systems in some so-called primitive societies are monogamous and very similar to those in 'modern' societies and the extended family still survives in modern in-dustrial societies, though it is less often a residential unit than in the past.

Full isolation of nuclear families, with complete dependence on their own resources and no contacts with kinsmen, is rare. Most young people in Britain and America as in Africa consult their parents about important decisions such as marriage, are helped to set up their new household, maintain fairly frequent contact with their parents and help to support them in their old age (though state pensions make this last less necessary than in Africa). Other kinsmen are less often part of the household today, but contact is often maintained with a fairly wide circle (especially among couples who are not geographically or socially mobile), mutual aid is given and there is a certain amount of interference in family affairs. Studies of household com-position in various African towns indicate that from 15 to 50% of households include at least one kinsman, and most migrants living alone or as a nuclear or stem family have a kinsman in town who is visited regularly. Thus, the extended family remains meaningful in terms of social interaction.

What functions does the family perform and how have these changed over time?

1 Sexual access for the production of new members of the society is con-trolled through the family.

2 The family socialises new members.

3 The family provides economic support and a basic division of labour for the organisation of production, distribution and consumption.

4 The family may also have political and religious functions as the most basic corporate group in the society.

Sexual access outside marriage is always possible, but most societies

(58) Goode 1963, pp.1–2. See Barrett 1974 for an extensive discussion of the effects of a strong socialist orientation on family roles in a Nigerian village.

officially disapprove and some have strong sanctions against it. In many societies it is an important point of honour that the bride be a virgin, though in others proof of fertility is considered a necessary base for a stable marriage. A double standard operates here, in that men are allowed considerably more liberty than women both before and after marriage. Insofar as there is a trend toward monogamy, it can be seen as limiting the sexual access of men, but where polygyny is replaced by serial monogamy (a succession of wives but only one at a time) it might be questioned whether a real change has been effected.

A more important change may be occurring as a result of the introduction of birth control technology. The growth of population can now more easily be controlled and it is easier to prevent the unintended consequences of sexual activities, either inside or outside marriage. While opponents of birth control often fear that this will deprive the family of an important function and that the strong norm against sexual relations outside marriage will inevitably be weakened, the evidence is not very clear. Data available for the past are very limited, but seem to indicate that at least in some areas illegitimate births were as prevalent as they are today. The higher survival rate of infants today and the greater permissiveness of society whereby there is less pressure to marry because a child is on the way means that there will be more children known to have been conceived outside marriage than fifty years ago.

Where family and lineage ties remain strong, children are seen as important for continuing the lineage and usually find a welcome regardless of their origin. However, as these ties break down and children are seen as an economic burden, families become less willing to take in 'outside' children. Unless the state can make arrangements to care for them, they may be left to die. Thus, in recent years it has been necessary to set up orphanages and establish formal procedures for the adoption of children by anyone who wants them, though the need for this is still far less in Africa than in Europe.

Socialisation was discussed in Chapter 3. Since such a large part of an individual's socialisation takes place in the early years, the family continues to be very important in this. As the size of the residential family declines, children are socialised into a different view of marriage and family than in the past, which may affect their own marital relationships. People who grow up in a large extended family compound may find it harder to adjust to the close ties of a relatively isolated nuclear family than their own children, who are socialised into it.

Although individual families have only rarely been economically self-sufficient, either now or in the past, the farm family remains a producing and consuming unit, with father, mother and children contributing to its economic functions. In the urban family, on the other hand, production functions usually take place outside the family – the father and often the mother works away from the household. This is less true in African than in European cities, because many self-employed people such as carpenters and tailors work in their own compound and women traders can set up a table at the door. But with the increase in wage employment, this type of activity may include a declining proportion of adults. Whereas a child on a farm learns about adult economic roles by participating in them, urban children often know little about the work their parents do and in any case take up different occupations themselves. Formal education becomes more important than the family in providing training for these occupations.

Generally, complex industrialised societies have developed special religious and political institutions so that the family has little need to carry out these functions. The state bureaucracy and various churches have separate hierarchies of authority and family members are expected to participate in these wider structures. However, children usually receive their first introduction to religion and politics through their family and develop their religious and political values within the framework of the family. Thus, although the family is not autonomous in these areas (and in most ethnic groups it never was), it still retains important socialisation functions in politics and religion. All in all, it can be said that the functions of the family have been somewhat modified, but none has been lost.

Since there seems to be increasing emphasis on conjugal as opposed to extended families, we can examine the factors which make this functional. An industrial society relies on bureaucratic authority, appointment and promotion without regard to particularist characteristics. Widespread social and geographic mobility are encouraged so that people will be available for new roles as the technology develops. Thus, if mines are developed in a relatively uninhabited area (as in Liberia or Mauritania), people must be willing to leave their family and kinsmen to take up jobs there. Also, the society benefits if people of talent who are born into less advantaged families can obtain training and be upwardly mobile and if people born into families of high socio-economic status who are of only average ability are allowed to be downwardly mobile.

The conjugal family system allows people to move away more easily from their family of orientation (birth), though this partly depends on where one starts. Young people in elite families generally get considerable help to make sure they stay at the top, especially in the provision of education (see Chapter 6). Less help is available to children in ordinary families, so that upward mobility tends to be based on individual achievement. However, a young man who has to finance his own education has more limited opportunities for upward mobility than one with family or government support. Most families expect to share in the economic and political resources of their successful members, and it is a measure of the continued value of kinship ties that so many do so. There are many complaints, of course, since the extent of assistance often falls short of expectations. But the principle appears to be widely maintained.

There are varying reports as to the extent to which elite couples separate themselves from their families of orientation. Caldwell[59] reports that 88% of the Ghanaian university students in his sample had received considerable financial support for their education from parents and/ or kinsmen and only 4% expected to spend less than 10% of their income after graduation helping relatives. Few resented this; it was seen by the majority as a moral obligation. Oppong[60] found that two fifths of the Akan senior civil servants she studied sent at least £5 monthly to their kinsmen, over half had educated a relative's child and most made frequent visits home and were visited in town by their kinsmen, some of whom received long-term accommodation. First-generation elite couples were less likely to have joint bank accounts than members of second- or third-generation elite families because the former had more calls for assistance and spouses did not want money they saved to be spent on support of their partner's kinsmen. (Longer established members of the elites had less calls for help because their parents and siblings were more often at the same economic level as themselves.) Lloyd[61] confirms that successful Yoruba also maintain close ties with parents and siblings, with frequent remittances and visits and Ross[62] found that contacts between Nairobi residents and rural kinsmen (visits and sending money) increased with the individual's education and income; poverty was the most frequent reason for loss of contact.

On the other hand, Lukhero[63] gives examples of families in Salisbury which prefer isolation and Chilivumbo[64] reports that elite families in Blantyre shun their poor relations, whom they consider 'a source of shame and embarrassment.' Parkin[65] suggests that the importance of helping kinsmen varies with the ideology of kinship. This is based on customary norms, colonial experiences and involvement in wider economic and political developments. The stratified social system of the Ganda minimised extensive lineage ties, so high-status Ganda do not feel obliged to support distant kinsmen. The Luo lineage system was reinforced by colonial territorial divisions, and hence has remained strong.

Non-elite couples may achieve some separation by migration far from

(59) 1965, pp.188, 191. (60) 1974, pp.55, 63. (61) 1974, pp.119–20. (62) 1975, pp.48–90. (63) In Lloyd 1966. (64) In Parkin 1975, p.312. (65) 1975, p.38.

their kinsmen. While this migration tends to be for an urban job, Fortes[66] reports that Asante cocoa farmers sometimes found land away from their kinsmen to avoid excessive demands on them. Lux[67] found that some Yombe migrants send money home to maintain solidarity and avoid magical sanctions but visit rarely so as to maintain their independence. The majority of migrants, regardless of their isolation, maintain some contact with their extended families. Those who can afford it usually send money home, at least for emergencies; where the distance is not too great, they usually visit at least once a year. Thus, the nuclearity of the residential family should not be taken as an indication that the extended family is a thing of the past.[68]

A second factor in the functionality of the nuclear family in industrial society is the greater need of industrial workers for emotional and psychological satisfaction which they do not get from their work and their lower need for the economic security which an extended family provides. A farmer often gets considerable satisfaction from working his land, and a craftsman from making things at his trade. The extreme division of labour common in factory work makes it more boring and provides little intrinsic satisfaction for the worker; hence he looks to his family for it. As mentioned above, the nuclear family provides better opportunities for strong emotional ties than a residential extended family. Strong emotional ties may also develop within the extended family (and often do), but the less intense contacts implicit in a larger group make it more difficult.

Regardless of the degree of affection they have for various kinsmen, most African migrants do maintain many kinship ties. This is partly because it is expected of them, but there are also economic reasons. As there is as yet little state provision of social welfare, it is well to help the family whenever possible because one may need help at any time. Workers who cannot support themselves in their old age must rely on family assistance. The same is true, over a shorter period, in sickness and unemployment. Obviously, members of the elites who can count on remaining in well-paid government jobs until they retire on a pension can afford to isolate themselves from their kinsmen much more than the lower-level wage-earner. Self-employed workers are the most at risk and thus have the greatest need to seem helpful, but they may be better able to minimise demands on their resources because the level of their income can more easily be hidden. When the government announces a wage rise, everyone knows how much wage-earners get. But a trader or craftsman can apologise for the small size of his gift, saying that times are bad or customers have not paid their bills.

Although the extended family is an important source of support in times

(66) *et al* 1947, p.164.   (67) 1971, 1973.   (68) Peil 1972a, pp.203–15.

of difficulty, it may occasionally be seen as a sign of oppression by young adults who want to make their own decisions. The ideology of individualism also gives increased prestige to the nuclear family. In this sense, an increasing proportion of nuclear families in a society has often been allied to demands for political and legal change, and changes in values and ideology concerning the family have often preceded rather than followed industrialisation. Nuclear families were common in Europe for generations before the industrial revolution, as the feudal society broke down and the common people gradually got rights to free movement off the land and political representation. Where family change took place in colonial territories, it often started as a result of the preaching of Christian missionaries (who separated converts from their families to help them avoid pagan religious customs), the example of colonial rulers (whose extended families were far away) and Western education (with its emphasis on European culture).

As family patterns change, there are demands for legal changes to confirm the new situation. Women may demand the right to own property, when this has formerly been denied, or to sue for divorce. Women in several countries have agitated for an end to polygyny. This was granted in Guinea, but later men were allowed to marry polygynously if they inherited a brother's widow, as some of these women had no other means of support. Laws have also developed requiring men to support their wives and children and providing for equal inheritance of all children if this is desired by the parents. Initially, these laws are not well known among the people and there may be no effort to enforce them, but over time they do exert an influence.

Matrilineal societies in Ghana have been under considerable pressure to change their rules of inheritance. The custom of children inheriting from their mother's brother rather than from their father made relatively little difference when there was not much to inherit, but it can be much more important if the children's father has spent his lifetime building up a large cocoa farm or business whereas their uncle has barely been able to support himself. Children say, 'Everyone has a father but not everyone has a mother's brother', and see no reason to work hard on their father's farm if the result will go to their cousins. A law providing that a father can leave one third of this property to his wife and children by making a will provides some help, but it may be difficult to enforce if the man's mother, sisters and nephews quickly claim everything when he dies. Because of the disadvantages of a matrilineal system in an economically differentiated society, its disappearance has long been forecast. However, it seems more likely that it will continue in modified form, gradually being adjusted to new conditions.

The most important point to remember about family change is the great variety of family structures which exist, even within a single society. It is easy to think of change from a 'traditional' system of large, extended, poly-gynous families living together in perfect harmony, with low divorce and illigitimacy, marriage by almost all adults and absolute control by the elders to a 'modern' system of small, monogamous nuclear families, high divorce and illigitimacy, many people remaining single throughout their lives, freedom of the individual to choose his spouse and make other personal decisions and the absence of harmony. But the facts, as we know them, pro-vide examples of both extremes and many points in between in most coun-tries. Happiness is more dependent on individuals than on the system. Marital discord occurs in all societies, though the conjugal bond is more easily broken in some than in others.

Population growth

Africa has been a continent of low population density, with some societies being threatened by extinction through a high infant death rate. Some women have had ten children without one living until adulthood. Thus, children are highly valued. Recent improvements in health services (allowing a much higher proportion of children to survive) have resulted in high rates of population growth. European nations have gone through a 'demographic transition', whereby birth and death rates gradually fell and the population now grows very slowly. In Africa, as in Asia and Latin America, death rates have fallen rapidly in the last thirty years while birth rates have remained high. The resulting growth rate is between 2 and 4% per year, leading to a doubling of the population in between twenty and thirty-five years. A rate of 4% means that for every one million people in a country there will be 40 000 more people at the end of the year. Some areas are already short of land, with large numbers of young adults having to migrate because there is no room for them to remain on the land. This pattern has been noted among the Frafra of Ghana, the Ibo of Nigeria and the Luo and Margoli of Kenya. Other areas where cash crops are grown are quickly filling up.

This rapid growth also means that a high proportion of the population are under fifteen years of age (42% of the African compared with 26% of the European population in 1960). Some of these young people are self-support-ing, but most must be supported – fed, clothed, housed, educated – by the adults. Efforts to provide primary schooling for everyone are hindered by the very large increases in the school-age population and the unemployment situation is worsened by the large numbers of young people coming into the labour force each year. The most advanced areas, where land must be bought and schooling provided, often show the most rapid population growth.

In the face of this rapid increase in population, some countries have begun birth control programmes to encourage their people to have fewer than the six children which is now the common average. (The intention is not to stop population growth, which would be against the country's best interests, but rather to slow it somewhat.) These programmes run against strong societal values, but economic considerations and the spread of higher education seem likely to bring the birth rate down in the long run. It is more expensive to rear children in town than on the farm and even in the rural areas many children expect to be sent to school. Thus, some parents are beginning to think that four children might be a more satisfactory number than six.

Second, many studies have shown that women who have attended secondary school or university tend to have slightly fewer children than uneducated women. They are more aware of contraceptive practices and more likely to use them. They do not want to interrupt their employment careers too often for childbirth, and feel that it is better to provide liberally for a smaller number of children rather than less well for a larger number. While the pronatalist view is still widespread (and many women use family planning clinics to improve rather than limit their fertility), the interest in somewhat smaller families seems to be growing slowly.[69]

People continue to value large families because they bring prestige; barrenness is a sign of punishment. Caldwell's study found that rural Ghanaian couples wanted children for the help they provide on the farm and in the house, for their support in old age, for prestige and respect, and for their pleasure and company. The chief difficulties of a large family were the cost of support and education and the trouble, sorrow, overcrowdedness and noise. Elderly Ghanaians needed at least four children to be sure that one would survive.[70] Although a child born today has a better chance, grandparents continue to urge their children to have a large family because of their own experience. Four fifths of those supporting elderly retired people were their children or grandchildren, but some parents were beginning to realise that they could get more assistance from one child who was educated to a high level than from a large number who barely earned enough to support themselves. This may in time lower the size of completed families, but it seems unlikely that the 'small' family (less than four children) will become common in less than a generation.

Conclusion

Although it has undergone considerable modification of function in recent

(69) Caldwell 1967a, 1968; Okediji 1967. (70) Caldwell 1966, p.17.

years and seems likely to continue to change, the family remains the most basic social institution, responsible for the production and integration of new members without whom the society could not continue. This chapter will be concluded with a brief discussion of the ways in which national planning is likely to affect the families of its citizens.[71]

1 Families are seen as agents of social control over the nation's youth. Parents are expected to enforce national laws governing children. They are expected to train their children to be law-abiding, tax-paying, hard-working, respectful of government authority, etc. Changes in laws governing divorce and inheritance or equality of educational and occupational opportunity can affect the relative authority of the father and mother. Further state concern for the personality of its citizens is inhibited by the lack of knowledge as to the effects of various patterns of child-rearing.

2 The state is concerned to minimise disputes between family members. This leads to attempts to develop nationally accepted family law out of a wide variety of local customs, especially in relation to inheritance. Such laws also facilitate interethnic marriage and national integration. Family counselling may substitute for an absent extended family in attempting to prevent marital breakdown. The state is also concerned that rules of inheritance promote national development. It may legislate for individual rather than corporate (family) inheritance so that businesses will be passed on to an individual able to run them rather than to a lineage. It may also promote a more equal distribution of wealth through high taxes on inheritance.

3 The social welfare functions of the family may be fostered or supplanted. The elite may support the ideology of the extended family by being regularly reported as participating in family activities, or they can demonstrate that they consider the nuclear family more important by appearing in the newspapers with only a wife and children. Speech day pronouncements about the joys of family life must be balanced against reports of selfishness when faced with requests for aid. In addition, the government must decide how much of its scarce resources it can spend on providing welfare services for the young, the old, the ill, etc., services which are in most cases still provided by families. If most of the available funds go for staff salaries, it may be better to postpone a formal family welfare service and spend the money on more immediate needs, such as medicines and roads.

4 Governments are becoming increasingly concerned with family planning programmes. Many areas are seriously overcrowded for the ecology and level of agriculture being practised. But large-scale programmes are only likely to be successful if people have good reasons for changing their prefer-

(71) Dore 1970

ence for large families, because of economic pressures or greater success in rearing the children who are born. Insofar as family planning clinics assist barren women as well as those who wish to limit the size of their families, they support customary values and may have the latent function of cutting down polygyny.

Lastly, governments often promote small, monogamous, individualised, nuclear families because they have been led to believe that these will somehow make the country more 'modern' rather than because there is any evidence that they will prove to be the best patterns for their own society. There is a great deal of value in customary patterns, and not nearly enough data on the causes and effects of family change in specific societies.

Suggested reading and discussion topics
1. Compare the kinship structure of your own and another ethnic group.
2. Read Boserup (1970), LeVine (in Middleton 1970), Gugler (1972) or Ottenberg (in Bascom and Herskovits 1959). Discuss changes in the role of women in African society.
3. How do patterns of residence affect the social structure and relationships in the family?
4. Discuss the application of Goode's hypothesis to your own country.

6 Education

An increasing number of children are exposed to at least a few years of formal education. Providing this education, even for a minority of its youth, often taxes the financial resources of the country. Sociologists should therefore be concerned with the effect of education on a society and on the individuals who pass through the system. What are the manifest and latent functions of education? If the goals of education as seen by the government, the parents, the pupils and the educators are not identical, how do these and other pressure groups influence the educational process? Schools are also organisations which attempt to maintain a certain autonomy from societal pressures; their style of bureaucracy, boundary-supporting devices and methods of socialisation will be examined in this chapter. Finally, teaching as an occupation will be considered. To what extent does it fulfil the characteristics of a profession? What factors affect the status of teachers?

By no means all education is institutionalised or takes place in schools. Primary socialisation in the family is the most important education we receive, and anyone who is alive to his surroundings continues his own education throughout his life. We sometimes speak of 'informal' education or 'out of school' education to refer to learning situations which lack formal organisational characteristics. In an apprenticeship, for example, the trainee is assigned various tasks of increasing difficulty until, over a period of years, he learns his trade and becomes a master in his own right, able to pass on his knowledge to other apprentices. The apprenticeship usually has some formal features, such as a ceremony at the beginning and/or end and an institutionalised relationship between apprentice and master, but there are usually no examinations, no special building, no bureaucratic regulation as to what is to be taught and when and no central headquarters which hires and pays the teaching personnel. 'Bush schools' for adolescents are also on the continuum between the casual teaching of one individual by another (as a child is taught by its mother) and the closely regulated system of 'Western' education.[1]

(1) See Brown and Hiskett 1975 for discussions of indigenous education in several West African countries. For the relationship between culture, language and education, see Irvine and Sanders 1972.

Koranic schools, which have an important educational role among Muslims, vary considerably in formality and institutionalisation from the mallam with three or four students sitting under a tree to the Ecole Supérieure Coranique in Bamako and the School of Arabic Studies in Kano, which are part of the national educational system of their respective countries. The former type are concerned with the memorisation of religious texts, often for only an hour or two per day; the pupils may not even become literate in Arabic. The latter provide full-time training to a high academic level and have the bureaucratic characteristics of other large organisations.

This chapter will be mainly concerned with the system of formal education imported from abroad during the past 200 years. So far, there have been few studies of the sociological aspects of indigenous or Islamic education, whereas 'Western' education has attracted considerable interest as an agent of social change and because of its implications for manpower development. For convenience, 'education' will henceforth mean 'Western', formal education, but you should remember that other types of education continue to exist and exert an influence on the imported system, though they tend to be less important than in the past.

It is because of these influences that the educational system found today is as much a part of African society as it is. Colonial governments often tried to limit the expansion of the school system or to shape it for the needs of a farming community as seen from above. The people countered by opening private schools wherever these were allowed[2] and resisting adaptations which hindered the achievement of their aspirations. While there is still need for further adjustment, schools appear to have been more responsive to societal than to official demands. The Harambee movement in Kenya is a current example of educational reform led by the people.[3]

Functions of education

The early development of educational systems in Africa was largely in the hands of missionaries. They often arrived before colonial authority was established and built up their schools as a way of reaching people who were not interested in Christianity. But in the early days most people were not interested in formal schooling for their children either; the first pupils were often orphans or slaves. Parents needed the help of their children on the farm and saw no advantage to be gained from learning to read; chiefs saw a

(2) See Foster 1965, pp.101-3 for Ghana; Abernethy 1969, pp.63-5 for Nigeria; and Cameron in Brown and Hiskett 1975, p.359 for Tanzania.   (3) Brown and Hiskett 1975, pp.422-30; Court and Ghai 1975.

strong disadvantage in their sons being attracted to foreign ritual rather than following in their father's footsteps. However, in a few areas, such as Buganda, the introduction of literacy was welcomed because it facilitated communications between various sections of the kingdom. The Ganda were already operating an educational apprenticeship system in which promising young men served as pages at the royal court to prepare for positions of leadership. This gradually changed over to a formal educational system. The general response to the introduction of education has been instrumental; while a few students are interested in knowledge for its own sake, the majority want education because of the opportunities for an improved standard of living which it offers. Schools must be seen to be useful before they will be patronised.

The functions of education are broadly similar in all societies. President Nyerere[4] has summarised them as: 'to transmit from one generation to the next the accumulated wisdom and knowledge of the society, and to prepare the young people for their active participation in its maintenance of development; . . . to liberate both the mind and the body of man.' This broad definition can be related to specific tasks. The educational system is responsible for basic literacy. It is also an important agent of socialisation, shaping values and attitudes to the needs of contemporary society. It widens the mental horizons of pupils and teaches them new ways of looking at themselves and their society. It may be an agent for promoting a better understanding of societal traditions and for the development of local culture in the forms of art, music and literature; it has been used to politicise future citizens and foster national integration through the inculcation of a common culture and, by the missions, to foster religious conversion. It is a direct and indirect means of training the future labour force and hence is important in manpower planning and in fostering social mobility. Lastly, it acts to maintain and strengthen its position within the society; in this it is a strong force for preserving the *status quo* and resisting change.[5]

Literacy
Most African children are lucky to get a few years of training in reading, writing and arithmetic. Although the proportions attending school have risen greatly in recent years, there are still many countries where a majority of children either are not sent to school at all or do not stay the three to five years it usually takes to become permanently literate. The rate of enrolment varies from less than 10% to over three quarters of the primary age group; secondary education for more than 10% of the age group is still rare. In

(4) 1974, p.47. (5) Anderson 1970, p.7; Dore 1976.

countries such as Mauritania, where most of the population are migrant pastoralists, it is very difficult and expensive to provide primary schools; they must either cater for very small numbers of children or provide boarding facilities and separate the children from their parents for long periods. Since the uses of literacy in a pastoral economy are difficult to demonstrate, parents are generally unenthusiastic. At the other extreme, white governments in southern Africa usually provide a few years of education for a large proportion of the child population to facilitate basic literacy, but make it very difficult for blacks to get higher education; their goal is a literate labour force which is ineligible for promotion.

There are differences in access to education within as well as between countries.[6] Coastal areas, which were easier for missionaries to reach, generally have a longer educational history and higher enrolment figures than inland areas. Insofar as the cities with their employment opportunities are located in these coastal areas, people living there have a better appreciation than inland peoples of the payoff for education and are more anxious that their children should participate. Muslim areas have generally been resistant to the introduction of 'secular' schools, since the Koran is considered to contain all necessary knowledge.[7] British officials kept missionaries out of parts of northern Nigeria controlled by the Emirates, with the result that education there is far behind other parts of Nigeria. There was a genuine fear on the part of many parents that children sent to school would be converted to Christianity; this is hard to overcome even when all the schools are run by the state. As women are ideally secluded in the house after marriage, many Muslim parents see little point in sending daughters to school. However, Peshkin[8] found that Kanuri parents (in northeastern Nigeria) were beginning to see the benefits of education for girls; it improves their chances of finding a good husband and their marital skills, and literacy is an asset to self-support in case of divorce. As a result, the proportion of girls attending school in the area is gradually increasing.

Males receive more education than females in all countries, but the differential is greatest where participation in education is lowest. Girls only begin to catch up when education is almost universal, and they are always furthest behind in the highest part of the system. Thus, where most boys attend primary school most girls usually do so as well, but there will be a smaller proportion of girls than boys in secondary school and they fall

---

(6) An interesting sociological study could be made in most countries of the differences between people living in the north and in the south. Ecological and cultural differences have often resulted in distinctive attitudes towards education, occupational and religious preferences and other notable social differences. These are as evident in European as in African countries. (7) See Fisher in Jolly 1969. (8) 1973, pp.153–4.

even further behind equality in the university population.[9] For example, the proportion of females in the Nigerian primary school population in 1971 varied from 25% in Benue/Plateau State to 48% in Lagos.[10] Table 3 shows how girls catch up as education becomes more widespread; nevertheless, they still contribute only about 15% of the university population.

Table 3 Percentage Who Had Attended School by Age and Sex, Ghana 1960 and 1970

Age	Males		Females	
	1960	1970	1960	1970
6–14	53	66	33	58
15–24	59	74	21	45
25+	21	33	6	12

Source: 1960 and 1970 *Population Census of Ghana*, Census Office, Accra.

The educational differential in favour of males ensures that they dominate the higher levels of the labour force; few women qualify for such posts. This both reflects and supports the attitude toward women in the society concerned. Where women have relatively high prestige they are more likely to get equal access to education than in a society where their prestige is lower, and where women are able to compete on relatively equal terms this is reflected in relatively high prestige.

What is the social importance of literacy? A society which lacks literacy can pass down its traditions orally, but there are limitations to the amount which can be remembered and societies which are literate have scope for much greater complexity in the transmission of their heritage to succeeding generations. Literacy makes possible governmental control over a large area because written messages can be sent and received. Literacy in a common language also facilitates communication between members of different ethnic groups. Finally, literacy fosters social change because new ideas can be widely and quickly spread; literates are 'available' to change in a way that people who are dependent on verbal communication are not. This is somewhat less true since transistor radios have become popular, but the ability

(9) See Mbilinji 1969 for a discussion of female education in Tanzania. (10) Nigeria 1971, Table 1.

to go over a piece of information again at one's leisure, to understand pictures through their accompanying text and to store the information for use when needed still give the literate a considerable advantage.[11]

Even with a fairly low level of educational achievement, men and women who become literate, either by attending primary school or an adult literacy course, or through their own efforts, have access to government information and a useful tool for small-scale business and for dealing with the demands of bureaucracy. The ability to read and fill up forms is not emphasised in primary schools, yet this may be the most important use to which literacy is put in future years.

Socialisation

The socialisation which a child receives in school may supplement or supplant what is learned at home. Children starting school often go through a stage where 'teacher says' is all-important; this challenge to parental authority is particularly threatening if the parent is illiterate. Conflicts are increased when the society values age as a prime factor in authority and most of the teachers are better educated but younger than the parents and community elders. The parent may respond by withdrawing the child from school, by abandoning his task – leaving all future socialisation to the school – or by accommodating, helping the child to understand that adults may disagree on certain things but that no one is correct all the time.

Education can be influential in promoting new values and stimulating adaptation to changing conditions. Inkeles[12] found that education was the most important factor in the development of what he terms psychological modernity (see Chapter 10). Schools teach the importance of time and introduce the child to a bureaucratic organisation where achievement matters more than ascription. Schools promote individualsm through competition to succeed, especially in examinations. Students often assume that the shortage of places at higher levels means that they can be successful only by doing better than others. In societies where cooperation is strongly stressed, students often feel threatened by this competition and may refuse to 'play the game', thus lowering their chances for academic success. The discovery that everything written down is not necessarily true and pressure to think for oneself may be useful in developing an independence of mind which makes an individual open to new ideas rather than merely willing to follow the crowd.

However, many schools, especially primary schools, do just the opposite. Untrained teachers who rely on rote memorisation may make students less

(11) Goody and Watt 1963.   (12) 1969, p.212.

independent of mind than their fathers. Too many students at all levels blindly accept what they read rather than thinking about it critically and testing it against their own experience. In this case, children are being socialised as sheep rather than intelligent adults. Peshkin[13] found that, beyond developing a preference for urban life and a non-farming occupation, classroom experience had little effect on a Kanuri child's life: 'He was not intentionally instructed to consider either new goals or new ways of thinking, improving his society, or ordering his life.'

There is increasing evidence that African parents generally value the socialisation function of schools. Records show that the Gisu welcomed education because 'to read is to become a Muganda, a superior person.'[14] Anderson[15] reports that a Kenyan father whose son was doing badly at his secondary school wanted him to continue because it 'would improve his ability to cope with life.' Parents expect the teachers to pass on far more than reading, writing and arithmetic. Traditional socialisation patterns and the mission background of education are evident in their concern that schools should teach moral values. Blakemore[16] found that northern Ghanaian parents were concerned that schooling should not make their children less sociable or dutiful than their uneducated siblings. Peshkin[17] reports that Kanuri parents expected school children to learn correct behaviour (to be

Table 4 The Effect of Education on Children by Educational Attainment of Respondent, Lagos 1971 (Percentages)

	None	Primary	Secondary	More
No effect	3	8	0	3
Morals, deportment	55	37	40	22
Knowledge, awareness increased	15	29	50	51
Intelligence developed	15	8	1	13
'Better', other changes	24	32	23	20
Total*	112	114	114	109
N	34	38	111	164

Source: Survey results.
*Totals are over 100% because of multiple answers.

(13) 1972, p.18.   (14) Twaddle in Gulliver 1969, p.196.   (15) In Jolly 1969, p.121.
(16) 1975, pp.246–7.   (17) 1973, pp.54–6.

clean, well-dressed, respectful, disciplined) and how to take advantage of changing times ('to know what is happening in the world'). They also learned about proper Islamic observance, which increased the attractiveness of these schools to the Muslim parents.

Parents and students in Lagos were asked, 'What effect does education have on children?' About two fifths said it affected their morals or deportment, usually for the better. About a third of the parents and half the students thought it improved their knowledge, curiosity and/or awareness of the world about them. These factors appear to be as important as 'book learning' for many parents, and encourage them to support the schools in the face of increasing unemployment of school-leavers. Table 4 shows that the teaching of morals and deportment in schools is more important to uneducated than to well educated people, whereas the emphasis on the acquisition of knowledge increases with the education of the respondent. This suggests that many parents judge schools on different criteria than students, teachers, or school administrators. If school children are observed to be badly behaved, not conforming to community norms of conduct, the parents will blame the school even though the cause may be their own more lenient treatment of their children who are 'scholars'. On the other hand, parents may be less disappointed with failure in examinations than their children, especially if failure means that the child will now join the labour force instead of wanting still more expensive education.

Comments on intelligence show a curvilinear relationship. Respondents with no education at all and those who had gone beyond secondary school were more likely than those who had a primary or secondary education to say that schools develop a child's intelligence. Illiterate parents may see the schools as giving the child a chance to make the most of his natural talents, whereas those who have post-secondary education have specialised at a fairly high level. People with only a moderate level of education, on the other hand, may feel frustrated because they could go no further, or may see the memorisation which characterises this level of education as having little to do with intelligence.

The missionaries who started schools in most parts of Africa were very aware of the possibilities of religious socialisation which could be achieved through them. Bishop Shanahan, who strenuously promoted education in eastern Nigeria, saw schools as the most important means of religious conversion: 'Those who hold the school, hold the country, hold its religion, hold its future.'[18] Muslim parents often agreed, and kept their children away from Christian-run schools. Although the state has taken over and secularised

(18) Cited by Abernethy 1969, p.41.

the schools in many places, religious education often remains a part of the curriculum because both Christian and Muslim parents want their children to have some formal instruction in their faith. Where the children do not all belong to the same religion, separating classes may be a divisive factor, but mixing in one school is probably less divisive than allowing each religious group in a village to run its own school.

National governments also rely on the schools to socialise their pupils into loyal and active citizens. Singing the national anthem, saluting the flag and greeting national and regional leaders teach the pupils that they are part of something larger than their local community. Colonial education was often designed, consciously or unconsciously, either to teach the students to accept the *status quo* or to assimilate them into the culture of the metropolitan country,[19] whereas attempts are now being made (notably in Tanzania) to produce a new type of citizen.[20]

There is a great deal of literature on political socialisation through the schools. It is fairly clear that most students acquire a diffuse allegiance to their nation which may be particularly important when the majority of adults have little sense of belonging to such a large and abstract entity. However, special programmes of political education usually have less effect on political behaviour than other institutional arrangements of the school and the daily life of the pupil both during his school career and after leaving. There is often considerable disagreement among government and educational officials about what the content of a political education course ought to be. Prewitt[21] found that many Ugandan schools were run on lines which directly contradicted the democratic, cooperative emphasis of the civics syllabus. In addition, students paid little attention to civics because it was not an important component of the School Certificate. Examining the social relations within the school (for instance, the contacts between teachers and pupils, or what types of student activity are rewarded with prestige) may tell us more about the political values being passed on by the school than the content of formal instruction.

An example of the latent role of education in political socialisation is the connection which is often made between the spread of higher education and the growth of African independence movements. Young men reading philosophy, history and literature found out about the political development of other peoples. This supported their view that a people should run its own affairs rather than being dominated by outsiders. Education abroad provided opportunities to discuss these conclusions and possible action with young men from other areas. Fully accepting the ideas of equality and

(19) Clignet 1970.   (20) Nyerere 1967; Mwingira in Jolly 1969.   (21) 1971.

democracy which were implicit in their academic training, they returned home to find themselves denied employment which was given to less well trained colonial officers. Thus, their education socialised them to a certain view of society, which they had to work to create.

The present generation of university students is also often disillusioned to find that the achievement they have learned to value is less important than ascription in many sectors of national life. Those who find their educational socialisation disfunctional to success may react in several ways. Some withdraw as a means of expressing their alienation from local society, especially its political aspects. Others become reformists, attempting to introduce new norms, or rebel, actively pursuing new goals in a spirit of alienation from authority which they no longer consider legitimate. The most common response is opportunism, either initially or after a period of withdrawal, reform, or rebellion. The graduate decides, 'When in Rome, do as the Romans do'; he might as well put his new norms aside and make the most of his qualifications and contacts as everyone else seems to be doing.[22]

On the whole, African university students have tended to be rather passive politically, waiting for their turn to join the elites rather than aiming at fundamental changes in the power structure. Prewitt[23] claims that this is due to the authoritarian nature of secondary schooling and the students' goal of security rather than power, which equates well with the British model of a non-political civil service. Barkan[24] found that Tanzanian university students were somewhat more concerned than students from other countries with finding jobs which were serviceable to their country and the necessity of hard work as a component of success (see Table 5). This reflects the communal orientation of their country's ideology, but the differences were not as great as the efforts put into educating students for service might lead one to expect. Students who started school after the Arusha Declaration may show a stronger commitment to its goals.

The extent to which education fosters national integration may also be questioned. Many Nigerians feel that conflict among the educated elite was mainly responsible for the civil war. While this is too simple an explanation, it has been noted in several countries that competition for power, resources and jobs has led to emphasis on sectoral divisions rather than on national unity. Although interethnic marriage generally increases with education because educated young people have better opportunities for meeting members of other groups at school or in the towns, this continues to characterise only a small percentage of marriages among well educated people and is often not notably higher than among uneducated people who have similar

(22) Levine 1965, pp.204–6. (23) 1971. (24) In *ibid*.

Table 5 The Two Most Important Things a Person Can Gain with his
Education, East African University Students (Percentages)

	Kenya	Tanzania	Uganda
Security; to earn a good living	42	49	37
Knowledge; ability to think critically	29	22	29
Status, respect	23	20	15
Wealth, money	14	19	15
Contribute to country's development; service to community	12	14	10
Improve my personality	11	10	12
Good citizen; moral and tolerant man	8	6	11
Practical knowledge; ability to work well	7	7	9
Satisfaction, happiness	14	5	5
Power, influence, leadership	6	7	4
Total*	166	159	147
N	132	430	297

Source: Barkan in Prewitt (1971, p. 181). Students were interviewed in 1966
(Makerere) and 1967 (Dar es Salaam).
*Totals are over 100% because of multiple answers.

opportunities for mixing. In addition, differential educational opportunity
in various parts of the country is increasingly seen as divisive rather than used
as an occasion for developing a spirit of sharing. People in those areas which
are behind demand quotas or other special opportunities to increase their
share of top jobs, while the more advanced areas emphasise qualifications.

Manpower development
Both educators and parents tend to think of schools as providing training for
jobs, and arguments about the expansion of education are often in terms of
the nation's need for an educated labour force. The very considerable efforts
of parents and community leaders in many countries to provide education
for their children have been motivated by a desire for the social, economic
and political benefits which education can bring. Governments must somehow balance social demands for more schools against the likely manpower
demands of the economy. So far, vocational education has met with only
very limited success because the expectations which both parents and students

have of education are not fulfilled by purely vocational training.

The social demand for education is based on the individual aspirations of children and their parents and the communal aspirations of the society as a whole. Education is desired because it leads to an improved standard of living and because it is seen as a 'good thing' which gives prestige to those who participate and to the country which provides it. Manpower demand, on the other hand, is based on the country's labour force needs; the educational system should produce, over time, the number of people needed for each of a wide variety of jobs: so many doctors, engineers, accountants, clerks, etc. Several problems and points of conflict arise. First, education takes many years and the forecasting of manpower needs is often grossly mistaken because of changes in technology, changes in the economy and occupational mobility. A new invention may put large numbers of people with a particular skill out of work or lead to the need for many people with a new skill. Good economic conditions may increase the demand for certain skills because the public can now afford to pay for these services, and poor economic conditions can put many people out of work. An ill-paid, low-prestige occupation may have a high turnover, so that even if an appropriate number of people are trained there continues to be a shortage of workers.

Second, manpower planners have been concerned almost exclusively with high-level skills, requiring post-secondary education and training, whereas social demand is mainly for more primary and secondary places. Thus, there are conflicting demands on government resources which are increased by rapid population growth. This can be demonstrated by comparing the educational pyramids of manpower planners and of social demand (see Figure 11). If the aim is for a small number of well-trained people (A), one must start with just enough so that, after drop-outs and failures, the required number will complete the course. If the aim is universal primary education with substantial numbers going on to secondary school (B), there will be few resources left for higher education, including the training of teachers. Since emphasis on manpower demands at the cost of social demands might lead to political unrest, the government usually sets aside some of its manpower needs in order to satisfy, at least partially, the demand for expansion of primary education. However, if the population is growing relatively slowly there will be fewer children of primary school age and therefore more resources for high-level education; the two pyramids will be closer together (C).

The population growth rate is therefore important planning for the expansion of education. To take an example: about a third of the Ugandan children aged between six and twelve were in school in 1967 and social demands were being made to raise this to half. Shortages of skilled manpower, on the other hand, made it important to raise the number of university places. Assuming that it costs about 150 times as much per student year at university as per pupil year at primary school, the country was faced with a demand to spend almost half as much to maintain 2 150 students at university as to support 700 000 primary pupils; doing both was beyond its capacity.

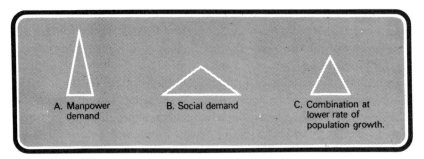

A. Manpower demand   B. Social demand   C. Combination at lower rate of population growth.

Figure 11 Population pyramids and the demand for education

However, if five to fifteen years earlier there had been a 30% lower birth rate, the 480 000 places in primary schools would have satisfied the social demand and extra government money could have been used to expand university education. Other factors must be considered. For instance, the social demand for education tends to be inversely related to fertility levels; as parents have fewer children they want them to be better educated. Thus, if the Ugandan parents of five to fifteen years earlier had decided to have only three children rather than six they might have demanded primary places for all of them. In this case, the demand for 700 000 primary places would be maintained, though the number of children of primary age was halved.[25]

The other side of the manpower question involves the content of education. How 'practical' should education be at the primary and secondary level? How closely should the curriculum in rural schools be tied to agriculture? Should technical or vocational education be provided for all children attending school? Foster[26] shows the history of 'applied' education in Africa and why it has generally failed. Since at least 1842, governments have been recommending agricultural and trade training for African pupils, and these pupils and their parents have been rejecting it as inferior to an 'academic' programme because the latter clearly leads to better jobs. Both parents and children see the schools as the route out of agriculture; their basic contribution is literacy, which led to clerical and teaching posts during the colonial period and leads to urban jobs (for many if not all school-leavers)

(25) Muhsam 1971.   (26) 1966.

today. With the rise of school-leaver unemployment, considerable efforts are made to persuade the general public that not all school-leavers can expect wage employment (especially in 'white collar' occupations), but the relative lack of success of this programme is hardly surprising. Drucker[27] reports:

It has always been axiomatic that the man of even a little education would forsake the hoe and the potter's wheel and would stop working with his hands. After all, our word 'school' – and its equivalent in all European languages – derives from a Greek word meaning 'leisure'.

This is not to say that school-leavers do not take manual jobs, or even sometimes prefer them to the alternatives available to them, but rather that while they are at school they prefer to spend their time preparing for non-manual work and see vocational schooling as denying them opportunities for advancement. In addition, vocational schooling has often failed to protect students from unemployment and has not generally been a good preparation for the manual jobs available because of its theoretical nature and inflexibility, inexperienced teachers and the lack of information on manpower needs.[28]

An example from Ivory Coast demonstrates this. Ivory Coast has a particularly well-developed system of post-primary institutions with long and short courses: academic, technical and agricultural. There is a distinct hierarchy in these institutions, with the long academic course at the top, since it is seen that the best jobs are available only to those who manage to get university degrees. Students accept places in lower-status institutions (with the agricultural schools at the bottom) in the hope of moving from these to higher-status institutions, though most mobility is in the opposite direction. A majority of the students at apprenticeship centres did not enter directly but were drop-outs from academic courses. A majority of those who had left apprenticeship centres were either employed in jobs which did not utilise their training or were unemployed. On the other hand, most graduates of the long academic course were employed.[29]

Kenya's village polytechnics seem to have done somewhat better than this, but the results have also been disappointing. They were started with considerable enthusiasm as a way of providing training for unemployed school-leavers. However, they have been seen as a place of last resort for those who could not get into an academic secondary school or find wage employment, and fewer trainees than was hoped have been able to use their training to provide a regular income. Court[30] reports that a third of the trainees he studied had found wage employment using their skill and another

(27) 1961,p.15.   (28) Rado 1972.   (29) Clignet and Foster 1966.   (30) 1974, pp.92, 95.

third used it at least occasionally for self-employment. Lack of tools and working capital made it difficult for many to utilise their training, and village people provide only a limited demand for most skills. The proliferation of village polytechnics and institutes of technology could easily lead to the same overproduction as is evident in secondary schooling.[31]

The general preference for academic education has been rational in the light of opportunities available. A majority of wage jobs in most countries are still government clerical or teaching positions, so academic education is more 'vocational' than technical education. In recent years, the proportion of government jobs has tended to increase rather than decrease. Foster[32] reports that the technically trained have always faced more unemployment and lower salaries than the academically trained, partly because until recently there was little industry in most African countries and partly because the technically trained are dependent on openings in the specific job for which they were trained, whereas the academically trained are considered more flexible. Employers often prefer to train workers on the job because they are then accustomed to the equipment and methods of the firm concerned. Technical schools often use machines which are more complex than those used by local businesses.

Technical schools can also be extremely expensive even though they produce few qualified workers. An Ivory Coast course for printers cost 2·7 million francs, but only three of the thirty-two students passed.[33] Other schools have been more successful, but generally training on the job, either in industry or with a self-employed master craftsman, is better suited to local needs and attracts pupils who are better motivated to make the most of their training. Such training is much cheaper than that provided by technical schools and trainees soon contribute to production rather than being a drain on the economy for several years. The apprentice who is trained by a small-scale craftsman learns how to make do with little equipment and how to conduct a small business; he is thus less dependent on wage employment than the product of a technical school.[34]

The argument for extension services to practising farmers rather than trying to teach modern farming to schoolboys also seems reasonable. While at school, pupils are still oriented towards getting out of farming. Later, when they have decided to settle down and farm, they are more receptive to ideas about improving their crops. Too often teachers have no special training in agriculture, so parents are right in saying that their children can be taught this subject as well out of school as in it. In addition, school farms are often used to supply the teacher with food and to punish deviant pupils

(31) Court, Godfrey and Mutiso in Court and Ghai 1975. (32) 1966. (33) Berg 1965, p.263. (34) Callaway 1964; Peil 1970; King in Court and Ghai 1975.

rather than to teach better farming methods. If recent school leavers are dependent on their parents or kinsmen for farmland and income from farming, they may have no opportunity to practise what they have learned and will want to migrate for an independent income.

However, where pupils have access to land and the prospect of growing cash crops on their own, a school agricultural programme can be welcome. Wood[35] has described a carefully designed programme in northeastern Nigeria where primary pupils demonstrated the efficiency of simple techniques on land made available to them by their parents. He also reports on many other farming and technical programmes, mostly for school-leavers, in other English-speaking African countries, and evaluates their relative success. Most of the programmes were very expensive and produced few permanent farmers. There is little available on Tanzanian programmes to combine schooling and active participation in rural life, but children in many countries play an active part in rural life outside school hours. The important factor seems to be awareness of relative opportunities and relative deprivation. Acceptance of farming as a career will be directly related to improvements in the rural standard of living in comparison with the cities.

In summary, the relationship between schools and the labour force is reflected in the government's concern for higher education and the public's demands for wider availability of lower-level education. So far, the schools have been far more successful in providing the fundamentals on which occupational training can be based (literacy and numeracy) than in training for specific jobs. This seems likely to continue as long as academic education is seen as providing the best chance for improving one's position within the society.

Education and social mobility

Both parents and pupils tend to think of education as closely related to social and geographic mobility. The migration of school-leavers will be discussed in Chapter 8; this section will deal with the use of education for social mobility. The role of education in aiding or hindering social mobility can be assessed at three points:

1 Recruitment. How equal are the chances of all members of the society to enter a given level of education?

2 Achievement. Once a given level of education has been started, how equal are the chances of success?

(35) 1974, pp.165–57.

3 Placement. To what extent is occupational placement determined by educational achievement?

Two extreme contrasts can be proposed:

1 A society where recruitment is strictly related to social background (the elite children get almost all the places in high quality schools and have a far better chance than ordinary children to reach higher education), where success in the system is also closely correlated with social background (elite children do better in examinations) and where occupational advancement is related more closely to social background than to educational achievement (jobs go to those with elite status rather than to others with equivalent educational qualifications). In such a society, the educational system serves to confirm status, not to foster social mobility, and many able people are denied a chance to contribute to national development.

2 A society where recruitment is open (all children have an equal chance of schooling at all levels); achievement is related to ability, not to social background (all those of equal ability have the same chance of success); and jobs are closely related to educational achievement. In its perfect form, this would be a meritocracy with no scope for appointment or promotion based on performance since leaving school or ability to perform the job in question. This could be highly dysfunctional. Neither of these extremes exists in practice, but educational systems vary in their position on each of the variables.

Recruitment

Access to education is increasingly selective as one moves up the system. Parents usually strive to provide at least as much education for their children as they received, which means that differentials are often passed on from one generation to the next. A study of a Kenyan village[36] found that most farmers' children had only primary education or none at all, whereas children whose fathers were clerical workers or professionals all reached Standard V and were the only ones to go beyond Standard VIII. These parents saw the need for education more clearly than the less educated farmers and manual workers and strongly encouraged their children to remain in school. Farmers' children may have to overcome parental resistance in order to start school, but those who do go may be more committed to schooling than children who take it for granted.

Recruitment to secondary and university education has been of considerable concern in several countries, especially in Ghana.[37] Since most well-paid jobs, especially in the civil service, require secondary schooling (and,

(36) Moock 1973, p.307.   (37) Jahoda 1954; Foster 1963; Peil 1965; Hurd and Johnson 1967; Bibby 1973; Kaufert and Peil 1976.

increasingly, a university degree) sectors of the population which are grossly over-represented among students may monopolise these jobs. Recruitment is affected by social background (parental occupation, education and income), by sex and religion, and by regional and rural or urban place of residence.

Table 6 Occupations of students' fathers by country, university, entry year and sex

Fathers' Occupation [a]	Ghana			Nigeria					Uganda
	Legon		Cape Coast	Ibadan, 1948-66		Ife, 1969-72		ABU [b]	Makerere
	1951-3	1967-9	1967-9	M	F	M	F	1970-1	1968
Farmer	26	36	49	32	11	44	19	56	43
Manual	7	19	15	8	5	4	2	0a	20
Commerce	20	12	15	17	11	21	24	12	37
Non-manual	36	33	21	40	66	31	55	24	
Other	11	–	–	3	7	–	–	8	–
Total	100	100	100	100	100	100	100	100	100
N	430	230	142	2 487	212	1 034	228	885	122

Sources: Legon 1951-3: Jahoda 1954, p. 360. Ibadan: van den Berghe and Nuttney
Legon 1967-9: Kaufert and Peil 1976. 1969, p. 368.
Ife: Aluko 1974, p. 11 ABU: Beckett and O'Connell 1972, p. 18.
Makerere: van den Berghe 1968, p. 59.

[a] Manual includes unskilled, semi-skilled and skilled. Non-manual includes clerical, semi-professional and professional. Other, where used, tends to refer to army and police and no information. At ABU, manual workers seem to have been included with 'other'.
[b] Ahmadu Bello University.

Table 6 compares students in six universities according to the occupation of their fathers. Ibadan appears to recruit more high-status students than Ife or Legon, and these, in turn, have less representative student bodies than Makerere, ABU, or Cape Coast. The high proportion of Ibadan students with fathers in non-manual occupations may be partly due to the inclusion of the early years, when few Nigerians completed secondary school, though the change over time at Legon is less in the non-manual than in other categories. The differences in social background between men and women students (shown for Ibadan and Ife and very similar at Legon) reflects the lower proportion of girls attending school at any level and the inability of low-income parents to pay for higher education for their daughters.

The occupational classifications used are too wide to show some of the important differences. It would be useful to differentiate between large and small farmers; between unskilled, semi-skilled and skilled manual workers; between petty traders and large-scale businessmen; and between clerical workers, teachers and nurses, and professionals. However, these divisions are missing in several of the reports, so grouping was necessary to make the data comparable.

Where more detailed data exist, it can be seen that the children of professionals, large farmers and businessmen are (as expected) better represented among the students than in the population as a whole; unskilled workers are least likely to send their children to university. The proportion of students whose fathers are professionals appears to be declining somewhat, but one would need figures on the numbers going abroad for a true picture of access to universities by this sector of society. The proportion of students from farming families seems to be increasing at a time when the farming population is declining or growing less rapidly than the urban population. This is partly due to increased incomes for cash crops and the spread of primary schools through the rural areas, but it may also be related to an increasing average age of farmers. If the average farmer is over forty, he is more likely to have a child of university age than the average manual worker in town, who is probably under thirty-five.

Since the majority of the parental generation in all these countries are farmers, fishermen, or pastoralists, the proportion of students from such families is an important measure of selectivity. Farmers are everywhere under-represented, but they contribute a large proportion of the male students in all the universities, especially at ABU. It has been argued[38] that farmers who manage to send their children to university tend to be wealthy cash crop farmers rather than subsistence farmers, but sons of cash crop and subsistence farmers were found in equal numbers in all three of Ghana's universities in 1969; a fifth of the university students sampled had fathers with an income of less than £20 per year.[39] Beckett and O'Connell[40] found that 40% of the fathers of ABU students (62% of the farmers) had incomes of £50 per year or less. A study of six Nigerian universities[41] showed that 58% of the 2 852 students sampled had fathers earning less than N500 (about £280) per year. Only 13% had fathers earning over N2000, which all would expect to pass within a few years of receiving their degree. Thus, the evidence suggests that, while there is considerable inequality in educational recruitment, farmers and manual workers' children have relatively as much chance of a university education in Africa as in many developed countries.

Attempts to detect a trend in university or secondary recruitment have not yet produced convincing results, though the direction of change seems to be shifting from increasing openness to some closure and increased advantage for children of elite families.[42] A change of direction in a single sample (as in Currie's results for 1969) is not enough to establish a trend. She

(38) Hurd and Johnson 1967, p.72.   (39) Kaufert and Peil 1976.   (40) 1972, p.10.
(41) Human Resources Research Unit 1973, p.10.   (42) Bibby 1973; Currie 1974.

also assumes increasing closure of recruitment among the Ganda (and generalises this to all Ugandans) because there was a decline in the proportion of fathers with no education, but this is bound to occur as the first generation to achieve widespread primary education becomes parents. Another problem is the use of varying occupational categories; 'professional' and 'skilled' may be given a wide or a narrow interpretation and parents classified as 'other' in one sample may be distributed among named categories in other studies; this can have a notable effect on the proportions reported. Where students have access to more than one university, there can be considerable differences in recruitment between them, as shown in Table 6.

Recruitment to the educational system can also be examined by using education rather than occupation as a criterion and by studying parents rather than students. This is less often done because contacting parents is more difficult than checking on the background of students, but it is valuable for the data it provides on the education of all children in a family. As education at a given level becomes more widespread, the elites tend to retain their predominant position by ensuring that their children get more education than other children. Hence, when the proportion of children attending primary school begins to grow, parents who found primary school enough for themselves see that their children at least complete secondary school. When this sector in turn becomes more widely available, elite parents do their best to get their children into university. Insofar as they are more successful than ordinary parents in upgrading their children's education, equality of education never becomes a reality.

Parents who only provide as much education for their children as everyone else are likely to be disappointed because many jobs are upgraded as applicants with more education are available; clerks and teachers must complete secondary rather than primary school and the government and large businesses recruit graduates rather than secondary school leavers for management posts. Many parents are aware of this devaluation of education, but cannot make provision against it. When members of the public in Lagos were asked, 'How much education is necessary to get a good job today?', only 1% said primary and 45% said university, yet most of their children will not go beyond primary school.

Table 7 shows that fathers living in a low-income suburb of Lagos who had gone beyond primary school were more likely than parents with less education to have had at least one child who reached university. Fathers with no education were least likely to have a child go beyond primary school, but a tenth had managed to send a child to university, indicating that considerable opportunity for long-distance intergenerational mobility still exists, even among the urban disadvantaged who appear to be least repre-

Table 7 Education of Children by Parental Education, Lagos 1971
(Percentages)

Highest Level Reached by Children Aged 15+	Father's Education			
	None	Primary	Secondary 1–4	More
Primary	38*	18	19	5
Secondary	52	82	62	75
University	10	0	19	20
Total	100	100	100	100
N	63	63	16	20

Source: Census of 120 houses in Ajegunle, a Lagos suburb.
*Includes 6% who did not go to school.

sented in higher education. The proportion of fathers who had not sent their children beyond primary school is probably a better measure than the proportion sending a child to university, because many of these children were not yet of university age. Only one in twenty of the well educated fathers had limited their children's education to primary school, compared with two fifths of the uneducated fathers, but it is notable that a majority of fathers with no education had managed to provide secondary schooling for at least one of their children and that there was no difference between fathers with primary and secondary education in the proportion sending children only to primary school.

In the light of what was said earlier about the disadvantages girls have in obtaining an education, it is notable that the mother's education tends to be an important factor in access to schooling, especially for girls but also for boys. If the mother has been to school, she will persuade the father to send her children or, if necessary, pay the school fees herself.[43] Religion is important in that the Christian bias of the schools has made them more attractive to Christians than to Muslims or followers of local religions. Many of the first generation to be educated became Christian at school; parents who have resisted Christianity tend to see little need for education either. Muslim parents often feel that Koranic education is preferable to 'English' education, though increasing numbers provide both for their children.[44]

Other factors in selectivity are fees, place in the family and place of origin.

(43) Wallace 1974, p.35 (44) Currie 1974, p.55; Blakemore 1975, pp.246–7.

School fees may be necessary from the standpoint of the national economy, but they introduce an economic barrier into educational selection, especially where the highest status schools have higher fees than ordinary schools. Abernethy[45] reports that fees charged for primary school were a direct cause of the high dropout rate in eastern Nigeria compared with other areas. Ghanaian primary education lost 100 000 students the year primary fees were re-introduced. Many fathers of large families can afford fees for only a few, so they must select which children are to be sent. They may choose on the grounds of demonstrated intelligence, but other factors are sometimes more important; the child who is troublesome, or not strong enough to work on the farm, is sent to school. The first son is often sent, as an investment for the future. By the time the second or third son is ready for school, the expenses of a large family and/or the need for help in the fields mean that he must remain at home or at least delay starting school. Later, if family income increases because there are more older children to help with the farming or the eldest child has finished school and found wage employment, there will be money available to pay the school fees of the youngest children. Thus, middle children are often denied schooling.

The selectivity of secondary schools varies from one country to another and according to the size and nature of the educational system and method of recruitment. Clignet and Foster [46] show that children of non-manual workers were over-represented to a greater extent in the relatively small Ivory Coast secondary system than in the larger and less centralised Ghanaian system. However, the greater concentration of secondary schools in Abidjan than in Accra seems to have given more equal opportunities to able children from all over Ivory Coast than was true in Ghana; the relatively late and slow development of schools in northern Ghana compared with the south may be a factor here.

Regional and rural/urban variances in school recruitment are partly due to the nature and timing of the introduction of schools into an area, but are also related to religious preferences and the availability of cash crops or other sources of income to provide money for school fees. Although regional differences appear to be declining in some countries,[47] they often remain considerable because some areas are much better equipped with schools and parents in other areas continue to be unenthusiastic about education.[48]

Rural areas are less well served with schools than urban areas because there has been less demand (urban people have been more aware of the value of education and more able to pay for it) and because the lower density of population makes provision more expensive. Children must either walk a

(45) 1969, p.356.   (46) 1964, p.237. (47) Currie 1974; Kaufert and Peil 1976.
(48) Blakemore 1975; Prewitt in Court and Ghai 1975, p.205.

long way to reach the school or the school must serve only a small number of pupils. Rural children, like girls, catch up as schooling becomes more widespread in the area. Where schooling is rare, they are usually far behind; where a majority of children go to school, the rural children are usually only slightly behind urban children.

Only in fairly large towns is it feasible to have secondary schools without expensive boarding facilities. Nevertheless, there has been a growing awareness in recent years that rural children are disadvantaged by the urban concentration of schools and more post-primary institutions are being built in rural areas so that rural children can be educated without being completely urbanised. If the school is a self-contained boarding institution whose students have little contact with people in the neighbourhood, it does not matter where it is built, but a programme of participation in local affairs (as in Tanzania) increases the relevance of the environment. However, if students expect to move into urban jobs after leaving school, their anticipatory socialisation will be to urban rather than rural life regardless of where their school is placed.

Achievement

Entering a given level of education is not enough. In a world increasingly based on achievement, certificates proclaiming success in examinations are also required. The child of elite parents usually gets a head start in educational achievement. His parents are well educated and may teach him to read before he enters primary school; child-rearing patterns emphasising self-reliance, working towards remote goals, periods of quiet and ability to work and play on his own socialise the child for schooling. The emphasis in poorer, illiterate homes, on the other hand, is on group activities, instant obedience, ascription and the satisfaction of short-term needs which makes adjustment to school life more difficult.[49] Parents who lack education do not understand their children's need to be alone to study and expect them to help with work on the farm, in trade, or around the house. They see education as a 'good thing', but do not know how to help their children succeed.

Thus, it is hardly surprising that the elite children tend to be most successful in primary leaving examinations. If, on the basis of these examinations, the elite child goes to a long-established boarding school with well qualified teachers and a good library while the poor child attends a new day school with a small library and teachers who have only a few years of secondary schooling themselves, then the former is much more likely than the latter to succeed in the secondary leaving examinations.

(49) B. Lloyd in Lloyd 1966; Prewitt in Court and Ghai 1975, p.206.

Social advantages become less important the further one moves up the system. Since children with initial disadvantages must be more able than elite children in order to succeed in the first stages, they often equal or pass them at the upper levels. Clignet and Foster [50] show that 55% of the children of both subsistence farmers and of managerial and clerical workers in Ivorian secondary schools were in the long academic stream, indicating that farmer's children are not being relegated to the less prestigious sectors of the secondary system through inability to cope with entrance examinations. Social background helps elite children to do well on the Ghanaian Common Entrance Examination but performance on 'O' Level examinations after five years of secondary school is more closely related to the quality of the school than the social background of the pupil. Boys from elite families who only managed to get a place at a low-quality secondary school failed their 'O' Level examinations; boys in high-quality secondary schools did about equally well regardless of whether they came from low or high-status backgrounds.[51] This suggests that lack of success in the educational system will result in downward mobility for some children of the elite; they will lack the educational qualifications for most elite occupations. It likewise points to the importance of equality of opportunity at the point of entrance to secondary school. As secondary education becomes more widespread, the critical point will move up to university entrance, but at the present stage of development secondary entrance is more crucial. If a highly intelligent child gets into an adequate secondary school, he will probably get the help he needs, academically and financially, to reach a degree.

One important question, then, is whether a six-year primary course is long enough to enable children with initial disadvantages to catch up. Heyneman's study[52] of success in the Ugandan Primary Leaving Examination (UPLE) suggests that the nature of the examination may be more important than home background by the end of primary school. Private preparatory schools for elite children may give them better training for the examination than is available in ordinary schools, but in a large sample Heyneman found no relationship between socio-economic background (father's occupation, the education of both parents and household possessions) and success in the UPLE. Children from rural schools did as well as those from urban schools. He feels that this is because the examination relies heavily on memory for the mathematics and general knowledge sections. Only the English language section favours children with well educated parents, and even here the relationship was weak. The strongest influence on success appears to be the English ability of the primary teacher, and here urban schools may have some

(50) 1966, p.82.   (51) Bibby and Peil 1974.   (52) 1976.

edge over rural schools if better qualified teachers tend to find jobs in the towns. He suggests that examinations for which students can prepare are fairer than those emphasising skill in the metropolitan language, but that true equality of access is probably more related to parental ability to pay secondary fees than ability to perform well on entrance examinations.

Somerset[53] found that the Kenya Certificate of Primary Education (CPE) examination is more efficient in measuring the ability of the small proportion of students in high status schools than for the rest of the population. There is a relatively low correlation between performance on the CPE examination and subsequent performance on secondary leaving examinations,[54] suggesting that many able young people are not admitted to secondary schools. A high proportion of Standard VII students repeated the year in order to have a better chance of doing well and entering secondary school, and this considerably increased the primary population at no benefit to the nation. The very high commitment of parents and pupils to the goal of passing the examination is clear. The main difference between this and former rites marking the passage to adulthood is that only a minority can pass through this new gate.

Placement

The influence of social background on occupational attainment tends to be indirect rather than direct, with educational attainment as the intervening variable (see Figure 12). The earlier discussion has shown how parents of high educational and occupational achievement are able to provide better

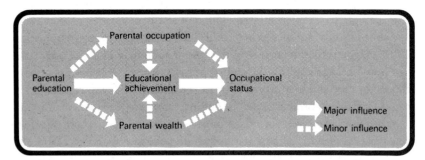

Figure 12 The relationship between social background, educational attainment and occupational placement

educational opportunities for their children than parents who lack these advantages. Children of the elites are unlikely to leave after primary school because a place in some secondary school can usually be found for them.

(53) In Court and Ghai 1975.   (54) As in Ghana, see Bibby and Peil 1974, p.410.

Parents may also pay for a child to study abroad if he has failed to get into a local university. Thus, by pushing the child into a higher level of education than he would have attained by his own ability, the high-status parent can improve his child's occupational opportunities even though these are directly related to educational achievement. A high-status parent may also help his children's occupational placement more directly by providing contacts to help make the most of rather mediocre educational attainment. A successful businessman or higher civil servant may be able to find a clerical post for a son who has not managed to get into sixth form, whereas the son of a small farmer in similar circumstances may face unemployment.[55]

The relationship between educational achievement and occupational placement is generally closer in Africa than in Europe or North America. The development of the bureaucracy during the colonial period, with its attempt to limit access of Africans to higher-level occupations, resulted in an emphasis on meritocracy which has been maintained and even strengthened. Standards were lowered somewhat with the mass Africanisation of posts at independence (though many posts were kept by Europeans until appropriately qualified Africans were available, especially in the former French territories). But after the initial rapid growth of the civil service, new openings have been much more limited. This narrowing of opportunities has increased the dependence on formal qualifications.

Similarly, the more rapid expansion of the educational system than of industry has meant that employers can upgrade their requirements; factory jobs for which illiterates or men with a few years of primary schooling were hired now often require some post-primary schooling. In some cases, the job is more effectively performed by someone with more education (this applies particularly to clerical posts), but not necessarily. The higher qualification may be merely a means of cutting down the number of applications, facilitating choice. On the other hand, those with considerably more education than a job requires are often dissatisfied and work less efficiently than those whose qualifications (and hence aspirations) fit the work more closely.

Nevertheless, although certain occupations are closely tied to a specific level of educational attainment, other factors are also important in occupational placement. Nepotism, tribalism and patronage are important in many areas, but the type of job sought, the size and nature of the labour force in the place of residence, age and experience can also be as important as certification by the educational system. There are many jobs (such as the skilled trades) which attract people of widely varying education and some people of considerable education are doing unskilled work because they have

(55) Unemployment at this level varies considerably between and within countries. See Chapter 9.

been unable to cope with better jobs. Farms and businesses are run both by graduates and by men and women with no education at all. A study of occupational placement in four Nigerian cities showed that occupational opportunities differed considerably between them, making a given level of education more useful in one town than in another. Someone with a moderate level of education has more opportunities in areas where education is still limited than in a metropolis where higher education is common. Older people who got their jobs ten or twenty years ago needed less education than a young man looking for the same job today, and an employer may choose an older and more experienced man with less education rather than a recent school leaver who would have to be trained.

Education and equality
There is considerable evidence that educational recruitment, placement and, to a lesser extent, achievement provide greater opportunities for some members of the society than others. While it acts as a vehicle of social mobility, it can also help to preserve the position of those who are born into high-status families and make it more difficult for those from low-status families to improve their position. In spite of this, governments proclaim their dedication to equality for all citizens. This poses an interesting problem for the relationship between consensus and conflict in society.

If this were a straightforward case of differential advantage, educational privilege could give rise to considerable protest. But the educational system emphasises selection by *ability*. People recognise that not everyone is equally gifted intellectually, and that the prizes of certification should go to those who can prove their worth by success in examinations. It is thus not difficult to get societal consensus that schooling must have an element of selection and that some should get more of it than others. So long as the criteria of selection are widely acceptable and seen to be fair, conflict is minimised and the resulting social differentiation is tolerated in spite of its interference with equality.

Acceptance becomes more problematic when selection and placement are seen to be less than fair. So far, parents and students have been so committed to the goals of educational achievement that they have ignored the low chances of success if, indeed, they have been aware of them at all. Students are often ignorant of their school's poor record;[56] because the reference group is usually local, an occasional success raises the hopes of several cohorts of aspirants. The most disadvantaged often have the least clear view of the system as a whole and therefore cannot appreciate their position.

(56) Bibby and Peil 1974, p.403; King 1974, p.50; Somerset in Court and Ghai 1975, p.90.

At the same time, the government emphasises patriotism and service to one's country in the schools, encouraging those who succeed to see themselves as responsible leaders and the rest (the failures) to see themselves as good citizens, willing followers of those whose merit has put them at the top. Thus, a functionalist ideology helps to explain the persistence (and increase) of social differentiation in spite of a commitment to social equality. Conflict is most likely to arise when members of the best-served and best-informed sector of the disadvantaged population become aware of the odds against them and withhold their consent; they will continue to agree on the goal but deny legitimacy to the means until adjustments favourable to them have been made. This may require changes in both the structure and content of the educational system,[57] or may merely aid those who are objecting at the expense of those who are even less represented.

Schools and universities as organisations

The school is the first formal organisation to which many children are exposed, their first experience of secondary rather than primary relationships and of bureaucratic authority. Therefore, socialisation of the child within the school must include adjustment to the requirements of a formal organisation. A boarding school requires even greater adjustment than a day school, because it forms a small-scale society with its own history, hierarchy of leaders, norms, values and relations with other societies. Even though students interact with people living in the neighbourhood, their attitudes and behaviour are shaped by the organisation of which they are a part.

The organisational aspects of education may be examined at the macro-level (the national or regional aparatus controlling the educational system) or the micro-level (the individual school). Every nation has a large educational bureaucracy headed by a Minister or Commissioner of Education with centralised civil servants and localised Education Officers to regulate, control and assess what goes on in the schools. African nations inherited a fairly high level of centralisation from the colonial era, though this was generally stronger in those countries following the French tradition than in those whose educational systems were organised on British lines. Local diversity has generally received little encouragement because central officials have taken the paternalistic position that they know better than the local people what is best. Tanzanian schools are now encouraged to become active partners in local development, but centralised direction of curriculum and

(57) Prewitt in Court and Ghai 1975.

examinations inevitably restricts local initiative. The Harambee schools of Kenya are very much local creations,[58] but they model themselves on the state system and their goal is usually government take-over.

The two factors most important in consolidating centralised control of education are examinations and funding. The goal of most students is passing examinations in order to move to the next higher level, and the whole school programme, especially at upper primary and upper secondary levels, tends to be geared to this.[59] The innovative school which puts examination success at risk in order to pursue other goals such as helping the child to understand his own society, become a better farmer, experiment with nature or science, or become a creative artist may quickly lose support of parents and pupils.[60] Funding is equally important, because so far it has proved very difficult to collect enough money to support local schools fully. A drive for funds and communal labour can produce a school building, but continuing support for salaries, books and equipment is much more difficult to achieve, especially for primary schools. These are felt to be the responsibility of the government rather than the local people, and when the government pays the bills it has the right to make the rules. Community secondary schools are seen as sources of prestige, but many are severely hampered by a shortage of funds.[61]

At the level of the individual institution, there are interesting differences which are related to their size and functions. Universities are complex institutions which have market, bureaucratic, democratic and collegial functions.[62] In its function as an economic marketplace, the academic staff are the producers. While the most obvious consumers are the students, staff products are also consumed by the general public (where research has practical applications) and their academic colleagues around the world. The staff often have conflicts of interest in relation to their several markets; they may be accused of not spending enough time on their teaching, of not carrying out relevant research, or of not furthering their academic discipline.

While a university has obvious aspects of bureaucracy, these are in its non-academic rather than its academic organisation. The bureaucracy provides the buildings and equipment, organises the admission of students, and arranges for the teaching to take place. The core relationships of the univer-

---

(58) See Anderson in Jolly 1969 and in Brown and Hiskett 1975. (59) King in Court and Ghai 1975; Dore 1976. (60) Van Rensburg 1974 suggests, on the basis of his experience with an employment-oriented secondary school in Botswana, that education is better able to respond to societal pressures than to initiate social change. (61) See the chapters by Anderson mentioned above and the chapters on Harambee schools in Court and Ghai 1975. Some Ibo communities have been relatively successful in maintaining secondary schools; see Smock 1971, p.33. (62) Parsons and Platt 1974.

sity, interaction between teachers and students, cannot be merely bureaucratic because they must be based on professional expertise and the fostering of individual talent. Bureaucracy is fostered by the increasing size of universities. An institution with a few hundred students needs relatively few rules because it is possible to know the students as individuals, at least within a department. But more formalised organisational arrangements are necessary when there are several thousand students and when two or three hundred are taking courses in some of the more popular departments. In a period of rapid growth, the quality, social background and/or expectations of the students may change, requiring adjustment of teaching methods, or expectations of tuition may be maintained when such attention is no longer possible. Such a situation often gives rise to conflict.

A prevailing democratic political ideology has led to demands for more democracy in the universities, for a minimising of the strict hierarchy which puts junior students at the bottom and professors at the top, with only the latter having a say in university government. While some changes can be made, universities are basically stratified by differential competence, knowledge and experience. Academic staff and disciplines are also stratified according to prevailing views on their contribution to knowledge. (An international reputation adds to the prestige of a member of staff; sociology is usually considered less important than physics.) The system provides more rewards in prestige and resources to those who perform best and relegates to less important roles those whose performance is inferior. Full democracy would interfere with the achievement of the primary goal of the university. Therefore, Parsons and Platt suggest that universities are best considered as stratified collegial organisations, run by specialists in various fields who cooperate in order to maximise their joint contribution to knowledge. Economic, social and political factors necessarily affect university functioning so that it takes on market, bureaucratic and democratic features, but the core of the university and its national and international academic standing lie in its operation as a community in pursuit of higher learning.

Primary and secondary schools are smaller and less specialised than universities. They are also much less autonomous; considerable time must often be spent by teachers filling the requirements of the central bureaucracy. The age differences between students and teachers and the fact that the latter are legally minors make a hierarchical organisation more acceptable. However, older secondary students often demand more say in matters affecting them and greater freedom from the petty rules of boarding institutions that is allowed younger students. While some secondary schools still maintain the colonial/mission heritage of emphasising hierarchy and obedience to authority, the increasing competition for success and interest of the students in democratic politics have led to some schools being run cooperatively by students and teachers. As in universities, this cooperation works best in questions of discipline and living arrangements; teachers must take greater responsibility for academic aspects, but students may take the initiative in demanding reform if they feel the school is inadequately staffed or equipped. The lower emphasis on competence and specialisation by secondary than by university teachers makes a democratic form of organisation easier to achieve.

Classroom organisation has generally been very autocratic in African primary schools. Untrained, uninterested teachers tend to use harsh discipline because this is the only way they can maintain control over the classroom. More professional, trained teachers can use other techniques to maintain attention and encourage the pupils to learn, but this is still likely to reflect prevailing local norms on proper relationships between adults and children. Peshkin[63] illustrates patterns of discipline in Kanuri primary schools and the interaction between pupils and their teachers and peers. Some of these patterns were inherited from the British (systems of prefects and monitors), but others come from the Islamic norms of northern Nigerian society.

Primary pupils are generally grouped according to age, with children of a wide range of abilities studying together. However, where passing to the next class is not automatic and where primary education is only beginning to expand, children of widely differing ages may also be in the same class. This age range may present discipline problems for the teacher and will cause stratification problems for the pupils because position in the class hierarchy of ability is often quite different from position in the age hierarchy of children outside the school. The changing interests and physical and mental abilities of children as they grow up and especially as they move from childhood into adolescence make it as difficult for a teacher to handle a class with a wide age variance as one with a wide ability variance.

In large urban primary schools and in secondary schools, students may also be streamed according to ability, since this simplifies teaching. The evidence suggests that less able students do less well in streamed than in open classes. Assignment to a C or D stream lowers their self-esteem, and they generally profit from contact with more able students. Different streams often develop separate subcultures, norms and goals; the A stream is highly oriented towards academic success, whereas the D stream may become strongly anti-academic, uninterested in school and concerned to demonstrate social or physical prowess. Somerset[64] shows that secondary students' aspirations to continue in school are related to their position in the class; the better students have higher aspirations than those who realise that they are

(63) 1972.   (64) In Court and Ghai 1975, pp.80–6.

not performing well. (Type of school attended is probably a more important influence in setting a general level for aspirations.) Self-perception resulting from relative position in the school hierarchy can serve as a stimulus for some students to perform at their best and for others to lose interest or at least perform less well than they might.

The teaching profession

Teachers constitute the largest single group of government employees. They often have a strong sense of occupational identity and they play an important role in passing on the learning of the past and in training the nation's youth for the future. Teachers are often dissatisfied because they feel that they are denied the status and economic rewards which should be theirs. This section will provide a brief introduction to the sociology of the professions by examining the extent to which teachers are a profession. It will conclude with a discussion of the social background of teachers and factors affecting their relative prestige.

Professionalism

The word professional is used in Africa for a wide variety of activities. Drivers, carpenters, teachers and doctors all refer to 'my profession', so it may be difficult to separate 'profession' from 'occupation'. Sociologists use profession in a more restricted sense for occupations that have four characteristics:

1 a defined field of knowledge;
2 a long period of specialised training;
3 an ethical code governing relationships between the professional and the clients, this relationship being based predominantly on service to clients rather than profit for the professional;
4 autonomy, so that the group controls entry and conditions of practice. If teaching is examined on each of these points, we can see that it is only margially a profession.

Unlike law or medicine, teaching has no special field of knowledge; of its nature, it covers all fields of knowledge. Its distinctive training applies only to methods of imparting knowledge, but there is considerable disagreement on these methods and, in any case, they differ with the level of education and many teachers have no training at all in methods. The specialised training of teachers is also much shorter than that devoted to law or medicine and at a lower level. In countries where lawyers and doctors practise after a first degree, teaching is not usually studied at university level; where teachers are expected to have a degree (e.g., the U.S.A.), medicine and law require a higher degree. There is also the paradox that teachers with the most prestige have the least training in methods. Instead of instruction in teaching, university lecturers have long training in a specialised field of knowledge. This encourages them to think of themselves as professional sociologists, psychologists, chemists, etc. rather than professional teachers.

Teaching comes closest to being a profession in its ethical code and attitude of service, though cases of male teachers taking advantage of female pupils have been sufficiently common in some areas for parents to resist sending their older daughters to school. The profit motive enters into teaching mainly in the provision of private tuition, and it is here that it comes closest to law and medicine in relatively autonomous provision of service.

Generally, teachers are at a serious disadvantage to members of the 'free professions' in regard to autonomy. Doctors and especially lawyers tend to be self-employed, and entry into these professions is regulated by the members through their Medical and Bar Associations. These set professional standards and enforce the ethical code. Teachers, on the other hand, are certified by the state (Grade II Certificate, etc.), employed by the state (or by private educational authorities such as the missions) and closely controlled by school managers, local authorities and the Ministry of Education. This control may even extend to their clothing and behaviour outside the school. The state approves the syllabus which regulates what must be taught and sets the examinations by which the teachers' efficiency is measured. University lecturers (or at least their departments), have more control over what is taught and who is hired to teach it than primary or secondary teachers, but their results are also monitored by external examiners. They have a considerable measure of self-government through the Faculty Boards or university Senates (their collegial form of organisation), but there is always some outside authority representing the government or the public which can overrule decisions which are not felt to be in the general interest.

Teachers have made various attempts to improve their autonomy, but their associations tend to be closer to trade unions, through which workers can negotiate with management, than to professional associations, which are self-regulating. National unions of teachers have often been among the first unions to be organised; several have become increasingly militant in recent years, attempting to halt the falling status of the 'profession'.

Social background
The social origins of people in a given occupation reflect the ease of entry and level of prestige; the rewards and prestige of the occupation in turn encourage people at certain levels to undertake it. The background of teachers

varies at different levels; it is lowest in the primary schools and highest in the universities. This is partly because of the length and expense of the training required and partly because of the alternative opportunities available to young people who might aspire to be teachers.

Teaching has been used in many countries as a means to social mobility. It is attractive to the poor, women and rural aspirants, who have fewer opportunities to enter more rewarding and prestigious occupations. The bright child of poor parents may not be able to afford the education necessary to become a doctor or a lawyer, but he can become a teacher and so help his children to move further up the social hierarchy. Primary teaching has often been used as a route to university by young men who lacked the money for secondary fees. Training college provided them with a good start toward 'O' Levels or School Certificate, and private study enabled some to reach their goal. Some returned to teaching at a higher level after university, while others left teaching entirely. As secondary enrolment has expanded and requirements for entry to training colleges have risen, this route to social mobility for children of the poor has increasingly been cut off. This may in time raise the social background of primary teachers, depending on the openness of access to secondary schools.

At each level of education, women teachers tend to have a higher social background than men. Women tend to get less education than men of the same social status and hence find teaching more attractive. There are also more women teaching at primary level because women have fewer alternative occupations than men. Primary teaching is considered well suited to women because they are experienced in dealing with small children and because they can move fairly easily when their husbands are transferred. Primary teachers tend to come from rural places because rural children know about fewer possibilities of wage employment than urban children and are less likely to object to teaching in a rural school. Primary teaching has also been popular among school-leavers in areas where educational provision is limited, because the first products of the schools see teaching as directly relevant to the formal education they have received.[65]

The social background of secondary teachers depends on the type of educational system. If secondary education is highly selective, catering mostly for elite children (as in France and in African elite schools, especially during colonial times), secondary teachers may be of relatively high social background; the aim is to have teachers who will 'set a good example' for the students, teaching them to speak and behave properly. Where little distinction is made between primary and secondary education (as in the U.S.A.),

(65) Peil 1968.

there is little difference in the social background of teachers at the two levels. In many parts of Africa, expatriate teachers have left the secondary schools before sufficient local graduates were available for their posts. This gap was largely filled by volunteers from abroad and local students who were either waiting to enter university or studying for pre-university examinations. While these young teachers filled a vital need, their presence in large numbers tended to lower the status of secondary teaching. They seldom stayed long enough to become experienced teachers and were often less concerned with providing the best possible service to their students or with the school as an organisation than those for whom teaching was a career.

Prestige

The prestige of teaching is affected by its psychological and monetary rewards; qualifications for entry; the demand for teachers, numbers employed and proportion of women; the diffuseness of the role and amount of self-determination. In the initial expansion of primary education, teachers had an important role in vertical integration, acting as mediators between the general public and the elite. They introduced their pupils to the national language and principles of citizenship and demonstrated new norms of behaviour in rural communities. At the same time, they could transmit community demands upward to the political elite, many of whom were ex-teachers. Their status was high and their position seemed secure. However, post-independence expansion brought in many unqualified teachers. These got less respect from the local population, and their position was further undermined because their integrative function was no longer necessary; many other local people were able to communicate directly with those in power. As more teachers were trained, uncertificated teachers lost their positions, often to their ex-pupils. Declining status and security brought low morale, which was intensified when salaries were not paid on time. Many teachers simply left the field; those who stayed were often unable to move rather than deeply committed to teaching. Widespread dissatisfaction, in turn, decreased the status of teaching still further.[66]

Teaching is usually seen as having fairly high psychological but relatively low financial rewards. This causes a circular deterioration in the social position of teachers. Remuneration is used as a measure of the society's esteem, and low pay signals that the job is not ranked highly. This makes teachers dissatisfied, lowering the quality of their work and discouraging the most able young people from going into teaching. This, in turn, further lowers the prestige of teachers. (The converse is not necessarily true. High

(66) Abernethy in Melson and Wolpe 1971, pp.418–24.

pay will not ensure that teaching has high prestige and job satisfaction.)

Occupations practised by small numbers of highly selected people generally have more prestige than more common occupations, and teaching suffers because large numbers are involved. There are too many teachers for the general public to think of them as a special category. In addition, work which is done by women generally has lower prestige than work done by men and primary teaching is attracting increasing numbers of women. Teaching also suffers because its clients are children; people who work with children usually have less prestige than those whose clients are adults.

The large number of teachers and the high proportion of women are also used as an excuse to keep salaries low, especially for primary teachers. Women tend to be less concerned about salary than men because they are usually providing a second rather than a primary income for the household. The government resists raising teachers' salaries because even a small rise represents a large drain on the economy. African teachers have generally expected to be paid considerably more than the 'common man' (farmer, carpenter, etc.) whereas in many developed countries the remuneration for primary teaching is fairly close to average, reflecting a similar level of prestige.

Finally, the teaching role tends to be diffuse and controlled rather than specific and autonomous, though the latter characteristics increase as one moves up from primary to university level. Many things are expected of primary teachers: discipline and character training, leadership in sports, administrative ability and clerical skills as well as the dissemination of knowledge. As pointed out above, they have relatively little autonomy, even in the classroom.

Studies of occupational prestige (see Chapter 4) show that primary teaching has about the same ranking as skilled trades; secondary teachers, education officers and headmasters have a higher rank, but are below elite occupations such as judge, doctor and Member of Parliament. Entrants to training colleges and craft apprenticeships often have about the same amount of schooling, and their training takes about the same length of time. Primary teaching may gain some prestige from being a white collar occupation with relatively short hours, but remuneration has lagged behind that of the more successful craftsmen and they lack the independence of self-employment, which is often highly valued. Higher levels of teaching carry more prestige because of the longer training, higher entry requirements, greater autonomy and higher remuneration.

Conclusion

Education has played, and will continue to play, a large role in shaping

African societies, though perhaps not as large a role as is imputed to it because the educational system is itself shaped in many ways by the society in which it operates. This can be illustrated by examining the role of education in providing skilled manpower and in fostering social mobility. The government and industries look to education to provide a trained labour force which meets the needs of a particular time. But training through the educational system takes many years, and popular demand for courses is strongly affected by the perception candidates have of opportunities for employment at the time they start their course. It is likely that either too many or too few people with a particular skill will be produced, and the educational system will then be blamed for inefficiency in producing 'educated unemployed' or causing a shortage. Some types of education never attract much popular support because the jobs for which they prepare are not seen as sufficiently rewarding, whereas other types are oversubscribed because these seem to lead to the most prestigious positions in the society. Thus, the societal stratification system has a strong effect on manpower production by the educational system.

Similarly, education does provide opportunities for social mobility, but it also provides for status maintenance. Educational participation varies in all societies for which we have measures by culture and social status, but also by intelligence, school achievement and aspirations, which tend to be inter-related and partially independent of socio-economic background.[67] The structure of the occupational system of the society may open or close opportunities for mobility through education quite independently of the nature of the school system. For example, if new occupations arise or the economy expands rapidly there are likely to be many openings for people with a moderate level of education. If there are relatively few openings in another country or at a different period of time, people with exactly the same amount of education may find it of little use to them in their struggle to improve their social position.

Societal ideology also affects equality of opportunity available through the schools; some educational leaders might prefer a more elitist approach but be constrained to emphasise quantity rather than quality. On the other hand, the shortage of economic resources may force the government to limit educational expansion even though this interferes with equality of access to the system. Thus, the educational system cannot be examined in isolation from other institutions of the society.

Schools and universities can be studied as formal organisations having manifest and latent goals, patterns of authority and relationships with other

(67) Boudon 1974.

organisations and with the wider community. Conflicts over academic freedom or changes in university structures suggest that there has been little thought on either side as to the basic goals of a university, or that there is considerable disagreement about the nature of these goals.

Teaching may be seen as a semi-profession whose members aspire to improve their position in society by professionalising their role. Teachers are seldom from a high social background, but they often aspire to have their children reach such a status. Teaching is thus used as a stepping-stone to inter-generational mobility. It has also been used for intragenerational mobility; men who have taught early in their career have been able to move up by leaving teaching for the civil service. With the great expansion of higher education, the rise in entry requirements to universities and the slower expansion of higher government posts than in the past, teachers will find it more difficult to achieve further mobility in future. This is likely to lead to a greater commitment to teaching and increased pressure to improve the pay, conditions and status of teachers.

Brown and Hiskett[68] suggest that Islamic education differs from Western education in five ways:

1 It is available to anyone seeking knowledge; there is no 'school age'.
2 There is no examination or certification; the scholar seeks only knowledge.
3 There are no fixed fees, so the poor can be accommodated; there is equality of access to anyone who desires it.
4 Teachers attract students by the quality of their instruction, not through bureaucratic appointments or formal qualifications. Formal organisation is minimised at the lower levels.
5 It emphasises social cohesion rather than competition, a fuller assimilation into the Muslim community rather than individual achievement.

These aspects spotlight many of the problems of Western education which await solutions. Its literacy, socialisation and manpower functions could be more beneficial to the population as a whole if they were available at any time when they were needed rather than being limited to children, if they were open to the needs of pupils rather than being tied to examinations, and if the needs of the community took primacy over the competitive aspir-ations of individuals. Some of the new forms of education now taking shape are steps in this direction, but societal pressures for a continuance of metro-politan patterns remain strong.

Suggested reading and discussion topics
1. Describe the power structure or patterns of group formation in your

(68) 1975, pp.95, 101.

secondary school. (See Elliott 1970 or Masemann 1974.)

2. Which is a more important goal for education, equality or excellence? Consider the advantages and disadvantages of each of these goals for national development.

3. Discuss the effect of recent political decisions on the role of teachers.

4. Comment on the problem of multilingualism in African education. (See Strevens and Parren in Jolly 1969 or Tiffen in Brown and Hiskett 1975.)

5. Examine the effects of cultural background on the acquisition of Western education. (See Cole *et al* 1971; Gay and Cole 1967; Horton 1967.)

7 Religion

Religion may be seen in a narrow sense to refer to a set of theological beliefs held and rituals performed by members of a particular group: Anglicans or Muslims, for instance. Or it may be used in a broad sense for the belief systems, moral norms and values held by members of a society. This chapter adapts the broader meaning to examine religion as an integral part of the culture of a people. It introduces some aspects of the sociology of religion: definitions or religion, the effect of society on religion and of religion on society, the development and change of belief systems and their relevance for attitudes towards disease, and the formal organisations developed by various religious groups.

The sociological meaning of religion

There has been considerable disagreement between scholars as to just what constitutes religion, how it differs from magic and whether it has been superseded by science. Tylor's *Primitive Culture* presented a 'minimal definition' of religion as 'a belief in Spiritual Beings'[1]. He drew his theories from the limited ethnographic material available in the 1860s and the evolutionist ideas of Social Darwinism current among the intellectuals of the period. He distinguished magic from science by saying that a scientific association can be objectively demonstrated (cause and effect can be empirically proved, as when blood flows from a knife cut) whereas in magic the link is subjective (there may be symbolic or other reasons for believing that the act and event are related, as when a mother believes that another woman has caused her child's death, but the connection cannot be proved).

Tylor did not attempt to separate magic and religion except in that anything supernatural beyond the 'belief in Spiritual Beings' was held to be magic. He then developed a theory of animism, which is essentially endowing animals, plants and even non-living things such as stones with a spirit.

(1) Bohannan 1969, p.313.

213

Any religion which includes the belief that mountains, trees, or animals have the power to influence man's destiny and should therefore be worshipped was labelled 'animist' by Tylor. He suggested that 'savage' peoples did not realise that their religion and their magic were false because proof was very difficult, failure could be explained and success sometimes occurred in the natural course of events. Although religion and magic are gradually being replaced by science, he argued, this replacement will never be complete because there are many events in life which cannot be scientifically predicted or explained.

Followers of Tylor took up his idea of the necessity of religion to explain dreams and death and to handle fear and insecurity. Books such as Frazer's *The Golden Bough* and Burton's *The Mystic Rose* propounded theories of the 'primitive mind', filled with superstitions, blindly following irrational beliefs and living in constant fear of beings they could not understand. These men of the 'Age of Enlightenment' tended to think of religion as gross self-deception resulting from the insecurity of life for these illiterate peoples. They made no attempt to fit 'primitive religion' into the same framework as their own religious experience or that of ancient Asian civilisations. They tended to see religion as the experience of an individual rather than as an institution of a society.

In trying to interpret what goes on in the mind of a magician or man practising his religion, they went well beyond the limits of the data available. They missed the most important point of difference between science and magic, that the scientist is constantly adjusting his ideas of reality as a result of his experience whereas the magician applies no such tests; failure is not blamed on the magic itself. (Individuals seeking aid from magicians are somewhat more empirical in that they will try a series of specialists until they get the result they seek.) Finally, these early theorists used inadequate comparisons. They contrasted magic behaviour in 'primitive' societies with scientific behaviour in their own. It would have been much more valid to compare magical behaviour in several societies or compare magical and scientific behaviour in a single society.

Levy-Bruhl and Durkheim took a step forward in seeing religion as something larger than the individual, standing for the 'collective representations' of the society. Individuals are socialised into a particular culture and tend to see things and events as they have been taught to see them. A young Akan boy growing up on the shores of Lake Bosumtwi sees the lake as the home of a spirit who demands certain actions of those who wish to live in peace. He can cite examples of misfortune which befell people who ignored the fetish. A visiting Englishman may laugh at such ideas and see the lake only as a water reservoir, a source of fish, or a tourist attraction. This makes it easy to understand why 'armchair theorists' in Europe should misunderstand the religious ideas of non-European peoples; their 'collective representations' of reality were widely different. Durkheim suggested that one should study religion by examining what the ritual specialists do, what goals they set out to achieve and why they choose these goals. This should tell us a great deal about their ideas of their own society; economic, political and social institutions of a society are reflected in its religious institutions. More than this, Durkheim's study of Australian Aborigines convinced him that men created religion as an expression of society; as a rationalist, he denied the possibility of supernatural reality. This is going too far; religion arises in society but includes more than society.[2]

Religion involves a belief in something beyond humanity, in the supernatural. It sets the sacred apart from the secular, the holy from the profane, but it is also closely bound up with the society in which it is practised. It aims at universal reality, but can never be completely free of daily experience. Durkheim's often-quoted definition provides a useful base for understanding the role of religion in society:

A religion is a unified system of beliefs and practices relative to sacred things, that is to say, things set apart and forbidden – beliefs and practices which unite into one single moral community . . . all those who adhere to them.[3]

This definition necessarily ignores many important aspects of religion (its theology, philosophy, history, etc.) in favour of its sociological aspects. We are interested in the way religion both affects and reflects the society in which it is practised. All men face problems of life and death, success and failure, which they see as relevant to their religion. Religious rituals help them to cope with fear and anxiety, but also with joy and hope fulfilled. While this might be done as an individual, it is more often communal. Most religions allow for the solitary man communing with God, but it is assumed that the majority will practise their religion as members of a group and that their religious ideas will be influenced by the society of which they are a member.

Religion in society

The main social functions of religion may be summarised as integration, explanation and the making of symbolic statements about society through ritual. Religious rituals certify the passage of various stages of life and the achievement of new status. These rituals are patterns of behaviour recognised

(2) *Ibid.*, Chapter 18.　(3) Durkheim 1915, p.47.

by the community and include the celebration of individual and communal events. Religion fosters social integration by upholding the values and norms of the society. It helps men to overcome their fear and anxiety by providing a theological explanation of success, failure and man's place in the universe.

Ritual

Radcliffe-Brown[4] suggested that while beliefs may be vague and variable, rituals often continue to be meaningful even though the participants no longer believe in the religion on which the rite was originally based. For example, educated Christians often continue to participate in rituals honouring local spirits they no longer believe in, 'just in case', or because the rituals symbolise membership in the local community quite apart from religious allegiance. Many Muslims and Christians also continue to observe local religious customs in addition to the practices of their world religion because they still believe in both systems.

Ritual activities are useful for symbolising that an individual has achieved a particular status in the community; these may be called life cycle rituals or rites of passage. Infants are formally accepted as members of the society by outdooring or baptism; adolescents become full adult members through puberty/initiation ceremonies; marriage rituals (which may extend over a long period of time) formally tie the two families together and legitimate the children by giving them a specific position in the society. Finally, the rituals of death provide an organised way for the community to adjust to the loss of members, including highly valued leaders.

Early studies of religion in various societies often mentioned the importance of religious ritual in helping individuals come to terms with death and disaster. More than any other crisis, death faces man with questions of ultimate meaning and also with the need for rearranging social networks. From a sociological point of view, assistance given the deceased through various rituals is less important than the reorganisation of social relationships and the support given to societal norms of affinity, inheritance, etc. through the carrying out of these rituals. This is less of a problem in the case of elderly people whose death is anticipated or of young children who are not yet full members of the society, but illness and accidents carry off many young and middle-aged adults whose roles must somehow be filled by siblings or other kinsmen. Children are fostered, brothers take over widows, political roles fall to the next in line, new members are found for work groups, the extended family separates as sons set up new compounds after the death of their father. In the midst of all this change, elaborate funeral

(4) 1952, p.155.

ceremonies and memorial services (sometimes lasting over several years) provide a framework which emphasises the continuity of the social system.

Another focus of religious ritual is war. Large or small-scale intersocietal conflict involves considerable risk and insecurity; most societies try to minimise this by assuring participants that Spiritual Beings are on their side. Sacrifices are made, rituals are performed and calls are issued for a reform of moral life so that victory will be deserved. The exterior threat heightens societal cohesion, and this cohesion is symbolised by the communal rites which are led or at least notably attended by political and military leaders.

In agricultural societies, religious ritual has an important role in planting and harvesting. Man recognises his dependence on nature, especially for adequate and timely rain. He calls on god(s), spirits and/or ancestors to provide a bountiful harvest and then expresses thanks by celebrating the earth's fruitfulness. Some societies have an earth goddess who is responsible for the fertility of the soil, animals and women. Others have rain-makers whose speciality is to preserve the area from drought (and occasionally to stop excessive rainfall). In some areas there is a mountain, river, tree, etc. whose spirit must be propitiated. The similarity in all these beliefs and their expression in rituals is that individuals and the society declare their subordination to supernatural forces which vitally affect the future of the community. Whereas fertility rituals are often performed by individuals or heads of families, harvest rituals are usually a community affair, symbolising a wide identity.

Integration and conflict
The socialisation of children provides them with a 'collective consciousness' of what is right and wrong in their society, but this is greatly strengthened in societies where common membership of a single religion adds moral support and supernatural sanctions to parental teaching. Parsons[5] shows that ideology and religious belief systems are important in solving integrative problems because they legitimate value patterns; they provide reasons why certain values should be preferred to others. For instance, in a society where the economic and political system foster collectivist values (a socialist or communist society), religious institutions are also likely to support communal rather than individual action, to encourage people to work together for the common good and worship God as a community rather than trying to contact Him as individuals. (The practice of world religions is often proscribed or severely hampered in such societies, but the ideology and ritual of a state-sponsored religion are substituted.) In a more individualist society where

(5) 1951, pp.350-1.

economic and political entrepreneurship are highly valued, religious institutions are likely to emphasise the individual relationship between man and God and that societal progress is a reward for the hard work and high morality of individuals.

A common religion can be very useful in holding together a group of people who would otherwise be competing economically and/or politically. The role of religion in integrating individuals into the society and the interaction between religious and other institutions is well demonstrated in Hausa society. Allegiance to Islam facilitates Hausa long-distance trade by providing a moral community on which trust can be based. Thus, traders can safely deal with non-kinsmen hundreds of miles away even though no written records are kept. The Hausa of Sabo (a section of Ibadan) managed to avoid the threat which Nigerian independence posed to their monopoly in the cattle and kola trades by conversion to the Tijaniyya Brotherhood, a strict Islamic sect which emphasises group participation in ritual. This intensified interpersonal relations between the Sabo Hausa and set them apart from the rest of the Ibadan population. It strengthened moral obligations to the community and the Chief of the Quarter. The new religious ideology, which was not available to local people, provided considerable political and economic advantages by further integrating this community of strangers and preventing their mixing with outsiders who otherwise shared their religion.[6]

Paden[7] found an even fuller integration of religious, political and social life in Kano. Only a small proportion of the Kano population are not Muslims, and these were isolated socially by the requirement that they live in the Sabon Gari (stranger's quarter) and politically because the Emir of Kano is a religious as well as a political leader. Competition for power between the leaders of various Muslim brotherhoods active in Kano has sometimes been intense, but the success of various reform movements and pressure from Muslims with a high level of Western education appears to be leading to greater toleration of other Muslims and even willingness to improve relations with Christians. Eventually, this is likely to weaken the authority of the Emir and sense of community of the Kano people in favour of greater allegiance to a wider Nigerian society.

However, the integrative role of religion can be overemphasised. Differences of religion have probably been responsible for deeper divisions within communities than any other source of conflict. There is always a tendency to feel that if one's own religious beliefs are true all others must necessarily be false; duty to one's own group and to outsiders lies in eliminating these false beliefs. Religious conflict is often related to a struggle for

(6) Cohen 1969.   (7) 1973.

power – another indication of the close relationship between religious institutions, as supporters of the values of the moral community, and political institutions, which use these values to organise the community for goal attainment. There are many examples of this in the struggles between followers of local religions and of Christianity (seen as an incursion of European power), between Christians and Muslims, and between followers of various branches of Christianity and of Islam. Horton[8] distinguishes between militant and non-militant Muslims; the latter carried out a series of *jihads* in order to spread and purify their religion. Various aspects of this conflict can be examined by focusing first on religious change (conversion) and secondly on political change (colonialism, independence).

Conversion
Pressure for conversion has often accompanied political change, as during a *jihad* or other periods of conquest such as pre-colonial expansion of kingdoms and the establishment of colonial empires. Where the local god(s) have failed, it may seem reasonable to follow the seemingly more powerful god(s) of the conqueror. Some will cynically change religion in order to improve their position with the new rulers.

Conversion generally is independent of political change, but it is likely to be more widespread in times of social change, when people question their habitual ways and look for answers to new problems. Peel[9] shows that the Aladura churches grew rapidly during the depression of the 1930s, especially in the towns where migrants were facing new patterns of social and economic organisation. Similarly, Cohen [10] shows how membership in the Tijaniyya Brotherhood spread among the Hausa in Ibadan in response to increasing economic and social competition with the predominant Yoruba.

Horton[11] criticises Peel's contrast between 'this-worldly', non-rational, unorganised traditional religion and Western Christianity as it was introduced to and is practised by Africans. He argues that traditional African religions emphasise 'explanation-prediction-control' and communion with individual spirits as a help in relations with one's fellow men, both focusing attention on this world rather than another. Christianity and Islam have some monks and mystics who are pulled into other-worldly communion (away from their fellow men), but the majority are more concerned with their everyday life in a way that is very similar to traditional religion. Second, Horton finds it difficult to quantify a difference in rationality between followers of traditional religion and Christianity. If religious beliefs are rationalised by organising them in line with one's knowledge and experience,

(8) 1975.   (9) 1968.   (10) 1969.   (11) 1971.

then the similarity can be demonstrated by the coordination between religion and social structure and by the regularities in expectation of performance of various types of spirits. This is closer in some societies and traditional religions than others, but it can always be demonstrated.

Horton's Intellectualist Theory [12] suggests that the change from emphasis on a multitude of lesser spirits to a supreme being can be the result of social change; he feels that conversion to Islam or Christianity is an accidental by-product. In a traditional society life is lived within the local community and moral rules tend to apply to the community. (Take, for example, the wide-spread norm that trickery, theft and even murder are not crimes if they involve outsiders but are grave offences if committed against someone in one's own group.) Traditional cosmology gives the lesser spirits and ancestors jurisdiction over the local community and its morality; the supreme being is usually seen as remote and not directly approachable by humans. Thus, although traditional religion has an idea of a supreme being, it is not very important. Social change, through which large numbers of people move outside their local community and face new experiences requiring 'explan-ation-prediction-control', will force followers of traditional religion to expand their ideas of a supreme being. They must move from a local to a universalist moral code, which is under the control of the supreme being. The lesser spirits may become less important, or may be changed from largely benevolent to mainly evil forces. New forms of ritual will be needed as the cult of the supreme being gradually replaces that of the lesser spirits. As it happened, Islam and Christianity were available and many people found it easier or more convenient to change their allegiance rather than expand and develop their traditional cosmology. Many traditional beliefs are taken with them into the new faith.

Fisher[13] disagrees with Horton and argues that Islam and Christianity were much more than catalysts which happened to be available to individuals looking for a more reliable contact with the supreme being. He points to several societies (such as the Nuer and Dinka of the Sudan) where the supreme being was an important part of traditional religion even though most indi-viduals' contacts were limited to the local community and others (such as the Asante of Ghana) where there was considerable contact with international trade and associated social change without mass conversion to a world religion. He suggests that religious reform movements probably occur from time to time in all religions, but the enthusiasm for witch-finding and similar activities in traditional religion may have been short-lived and relatively fruitless, at least partly because these societies lacked literacy. Both Islam

(12) 1971, 1975.   (13) 1973.

and Christianity are 'religions of a book', which facilitates codification and relatively stable organisation. Missionaries can pass on a set of doctrines which have been developed and studied over a long period and reformers can remind adherents of former standards. This is not to say that 'religions of a book' are practised in the same way everywhere, but the scriptures provide a standard against which to assess the changes which have taken place.

In response, Horton[14] presents several detailed case studies to illustrate the usefulness of his Intellectualist Theory in explaining religious orientation and change in Africa. Available evidence seems to suggest that traditional religions are more oriented toward a supreme being if the local community has considerable contact with outsiders (as in pastoralist and trading societies) and that lesser spirits are much more important in societies where members seldom venture beyond the local community (as among settled subsistence farmers). Acceptance or rejection of a world religion (Islam or Christianity) can also be seen as related to relative emphasis on the microcosm (the local settlement) or on important and continuing contacts with a wider society. Groups which have maintained their attachment to traditional religion in the face of considerable pressure from Islam are almost always isolated and able to maintain economic independence. Salamone[15] demonstrates this principle in the rapid conversion of formerly isolated peoples in northwestern Nigeria following their resettlement on the mainland and increasing social and political contact and communication with government authorities, who are all Muslims.

Religious conversion is often a long-term process rather than a rapid change. It can be visualised as a gradual mixing of new ideas with old. Before the first contacts have been made, we see an individual totally immersed in his own culture:

When the new teaching begins, there is a first crisis. The preachers have behind them their prestige as foreigners and, if Europeans, their knowledge of modern technology. Both Christian and Muslim teachers often accompanied soldiers, traders and administrators who sought power over traditional elements in the society. Formerly dominant elements sometimes accepted the new faith if they saw in it a guarantee of their position and of equality of treatment with the newcomers. In other societies, those at the bottom were the first to accept; they had little to lose. Chiefs and ritual specialists generally resisted because they saw the new faith as a threat to their position. Variable acceptance introduces disharmony into the society, as cultural changes accompany religious change. Masks and ritual places may be destroyed, initiation suspended and offerings to the spirits

(14) 1975   (15) 1975a.

stopped; the traditional culture has now been changed: 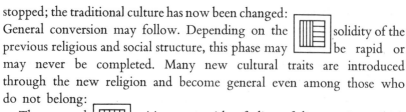 General conversion may follow. Depending on the solidity of the previous religious and social structure, this phase may be rapid or may never be completed. Many new cultural traits are introduced through the new religion and become general even among those who do not belong:

The second crisis comes with a feeling of dispossession, which was often inten- sified with the struggle for independence. Many people feel that the new rites do not fill all the functions of the old ones; disasters are sometimes attributed to the anger of spirits no longer being propitiated. Prestige and economic power equal to that of the foreigners have not been achieved. Various rituals are revived, but traditional forms have often lost their meaning and become artificial by being cut off from their original context in the homogeneous, pre-contact society. The new society is much less integrated, and Christians often feel this tension in their daily lives. They may alternate between Christian and pagan practices, abandon their faith, or join syncretic churches. At this stage, traditional culture retakes some of the field:

Fusion or acculturation takes place to a greater or lesser extent. The new re- ligion becomes fully a part of the culture, with local leadership and the integration of local music, art and philosophy into the rituals. A universal religion can never be as fully a part of a society as a local religion, but the variance of both Islam and Christianity from one place to another show that even universal religions are shaped by society in the process of acceptance:[16]

Fisher[17] divides the ac- ceptance of a new religion into three stages: quarantine, mixing and reform. These are best seen not as an evolutionary development where the second stage automatically follows the first and the third the second, but as differing patterns which may be important in varying order over time. During the quarantine period, which usually coincides with the introduction of a new religion, the few members (often strangers to the society) keep apart from the 'pagans', so preserving their faith intact. The few converts, often marginal to the local society, slaves and misfits, find it fairly easy to separate themselves from a community which rejects them; the low status of their new religion is no particular problem.

In the mixing stage, more local people join the new religion as it becomes more attractive. Fisher does not explain how the barriers are lowered and the new converts drawn in except to suggest that widespread slavery in Muslim areas detached many individuals from their communities. Horton[18] argues

(16) INADES 1964, pp.83–5.   (17) 1973.   (18) 1975.

that the new religion attracts because it seems to provide a better answer than the old religion to political and economic problems resulting from change in the society. People learn about new religions from contacts of trade or military service, migration and intermarriage as well as through conquest and slavery. Some are attracted, often more in terms of adding practices to their present ones than a full conversion to the new faith.

In the process of widespread acceptance, orthodoxy is often lost because the new converts bring many of their cults with them. This has been more true of Islam than of Christianity because very little has been asked of or taught to the Muslim convert whereas the Christian has often had a long catechuminate. But beliefs and practices which have been central to the convert's society are likely to persist even though strongly opposed by his new faith; ancestor worship and polygyny are probably the most important African examples. Skinner[19] shows that propitiation of the ancestors was so important to the Mossi of Upper Volta that chiefs responsible for the ceremonies could not become either Muslim or Christian because the dire consequences of omitting their duties threatened the whole community. Aryee[20] found that there was only a small (though statistically significant) difference between Christians, Muslims and followers of traditional religion in the proportion of men reported as polygynous by the 1960 Ghana census. In spite of strong preaching against polygyny by the Christian missions, it continues to receive considerable societal support.

The mixing stage may attain relative stability or be followed by further quarantine or by a reform movement. The religion gradually becomes integrated into local culture (diet and dress as well as prayer style often distinguish Muslims from Christians). Change to a short or long period of reform may arise through social, political, or economic pressures. The scriptures may be used either to maintain the *status quo* or as a spur to revolution. Fisher points out that the written word can be a strong conservative force so long as its precepts are observed; it can be a revolutionary force if the teachers object to the ignoring of precepts and call for a return to the fervour of the beginnings. He suggests that this is what happened with the *jihads* and with Christian calls for charity and social justice. Christians have generally objected more strongly than Muslims to mixing, but have been unable to avoid it; the mixers merely join one of the separatist churches or the more tolerant Muslims.

Since religion must be integrated into culture if it is to survive, religious conversion may be seen as a process of social change. Theories of conversion have generally either emphasised the individual, who is then segregated from

(19) 1958.   (20) 1967.

his former associates, or the group as a whole.[21] Some missions treated conversion as an individual response, but felt that it was very difficult for such individuals to continue to live in their old environment because they would be constantly tempted to continue their former practices. The solution was quarantine; they set up a separate village or part of a village where all the converts would live together under the supervision of the missionary or a catechist. This is a convenient way to socialise the new convert, but it is impossible to maintain such a system in a period of large scale conversion. In the enthusiasm of such a time, converts are not adequately taught or socialised and considerable mixing is inevitable. In a period of reform, there may be pressure to again segregate the 'true believers' to maintain purity of belief.

The alternate theory suggests that it is impossible to separate out individuals; the whole society must be permeated by the new values and culture even though this takes much longer before there are any conversions. If individuals are converted, they are urged to continue their old associations in order to convert their families and friends to the new faith. Islam has generally worked in this way, with each member rather than just religious specialists being responsible for spreading Muslim teachings. Although (or perhaps because) it has allowed considerable mixing with local culture, Muslim culture has permeated areas in which Islam is widespread more thoroughly than Christian culture has penetrated areas where Christianity has become prominent.

Explanation
Religion provides a focus for explanations of the good and bad fortune that both individuals and groups experience. It is particularly important in societies with a low level of technology because such a large share of their life cannot otherwise be explained.

> In the most primitive societies it is magic that gives man confidence in face of the difficulties and uncertainties, the real and imaginary dangers with which he is surrounded. . . . Religion develops in mankind what may be called a sense of dependence. . . . We can face life and its chances and difficulties with confidence when we know that there are powers, forces and events on which we can rely, but we must submit to the control of our conduct by rules which are imposed. The entirely asocial individual would be one who thought that he could be completely independent, relying only on himself, asking for no help and recognizing no duties.[22]

(21) See Beidelman 1974, p.242.　(22) Radcliffe-Brown 1952, pp.174–6.

Man's dependence on outside powers is first encountered in the child's dependence on his parents. The infant soon learns that he *can* depend on them (they will provide for his needs) and that he *must* depend on them (he cannot do without them and therefore must obey their commands in order to avoid trouble and misfortune). These two attitudes are carried over into his dealings with the supernatural world. Both magic and religion express the dependence of the community on the favour of more powerful beings. Manipulation of the spirit world through witchcraft and sorcery and the use of natural resources for divining and healing will be discussed in the concluding section.

It is obvious that some people's lives are marked by good fortune and opportunities for success whereas others seem destined for poverty and face ill-fortune no matter how hard they try. Religion is often used as a means of justifying the social and political order. Success may be legitimated as a sign of predestination to heaven or virtue in a past or present life; failure suggests that God or the ancestors are displeased or that one is being tried in order to earn a heavenly reward.

Many attempts have been made to demonstrate the role of religious attitudes and religious activities in men's desire to achieve success and avoid failure. The best known of these is Weber's theory that Calvinism was essential to the rise of capitalism in Western Europe. The key to the Calvinist spirit (or Protestant ethic as Weber called it)[23] is the belief that the diligent pursuit of gain is a virtuous thing, linking material and spiritual success. Whereas Catholic and Lutheran doctrine had encouraged members to passively accept their position in society in the hope of a future reward, Calvinists were taught that they were called to achievement and must make the most of any opportunities. There should be no religious withdrawal from the world because salvation must be won in the world; their reward would come both in this world and the next. It was a matter in which each individual stood alone – the community could not help or intercede. The anxieties of daily life were to be overcome through self-discipline and dedication to duty. Convinced followers of Calvin avoided entertainment and practised thrift and sobriety, which gave them economic advantages over their more easy-going competitors and made many of them leaders in the development of industrial capitalism.

Weber's theory has been widely criticised for overlooking widespread capitalism before the development of Calvinism and in many non-Christian areas of the world and for ignoring many economic and intellectual factors which promoted industrial capitalism during the period of early Calvinism.

(23) 1930.

Nevertheless, the connection between religious values and economic activities has proved a fruitful area for study. If one wants to examine why some people have been more active traders and entrepreneurs than others or why some people have been more ready to accept changes which have implications for social mobility, it is often useful to include religious beliefs as an independent variable. Those who believe that fate determines one's place in the world and that there is no chance for an individual to overcome his fate are unlikely to take risks to improve their position. Others who believe that God, the ancestors, or lesser spirits can be propitiated or cajoled into helping an individual to succeed may carry this manipulative attitude into their dealings with their fellow men and put considerable effort into making the most of their opportunities.

Both Hart and Parkin[24] found that conspicuous generosity is an important component of successful entrepreneurship in Africa. Some asceticism is necessary to accumulate capital and expand the business, but those who do not share some of the proceeds with kinsmen may lack support at a vital moment. Marris and Somerset[25] suggest that the influence of ideology and religion on economic achievement in Africa is very complex. Frustration and a sense of relative deprivation seem to be as important as religious motivation in the success of the East African businessmen they studied. Sometimes moral behaviour is justified as contributing to economic achievement rather than the other way round. (Drinking wastes money which should be put into the business.) Jehovah's Witnesses in Zambia have been a prominent example of a religious group which has prospered economically;[26] but, as with the Asians of East Africa, the Witnesses seem to have profited by the sense of community resulting from their marginal position in the local society rather than from values stemming from their religion *per se*. There is considerable evidence that new converts are often concerned to escape societal constraints; they should therefore be oriented toward change and able to cope with the risks of entrepreneurship. More research needs to be done on businessmen who are second or third generation members of their religion rather than recent converts.

There have been many cases where men have used religious means to explain and work for change in a political situation. Religious activities can be used as an outlet for social mobility and expression of aspirations in areas where political activity has been forbidden. An early study of this phenomenon is the classic by Sundkler[27] on the independent churches of the South African Zulu. He shows that the great proliferation of separatist churches in South Africa was a response to apartheid and the lack of opportunity for

24 In Goody 1975; 1972. (25) 1971, pp.79–84. (26) Long 1968. (27) 1948.

political and civic activity there. Potential leaders gravitate to religious roles because no other legitimate leadership roles are available. This has been noted in other parts of Africa, but is only part of the explanation because separatism has continued to grow in both East and West Africa since independence (see below).

The most notable case of the combination of religious separatism and nationalist feeling has been the growth of Kimbanguism in what is now Zaire. Simon Kimbangu taught for only six months before he was imprisoned by the Belgian authorities; he died in gaol. His followers were dispersed, but this only served to spread Kimbanguism throughout the territory. At its inception Kimbanguism was not concerned with a political, anti-colonial struggle, but the emphasis on a religion for blacks led the colonial government into a self-fulfilling prophecy – the action they took caused the spread of precisely the attitudes they feared. As Kimbanguism grew, the treatment of its founder made people more aware of colonial oppression than they might otherwise have been; several of the leaders were prominent in Abako, the nationalist party of the Kongo. Since independence, it has dropped its political side and become similar to most Protestant mission churches except for its lack of ties to a world church; this was remedied by joining the World Council of Churches.[28]

Belief systems

It is often claimed that change from a 'primitive' to a 'modern' society is accompanied by change from belief in witchcraft and magic to adherence to scientific principles. In reality, people in all societies have a variety of beliefs which they apply as the situation seems to demand, some of which can be classified as magic or witchcraft and some as science. These beliefs are often demonstrated in attitudes toward health and sickness, since here man faces his most fundamental problem of life and death. It was shown above that religion functions partly to help man overcome fears and insecurity; so also beliefs about witchcraft and magic are a response to the dangers and difficulties which men experience. Much can be learned about the social structure of a people by examining the patterns of witchcraft accusations and the type of action undertaken when a member of the primary group falls ill.[29]

(28) Banton in Middleton 1970. (29) See Mbiti (1969) and the section on Value Systems in McEwan and Sutcliffe 1965.

Magic and witchcraft[30]

Magic and witchcraft can be distinguished chiefly by their method. The magician attempts to coerce supernatural powers by performing certain rituals. He uses natural materials in specified ways (often accompanying his actions with verbal formulae) to affect a specified goal (make rain, cure a sick person, ensure success in business or an examination, restore harmony in a family). Some magic can be carried out only by specialists, but many activities of ordinary individuals could be included, such as putting something into the field to protect the growing crops from evil or hanging a charm on the bed to promote conception. If the magic is designed to attain an evil end (preparing potions to induce illness, death, failure of crops), it is known as sorcery. Sometimes the action of a sorcerer may be socially approved or considered socially neutral, as when his evil magic is used to kill another sorcerer or to protect property which has been attacked, but generally his activities are considered illicit.

Sorcerers tend to be men. Witches, on the other hand, are often but by no means always women. Whereas the material aspects of magic can be observed, there is nothing to see in witchcraft and because of this its reality has often been denied. Witchcraft is a power which is part of the personality of the individual, often from birth. It may be thought to have a material form, such as a python in the stomach, but this is never visible to outside observers. Sorcerers do their work deliberately, but witches may be unaware of their evil activities or of the fact that they are witches at all. Their activities are usually in their own interests, whereas sorcerers are hired by others. Witchcraft accusations are impossible to disprove and tend to have more serious implications for the individual concerned than allegations of sorcery. Both tend to arise in situations of conflict-ridden interpersonal relations. The most characteristic example is the accusation by a bereaved mother that her mother-in-law or a childless co-wife is a witch.

A person who becomes ill or has some other trouble often has a fairly clear idea of the proximate cause: an animal bit him or not enough rain fell on his fields. But this does not satisfy the more basic question: why me? Why wasn't someone else bitten? Why did the rain fall half a mile away but not on my farm? It is useful to blame such occurrences on witchcraft or juju. If the witch can be found, or the source of the juju uncovered, then the situation can be remedied and all will be well. Theories of witchcraft, identifying patterns which occur in many societies, are mainly psychological or sociological. Psychological theories concentrate on the use of witchcraft accusations as a socially approved form of aggression, a means to satisfy the

(30) Only a few of the basic principles can be discussed in this brief introduction; a useful selection of the relevant literature has been included in Marwick 1970.

need for success and importance, and the result of child-rearing patterns.

Jahoda[31] found that both educated and uneducated Ghanaians used magic and feared witchcraft in many situations connected with actual or hoped-for social mobility. Appropriate charms could be bought to improve performance at work and in examinations, to influence superiors to look favourably on the purchaser and miraculously to inform him of questions to be asked. Belief that those who are successful attract envy and witchcraft helps individuals explain their failure to advance as due to outside causes. This may also facilitate the break between a successful man and his kinsmen; some secondary schoolboys in northern Ghana believe that returning to their villages after completing the sixth form could endanger their lives.

Although evidence is as yet limited, it appears that supernatural beliefs, especially in witchcraft, are related to child-rearing patterns. The rage of a child who has been displaced by a younger sibling may be a fruitful foundation for the belief that women are witches. As parents place less emphasis on the obedience and subordination of their children and make less use of threats that misbehaviour will be punished by supernatural beings, belief in witchcraft may decline.

It is important to note the characteristics of the accuser as well as those of the victim and the witch.[32] A wealthy person may demonstrate his importance by claiming to be a witchcraft victim, or he may be accused of witchcraft by others who resent his treatment of kinsmen or his power. In most societies, one is expected to remain on good terms with kinsmen; witchcraft accusations provide an opportunity to express hostility and aggression which has no other socially approved outlet. The accused witch is almost always someone in the primary group; aggression toward outsiders can be expressed in other ways.

Sociological explanations usually relate witchcraft to social norms or social change and tension. (These necessarily overlap somewhat with each other and with psychological explanations.) The witch can be held up as a prime example of someone deviating from the society's norms, thus warning people of moral precepts which they are expected to follow. If the witchcraft is seen as the result of improper behaviour in the past (an old lady has caused her nephew trouble because he ignored her when she needed help), then the accusation is a projection of guilt and remedying the situation requires positive action to uphold moral values on both sides. Alternatively, accusations can be seen as reflections of the role conflicts and tensions of the society (disagreements between a man and his heir, between co-wives, between the successful and the unsuccessful).

(31) In Lloyd 1966.   (32) See Marwick 1970, p.285.

Nadel,[33] for example, shows that among the Nupe accusations of women by men and attempts to control witches by the male secret society are due to the greater economic success of women traders than of their farming husbands. The sex antagonism expressed in witchcraft beliefs is a projection of the male wish for superiority in a situation where there is little scope for practical remedies. The Gwari, a neighbouring people who are similar to the Nupe in many respects but lack this source of tension, show no sex antagonism in their witchcraft beliefs; either males or females may be witches, accusers, or victims.

Whereas magic may be used on strangers, witchcraft is assumed to operate between people who know each other well. Hence, it is inevitable that a large share of accusations are of kinsmen. Comparisons between matrilineal and patrilineal societies show that patterns of accusations often follow tensions associated with the lineage system. Accusations are more frequent in rural areas than in towns because the close personal relations in villages give rise to strains which cannot be resolved in other ways. Crawford[34] shows that among the Shona kinsmen, workmates and schoolmates may be accused of sorcery; generally women and elderly men who are not chiefs are accused of witchcraft. The latter is a more serious allegation, but is more often directed at those who are less able to defend themselves because of their relatively low social status. Some Shona use accusations to mobilise public opinion against someone with whom they have a private quarrel, usually someone with whom they have considerable personal contact and who is of roughly equal status. One does not accuse a chief because public opinion might easily be deflected towards oneself. People in power are often held to have reached their position through the possession of supernatural talents and are therefore considered unassailable. The assumption that the powerful have access to supernatural sanctions is found in many other societies as well, such as the Tiv.[35]

In examining the role of witchcraft and magic in a society, it is important to separate what people say from what they actually do. Most people have some idea of a norm, but this is often quite different from reality. Many entertaining stories can be told of witchcraft and informants will state that witches are always women, that they are found only in certain types of cases or certain relationships, etc. But if one actually records accusations over a period of time, quite a different pattern is likely to emerge.[36] Statements about beliefs may give a useful idea of an individual's view of social structure, but the actual pattern of accusations will reveal more about how the social structure is functioning. If the norm states that men are never witches but in

(33) 1952.   (34) 1967, pp.278–90.   (35) Bohannan in Gibbs 1965, pp. 542–3; see also Price-Williams 1962.   (36) Marwick 1970, pp. 284–7.

fact they are often accused, this may indicate conflict over male social status, for example because they are exercising increasing dominance over women because of a spread of wealth from cash crops which only men can grow, or because some men are taking on new roles which clearly differentiate them as more successful than the rest of the community.

Science[37]

Men's approach to medicine may be either magical or scientific, so before discussing healing it is necessary to clarify the difference between these. Both magic and science arise from an attempt to explain the 'whys' of human experience, to share some orderly view of the complexity of daily life. Horton points out that common sense is enough for handling most occurrences, but unusual circumstances require going beyond common sense to theory. This theory may be religious, magical, or scientific; which type and level of theory is chosen depends on the need of the moment. For instance, the aid of local spirits of fertility may be solicited at the start of the growing season, but if some danger threatens the existence of the whole society sacrifices would be made to the supreme being.

Horton suggests that the basic difference between the magical theories of traditional cultures and the scientific thinking used in industrial cultures is the latter's relative openness to new ideas and options. An outside observer may wonder why people continue to rely on magical explanations which can be proved ineffective; the answer is not stupidity but a lack of alternative ways of conceptualising. In a closed society, where everyone shares the same world view, there may be no words for expressing doubt about established beliefs or any possibility of imagining some other view of reality. In scientifically oriented cultures, on the other hand, ideas tend to be separated from reality; abstractions of almost infinite variety are possible. This gives the thinker an opportunity to test out a series of models until he finds one that fits his particular situation and encourages him to continue testing whenever the facts he observes do not seem to fit his theory – the classic case of scientific thinking.

A member of a closed society whose theory does not provide satisfactory results has no alternative theory, so he must rely on secondary elaboration. This involves the use of *ad hoc* excuses for failure. Rather than admitting that shrines are useless or that diviners cannot cure an illness, one can suggest that this particular diviner is a cheat, that the ritual was not performed correctly, or that more than one spirit is involved in the trouble and therefore further action is necessary. People pay for more elaborate ceremonies in an attempt

(37) This section is largely a summary of some of the points raised by Horton 1967.

to get a full answer to their problem; they do not think to count the number of cases of various types that the diviner is able to help and the number of his failures. The scientist, on the other hand, remains sceptical about all beliefs, since most are subject to change and improvement; if the theory fails to predict as it should it is demoted or abandoned. Failures are not explained away, but investigated as to their cause.

The magical thinker cannot admit that there is no known answer to any problem which he considers important; such an admission would imply that the theory is inadequate and would cause extreme anxiety and a threat of chaos. The scientist's world view is far less comprehensive, and he readily admits that there are many important things which he cannot (as yet) explain. Since his theory is open to change, he can hope that an answer will eventually appear. In addition, the scientist holds that some situations are accidental rather than predictable. For example, a driver may skid and crash. A scientist would suggest that an 'accident' had happened because the road was wet or because the driver was not thinking about where he was going. For a man who accepts only a magical system of thought, coincidence or chance is not an acceptable explanation. There must be a 'true' reason which can be found if one tries hard enough. Perhaps the driver is being punished by his ancestors for not sending enough money to his aged parents or perhaps someone with whom he is in conflict arranged for a sorcerer to cause the 'accident'. Why did only this man crash?

Magic and scientific systems of thought have been described as ideal types; individuals and societies often utilise both, and are therefore best seen as somewhere on a continuum between the two extremes. Horton suggests that the gradual change from a closed to an open society is largely the result of the spread of literacy and extensive interaction between people of different cultures. If beliefs are not written down, gradual changes will not be noticed and the impression that they are comprehensive and immutable can be maintained.[38] However, once beliefs are written down, changes over time cannot be hidden and the possibility of alternatives must be faced. Similarly, if people have only a very limited contact with anyone holding other beliefs they may remain unaware of alternatives. This includes situations where people trade with each other but where the traders are effectively segregated from the local society, as happened with the establishment of *zongos* for strangers in West African towns and enclaves for Asian traders in East Africa. However, in the heterogeneous towns which have arisen in recent years, migrants from many places mix on terms of equality and have an opportunity to learn about each other's beliefs. This generally leads to greater openness,

(38) Goody and Watt 1963.

but the individual who has begun to question his former world view may still feel more comfortable with it than with any alternative. He tends to settle for a mixture, relying on magical or scientific explanation according to which seems to best fit a particular situation. The same applies to the large numbers of Africans who have acquired scientific ideas from Western education or the radio.

People in scientifically oriented cultures are seldom completely divorced from patterns of magical thought. These are in fact often applied at the 'common sense' level because they give a feeling of security which the acceptance of continual change in the interests of 'progress' lacks. They often yearn for the 'good old days' just as much as elders in traditionally oriented societies do, fearing that the scientists' future may not be an improvement on the present. Nearly everyone explains ordinary events in terms of familiar categories; the 'scientific' explanations of ordinary people are often a folk version which owes little to the scientist and has never been personally tested. Even scientists often think magically. Failure to prove an hypothesis, for instance, may be attributed to using the wrong instruments rather than to its falsity. Specialists may be as convinced as the elders that their beliefs are absolute (the great advance that is expected certainly exists and is just waiting to be discovered) and just as immersed in their terms and techniques, preventing them from seeking solutions from an entirely new point of view. Thus, it is probably better to look at the way an individual arrives at his conclusions in a particular situation rather than characterising the beliefs of a whole society as scientific or magical.

Healing

Illness and death represent very serious sources of insecurity for most people, because they are important for continued well-being and even existence yet are subject to many influences not under an individual's control. It is therefore not surprising that religious ideas are carried over into the medical sphere. Scientific and magical belief systems are reflected in one's response to serious illness. The man who is ill (or whose kinsman is ill) has several possibilities in seeking a cure. He may consult a local herbalist, diviner, oracle or medicine shrine; try a healing church; or go to a hospital or clinic for 'modern' medicine. Some try several of these. People in isolated areas may lack this range of choice, but if the patient is not too ill there is always the possibility of a trip to a famous prophet, shrine or hospital. There is considerable travelling for medical purposes in most parts of Africa.

Most peoples have traditionally seen illness as due to supernatural causes and as having moral and social implications. Healing, therefore, requires propitiating the spirits and improving social relationships within the group.[39] It can often be shown that the sick man has committed some offence or is in conflict with someone. Treating his medical symptoms may not result in a cure because the more basic cause has not been attended to; the supernatural aspect of medicine is seen as more important than any natural aspect. While herbalists use biological means (which are sometimes as specific to the disease as any medicines dispensed in a hospital), they and their clients tend to see medicine as only part of the cure. The 'real' cause of the disease (in the spirit world) must be found, and appropriate action taken, often by seeking to reduce conflict within the patient's primary group.

Traditional medicine maintains its following because it provides what its users expect. For example, if the sick man believes that his disease is caused by something in his blood and he gets well after the healer draws blood, he is convinced that the method caused the cure. If he is treated to stop someone from bewitching him and remains healthy, his belief in the efficacy of the treatment is strengthened. If he becomes ill after doing something he shouldn't and becomes well after confessing and sacrificing to an offended spirit, again the results have supported his beliefs. Even users of Western medicine can interpret its practices in terms of traditional beliefs; a cancer removed surgically may be reported as a source of witchcraft. Young [40] shows that the Amhara of Ethiopia believe in varying levels of efficacy among healers and strength among disease-causing agents. Any failure to heal merely indicates that the agent is stronger than the healer chosen. This does not mean that traditional healers never carry out 'real' cures. They are sometimes able to provide more relief than Western-trained doctors, but on other occasions they do considerable harm by delaying or denying the opportunity for more effective treatment.

Partly as a result of the spread of scientific beliefs and partly due to the greater availability of Western medicine, many peoples now distinguish between diseases, some being considered more amenable to European medicine and some to local medicine. For example, the Ganda put pneumonia, influenza and smallpox in the European category because they were unknown before the Europeans arrived.[41] Faiwoo[42] reports that the Ewe distinguish between natural and supernatural disease. The latter is diagnosed when a disease is prolonged and 'does not make sense'. Doctors are useful for natural diseases, but priests or diviners are better for curing supernatural diseases. Maclean found that most residents of Ibadan, educated and uneducated, make use of both traditional remedies and hospitals. The latter are considered the best place for severe cases and diseases of sudden and un-

(39) Twumasi 1975, pp.8, 40.   (40) 1974.   (41) Zeller 1974.   (42) 1968, p.82.

explainable onset, such as cholera, acute infections, obstetrical complications and childhood diseases. Modern antibiotics are particularly efficient for these 'self-limiting' diseases where in the past recovery depended mainly on time and the patient's natural resistance.

Local medicine, on the other hand, is often helpful for chronic illnesses where Western medicine can offer little hope of recovery. It is also useful for simple illnesses such as the cold, which are easily treated at home and where recovery in a short time is likely whatever treatment is used. Treatment of mental illness by a local religious specialist is often more fruitful than committing the patient to a mental hospital. The personal attention of a healer in a fairly familiar environment gives the patient a greater sense of security than isolation from his/her family and the lack of attention which is inevitable in badly overcrowded government mental hospitals.[43]

As Western medical treatment has become more widely available and more accepted, there has been a certain amount of syncretism. Healers have begun to put their potions in bottles and sell them commercially, drugs stolen from hospitals are often on sale in the markets and injections have become part of the repertoire of healers who can acquire the equipment. Nurses and pharmacists often set up as independent practitioners, providing treatment which can legally be given only by qualified doctors. The government may attempt to stop such activities,[44] but often they receive considerable public support because of a shortage of official facilities and therefore continue to thrive.

Syncretism in the other direction (the use of local herbs by Western-trained practitioners and attempts to combine the best aspects of both systems for the good of the patient) have increased in many countries since independence, but are still rare. Imperato[45] shows that a large majority of Malian physicians and other medical personnel would support cooperation with *furatigui* (herbalists), but the physicians would refuse to cooperate in treating diseases with diviners, specialists in detecting witches and sorcerers, and Koranic teachers. At least some of the infirmiers and aids would cooperate with these as well. (Some lower-level medical personnel encourage patients to try a herbalist or healing church if Western treatment seems unlikely to succeed.) When the Malian traditional healers were asked about cooperation with doctors and midwives, the latter got more approval than the former and *furatigui* were far more ready for cooperation than the others.

Cooperation is partly a question of social status and prestige. Herbalists in several countries have reacted to the challenge from Western medicine by

(43) Maclean 1971, pp.78–9; see also Frankenburg 1969, p.581.   (44) See Janzen 1974 on Zaire.   (45) 1974, pp.49, 51.

forming associations and attempting to professionalise. The Dingaka (Society of Botswana Herbalists) has governmental authority to license traditional healers considered competent by the officers and is working toward the regulation of recruitment and training.[46] In many areas, recruitment is becoming a problem, as children who attend school are unwilling to spend many years learning the properties of herbs or rules for divination when the material reward is relatively low. Centres for the study of medicinal herbs in Ghana and Uganda add to the 'scientific' image of herbalists, and many healers now place less emphasis than formerly on the influence of magic and spirits.

Shrines and healing churches (and also hospitals) may be approached in a spirit of magic or science. If the patient expects health to return automatically and uses secondary elaboration to explain any lack of effect of the treatment given, he is relying on magical explanation of the healing process. This applies as much to the man who thinks any illness can be cured by an injection (without finding out whether medicine or plain water is being injected) as to the one who expects that a prayer from the local prophet or the killing of a chicken at a particular shrine will infallibly cure him. If, on the other hand, he is quite willing to test a series of methods until he finds one that works (making a sacrifice at a shrine and then seeking medicine from the nearest out-patient clinic, for instance), he is taking a scientific approach to his cure. This is particularly true of the man who keeps track of the best methods for curing various types of disease so that he knows which one he should apply to immediately if the illness recurs.

While one is based on Christianity and the other on local religion, there is considerable similarity in the procedures of healing churches and medicine shrines. In both, the patient may come for medical, psychological, or material help. He becomes, at least temporarily, part of a community which jointly takes up his cause. Serious cases live with the prophet or healer until they are cured or give up the attempt. The ritual differs more in detail than in meaning. Churches use prayer, sprinkling with water and anointing with oil; the prophet or prophetess of the shrine goes into a trance so that the spirit can give advice and/or animals are sacrificed in order to divine the cause. The patient is often asked to confess (essentially to give his interpretation of the origin of his difficulties) and some offering is expected in thanksgiving for the help received. A sacrifice to the spirits after the admission of guilt is particularly useful in cases of psychosomatic illness, and in taking action to restore harmony to his social life the patient gains the psychological peace he needs.[47]

(46) Ulin 1974.   (47) Field 1960; Baeta 1962; Twumasi 1975; Hastings 1976.

Popular shrines and churches may spread from one area to another. The Tigare shrines of southern Ghana and Atinga shrines of Nigeria both stem from northern Ghana and the Cherubim and Seraphim churches found in many parts of Ghana and Nigeria originated in southwestern Nigeria. Those who are helped by the shrine or church may decide to join the community. Some shrines require petitioners to join the cult by making an offering and agreeing to obey its rules as a condition of obtaining help. This places petitioners under the protection of the spirit of the cult so that they will avoid a repetition of their trouble.[48]

There have been reports of an increase in the numbers of shrines, especially for witch-finding, as a reaction to social change. By the 1940s, most Asante villages had at least one shrine, usually established within the last three years and owned by a fairly successful local man who was too young for traditional office. Whether he ran the shrine himself or left this to a kinsman, the shrine could bring the owner both money and prestige. Many of the problems brought to the shrines required 'medicine' in the widest sense; something was wrong which needed righting. Often the diagnosed cause of the trouble was the non-fulfilment of some kinship obligation. (A priest or healer with a local clientele knows far more about the background and social relations of his patients than would be possible for a hospital doctor seeing hundreds of patients every week; the former is therefore more able to explain illness caused by stress in terms his patient can understand and respond to.) A confession of guilt at the shrine often relieves the tension so that the individuals concerned can continue to live together.

Ward[49] suggested that the numerous shrines she found in Ashanti were due to a growth in anomie,[50] resulting from social change in the area. There were many causes of disturbance in Asante society at the time. Cash from cocoa gave many men more independence of their lineage than had been possible in the past, but the spread of swollen shoot disease threatened their livelihood. Migration to new farm land also weakened lineage ties and some were arguing that matriliny should give way to inheritance from one's father. Though there was a feeling that 'the gods have lost their strength', Christianity did not provide much help. Instead, it also threatened family and village solidarity because members of the same family joined different groups and competition for converts divided villages. Attempts to make Christian festivals such as Christmas occasions to express group solidarity were not very

---

(48) Faiwoo 1968.   (49) 1956.   (50) This term was used by Durkheim for a type of suicide resulting from a lack of clear norms of conduct. It has since been used more broadly to mean a state of mind which may arise when the norms of primary socialisation are no longer useful and the individual does not know what is expected of him.

successful. Christian guidance on family relations was not considered useful by the matrilineal Asante and the Christian interpretation of economic problems and illness was unsatisfactory to them.[51]

Goody [52] criticised Ward's interpretation on two points. First, there are medicine shrines in many areas which have had much less social change than Ashanti. People are very pragmatic in moving from one shrine to another if the medicine or the gods seem to be 'weakening', so most shrines are short-lived. Fame brings more difficult requests and an increase in the chance of failure. Witch-finding took many forms in the past, such as 'carrying the corpse', which colonial authorities forbade, so the spread of shrines may indicate merely the need for different techniques rather than an increase in accusations. In any case, many of the confessions made at shrines are of adultery rather than witchcraft. The shrines are also a response to an increase in wealth in the area. Services must be purchased, and there are usually many people willing to use ritual means for disposing of surplus wealth. *Safis* (charms containing verses of the Koran) sold to Muslims serve the same purpose.

Second, and more important, Goody holds that there is no empirical evidence that social change necessarily increases misery or anomie. Anthropologists and sociologists are often committed, consciously or unconsciously, to the *status quo*, since it is easier to theorise about relationships which remain fairly stable than about changing norms. Neither social scientists nor the general public are well informed about the past, and both tend to assume that the 'good old days' were a golden era. But they may be very wrong in this. For the Asante, former times included a bare subsistence standard of living for almost everyone, plantation and domestic slavery, frequent warfare and large-scale executions to provide companionship for a dead chief. The twentieth century has certainly brought the majority increased personal and material security. Though improvements in psychological satisfaction are more difficult to measure, he feels that an increase in anomie has certainly not been proved. Since there is no evidence on the level of anomie in the past and very little data which can be used for measuring it today, arguments about change over time cannot be fruitful.

Similarly, because no one counted or classified witchcraft accusations or the use made of magic in the past, there is no way to assess whether these have increased or decreased over time. What can be said is that the introduction of new methods for handling illness and the disruption of social relationships have largely been assimilated into traditional beliefs. Individuals treat each case separately and are quite prepared to try a variety of methods

(51) Williamson 1965. (52) 1957.

until a solution is found. There are still many matters over which a layman, or even a specialist, has little control, and this serves to increase societal tolerance of many varieties of healers. Although some sects which emphasise healing proscribe the use of all medicines, not all of their members are willing to rely on prayer alone if an illness appears serious. The same applies to devotees of a shrine cult and, in reverse, to those trained in scientific forms of medicine. An open belief system implies knowledge and use of alternatives.

Formal organisation

The amount of formal organisation and the authority patterns which accompany a set of religious beliefs and practices reflect the routinisation of charisma and the size of the group involved. When religion is a family affair under the leadership of the father, no special organisation is necessary. When an institutionalised church has adherents in many nations whose efforts must be coordinated, a complex bureaucracy is certain to develop. Some religions, such as Islam, which emphasise the individual or the small group, have little or no central authority. Others, such as Catholicism, emphasise community and centralised authority and exhibit much more formal organisation.

Churches, denominations and sects represent somewhat different approaches to religious organisation. Any religious group may be referred to as a church, but this term is generally reserved by sociologists for religious organisations which are highly institutionalised, with recruitment mainly by birth, and have a well developed hierarchy, routinised participation by ordinary members and relatively full integration into the society of which they are a part. The Catholic Church in Italy or Spain is the most obvious example. Denominations are chiefly found in societies practising religious pluralism where political and religious institutions are clearly differentiated, for example, Baptists, Methodists and Ismailis in East Africa. As with churches, membership in denominations is usually through the family and may involve only a low level of personal commitment.

Like denominations, sects survive best in pluralist societies. They are essentially voluntary and lay-oriented, with a highly committed membership which often emphasises withdrawal from the society, asceticism and/or mysticism and personal interaction with God (Tijaniyya and Madhi Muslims, Church of the Lord, Legio Maria). Sects may be hostile to secular society and the state, especially if the latter is strongly connected to a church.[53] For

(53) Troeltsch 1931; Broom and Selznick 1970, pp.425-7.

this reason, members of sects have often been persecuted. The Zambian Government has forcefully suppressed the Lumpa Church because its members refused to pay taxes; the Government of Malaŵi has taken similar action against the Jehovah's Witnesses. Sects usually arise by schism from churches and denominations. Some later become denominations; the charisma of their leaders is routinised as they grow and lose their isolation from the surrounding society.

Patterns of authority

Churches and denominations are large-scale organisations and, as such, generally have a considerable bureaucracy. Most church matters are handled by specialists, with a trained clergy as the chief decision-makers. Universalist criteria are emphasised and top leaders in each country maintain regular contacts with their colleagues in other parts of the world. This contact, and the greater control from the top which it promotes, has increased with recent improvements in transportation. This means that local branches of the church have less autonomy and scope for innovation than formerly.

At the local level, the congregation may be led by an elder, pastor or priest. Sects, which operate mainly at the local level, may also be led by a prophet. The pastor or priest is most characteristic of churches or denominations. He is specifically trained for his clerical duties, often for many years. His work involves administration, conducting services, and preaching in order to instruct members in church discipline. He may also be active in providing social services for members or potential members: running schools or clinics, visiting the elderly and the sick, etc.

Beidelman [54] points out that European missionaries were at first explorers and pastors over small communities. But as the numbers of converts increased they became increasingly separated from contact with ordinary people. Where charismatic preaching had been highly prized, administrative skills and the ability to keep records came to be more important. Catechists, clerical staff, trained teachers and medical personnel took over many of the tasks formerly performed by the missionaries. This task specialisation has largely been continued by local clergy, though in poorer churches the pastor's role is probably more diffuse than in those which can afford large scale organisation.

There is an interesting parallel here between the pastor and the nurse. Both are usually attracted to their occupations because they wish to work closely with people, to help them. But with success come increasing administrative tasks at the expense of personal contacts. Neither occupation attracts

(54) 1974, p.243.

the sort of person who prefers administration or supervision, with the result that those who rise to the top are often doing jobs for which their training did not prepare them.

Elders exercise authority in denominations featuring the congregational rather than the episcopal style of leadership. Whereas the clergyman gets his authority from the bishops and the hierarchy of the church, the elder's authority comes from church members. He may lead services or merely arrange for a pastor to do so. He is responsible for maintaining harmony among members and forwarding the needs of the local religious community. The prophet gets his authority directly from God through inspiration, visions, or dreams. He may act as elder and/or pastor as well, but in his prophetic role he is mainly concerned with catering for the needs of individual members through divination, healing and prayer. His is essentially a charismatic role, although if successful in attracting followers he may find himself becoming an administrator as well.

Because prophets prefer to leave administration to others, or because they are unable to provide the level of organisation needed, a sect may have dual leadership, the prophet and one or more elders. Where the prophet is a woman, as in the Lumpa Church of Zambia, administration is often taken over by male kinsmen. [55] Since enthusiasm is an important factor in attracting and keeping members, sects are inherently unstable and many last only a short time. Competing prophets arise within the group. These attract followers of their own and either set up branches or separate sects depending on the warmth of their relationship with the original prophet. However, neither prophetic nor gerontocratic authority is an adequate base for hierarchical relationships. Even sects which develop several branches generally have only a very simple organisational structure; each branch maintains considerable autonomy and resists attempts of the centre to exercise over-all authority. There is a loose coalition of peers rather than a tight, hierarchical authority. Where a trained clergy is introduced, on the other hand, hierarchical relationships beyond the boundary of the local congregation are possible. The organisation becomes more complex and integrated.[56]

The type of authority which is developed is also related to the level of literacy of the members. Peel[57] shows that the differences between the Cherubim and Seraphim and the Christ Apostolic independent churches in Nigeria can be traced to the fact that the founders of Cherubim and Seraphim had very little literacy or experience of bureaucratic organisation, whereas the Christ Apostolics had more education and took over the organisational forms of the Faith Tabernacle church of the United States,

(55) See Rotberg 1961.　(56) Horton 1971, pp.89–90.　(57) 1968.

which furnished early guidance. The Cherubim and Seraphim emphasise 'God's unwritten words'; beliefs and practices are easily adjusted to new inspiration and needs. Christ Apostolic pastors, on the other hand, preach a written doctrine which is tied to the period when the group was founded. Thus the authority of a trained clergy, based on written documents, produces a relatively static set of beliefs which may need periodic reform movements to maintain; prophetic authority is constantly being reformed but is inherently unstable and thus liable either to disappear or be routinised.

Separatism
Churches and denominations recruit chiefly through the family, though missionaries sent to promote conversions in new areas must attract members in other ways. They have often used schools on the theory that it is easier to change religious beliefs before an individual has been fully socialised into the old beliefs. Sects, on the other hand, are often too new to have second generation members and too poor to run schools. If the group is to grow, it must attract adults as well as children and must discourage schismatic tendencies.

Most of the African independent churches have arisen through their founders breaking away from one of the established mission churches or from another sect, though a few have been started completely independently of other religious groups. The Ethiopian churches (so-called after the Ethiopian Orthodox or Coptic Church, which broke away from Rome in the fourth century) share the same beliefs and rituals as the church from which they have separated, their goal being independence of authority. Other independent churches, known as Zionist or Aladura, have made more extensive changes. They may be messianic, millennial, or nativistic in emphasis (looking to a saviour or the ultimate overthrow of colonial rulers and the return to traditional ways), or emphasise healing or a revival of Christian faith and fervour. Many have syncretistic elements, combining traditional and Christian beliefs so that their members feel more at home than in churches which are culturally European.

A wide variety of reasons have been given for the spread of independent church movements in Africa. These can be summarised as historical, political, economic, sociological, cultural, religious and theological. The study of the historical aspect alone (what happened in a specific case) is less useful than looking for similarities or patterns in a number of schisms. Political factors have been particularly important in South Africa, where independency has had to serve as a substitute for the political activity which is denied most of the population.[58] That this is only a partial answer is suggested by

(58) Sundkler 1948; see Welburn 1961 for East Africa.

the spread of independency in areas with less repressive regimes and since the achievement of national independence. Social discrimination is also important in independency movements in southern Africa. Economic factors appear to be more important elsewhere than in Africa, where sects attract not only the economically deprived but also middle status people such as clerks and civil servants who find the movement attractive for other reasons, including the opportunities they provide to exercise leadership. The fact that sects are often small and approximate primary groups makes them attractive to migrants.

In addition to all these non-religious factors, independent church movements represent attempts to find a mode of religious expression which is psychologically and sociologically satisfying, which expresses the need to make religion an important part of daily life and to get religious support in times of stress and insecurity. While theological factors are seldom very important in the break, independent interpretation of the scriptures can lead to disputes over the relevance of cultural carry-overs: is this point basic to Christianity or merely a European explanation of what the Gospels mean? In any particular instance, several factors may combine. For example, a personality clash may coincide with theological and cultural differences between the parties. Generally, the number of factors involved and the intensity of conflict generated affect whether the dispute is contained or a break takes place.

The largest study of African independent churches was made by Barrett. After examining the literature on about 5 000 independent church movements in thirty-four sub-Saharan nations or colonies, Barrett developed what he calls a 'Scale of Religious Tension' to explain why these movements arise and why they are more widespread in some areas than in others. This scale runs from 0–18 depending on the tribal position on eighteen variables:

(A) Traditional culture: (1) Bantu, (2) size of tribe (over 115 000), (3) polygyny common.
(B) Traditional religion: (4) importance of ancestor cult, (5) earth goddess.
(C) Colonial experience: (6) colonialists arrived over 100 years ago, (7) white settlers on tribal land, (8) national per capita income over £25 per year.
(D) Missionary period: (9) missionaries arrived over sixty years ago, (10) some scripture translated into vernacular, (11) New Testament published, (12) entire Bible published, (13) New Testament published over sixty years ago, (14) more than twenty-two ordained Protestant missionaries per million population.
(E) Current period: (15) population less than 50% Muslim, (16) tribe at least 20% Protestant, (17) tribe at least 20% Catholic, (18) independency

in an adjacent tribe.[59]

Barrett found that tribes with a score of five or less had no independency at all. There were few movements in tribes with a score of six or seven, but more than half of those scoring between eight and twelve and all of those with scores over twelve had some independent churches. The Zulu of South Africa had both the highest score (17) and the largest number of separatist groups. Barrett sees independency as basically a reaction to the attack of colonial powers and Christian missions on traditional African culture. He argues that it is greatly facilitated by the translation of the scriptures into local languages because this makes it possible for people to read and assess their meaning for themselves. Religion and family life are closely related in traditional society, and mission regulations against pouring libations to the ancestors, honouring the earth goddess and polygyny have often been ignored or led to desertion in favour of sects which permit these customs. The prominence of separatism in Bantu areas is explained in terms of a misunderstanding of Bantu culture (Barrett does not show that non-Bantu culture has been any better understood) or the greater suitability of lands farmed by Bantu peoples for takeover by European colonists. Insofar as colonial rulers and missionaries contribute to tension through the regulations and changes they introduce into the society, we would expect separatism to grow as their period of residence lengthens.

Size of population and income are relevant to access to the scriptures because the economics of publishing make it better to translate the Bible for a large rather than a small language group and it is impossible to sell copies to people living in a subsistence economy. The spread of the scriptures is also facilitated by a large number of missionaries, who provide education and urge Western values on their converts. Numerous missionaries usually mean the presence of several groups; separatism is much easier when disunity is already visible. There are usually few Christians in areas which are over half Muslim, so they tend to stick together. Rapid growth of Christianity in an area often gives rise to independency because new converts are not well instructed or supervised; it takes much longer to train clergy than to baptise converts. Finally, independent church movements seldom learn from neighbouring groups, but the same causes of tension are often found in adjacent areas and hence similar movements can be expected to arise.

Barrett has been criticised for mistaking scripture publication for the more important factor of education. The spread of literacy makes it possible for people to read the scriptures in whatever language they are published. There are also many prophetic and healing movements which place little emphasis

(59) Barrett 1968, p.109 and in Baeta 1968, pp.276–7.

on the scriptures but have arisen in response to other sources of strain not included in Barrett's list, such as economic depression. In addition, there are many schisms within the separatist movement, a development which the theory does little to explain. (Conflict theory is more useful here.) Thus, while the theory brings out important variables, it is incomplete.

Like their members, separatist movements have a life cycle. They are generally organised by young men and women, often with one individual as leader. If enthusiasm cannot be maintained, the movement ceases to exist. If it is more fortunate, the movement grows in size and the founding members gradually age. This poses two problems. Charismatic leadership must be routinised, when the founder dies if not before, and new members (including the children of original members) must be incorporated into the group. The original members often become more conservative as they age, so that young people feel the need to hive off and form their own 'reformed' church. (Pressure for the acceptance of polygyny, for instance, increases as there are more older members.)

Success in terms of increased size also brings problems. The sect form of organisation assumes that all members will participate frequently and actively through societies based on age or sex, discussion or Bible study groups, etc. Members generally want an opportunity to know other members personally. But a growing sect soon reaches a size where primary relationships with all other members are impossible. At this point, some members are likely to find an excuse to establish a separate group in order to renew the sense of community which is important to their religious experience. These groups tend to encapsulate their members, so that all their time is taken up with religious activities and they feel no need for friends outside the sect. This is quite different from the attitude of many members of the older mission denominations, who participate only occasionally and whose religious ties are only a small part of their social network. Another difference is that membership in a sect is not usually seen as a life-long commitment to a particular religious organisation; the community aspect is more important than dogmatic beliefs and a member can easily join another group if he moves to another place.

Membership
The last paragraph suggests some of the factors which differentiate members of sects from people belonging to the longer established denominations. The desire for community (especially among migrants to large cities) and for support in times of crisis are strong factors in recruiting the low income, insecure members of the society into the separatist sects. Peel[60] found that

(60) 1968.

members of the Aladura groups he studied valued their emphasis on healing and prayers for wealth and success; spiritual values, such as eternal salvation and peace (which are considered more central by the established churches) appeared to be much less important to Aladura members than 'this worldly' benefits. Many members joined an Aladura group after a friend recommended it as helping to solve a particular difficulty. For example, a woman attends a meeting to pray for a child, or that a son will pass his examinations or her husband find a better job. If the prayer is answered, or if she sees that other members have their prayers answered, she attends more regularly and finally joins, often bringing in other members of her family with her. This is much the same attitude as many people have towards customary cults; if help is provided in time of need, the recipient often attaches himself formally to the cult.

The sects also attract people who feel disinherited by the established political, economic, social, or religious systems of their societies and want a chance to participate fully and be important. Young people often feel frustrated because they cannot find the well-paid employment their teachers and parents implicitly promised them, they remain 'small boys' in the eyes of community elders, and/or they are being manipulated by politicians for the latter's benefit. Other people feel that the austere liturgy of the mission churches denies them the opportunity to express religious enthusiasm through singing and dancing, activities which are taken for granted as part of traditional religious expression. In a large, bureaucratic organisation under the direction of trained specialists, ordinary members are often expected to be passive spectators who contribute largely in cash; opportunities for close primary relationships are few. But in a small sect everyone knows everyone else and all are expected to participate actively. The poor craftsman or labourer or seamstress can be an elder on whom others depend. The liturgy is flexible and expressive. Total commitment is demanded.

Sects are also particularly attractive to women because they provide opportunities for leadership which are denied them in the more male-oriented established churches. Several of the most successful sects (such as the Cherubim and Seraphim, the Lumpa Church and the Legio Maria) have been founded by women. European ideas of the role of women brought by the missionaries have often meant a decline in status for women. Those with strong personalities who object to a subordinate role in a church find participation in a sect more satisfying.

Strong proscriptions against polygyny have driven many men from the mission churches; some who want to continue participating in formal religion can join a sect which allows polygyny. The dichotomy is not complete, of course. Many churches are tolerant of polygyny because the alternative would be losing many of the older and more successful men. Some sects forbid it, but this rule is easier to maintain if all the members are young and poor. Nevertheless, it is notable that most full participants in many church and denominational congregations are either women or children because the men have been disqualified.

Statements in the last three paragraphs are largely based on impressionistic reports; there is little quantitative information available on the social background of members of various churches and sects. The membership of a local congregation is affected by the type of people living nearby (most people attend a church in the neighbourhood), the age of the religious organisation (new sects will have mostly young members) and the style of religious activity which it favours (where full participation requires literacy, few illiterates will be attracted). Peel[61] presents data on a sample of members of four Ibadan churches. Members of the Cherubim and Seraphim had much the same background as members of the Anglican church in the sample, though the former had fewer well educated members. The African Church chosen had a relatively well educated, high-income congregation because it attracted members of the elite from throughout the city. The Christ Apostolic congregation had a relatively large number of older illiterate men in spite of its emphasis on youth and education; its mass appeal stemmed from frequent revivals.

The religious affiliation of a larger comparative sample drawn from two Ghanaian and four Nigerian towns is shown in Table 8. This suggests that it may be misleading to draw conclusions based on small samples from a single locality. Sect members are older, less well educated and more often in manual occupations in the Ghanaian than in the Nigerian towns. It is necessary to keep in mind differences between countries and between men and women; Table 8 holds both of these constant. (Patterns of affiliation can be examined for members of one sex and one country at a time.) For example, Nigerian men are more likely to be engaged in trade than Ghanaian men, but for both countries the proportion of men in trade declines from Muslims to Catholics to Protestants to members of sects. The difference between Muslims and Christians is much larger in Ghana, where a high proportion of the male traders were Nigerian Muslims; much of the spread of Islam in West Africa has been due to the activities of Hausa, Mande and Yoruba traders.

The evidence that sects attract relatively uneducated manual workers is stronger in Ghana than in Nigeria; Muslims are more likely than members of other religions to be illiterate. (Those who continue to practise their

(61) *Ibid.*, pp.194–8.

Table 8 Religious affiliation of respondents by country, sex and demographic background

	Ghana				Nigeria			
	Muslim	Cath-olic	Protes-tant	Sect	Muslim	Cath-olic	Protes-tant	Sect
Males								
Age								
15–24	15.2	33.6	36.5	20.9	36.1	43.8	39.4	48.2
25–49	70.7	61.5	59.4	69.4	55.3	52.3	55.6	48.6
50+	4.1	4.9	4.1	9.7	8.6	3.5	5.0	3.2
Total	100.0	100.0	100.0	100.0	100.0	100.0	100.0	100.0
N	270	366	756	134	581	1002	902	436
Education								
None	47.1	14.9	8.3	18.7	21.4	6.4	10.4	9.1
Primary[a]	25.5	73.7	76.4	72.4	47.8	67.7	61.4	73.6
Muslim	23.0	0.0	0.1	0.0	11.7	0.4	0.4	0.0
Secondary+	4.4	11.4	15.2	8.9	19.1	25.5	27.8	17.3
Total	100.0	100.0	100.0	100.0	100.0	100.0	100.0	100.0
N	274	369	756	134	580	1009	905	439
Occupation								
Manual	71.1	61.8	56.2	71.6	46.8	43.6	43.3	54.8
Trade	17.1	5.4	3.4	3.0	22.3	21.1	20.3	17.0
Nonmanual	6.9	17.6	29.3	14.9	17.9	20.1	24.1	15.0
None	4.9	15.2	11.1	10.5	13.0	15.2	12.3	13.2
Total	100.0	100.0	100.0	100.0	100.0	100.0	100.0	100.0
N	263	369	754	134	575	1008	902	440
Polygynous marriage[b]	5.1	4.3	1.0	6.2	30.6	5.9	12.0	10.9
N	156	115	295	65	242	306	325	137
Migrant	100.0	99.7	99.7	99.2	69.0	87.2	82.8	86.8
N	269	361	752	130	581	1014	906	433
Females								
Age								
15–24	29.7	45.3	44.9	33.8	36.4	58.7	50.5	45.8
25–49	58.8	48.8	49.4	57.0	54.2	39.7	43.8	48.5
50+	11.5	5.9	5.7	9.2	9.4	1.6	5.7	5.7
Total	100.0	100.0	100.0	100.0	100.0	100.0	100.0	100.0
N	148	203	528	142	508	499	539	262
Education								
None	72.5	58.8	43.2	68.8	58.3	29.0	33.9	41.0
Primary[a]	10.7	33.7	45.5	23.4	27.1	56.6	47.8	48.3
Muslim	15.4	0.0	0.2	0.0	8.0	0.0	0.2	0.0
Secondary+	1.4	7.5	11.2	7.8	6.6	14.4	18.1	10.7
Total	100.0	100.0	100.0	100.0	100.0	100.0	100.0	100.0
N	149	199	528	141	513	507	542	261
In the labour force	63.1	53.5	65.2	63.6	58.5	40.7	51.5	46.2
N	149	198	529	140	513	506	542	260
Widowed/Divorced	1.3	0.5	1.7	2.9	4.7	3.4	3.9	6.9
N	150	201	532	139	515	507	544	260
Sex Ratio	184	182	142	94	113	200	167	168

Source: Peil 1975c; sample censuses of Tema and Ashaiman in Ghana and Ajegunle (Lagos), Kakuri/Makera (Kaduna), Abeokuta and Aba in Nigeria.

[a]includes middle school in Ghana and secondary modern or secondary 1–3 in Nigeria.

[b]Men aged 30+. These are minimum rates, as some non-resident wives were missed.

248

customary religion also tend to be illiterate, but there were too few of these in the samples to include in the table.) Protestants tend to be somewhat better educated and more often in non-manual occupations than Catholics. An exception to this is the somewhat higher proportion of Protestant than Catholic women in Nigeria who had never attended school. Those who did, however, tended to have gone further than the Catholic women. The latter have the lowest rate of labour force participation in both countries. This may be due to pressure from Catholic priests for married women to remain at home. Seclusion of married women is practised in many Muslim areas, but they may become house traders in order to provide an independent income;[62] many Catholic women are evidently satisfied to remain dependent on their husbands.

The preference of polygynists for sects is supported but not confirmed by these data. According to the 1960 Ghana Census,[63] 32% of married members of African Christian churches had two or more wives, compared with 21% of other Christians, 28% of Muslims and 31% of those practising a traditional religion. The figures in Table 8 are based on all men over thirty, including those not currently married; since polygny is rare before the age of thirty, younger men were excluded. Members of sects had the highest level of polygyny in Ghana, but not in Nigeria. However, if only men of fifty or over are considered, the rates for Nigerian men go up to 54% for Muslims, 18% for Catholics, 14% for Protestants and 42% for members of sects. Polygyny increases with age in both countries and all religions, but the increase is greater for Muslims and members of sects which do not prohibit it. Forbidding polygyny by no means stops it (societal values are stronger than the values introduced by a new religion), but it does inhibit some potential polygynists.

The hypothesis that sects attract women, and especially insecure older women, is partly upheld in that Ghanaian women over fifty and women who were widowed or divorced were somewhat more likely to belong to a sect than to be either Catholic or Protestant. The low sex ratio for sect members in Ghana (94 men per 100 women) also suggests that sects are attractive to women, but this differential was not found in Nigeria. The relatively high proportion of Muslim women over fifty may be due to the propensity of Muslim women traders to remain in town even though their husbands have returned home, or to the unwillingness of Muslim parents to let their young daughters go to town; the better educated Christians find it easier to get away.

(62) Hill 1969.   (63) Aryee 1967, p.104.

Conclusion

This chapter has dealt with religion in both a narrow and a broad sense. From the sociological point of view, men's belief in the supernatural, in powers outside themselves, is partly shaped by their societal experience (or that of their ancestors) and partly an expression of the fear and insecurity of their daily lives. Religion may help to integrate a society, especially when all members share the same religion. Religious pluralism, on the other hand, has often led to conflict because people who hold that their beliefs contain the ultimate truth find it difficult to be tolerant of those holding other beliefs. Religious conversion has sometimes accompanied conquest, but in order to be firmly established it is necessary for religion to be assimilated into the culture. This is why the role of Christianity is questioned in many areas. The integration of a new religion with an old culture may come about through religious as well as through cultural change. Religious prescriptions which conflict with valued customs may be ignored: Muslims carve masks and drink alcohol and Christians pour libations and marry two wives. Religious specialists often deplore this syncretism, but ordinary laymen can only occasionally be stirred to reform.

The role of religion in social change has not yet had much attention. Most people have assumed that religion is a stabilising force, supporting established norms and rulers. While claims of supernatural powers by leaders may succeed temporarily, they are less tolerable in today's plural societies than in the more homogeneous societies of the past and they will be strongly opposed by subjects who feel that their own religious beliefs are being suppressed. The gradual introduction of new norms by missionaries and prophets raises less opposition and results in greater long-term change but, as there is considerable variation in belief and practice between individual members of any religion, the amount of real change remains an empirical question.

Men's attempts to control nature lead them to both religion and science. Laymen tend to trust the esoteric knowledge of specialists, whether these are prophets or priests, healers or scientists. The ritual used gives them confidence that their needs will be met. Threats of illness, war, or agricultural failure and disturbances in interpersonal relations give rise to calls for help; the type of help sought and the interpretation of the results depends on the world view of the individual. Few people engage in speculative or scientific thought more than occasionally, so failure of a particular demand is usually seen as due to some lapse of technique rather than a basic fault of the system used. Thus, magic and science continue to coexist in all societies.

Healing has religious significance because in illness and death man faces his greatest challenge. Most Africans who have a choice now use both old and new sources of medicine. There is some tendency for healers to secularise and professionalise their services in order to compete with European medicine, but practitioners of the latter are also coming to see that older methods have much to offer. Many people still prefer the personal care and understanding of the old system to the aseptic impersonality of scientific medicine. Spiritual and moral aspects of illness continue to be important whatever medicine is used, and illness provides a warning to examine and improve social relationships. The rituals of death symbolise the changing nature of the community and help it to remain integrated in spite of the loss of members.

Religious groups have many things in common with groups organised on other bases, such as education or occupation. Study of the nature of authority patterns, the development of individual organisations and recruitment of members provides indicators of the nature of interaction within the organisation and of its relations with other organisations. The small group of followers of a new prophet will probably have much closer ties to each other and more commitment to the group than members of a large and well established denomination. Religious separatism is rife in several parts of Africa. Initially, it was fostered by the opportunities it provided for independence from European overlordship; it has continued to grow because its organisational style is attractive to many migrants to the cities. Further comparative study of the characteristics of members of religious groups and of their participation in religious and non-religious activities is needed for a better understanding of the role which religion plays in society.

Suggested reading and discussion topics
1. Attend a meeting of a pentecostal or healing church and talk with some of the members. What is their social background? Why do they find membership in this group a rewarding experience?
2. If you or a friend of yours have changed religion, describe your (their) socialisation into new religious beliefs and practices.
3. Read Nadel 1952 and/or Wilson 1951 (both are in Marwick 1970). Is this type of theory useful in explaining witchcraft beliefs in your own and/or neighbouring societies?
4. Read some of the literature by or about missionaries in your area (Christian or Muslim). What efforts did they make to understand local culture and what effect did this have on their work?

8 The Cities

Since the majority of Africans live in rural rather than in urban areas, it might be asked why there should be a chapter on urban sociology and none on rural sociology. There are several reasons for this. First, the urban revolution affects in ,ome way the lives of every member of the society. Cities are centres of power and technology and thus play an important role in development of rural as well as urban areas. Insofar as cities hold the key to the future, it is necessary to analyse carefully the nature of urban society and the implications of urban growth for all citizens of the countries concerned. Second, the process of rapid urbanisation creates many social problems and questions which sociologists are expected to solve, or at least to study. Third, urbanism is a relatively new social phenomenon; the most spectacular growth of cities all over the world has taken place within the last 200 years, just at the time when sociology as a discipline has been developing. Sociologists, who usually live in cities, could hardly ignore the urban explosion on their doorsteps.

This chapter will first discuss the reasons for the expansion of urban life and the meaning of urbanisation, urbanism and the city. Next, migration will be examined as a phenomenon with implications for both urban and rural areas and for both individuals and communities. Finally, the place of formal organisations in the urban environment will be discussed. These have often been studied in Africa because they are held to be important in the socialisation of migrants to urban life.

Urbanisation

The rapid growth of cities throughout the Third World is probably the most important social phenomenon of the twentieth century. Mankind has experienced permanent settlement for about 10 000 years, but few people lived in places of any size even 200 years ago.[1] This was particularly true of sub-Saharan Africa. According to tradition, Kano, Katsina and Zaria (in northern Nigeria) were founded in the first century A.D., but they appear to have been small and unimportant until the growth of trans-Saharan trade in the fourteenth century. Timbuctoo was an important centre of trade and scholarship

(1) Davis 1955.

at about the same time; today it is a small trading and administrative centre. Gao, in Mali, was the Bambara capital in the seventeenth century. Ife and Benin, the oldest towns in southern Nigeria, were probably in existence by the twelfth century; Kumasi in Ghana was reputedly founded in the seventeenth century. Travellers' reports suggest that these towns may have had between 10 000 and 100 000 people in the eighteenth or nineteenth centuries, but since no censuses are available the numbers are suspect.[2]

There is much less evidence of indigenous urbanism elsewhere in Africa. From the archaeological remains of Zimbabwe in Rhodesia, it appears to have been a religious and trading centre with a relatively small population. Kampala lacked permanence as the capital of the Baganda kingdom; new rulers changed their court from one hill to another. Mogadishu, Mombasa and Zanzibar have long histories, but these were Arab foundations for trade with India and China. There is a string of small Swahili trading towns along the East African coast which have experienced relatively little growth. Dar es Salaam was founded as a mainland slave camp by the Sultan of Zanzibar. Nairobi was established by the British as a railway camp and many of the towns of Zambia and southern Zaire are the result of copper mining operations.

There are also many towns in West Africa which are due to mining or the needs of colonial administration. Accra and Lagos were only villages until new economic and political functions made them important foci of migration. But urban life has everywhere been the exception; the majority of Africans continue to live in rural areas. As late as 1950 only 9% of the population of Africa lived in towns of 20 000 or more inhabitants.[3] However, since 1950 and especially since independence, many African towns and cities have been growing at more than 10% per annum, often more than doubling their populations between censuses. A notable case is Tema, a new port and industrial city in Ghana, which grew from 14 937 in 1960 to 60 767 in 1970, an increase of 307%.[4]

(2) Bascom 1959.   (3) Davis 1955, p.434.   (4)When figures for growth are given, always keep in mind that it is much easier to show a high growth rate from a small base than from a large base, especially when there is an upper limit, and that a small per cent increase may involve more people than a larger per cent increase. For example, the population of Accra increased from 388 396 in 1960 to 564 294 in 1970, a 45% increase. This is much smaller than Tema's, though in absolute numbers the increase in the Accra population was much greater. A country which has only 5% of its children in primary school can double this (a 100% increase) by bringing the proportion up to 10%; a country which already sends 75% of its children to primary school has only scope for a 33% increase, as this would mean that all of the children attend school. Percentage figures are often chosen to make a particular impression; by checking on the base, absolute numbers and possible upper limit, you will have a better idea of what they mean.

Towns have arisen, in Africa as elsewhere, in response to four developments:

1 increasing population,
2 new forms of social organisation,
3 increasing control over the environment, and
4 improved technology.[5] These are both causes and effects of urbanisation; they make it possible for people to live in cities and create pressure for cities to develop. If the population is very sparse it will be impossible to get enough people together for large cities. At the other extreme, if the density of population is very high, it may be difficult to avoid urban development unless people have a very strong preference for rural life (as in Rwanda). It is likely that at least some towns of fair size will develop (as in southeastern Nigeria, where dispersed settlement has also been preferred).

But large population is not enough. Without improved technology and control over the environment it would not be possible to grow enough surplus food to feed city-dwellers or to transport it to them. Diseases would spread rapidly and kill them off. As technology develops, fewer people are needed for rural occupations and the surplus must move to the cities for work. New social institutions are even more important. A bureaucracy is necessary to organise the supplies of food and other goods needed by the townsmen, the communications within and between towns and the contributions of religious, political and industrial specialists in the more complex division of labour. In addition, new types of social relationships develop when people live in large, dense agglomerations which are unnecessary in villages where everyone knows everyone else. Early towns were small because the levels of population, organisation, environmental control and technology were low; modern metropolises are possible because of developments in all these areas.

Urbanisation may be defined either as the proportion of the population living in urban places, the process by which these urban places grow, or the spread of a manner of life and values-which have come to be associated with such places. For example, Zambia is more urbanised than Niger; 30% of the Zambian population and only 3% of Niger's population in 1970 were defined as urban. Urbanisation as a process is taking place at a faster rate in Ghana (where the urban percent grew from 23 to 29 between 1960 and 1970) than in Somalia (where the increase was from 20 to 24% (see Table 9). These are both demographic approaches to urbanisation; a more sociological approach will be discussed below.

(5) Hauser 1965.

Table 9 National and Urban Population by Country and City

Country	Total Population[a]	Percent Urban	Cities over 100 000[b]	Latest Population[c]	Earlier Population
Angola	6 400 000(75E)	10.8(70)	Luanda	475 328(A,70)	225,000(A,60E)
Benin	2 948 000(73E)	13.1(73E)	Porto Novo	91 000(A,72E)	69 500(64E)
			Cotonou	175 000(72E)	109 328(64E)
Botswana	574 094(71)	9.9(71)	Gaborone	17 718(71)	
Burundi	3 800 000(75E)	2.2(70E)	Bujumbura	90 000(72E)	46 000(60)
Cameroon	6 400 000(75E)	20.3(70E)	Yaounde	274 399(A,75)	159 647(A,69)
			Douala	485 797(A,75)	125 000(56)
Cape Verde	272 071(70)		Praia	13 142(A,60)	
Central African Empire	1 800 000(75E)	26.6(66E)	Bangui	238 000(A,73E)	111 266(64)
Chad	4 000 000(75E)	12.5(70E)	Ndjamena	179 000(A,70E)	
Congo People's Republic	1 300 000(74E)	23.8(70E)	Brazzaville	289 700(A,74)	145 000(64)
			Pointe Noire	141 700(74)	
Equatorial Guinea	300 000(75E)		Bata	27 024(60)	
Ethiopia	26 076 000(73E)	11.0(73E)	Addis Ababa	1 083 420(74)	432 000(60E)
			Asmara	296 044(74)	119 000(60E)
Gabon	500 000(75E)	32.0(70E)	Libreville	251 400(75E)	31 027(60)
Gambia	494 279(73)	14.2(73)	Banjul	39 476(73)	27 800(63)
Ghana	8 859 313(70)	28.8(70)	Accra	574 194(70)	337 820(60)
			Kumasi	345 117(A,70)	180 642(60)
			Sekondi/ Takoradi	160 868(A,70)	75 450(60)
			Tema	102 431(A,70)	30 261(A,60)
Guinea	4 400 000(75E)	11.2(70E)	Conakry	220 000(A,70E)	112 158(60)
Guinea Bissau	800 000(75E)	18.1(70E)	Bissau	71 169(70)	18 309(A,50)
Ivory Coast	6 673 013(75)	29.0(70E)	Abidjan	650 000(A,73E)	155 000(58)
			Bouake	120 000(68)	45 000(58)
Kenya	13 300 000(75E)	9.9(69)	Nairobi	630 000(A,73E)	266 794(62)
			Mombasa	301 000(A,73E)	179 575(A,62)
Lesotho	1 100 000(75E)	1.6(70E)	Maseru	20 000(75E)	14 000(66)
Liberia	1 496 000(74)	27.6(74)	Monrovia	180 000(A,74)	80 992(62)
Malagasy Republic	8 000 000(75E)	14.1(70E)	Tananarive	377 600(A,71E)	
Malawi	4 900 000(75E)	5.0(66)	Lilongwe	19 170(A,66)	
			Blantyre- Limbe	160 063(A,72E)	109 461(A,66)
Mali	6 308 000(76)	9.0(70E)	Bamako	400 000(A76)	130 000(60)
Mauritania	1 300 000(75E)	10.0(73E)	Nouakchott	196 800(A,72E)	15 000(65E)
Mozambique	9 200 000(75E)	6.0(70E)	Maputo	383 775(A,70)	130 000(54)
Namibia	852 000(75E)	43.6(70E)	Windhoek	76 000(74E)	36 051(60)
Niger	4 600 000(75E)	4.0(71E)	Niamey	102 000(72E)	40 172(62E)
Nigeria	79 760 000(73E)	21.0(70E)	Lagos	3 500 000(A,77E)	1 113 392(A,63)
			Aba	300 000(72E)	131 003(63)
			Abeokuta	226 361(71E)	187 292(63)
			Ado-Ekiti	190 398(71E)	157 519(63)
			Benin	121 699(71E)	100 694(63)
			Ede	162 617(71E)	134 550(63)
			Enugu	167 339(71E)	138 457(63)
			Ibadan	758 332(71E)	728 380(63)
			Ikere-Ekiti	129 581(71E)	107 216(63)
			Ila	138 612(71E)	25 745(52)
			Ile-Ife	157 178(71E)	130 050(63)
			Ilesha	200 434(71E)	165 822(63)
			Ilorin	252 076(71E)	208 546(63)

255

Country	Total Population[a]	Percent Urban	Cities over 100 000[b]	Latest Population[c]	Earlier Population
			Iseyin	115 083(71E)	95 220(63)
			Iwo	191 684(71E)	158 583(63)
			Kaduna	181 201(71E)	149 910(63)
			Kano	357 098(71E)	295 432(63)
			Katsina	109 424(71E)	90 538(63)
			Maiduguri	169 180(71E)	139 965(63)
			Ogbomosho	386 650(71E)	343 279(63)
			Onitsha	197 062(71E)	163 032(63)
			Oshogbo	252 583(71E)	208 966(63)
			Oyo	135 785(71E)	112 349(63)
			Port Harcourt	217 043(71E)	179 563(63)
			Zaria	200 850(71E)	166 170(63)
Rwanda	4 200 000(75E)	0.3(71E)	Kigali	54 403(A,70E)	5 000(63)
Senegal	4 400 000(75E)	27.0(70E)	Dakar	800 000(A,76E)	374 700(A,61)
			Kaolack	100 000(75E)	
Sierra Leone	3 002 426(74)	14.0(70E)	Freetown	274 140(A,74)	127 917(63)
Somalia	3 200 000(75E)¹	24.2(70E)	Mogadishu	230 000(72E)	170 000(A,66)
Swaziland	500 000(75E)	7.1(66)	Mbabane	24 000(75E)	13 803(A,66)
Tanzania	15 400 000(75E)	5.5(67)	Dar es Salaam	343 911(70E)	272 821(67)
Togo	1 955 916(70)	13.0(70)	Lomé	200 100(71E)	86 400(66E)
Uganda	11 400 000(75E)	7.7(69)	Kampala	330 700(A,69)	46 735(59)
Upper Volta	6 000 000(75E)	6.2(70E)	Ouagadougou	150 000(74E)	59 126(61)
Zaire	24 500 000(75E)	30.0(75E)	Kinshasa	2 008 352(74E)	901 250(67)
			Bukavu	181 774(74E)	
			Jadothville	102 187(66E)	
			Kananga	601 239(74E)	140 000(60E)
			Kikwit	150 253(74E)	
			Kisangani	310 705(74E)	229 595(70)
			Likasi	146 394(70E)	
			Lubumbashi	403 623(74E)	190 000(60E)
			Luluabourg	506 033(72E)	
			Matadi	143 598(74E)	
			Mbandaka	134 495(74E)	
			Mbuji-Mayi	336 654(74E)	
Zambia	5 000 000(75E)	30.4(69)	Lusaka	401 000(A,74)	262 182(A,69)
			Chingola	190 000(A,74)	103 292(A,69)
			Kitwe	292 000(A,74)	199 798(A,69)
			Luanshya	121 000(A,74)	72 260(63E)
			Mufulira	136 000(A,74)	107 802(A,69)
			Ndola	229 000(A,74)	159 786(A,69)
Zimbabwe	6 300 000(75E)	16.8(69)	Salisbury	569 000(A,75E)	386 045(A,69)
			Bulawayo	340 000(A,75E)	245 036(A,69)

Sources: A large number of sources have been used. Most of the data come from Population Reference Bureau 1975; U.N. Demographic Yearbook 1974; World Bank 1972; Davis 1969; and national census reports.

[a]The number in parentheses indicates the year to which the data refer. An E after the year indicates that the figures are an estimate. If the E is omitted, data come from a census.

[b]The capital is listed first and is included even though it has not reached 100 000.

[c]An A indicates that the figure refers to the population of the urban agglomeration (city and suburbs). Where the latest figure is for the agglomeration and the earlier figure for the city alone, a considerable part of the increase may be due to the difference in boundaries.

Urbanisation in the demographic sense comes about from the movement of people from small settlements scattered across the countryside (dispersed compounds, hamlets and villages) into areas of concentration (towns and cities) or through the growth of these smaller places through natural increase (the excess of births over deaths) and in-migration. Thus, between one census and the next a place may cross the size boundary and be classified as 'urban'. Most countries have established a minimum size for a place to qualify as urban. This often depends on the number and average size of towns in the country; it is usually lower in countries where the people are relatively dispersed and higher in countries where towns are more common. The rural/urban line is at 2 000 in Sierra Leone and Kenya; it is 5 000 in Ghana. In some countries, a political rather than a size definition is used; Tanzania classifies all declared townships as urban regardless of size and in Zambia places of less than 500 can be designated as urban. International comparisons are often limited to places of 100 000 or more population, which can clearly be defined as cities.

A rough classification of urban places can be made according to size. Those of less than 20 000 or 50 000 are probably best described as towns. Places larger than this but having less than 500 000 or a million inhabitants are termed cities and places which are larger than this are usually called metropolises. It doesn't make much difference where one draws the line; providing it is consistent when comparing several countries the same picture of relative urbanisation will appear (the countries will come out in the same order). Size is by no means the most important characteristic of an urban place, but it is useful as an indicator of other characteristics. (These are discussed in the next section.)

Cities can also be differentiated by their functions. Preindustrial cities were usually trading centres and also had political and religious functions (often the political and religious institutions were united in the person of the ruler). The paramount chief or king and his courtiers and servants were sometimes the only permanent residents of the town. Towns of this type can be recognised by the central position given to the palace and market. Where religion was a separate source of power, as in Islam, religious buildings share this central position. Administrative towns founded by colonial rulers also tend to have governmental buildings in the centre.

Other towns grew up as transport centres, surrounding a dock or railway station (Nairobi, Port Harcourt and Sekondi/Takoradi). Cooley pointed out that towns tend to be located at breaks in transportation (between sea and land, rail and road); goods must be unpacked and often broken into smaller quantities; workers are needed for loading and unloading, buying and selling as well as for transporting. Sometimes the addition of new means of transport promotes the growth of older towns (Mombasa, Kumasi); other towns by-passed by new transport routes tend to decline in size.

Far more African towns have grown as service centres than as industrial centres. The sometimes accidental location of schools and hospitals provides an impetus for growth because migrants come for jobs or to provide food, housing, etc. to those using the services or employed in them. The most characteristic industrial centres are the mining towns (the Copperbelt and Rand, the gold and diamond mining towns of Ghana and Sierra Leone, Enugu, Jos and Lunsar). As most of these mines are developed by foreign capital, mining towns have tended to be European in style, but more so in Central than in West Africa because much tighter civic controls in the former inhibited the development of other functions and the introduction of indigenous customs. The diamond mining towns of Sierra Leone are an exception, as individual diamond diggers, smugglers and a variety of hangers-on have made Kanema an almost ungovernable haven for small-scale enterprise. The old indigenous towns tend to have a high proportion of craftsmen engaged in small-scale manufacturing. Large-scale manufactur-ing has been developed chiefly in the cities, whose populations provide most of the customers for mass produced consumer goods. Tema is unusual in being developed mainly as a manufacturing centre and port; most other cities added manufacturing after their governmental and trading functions were well developed.

Capital cities generally have all these functions; one reason they are grow-ing so rapidly is that migrants are drawn to them by their political, adminis-trative, commercial, industrial, service and transport functions. Industries locate there because it is easier to contact government officials, to obtain raw materials and to sell finished products; electricity, water supplies and skilled labour are more likely to be available than in a smaller and more isolated town; all of this lowers the cost of doing business. At the same time, concentration of development in one city is likely to bring far more migrants than can be placed, leading to excessive competition for resources, con-siderable social costs in unemployment, housing shortages and strain on civic amenities.

One other aspect of urbanisation must be discussed here, the spread of urban norms and behaviour to the surrounding countryside.[6] That urbanism does not start or stop at the city boundaries is quite evident when one sees many cities where because of rapid growth the density of population just outside the boundary is as high as in the central city. In other cities, the boun-dary has been extended well beyond present growth so that several villages

(6) Hart in Amin 1974, pp.322–32 demonstrates this for the Bolgatanga area of northern Ghana.

are included in the official urban area. (Only 69% of the Sekondi/Takoradi City Council population was counted as urban in 1960.)[7] Insofar as urbanism is a way of life, it is not dependent on living within a city at all. Patterns of social relations which are characteristic of cities may be practised in rural areas, as when elite landlords living on their country estates maintain the same sort of social life, the same relations with the peasantry and the same division of labour as they would in town. The social relations of a cocoa farmer may be little different when he is staying on his farm than when he is living in his Kumasi house, and his values and norms will be the same; the main differences will be in the amenities and increased social contacts available to him in Kumasi. (The last difference is, however, critical.)

Insofar as living in a city does affect values and beliefs, these ideas can be picked up by migrants and brought back to their villages; over time the villages come to share some aspects of urban culture. Cities lead the way in fashions and customs, but many village folk (especially the young) are eager to hear the latest news and copy city ways. Women learn new styles of dress and new techniques of cooking and child-rearing; men demand that their village should have a school, electricity, etc. Societies which are started in town sometimes develop rural branches. New occupations come to the village, often practised by individuals who are urban-oriented (teachers, clerks). All these factors, and the increasing possibility of villagers making regular visits to towns and cities, decrease the rural/urban differential.

This differential is lowest in areas of old urbanisation where contacts are frequent. (Many people in Yoruba areas spend part of each week, month, or year living in town and part maintaining dual residence on their farms.)[8] It is much greater for villagers living a long distance from any town and when the town has a European political and economic structure and an industrial pattern of social organisation. A squatter settlement on the outskirts probably seems much more like home to the migrant than the blocks of concrete flats on a government housing estate, but in both cases his previous experiences of living among a large mass of people will affect his adjustment to urban conditions, and this, in turn, will affect the extent to which he passes on urban ways to the people at home.

What is a city?

Sociologists have developed many theories about what it is that makes living in a city or town distinctively different from rural life. The main criteria

(7) Ghana 1960, Special Report A, p.vii. (8) Lloyd 1959, p.46.

studied have been size, density, heterogeneity, segmented social relationships, mental stimulation, social disorganisation and community. These are not all equally important and they have received varying amounts of attention, but together they can help us to better understand the nature of urban life. Some towns, especially in West Africa, which have passed 5 000 or even 10 000 in population seem to have little that is distinctively urban about them; life appears to be much the same as in smaller places. It is necessary to keep in mind that urbanisation, as with so many other sociological variables, is a continuum rather than a dichotomy.[9] There is very seldom a sharp difference so that one can say that a certain trait is only (or never) found in towns. Attitudes and behaviour which are seen as characteristically urban are found in villages and hamlets and other attitudes and behaviour which are said to be rural are often found in towns, cities and even metropolises. But it is still useful to try to set out a rural and an urban ideal type, looking for the features which are most often associated with one or the other. This is what the urban theorists have tried to do. We may argue that we know of towns or parts of cities which do not correspond to the type. Nevertheless, if the majority of urban people have these characteristics whereas only a minority of rural people have them, we have a useful tool for studying the social concomitants of life in town.

Wirth's contribution

The most famous definition of a city is by Wirth:[10] 'A city may be defined as a relatively large, dense and permanent settlement of socially heterogeneous individuals.' The first part of the definition, size, corresponds to the demographers' idea of a city. This is not enough, because a great deal depends on the type of economic, political and social relations which go on in the place. For instance, if 3 000 farming families built their houses close together and walked out to their farms each day, we would not call the place a town. On the other hand, if a group of shops, a post office, church and school were built at a cross-roads, we might call the place a small town even though only 500 people regularly lived there. Size is the most convenient descriptive quality for comparing places and it is often associated with other, more sociologically meaningful characteristics.

Density is easy to compute once size is known, but it is not a particularly useful criterion now that modern transportation makes it possible for people to live a long way from their place of employment. Population density (the number of people per hectare or square kilometre) is usually high in pre-industrial cities because people must walk from one place to another. It

(9) Yusuf 1974 discusses eighteen categories in the Hausa continuum, between stark wasteland and Kano, the 'capital of capitals'. (10) 1938, p.8.

remains high at the centre of many African cities because even if buses or lorries are available for transport they are expensive. The density of Lagos Island varied from 25 900 to 54 400 people per square km in 1950 and some other parts of Lagos had nearly 58 000 people per square km in 1972.[11] When the central density becomes so high that rooms cannot be found there, new migrants often have to go to the outskirts for the cheap rooms which they can afford. In 1940, Miner[12] found about 6 000 people in Timbuctoo, which is not much more than 2 square km in size. This is probably a more typical density for a preindustrial city, and is still considerably higher than severely overcrowded farm land. (Parts of rural southeastern Nigeria have nearly 400 people per square km.)

Table 10 Opportunities for interaction by density of population*

Population density (Persons per square km)	Place	Number of persons within a circle of radius 8 km
1.5	Rural Zambia, 1960	314
362	Mbale Township, Uganda, 1959	73 545
12 840	Lagos Federal Territory, 1963	2 611 067

*Adapted from Hauser 1965, p. 11.

In order to examine the importance of these criteria for urban social relations, we will adopt Hauser's 'size-density model'.[13] The city can be considered an independent variable affecting the social relations of its residents through the pressure of increased density. If we accept that people spend most of their time within 8 km of the place where they are living, we can compute how many people they could meet within this 8 km radius (an area of 203 square km); this will vary with population density. Assuming that the density of population is the same all over Zambia, the average resident could expect to find only 314 people living within 8 km of his village (including the residents of the village). He would probably know all or almost all of them by name and have blood or affinal ties with many of them. Mbale Township is smaller than 200 square km in size, so it did not have 73 545 people, but

(11) Bascom 1955, p.448; Peil 1974, p.5. (12) 1953. (13) 1965, p.11.

there were more than one individual could know personally. It would be even less possible to know more than a few of the 12 840 people living in an average square km of Lagos. Sharing space with this many people requires a more formal type of social organisation than that which is common in rural areas: more rules, more bureaucracy, more formal social control and less dependence on personal relations. It also allows an individual considerably greater choice in his contacts than is possible when only a few people live nearby.

However, this does not mean that many 'rural' forms of interaction do not survive in the cities; they do. This will be discussed more fully later. The important point here is that early attempts to clarify the distinctive characteristics of urban life were often mistaken in over-emphasising impersonality and formality. More recent studies have shown that kinship is an important base for social relations in the large cities of industrialised nations as in old quarters of less 'modern' cities. Kinship and long-established personal ties may be less important in cities than in villages, but they are by no means uniquely rural phenomena.

Permanency is necessary to develop the patterns of social organisation which cities require. If thousands of people crowd into a place for an athletic or political event, it does not become a city overnight. Some villages have become towns within ten years because the mining of minerals or the establishment of a factory there brought large numbers of migrants seeking employment or setting up small businesses, but it is their intention of staying and the network of relationships which they develop to make the place in some sense a community and which gives it its urban character.

Wirth's last criterion, heterogeneity, is by far the most difficult to quantify. He does not specify what he means very clearly, but seems to assume that the cosmopolitan nature of urban life is due to the meeting in one place of individuals of different norms and values arising from different ethnicity, religion, and/or education, and on considerable division of labour and specialisation. As a result, cities are identified by their secularisation, tenuous relationships based on segmented roles and limited agreement on norms. These criteria apply most fully to cities in the United States and pose considerable problems for those examining the level of urbanism in long established cities of the Third World.

Mitchell[14] sets out what he calls 'external determinants of urban interaction, including various types of heterogeneity' which provide a more fruitful framework for examining the social situation in which many African migrants to the city find themselves. Mobility of populations between rural

(14) 1966, pp.49–50.

and urban areas and between one town and another means that social relationships are less stable than in rural areas; one must continually accommodate to new people. These new contacts are less balanced in age and sex structure, so roles formerly handled by elders or by wives must be handled by young men. In addition, one meets people of widely differing cultural backgrounds and may even interact on a regular basis with non-Africans. The need for predictability in relationships with strangers leads to categorising and stereotyping and, especially in work situations, to structured relationships in which roles and statuses are closely specified and not expected to differ from one individual to another. This is facilitated by economic and political differentiation within the towns, resulting in the development of new forms of social stratification. Interaction in the towns of central and southern Africa has been strongly affected by administrative controls, which have been moderated but not removed since independence.

Preindustrial cities

Although these characteristics are present to some extent in most African towns today, they are less evident in truly indigenous towns than in those which were established to suit European administrative, commercial, or industrial needs. Southall[15] and Bascom[16] point to important differences between Yoruba towns of southwestern Nigeria or old Sudanic towns such as Timbuctoo and Kano and the new administrative centres such as Nairobi and Lusaka. Southall adds rate of growth to a long history, because it should be easier to retain indigenous behaviour patterns in towns which are growing slowly than where growth is rapid. However, this distinction was more appropriate in the 1950s than in the 1970s because most large African towns are now growing very rapidly, as shown in Table 9.

The necessity of assimilating large numbers of migrants every year does sometimes interfere with the maintenance of established customs in old towns, but the prevalence of 'social relations as usual' in many new as well as old West African towns indicates that the important factor may be the type of political control exercised over the town.[17] Where colonial authorities or European businessmen had the authority and the desire to run the town according to European norms (often emphasising racial segregation), a different type of town developed than where only minimal attempts were made to impose alien forms. These two types of town are still apparent because independent governments continue to enforce some colonial regulations; where they exercise little control over development, social relations in the new towns may become more like those in old towns and rural/urban

(15) 1961, p.6.   (16) 1962, in Kuper 1965; see also Mabogunje 1962.   (17) Epstein 1967, p,.278.

differences will be expressed by most migrants as a continuum rather than a dichotomy.

However, different indigenous attitudes toward urban life must be taken into account as well as different civic structures. These may be seen by comparing the preferred use of space in various areas. Several West African peoples (such as the Akan, Ga, Hausa and Yoruba) prefer to live in large villages or towns and commute daily or as necessary to their farms. Others, such as the Ibo and Frafra, are similar to most East African peoples in preferring to live on their farms (shambas), visiting marketing centres as necessary.[18] Thus, one finds the East African 'empty nucleus' village, where there is a market place and perhaps a school, church, and/or post office but almost no residents except Asian traders and missionary or transient civil service personnel. Administrative centres are often considerably smaller in East than in West Africa because a fairly large proportion of the work force commutes daily rather than living in town.

Sjoberg[19] makes a distinction between the pre-industrial and the industrial city. He agrees that cities can be distinguished from villages or towns by a larger and more dense and heterogeneous population, but emphasises that the latter must include a wide variety of non-farming specialists and especially a literate elite. He argues that the forms of social organisation prevailing in early cities were a function of the technological base. The more surplus there was to support the elite, the more they were likely to be separated from ordinary people. Their children received a literate, religious training which allowed them to maintain control over the society. The rural peasantry and the urban lower class in these societies had much in common: poor living conditions and little chance for mobility. Difficulties of communication further isolated the ordinary people from the elite. Such occupational specialists as there were (chiefly craftsmen and traders) had separate streets or sections for themselves; elite housing was in a protected central position. Strangers were also segregated. Thus, interaction between peoples of different background or interests was minimised even though interdependency was clearly necessary. Age and sex differentiation were also important at all levels of the society.

It is important to remember that industrialisation and urbanisation are not the same thing (one can exist without the other), but an industrialised economy can have a powerful effect on the type of urbanisation which develops. Industrialised cities using technology based on inanimate power require different patterns of social organisation from cities which lack this

(18) Some pastoral peoples, such as the Ila of Zambia and Masai of Kenya, reject towns completely; others, such as the Fulani and Toureg of West Africa, have found them useful. (19) 1955, 1960.

resource. This makes industrial cities unlike preindustrial cities in many ways. Industrial technology and a highly differentiated market economy need an emphasis on achievement and universalism rather than ascription and particularism. Cities and their hinterlands are no longer autonomous, but tied into a world system which provides pressure for social changes which might not otherwise be accepted. The kinship, education and stratification systems must be more flexible to allow for greater mobility; social control is based on more formal sanctions and religion is separated from political power. Thus, it should not be surprising that social life in industrial cities is somewhat different from social life in preindustrial cities.

Many African cities are somewhere in between, with elements of both, partly because any change from earlier patterns is slowed by the large influx of less urbanised migrants and partly because the categorisation of the industrial city is somewhat of an over-statement, an ideal type which is not found in reality. Even the largest and most industrialised cities have areas where familism and particularism survive, often allied with a lower level of education and higher level of religious participation than is characteristic of people in other parts of the city. Mengo in Kampala and Isale Eko on Lagos Island[20] have been less affected by social change than other parts of these cities.

There has been considerable discussion as to whether the old Yoruba towns were really urban; a more useful question would be to what extent do they fulfil various criteria of urbanism? Demographically, there is little doubt; they were certainly large and dense, though not as large or dense as they are today. With the exception of those displaced by war (such as Oyo), they have been permanent. However, their heterogeneity was certainly limited. Almost all of the residents belonged to the same ethnic subgroup and shared the same norms and values, religion and education. There were a few political, religious and occupational specialists, such as the *oba* (ruler) and blacksmiths, but most of the people were subsistence farmers who did some trading or craft work during the dry season. Social placement was largely hereditary, through membership in a lineage. Some secondary relationships and selective associations existed, such as the *ogboni* and *egbe* societies, but most relationships were primary and informal. Because of difficulties of storage and the requirements of hospitality, the standard of living of rulers was little different from that of their people.

There is little question that these towns were critically different in many ways from the present-day cities of industrialised nations, but is this the comparison which ought to be made? It seems more useful to take an

(20) Southall and Gutkind 1957; Marris 1961.

historical, evolutionary view of urbanisation and to recognise that cities will mirror the level of technological development of the society of which they are a part. Urban social systems are never autonomous, but are linked to the social system of their hinterland. It can then be shown that the old Yoruba towns had much in common with preindustrial cities elsewhere (though there are some interesting differences depending on which cities are being compared) and that most of them have changed considerably in this century so that they now have many aspects which are recognised as characteristic of present-day urbanism. One can conclude, then, that they were the urban manifestation of their time and place and that life in them had some demonstrable differences from rural life; they also lacked some aspects of urbanism which are considered critical in distinguishing towns today.

Contemporary Yoruba towns, or at least parts of them, still lack some of these characteristics; most are largely homogeneous ethnically and have only limited occupational differentiation. Secondary relationships are still relatively unimportant. One might say that they are less urban than towns such as Lusaka or Nairobi, which have a different and shorter history, or merely that they represent a different type of urbanism. Similarly, one might say that Lusaka and Nairobi are less urban than metropolises such as New York, Tokyo, or Calcutta, or merely argue that these cities are different because urban life must develop new forms to make possible an agglomeration of several million people. Examining the nature of the similarities and differences helps us to better understand the nature of urban life.

Socio-psychological factors
If you ask ordinary people about the difference between village and town dwellers, many will reply in terms of personality: rural people are 'bush', unsophisticated, trusting, friendly; urban people tend to be impersonal, cynical, proud. They will point to the high incidence of crime and other types of social disorganisation in the towns. Even people who like urban life often think of cities as a 'bad' place, especially for bringing up children. It is the sociologists' task to investigate why urban life should cause these problems (or, if the accusations are not true, why such things should be believed about cities).

An early article by Simmel[21] presents a general approach from which to examine urban behaviour. Simmel argued that the personality of people living in cities is inevitably affected by the population density; an individual must make many contacts every day with people he doesn't know and whose behaviour he cannot predict, and he must constantly react to new stimuli.

(21) 1950.

He protects himself in a constantly changing environment by substituting intellect for emotion (thought for feeling); this is the core of his sophistication. He can have many interests, but none of them goes very deep; he may have many friends, but does not know any of them very well. The second aspect of urban life is the concentration on money. People move to town to make money, and timing and calculation are important because time comes to mean money. But this means that people cannot afford to act 'naturally' or spontaneously; each action should be rationally directed towards a goal: 'What is in it for me?'

As a result of these pressures, urban folk often find it easier than rural people to separate themselves from their neighbours. They have what Simmel calls reserve. This deprives them of some support (increasing their insecurity), but it may also provide freedom to choose whom to associate with, a freedom the villager lacks. The urban division of labour fosters individualism and specialisation. People form associations to overcome loneliness as well as to forward goals, but if these groups become large they again reproduce the isolation of the wider society. Alienation (the feeling of being powerless to affect the political, social, or economic system) is more often found in cities because people there are usually more aware of power structures (power is centred in cities) and of their relative deprivation compared to the elite (who tend to live in cities). Schwab[22] commented that 'in many Rhodesian towns . . . passivity, repression, and lack of gusto are the most striking characteristics of these African people.'

From alienation, or from poverty, comes a tendency to commit criminal acts. At the same time, because people in cities are constantly exposed to new values and norms, they may develop anomie, a normlessness or confusion about values which may make deviant behaviour seem acceptable or at least not morally wrong. Merton[23] suggests that anomie occurs when individuals see society as lacking order, lose faith in officials and friends as able or willing to help them and feel that it is impossible to accomplish goals which they consider important. Since people who migrate to cities are often more aware of their goals than those who stay at home and since the technological base of urban life encourages them to think that they can achieve these goals, the realisation that they are failing (in a society where success is highly valued) comes as a psychological shock, and they may try to stop this failure by turning to crime. Clinard and Abbott found that crime was increasing rapidly in East African cities as they grew in size and suggest[24] that initial adjustment to urban life and social isolation are probably more important than economic deprivation in encouraging young men to become involved in crime (see

(22) Replying to Epstein 1967, p.291. (23) 1957,. p.164 (24) 1973, p.127.

267

Chapter 9).

The strongest criticism of Simmel's ideas comes from recent studies of 'urban villagers', people living in long-established, low income areas of large towns who maintain strong social networks with their neighbours. Marris[25] found these patterns in central Lagos and Parkin's report[26] on a Kampala housing estate suggests that although social ties may be somewhat less close in this type of settlement, individuals are seldom completely isolated. Cosmopolitanism seems to be related to income and education in that those who can afford to belong to several clubs, buy books, travel, etc. are more likely to encounter new ideas and people than individuals who must watch every penny. The latter tend to take their recreation by sitting in the shade with a few friends and encounter less of the 'mental stimulation' which Simmel considered so typical of urban life.

There is also an element of personal choice here; freedom of choice must be considered an important urban characteristic. An individual may choose to seek out new friends and new experiences (this is for some the reason for migrating to the city in the first place) or he can choose to stay with the old ways, associating mainly with people from home, and thus avoid much of the strain of change even though he lives in a town. Mayer[27] distinguishes two types of migrants to East London, South Africa: 'Red' and 'School'. The Red migrants (the traditional Xhosa wear a red blanket) kept very much to themselves in town, orienting themselves toward home and following customary ways as far as possible. The School migrants (most had been to school) wore European clothes, made new friends from other areas and were generally oriented toward change even though few cut off their ties with home. (In South Africa, such a break would not be realistic.) Although the distinction may be less clear in other towns, it is always possible to find people who have chosen in this way, suggesting that urban pressures can be accommodated to individual needs. Generally, the more educated migrants are better prepared for flexibility, tolerance and impersonality as well as having language skills which make it easier to contact people of other background than their own. Strain is minimised because people can choose the level at which they participate in urban life.

An aspect of urban life which is harder to avoid is limited interaction in segmented roles. Southall[28] distinguishes urban life as

'characterized by role relationships that are more narrowly defined, more specific, more unequally distributed between persons, more extensively developed in latent role structure, more numerous as a whole relation to persons who are themselves living at a high spatial density, more fleeting

(25) 1961.   (26) 1969.   (27) 1962, 1971.   (28) 1959, p.29.

268

in their duration over time. In short, the passage from rural to urban conditions is marked by a rise in the density of role texture.'

People living in towns often know little about people they meet. One acquaintance is known only at work, another as a neighbour seen only occasionally, another as a fellow church member, etc. Farmers in a village know each other as whole people; seeing them through good and bad times over many years and knowing their wives, children and kinsmen. Such close relationships are possible in town, especially in groups of long-distance migrants who live together and drink together. But the majority of migrants spend relatively little time even with close friends. The fact that they have close friends helps to prevent alienation, but most of their time is spent in secondary relationships, with people who know and care little about them.

This, and the possibility of changing friends, makes status mobility easier than it would be in a village. It may also lead to considerable status ambiguity because someone who has an important role in one aspect of his life (a church or hometown association) has only a low status in some other role (employment). In this case, the labourer may feel compensated because he receives prestige for non-working activities. In a somewhat different situation (a young man with a good job but no status in his hometown association), status deprivation may lead to the choice to avoid the low-status role (stop attending association meetings). People who cannot find a role with any prestige probably feel most alienated, and probably find segmented roles the greatest strain because their low status is continually being reinforced. For the more successful, there is often a carry-over from one role to another so that the 'big man' of politics or business can use this status in other aspects of his life.

However, although urban roles are more numerous, specific, segmented and impermanent than rural roles, this is more true of some urban dwellers than of others. New migrants may take some time to make friends, or may be surrounded from the first by kinsmen and others they knew at home. Some work in an impersonal factory; others work as a group with people they know well and spend their spare time with. Residents of long established neighbourhoods often have social networks which are diffuse and as permanent as they would be in a village (which gives these places the name 'urban villages'), though the fact that some residents go outside the area to work or shop and other people come into the area to visit or work means that it is more open to outside contacts than an isolated village. It is well to remember that all generalisations about society are subject to exceptions, so that in many specific cases the 'normal' may not apply.

The charge that cities are centres of crime, poverty, social disorganisation, mental illness, deprivation, etc. often stems from an ideology of 'the good old days', which holds that all virtues and joys are found in rural life. This myth is found all over the world, often among people who do not know rural life very well and would not choose it for themselves or their children. Crime and other forms of social disorganisation are more visible and more often reported in cities than in rural areas; the latter have few policemen and community or family social control takes care of the offender so that outsiders are often unaware of the offence. Some kinds of conflict are fostered by close, multi-stranded rural ties and can be avoided in the urban atmosphere of choice and single-stranded ties. Witchcraft accusations, for example, are probably more prevalent in villages than in towns. Most important, empirical data on this are lacking, so it is better to assume that both cities and villages have positive and negative characteristics which balance in different ways for different individuals. This may help us to avoid and alert us to criticise decisions based on this ideology: demands for rural factories so people will not have to migrate to the cities, attempts to halt the growth of cities because of the assumed exploitation and unhappiness of residents. Studies of urbanites, even the poorest, consistently find satisfaction as well as dissatisfaction and valid reasons for remaining in town. These will be further discussed in the section on migration.

The urban community

A final approach to urbanism is to examine the city as a community. Weber developed this idea in reaction to earlier theories that cities were based mainly on the primacy of one institution (religion, the family, law, the economy).[29] He felt that cities could be better understood by examining their social relations than by concentrating on a particular institution; they require complex interaction between participants in many institutions. As communities, cities are societies in miniature, possessing all of the institutions necessary for full human interaction. A true city, to Weber, is an urban community having partial or (ideally) full political and legal autonomy, a market and the means of protecting its interests (symbolised by fortifications). It should be administered by authorities elected by the citizens.

By Weber's criteria, cities which were centres of state administration (headquarters for kingdoms, as was typical in Asia and parts of Africa) were not true cities because they lacked the autonomy necessary for an urban community. A city may be an important distribution centre for goods, culture, knowledge, etc., but lack this aspect of community – a local organisation of individuals for communal goals – because residents have too many

(29) See Martindale's introduction to Weber 1958.

270

interests which lie outside their particular place of residence. Modern cities have lost their military protection and their local autonomy; residents are often caught up in national and international interests and thus miss the sense of belonging to an urban community.

Although Weber's theory of the city applies only to certain cities at a particular time, it is useful to examine present-day cities or parts of cities for evidence of this type of communalism. Residents of a low-income area may have a community identity which is expressed in informal social control, mutual aid and joint activity against outside threats. Ross[30] describes how squatters in Mathare Valley (Nairobi) organised a village committee to provide a social hall, nursery school and water supply. In other areas, where people have not developed a sense of community, social relations are often more strained and people are less concerned with their environment – refuse is thrown in the streets, thieves are allowed free rein and people are unwilling to help their neighbours. The sense of community could be present in upper-income areas because residents share the same employer (the government) and meet socially at the same clubs, but it is often missing because residents are transferred frequently from one town to another and therefore are more oriented to a national than a local reference group.[31] Since they have more economic security than low-income urbanites, mutual aid is less important to them.

Parkin[32] describes neighbourhood and locality ties built up in two Kampala housing estates, Nakawa and Naguru. Neighbourhoods within the estates were the main areas of socialisation for the women and primary ties were important there. Since men were away from the estate most of the day, their community ties (if any) were to the locality; these were sometimes expressed through membership in tenants' associations which were dedicated to improving conditions for residents. The proportion of the population active in such associations is one measure of the development of communal feeling.

Communities may be studied from the point of view of interaction in space or of social groups. With the interaction approach, we ask whether there are local goals which are commonly recognised and what collective activity or allocation of resources has taken place to achieve these goals. If the people living in an area can tell us about their goals and are working to achieve them, we say there is a community here; this was certainly true of the Mathare Valley settlement studied by Ross. In comparing communities, we can ask how various features of community structure and leadership affect the harmony or conflict within the community. It is easier for relatively small and isolated agglomerations than for areas which are large and have no

(30) 1973.   (31) Jacobson 1973.   (32) 1969.

natural boundaries to develop a sense of community.

The social group approach examines integration. How is the community defined? Is there a well developed sense of corporate group membership and recognition of community boundaries? How are local values implemented? In what sense is there a community status system? How does the size and structure of the community affect the interaction of people within it? Many of the books listed at the end of the chapter examine specific towns as communities, especially those by Bujra, Fraenkel, Marris, Miner, Parkin, Ross and Wolpe.

There are many definitions of a city, many ideas of what is most characteristic of urban life. The demographer's criteria (size and density) are much easier to measure than the sociologist's reliance on the nature of social relations and the amount of social heterogeneity. On these latter criteria, one may argue (if data are available) that one place is more urban than another, but it is impossible to draw any precise boundary between what is urban and what is not. Literacy and industry may vary in importance over time, depending on the level of technology of the society which supports the city. There is considerable disagreement as to the importance of segmented roles, isolation, anomie and crime, but these generally appear to be more prevalent in urban than in rural places. Nevertheless, urban residents often have a sense of community and anyone studying the nature of urban society must include factors which support integration as well as those which make for conflict.

Migration

Cities develop through natural increase (more births than deaths among the local population) and through migration. Where health standards are poor there may be more deaths than births in a city, making for net loss of population, but with improvements in medical knowledge in the past fifty years it tends to be easier to remain healthy in town than on the farm. Nevertheless, migration is largely responsible for the very rapid growth of African cities shown in Table 9. This section will examine theories of migration and its effects on the migrants and on the community they left behind.

Types
Migration may be divided into several categories based on origin and destination, distance travelled and length of stay.

Rural-rural migration may be greater in total volume than migration to the towns, but because it is spread over so much territory it usually makes less impact on the local population and has attracted less attention than rural-urban migration. Amin[33] estimates that in the early 1950s about 15 000 Nigerians moved each year to the Middle Belt from more crowded areas of the north and south for agricultural colonisation. While the majority of migrants move from less to more developed areas (from Upper Volta to the cocoa farms of Ghana and Ivory Coast, from Rwanda to southern Uganda), these Nigerians were moving in the reverse direction, to develop opportunities in a less advanced area than their own. Though more recent figures are not available, this type of migration continues because the areas of early cash crop farming are now often too crowded to absorb further population increase. Farm labourers move to earn money working on cash crops; individual farmers and whole villages move to obtain new land for farming, to avoid diseases such as trypanosomiasis or river blindness, or because dams are about to flood their lands; pastoralists follow their flocks for the best seasonal water supply; and wives migrate to their husbands' villages.[34] Urban–rural migration is more limited, but the last move of many migrants is in this direction, back to their homes. Teachers and civil servants also make urban–rural moves in the course of duty.

Migration to the towns has attracted considerably more attention because of the extremely rapid growth which has resulted; urban populations often double and sometimes treble within ten years. This migration is directed primarily to the capital city, which is often not only the largest city in the country but also a primate city, twice or more the size of its nearest competitor (see Table 9). A quarter of the increase in population for all of Ghana between 1952 and 1960 was absorbed by the Accra Capital District.[35] Rural-urban migration is also directed towards mining and industrial towns and, to a lesser extent, to provincial centres. Leaving one town or city for another is becoming more common as a higher proportion of the population lives in towns. Craftsmen often try their luck in various towns. The Kru who work as seamen along the West African coast and the Luo of East Africa have been noted as frequent migrants between towns.[36]

Long-distance migration, international or interregional, is mainly from the interior to the coast (both towns and cocoa or groundnut growing areas) in West Africa, to the Copperbelt of Zaire and Zambia and the South African Rand, and to the areas of greatest industrial or agricultural opportunity in East Africa (factories, railways, plantations). These patterns are shown in Map 3. Whereas long-distance migration used to require days and sometimes weeks of walking, the spread of modern means of transportation has made it much easier and meant that migrants can maintain contact with their homes, thus increasing the likelihood of a long stay.

(33) 1974, p.82. (34) Oppong 1967; Prothero 1968; Udo 1975. (35) Caldwell 1967b, p.132. (36) Parkin in A. Cohen 1974.

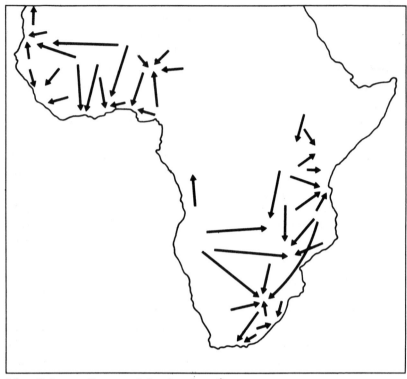

Map 3 Long-distance labour migration

It is useful to distinguish between long- and short-distance migrants and between migrants and immigrants because the social relations they establish at their destination tend to be different. Long-distance migrants (who often cross national boundaries) usually come from areas which are much less developed or urbanised than the area to which they move because people tend to go to the nearest place which offers adequate opportunities. They usually cross ethnic boundaries as well and, being distinctive in dress, customs and/or language from the local people, find it harder than short-distance migrants to settle down and fit into the urban society. Immigrants have been less welcome after independence than before because they usually resist assimilation into the new national identity. They are seen as outsiders taking economic opportunities which should be available to citizens, and as possible supporters of the political opposition. Various economic, social and political problems have led to deportations of aliens from Guinea, Ivory Coast, Niger, Sierra Leone, Zaire and, most notably, Ghana and Uganda (see pp. 127–30). Localisation of employment in Uganda and Zambia has also encouraged Kenyans and Malawians to return home.

The length of a migrant's stay is also an index of his adaptation to the community. Thirty or forty years ago, and in some areas even today, most migration was circulatory and often seasonal. Ideally, the migrant left home at the start of the dry season, worked in a mine or on a farm or plantation for a few months, and returned in time to plant his own crops. A few migrants stayed two or three years, but the majority were away from home for only long enough to save up money for the brideprice, or a bicycle, or whatever other consumer goods the family needed. They were known as target workers. They came alone, leaving their wives and children behind, and lived in very poor conditions so as to save as much as possible. They often migrated as a group and stayed together, having little to do with other residents of the town. Some made several trips, circulating between their homes and the centres of employment. Others made only one trip, earning enough to establish themselves as adults on a farm at home. In intention and in practice, both were temporary migrants.

Seasonal migration is particularly successful in West Africa because the harvest season for cocoa is during the Sahelian dry season; cocoa farmers of Ghana and Ivory Coast hire about 200 000 labourers each year, many of them from Upper Volta, Mali and Niger,[37] though in recent years citizens have largely replaced aliens among Ghanaian cocoa labourers.[38] These migrants often make several trips, returning home each year for their own farming. Thousands of men also migrated each year to grow groundnuts in Senegal and the Gambia, where the rainfall was better than at home, but this has declined considerably in recent years.[39] Rural-urban seasonal migration is described by Meillasoux[40] for Bamako and by Shack[41] for Addis Ababa. This depends on the availability of jobs in town for unskilled workers during the dry season. In Banjul, these are provided by the tourist industry. In other towns, building and services absorb workers.

In southern Africa, circulation is enforced by the employers rather than chosen by the migrants. Since it is cheaper to provide dormitory space for men rather than adequate housing for families and to ensure that migrants do not settle in the towns, employers and the government have required a return home on the completion of each twelve- or eighteen-month contract. This system is breaking down in the face of the need for more skilled workers, but so far ideology has taken primacy over economics.

In East Africa, short-term migration to the towns has been the result of the general distaste for urban living; migrants stayed only long enough to earn what they needed, and circulation appears to have been less common than in other parts of Africa. Seasonal migration for farming takes place on at least

(37) Amin 1974, p.73.　(38) Addo 1971.　(39) Amin 1974, p.74.　(40) 1968.
(41) 1973.

a small scale from most towns; low-income workers send their wives and some self employed men go themselves. Long-term migrants to the towns, such as the Luo and Kikuyu, often had little choice because of the shortage of land at home.

Both circulation and short-term migration have tended to decline in recent years (except where required by law) because migrants have seen the economic advantages of a longer stay and have found it easier than in the past to adjust to their new life. Farm labourers prefer to settle as tenant farmers if they can get access to suitable land.[42] With unemployment in the towns at present levels, it may take several months to find work; it would be risky to leave the job and have to start over again on another trip. This may be of relatively little concern to the self-employed (craftsmen, traders, providers of services), who can find some income wherever they go, but it is important to the new majority among rural-urban migrants, the educated. These are usually looking for wage employment (though many do not find it), and plan a longer stay because they see an urban career as providing a higher standard of living than life as a farmer. Through their school socialisation and talks with kinsmen and earlier migrants, they are better prepared than migrants of the last generation. Some arrive intending a long stay and others put off returning home because they enjoy urban life.

Another type of temporary migration is the transfer of government employees such as civil servants, teachers and nurses or the movement of building workers from one project to another. These migrants are not circulating between home and a place of employment but moving from one place to another as their job demands. For example, a Ga carpenter interviewed in Accra had lived in ten places in four countries by the time he was twenty-six.[43] Employees of the East African Railways expect to be transferred frequently from one depot to another.[44] Workers whose employers provide housing often form a community of their own, meeting at each post some people they knew before.[45] They may have relatively little to do with the town except as a market and source of services. If they live in ordinary rather than segregated housing (locations, Government Residential Areas), their experience makes it fairly easy to make new friends and fit into local customs. But the migrant who expects only a short stay generally remains somewhat aloof; he feels no need to join associations, build a house, or otherwise put down roots. Although data are still scanty, it appears that in recent years the time of temporary migration has lengthened; in some areas a majority of migrants have become permanent or semi-permanent residents.

When the migrant decides to stay, usually until retirement but occasionally

(42) Hutton 1973; Udo 1975.   (43) Peil 1972a, p.139.   (44) Grillo 1973.
(45) Jacobson 1973.

indefinitely, this facilitates absorption into the urban community. Some become active in the local politics of their ward, housing estate or party; others become leaders or active participants in voluntary associations. Their wives and children join them, so life can again be centred on the family. Those who can afford it acquire land and build a house. Over time, the migrant becomes a townsman, though home town ties are usually strong enough to ensure that most resist complete assimilation and continue to identify with their homes. Few would say, even after twenty or thirty years, that the city is home. This is partly for ethnic reasons; each city or town 'belongs' to a particular ethnic group or subgroup and it is more difficult socially and psychologically to be assimilated into an ethnic group (an ascriptive characteristic) than into an urban society (an achievement characteristic.).[46]

Reasons for migration

It is generally agreed that the main cause of migration is economic. Migrants hope to raise their standard of living above what it could be at home. This applies as much to the illiterate labourer as to the educated professional. It is evident in the drop in migration in areas where cash crops have been introduced and in increased migration when urban wages go up in relation to income from agriculture. Some economists have suggested that there is a 'backward-sloping curve' of labour supply; since workers aim at a target sum, they will respond to increased wages by working for a shorter period. This is a convenient reason for not raising wages, but has been proved false; even in the early period of wage labour, workers refused to migrate if the pay was too low and their length of stay bore little relation to the level of remuneration. As a result of this economic realism, forced labour was necessary to obtain a sufficient supply of labour, not only in colonial territories but also in Liberia and Ethiopia. International agreements against forced labour have helped to increase wage rates.

The migrant (or his sponsors) assesses the opportunities open to him. His information may not be too accurate, but he has some idea what he could earn at home and what his chances are of employment in the various places to which he might go. A young man whose contribution to the family farm would go to his father may feel that he has little to lose and possibly much to gain by migrating to a town. Unemployment would be difficult, but he will get some financial help at first and should he find a job the wages would be his. Why not stay abroad until he inherits the family farm? Where land

(46) A reverse identity also occurs among the Yoruba; villagers identifying with Abeokuta and Oyo expect to be buried in their town even though they have never lived there. See Olusanya 1969, p.6.

is available for young men to farm on their own, the decision to migrate involves balancing earnings from a cash crop against earnings as a migrant. The decision to migrate is more likely in moderately or well favoured areas than in the poorest ones, since assessment of alternatives is affected by relative deprivation. Potential migrants in the poorest areas may be satisfied with relatively little, whereas young men in cash crop areas (who are more likely to have some education and aspirations for a higher standard of living) tend to feel that they can only get ahead by leaving home. The introduction of new cash crop opportunities may bring many migrants home.[47] Udo[48] found that many Nigerian primary teachers had become tenant farmers because they could earn more than an uncertificated teacher's salary.

Population pressure is often important in long-term or permanent migration. The Luo of Kenya and Ibo of Nigeria leave home in large numbers because there is not enough farm land for all. Vanden Driesen[49] reports that 26% of the young men between twenty and thirty-five had left Ife Division in Western Nigeria because there was inadequate land for farming. As the population is growing at between 2 and 3% per year, it must be expected that many other areas will experience shortages of suitable agricultural land within the next generation. Migrants who find land elsewhere may remain permanently; other migrants will go home only when they inherit the family farm or retire.

While economic reasons may be primary in either pushing the migrant to leave or pulling him to the town, other reasons may also be influential in deciding who will go and when. The desire for schooling or training not available at home, leaving school or completing the harvest (signalling the achievement of independent adult status or the accumulation of enough money for fare), an accusation of witchcraft, or other trouble at home which makes it better to absent oneself are some of the precipitating factors. In times of political strife, a large proportion of the population may migrate to ensure their safety (Angola, Nigeria, Sudan, Zaire). Religious groups sometimes migrate because of difficulties with the national government (Jehovah's Witnesses in Malaŵi, followers of Alice Lenshina in Zambia). Many women migrate to their husband's village or join him in town when they marry.

Young people migrate to achieve independence from their elders, or because they want to 'see the world'. This attraction of the 'bright lights' is probably less important than many reports have suggested, especially now that migration is fairly common, but the idea that 'He who has not been to Kumasi will not go to Paradise' still inspires some to leave home. Likewise,

(47) Hutton 1969, 1973.   (48) 1975.   (49) 1971, p.51.

the idea that migration is an initiation to manhood which gives prestige to all who go has declined as migration has become more widespread. It is now just something which those who cannot find economic success at home must attempt. The most successful migrants do have considerable prestige at home unless they refuse to share their profits; they serve as a model of achievement to potential migrants and often help young kinsmen get started.

Imoagene[50] suggests that psycho-social factors are also important in migration, especially for villagers living near a town. As new ideas spread from the town, some villagers adopt new goals and become maladjusted for rural life. When these migrate, they are less likely than migrants with more economic goals to keep contact with home and are more likely to be permanent migrants. This appears to be partly a case of 'generation gap', young people who have been to school resenting the power of elders in their community. Relatively few migrate for this reason alone, but for many it reinforces the desire for economic independence and a higher standard of living, which are basic to what Imoagene calls labour migration. On the other hand, short-distance migrants find it easier than those from further away to maintain ties with home and therefore may be less involved in urban life than long-distance migrants who are equally committed to living in town.[51]

While there is considerable evidence of a desire for the 'civilising' aspect of urban life and of the social pull of extended family members who have already migrated,[52] there appear to be very few migrants who break their ties with home completely and the majority (with the possible exception of those over fifty years of age) say that they intend to return home eventually.[53] Mass migration to the towns is still too recent for reliable measures of the proportion who actually return to be developed, but urban success appears to be an important factor. The man who is very successful can go home to the prestigious role of 'big man', perhaps with a traditional title and certainly with a large house built for his retirement. The man of moderate success goes home on retirement because his pension or savings will go further if he does some farming and because kinsmen will help him in his old age as he helped them when he was able. The really unsuccessful man will go home if he can, but he may be unwelcome because he has not sent money home and he may have lost his land rights through his long absence.[54] There may be more of these poverty-stricken migrants staying permanently than migrants who remain for psychological reasons.

Caldwell[55] shows that rural-urban migration is selective of the males, the young, the educated and the single. Migrants are more likely to come from large villages near the town than from smaller places or further away and

(50) In Amin 1974, pp.351–3.   (51) Epstein 1967, p.280.   (52) Caldwell 1969;
Olusanya 1969; Peil 1972a.   (53) Peil 1976a.   (54) Plotnicov 1965.   (55) 1968a.

households which are above average economically have more migrants than economically disadvantaged households. The most notable difference between rapidly growing new towns and the older towns with more long established populations is the proportion of men. The sex ratio (the number of men per 100 women) is a good indicator of the migration status of a community. Sex ratios over 300 have been reported for mining towns relying mainly on short-term migrants, whereas the sex ratio of many southern Ghanaian and Nigerian towns is near 100 (a balance of men and women). High urban sex ratios are an indication of an early stage in rural-urban migration; ratios have tended to drop in recent years as migration of women has become more acceptable. For example, urban sex ratios in Zambia in 1963 were 282 for those over forty-five years of age, 162 for those between twenty-two and forty-five and 102 for those under twenty-two.[56] The sex ratio for Accra was reported as 117 by the 1960 census and 103 by the 1970 census. Villages with considerable out-migration may have a sex ratio as low as 50.

Young single men (and, increasingly, young women) are freer to undertake the risks of migration than older people who have spouses and children to look after. Attendance at school raises the expectations of both the young people and their parents that they will find better opportunities in town than at home. Caldwell shows (see Table 11) that rural-urban migration increases with education for both men and women; in a society where primary education and migration are both common (Ghana), sex makes little difference in the migration rate of those who completed primary school and two thirds of those who had gone beyond middle school (ten years of schooling) had left home, at least temporarily, for a town. Women with no schooling were more likely than men to stay at home, but even a few years in primary school brought the women's rate up to that of the men. While young people in advanced areas who get only a few years of education often stay home because they realise that their chances of competing with secondary leavers are poor,[57] it is likely that migration rates will increase over time as the educational level of the population rises. The primary leaver will choose a town near home or a city in an area less educationally advanced than his own; secondary leavers and especially those with university or specialised technical training will head for the capital.

Lastly, the choice of where to go is likely to be based on contacts even more than on economic opportunities. The new migrants need a place to stay and help finding a job and getting started. Leslie[58] reported that 'almost every African who decides to come to Dar es Salaam comes to a known

(56) Ohadike 1969, p.114.   (57) Peil 1968.   (58) 1963, p.32.

Table 11 Proportion of Rural Ghanaian Adults Who Migrated to Town, by Education and Sex (Percentages)

| Sex | None | Highest Level of Education Attained | | |
		Limited Primary	Extended Primary or Middle	Secondary or University
Male	27	31	49	67
N	1898	330	1305	215
Female	16	28	46	61
N	2767	324	592	30

Source: Adapted from Caldwell 1968, p. 370 and 1969, p. 64. Only respondents over age 20 are included.

address, where lives a known relation.' Only 8% of the factory workers interviewed in Accra and Takoradi and 13% of those in Tema and Kumasi had no contact when they arrived in town.[59] As migration becomes more common, the migrant probably has greater choice because he has kinsmen in various towns, which makes it even easier to go where one is known. Given several alternatives, migrants tend to pick the town where their economic opportunities are likely to be greatest.

Acculturation
The effects of migration differ considerably from one migrant to another; cultural differences between place of origin and destination, skills and education, length of stay, ease of contact with home, reasons for migration and many other factors make it easier for some than for others to settle down in the community. Gluckman's statement[60] that, 'an African townsman is a townsman, an African miner is a miner' has often been quoted in support of the argument that urban and rural social systems are completely separate and the behaviour of migrants in town cannot be interpreted in terms of their rural background. Mitchell[61] suggests that 'an urban social institution is not a changed rural institution: it is a separate social phenomenon existing as part of a separate social system.' Therefore, he argues that behaviour in town must be seen as demonstrating 'situational' rather than

(59) Peil 1972a, p.145.   (60) 1960, p.57.   (61) 1966, p.48.

'historical' or 'processive' change (see Chapter 10). This view of urban life owes much to its development in Central Africa, where towns were closely controlled by Europeans and segregated from tribal areas and where the migrant was often forbidden by law to bring either his wife or his institutions to town with him. Studies of West African towns, even those of recent development, indicate that such a view is too rigid. Urban and rural areas are, for many purposes, part of a single social system (though institutions may operate somewhat differently from place to place).

Nevertheless, becoming a townsman is often a much more gradual process than becoming a miner. A migrant does not become urban the day he moves to town, or on any other day, since he reacts to the various situations in which he finds himself according to the needs of the moment. He uses rural ties and institutions (in customary or in new ways) when they are useful, manipulates traditional values, and syncretises them with newly introduced traits (from whatever source) to suit his purposes.[62] Some people do this more easily than others; some find it very difficult.

Depending on the meaning one gives the term, there are various ways of estimating an individual's position on the continuum of acculturation to urban life. Several were developed in Central Africa, because the shift from rural to urban life caused particular problems there. The main measures are stabilisation, commitment, urbanisation and involvement. Stabilisation, a demographic measure, was useful to an administration which wanted information on the rate at which a permanent labour force was developing. Mitchell[63] computed stabilisation as

$$\frac{\text{Years in town since turned 15}}{\text{Years lived since turned 15}} \times 100$$

Thus, a migrant who moved to town at the age of fifteen and was still there would have a stabilisation score of 100. This had several disadvantages, notably that an elderly man with many years in town could have the same score as a new arrival and that it does not take attitudes into account. A man may spend many years in town but remain oriented toward his rural home to the extent of never considering his position stable or acting accordingly, while another may fit into the community soon after his arrival; whether or not he intends eventually to return home, he may be a stable resident almost from the beginning. Stabilisation, therefore, is easy to compute but less sociologically interesting than other measures.

Commitment is a psychological measure, usually referring to the length of expected stay in town. Migrants are divided into target workers (who intend to return home as soon as they accumulate a given sum of money)

(62) Skinner 1974, p.447. (63) 1954, 1969b.

and the temporarily or permanently committed; the latter do not expect to go home at all. Permanent commitment to town life has been rare in Africa. Migrants in other parts of the world have usually lost their farms and thus have no choice but to stay in town; Africans have tended to maintain their land rights and the ultimate security of subsistence agriculture. However, increasing population density, pensions which make it possible to remain in town during old age and acculturation to urban ways have meant a growth in commitment to the town, especially among peoples for whom farming has least to offer. The well educated, successful migrants are likely to be most committed, but even among them a majority are still likely to plan an eventual return home; they can at least return in style.[64] A compromise has been adopted by some of those returning to Malaŵi and Upper Volta. They settle in a town not too far from home, making it possible to see their kinsmen but also to enjoy urban amenities and opportunities.[65]

Urban involvement refers to the use the migrant is making of the social opportunities open to him. To what extent does he isolate himself with kinsmen and friends from home? Certain groups of urban residents, such as the Fula of Sierra Leone, Hausa traders in southern Nigeria and the Yao on the Copperbelt, are segregated through self-employment. These are all Muslim peoples, formerly slave owners, who maintain their sense of superiority over local people through isolation.[66] Although committed to urban life, they form a separate community which is in the town but not of it. They are fully involved at the neighbourhood level, but usually have little to do with the wider urban community unless their interests are particularly concerned. This often puts them at a disadvantage in local politics.

At the individual rather than the group level, Mitchell[67] used a series of measures to indicate involvement, including stabilisation and commitment:
1 the proportion of time in town,
2 the period of continuous residence (separating circulating from long-term migrants),
3 the presence of wife (established family life),
4 attitude toward town life (intention to stay indefinitely) and
5 occupation, education and wage level. (These tend to be correlated; those in well-paid, skilled, or other specifically urban-based occupations have more to lose by returning home.) An index built on these variables proved a good predictor of urban involvement and orientation among Copperbelt workers.

Imoagene[68] used friendship and associational participation as more direct measures of involvement. He found that education was the most important factor, followed by length of stay. Well-educated migrants adjusted quickly

(64) Peil 1976a. (65) Skinner 1960; Chilivumbo in Parkin 1975, p.309. (66) Epstein 1967, p.283; Cohen 1969. (67) 1969b, p.488; 1973, pp.303-5. (68) 1967a, b.

to urban life; the less educated ones were more adjusted the longer they remained in town. Independently of education and length of stay, members of clan associations were more adjusted than migrants who did not belong. This will be discussed further below.

Gugler[69] brought these approaches together. He suggested that the migrant's urban involvement should be measured by his residence, his economic support and his social field. Residence involves the stabilisation discussed above. Economic support refers to his sources of income. The migrant getting income from his farm at home as well as from urban wages has less incentive to immerse himself fully in urban life than the migrant whose total income is of urban origin. The continuing involvement of migrants at all socio-economic levels in the rural economy (from the small farmer who leaves a wife or a labourer to look after his crop to the elite professional who establishes a large plantation supervised by kinsmen) suggests that the majority of migrants are only partly urbanised in this sense. The social field is the most important factor; this refers to social networks, patterns of interaction and reference groups. As a migrant becomes immersed in urban life, his ties to people in town should increase and his extra-town ties should become less important. Insofar as this happens, a migrant is likely to stay in town longer than he originally intended and be more fully involved in and committed to urban life.

An important stage in this process is the movement of wife and children to town; the man separated from his nuclear family is under much greater

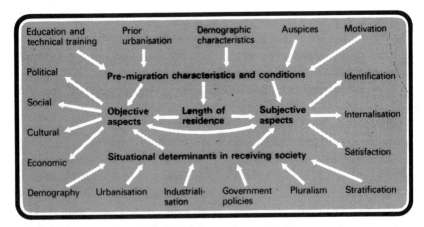

Figure 13 A model of the migrant adaptation process
(Source: Goldlust and Richmond 1974, p. 198.)

(69) 1970.

284

pressure to maintain contact with home than the migrant whose close family is all with him in town. It is easier for older men than for younger ones to decide to stay in town indefinitely because their parents and other close kinsmen of the preceding generation are dead and going home would mean leaving their children behind in town. (This is especially so for women, who often stay permanently in town to help look after their grandchildren.) In addition, their ties to friends at home have loosened over the years if they have been too far away to visit frequently. On the other hand, hometown ties are so valued in most African societies that migrants who cannot maintain these ties without disrupting their stay in town (because they come from a long distance, with poor transportation) are likely to be less involved in urban life and stay for a shorter period than migrants who can visit home easily and often.[70] The average migrant expects to go home at least once a year, to send gifts and messages and to receive visitors from home from time to time. No matter how caught up they are in the urban way of life, very few break their rural ties and even these tend to take a new interest in affairs, at home as the time for retirement draws near.[71]

Stabilisation, commitment and involvement are indirect ways of measuring an individual's urbanisation (the adoption of characteristically urban behaviour patterns) and, as such, none of them is wholly satisfactory. A more comprehensive approach to the problem of migrant adaptation is needed. An outline of such an approach has been suggested (see Figure 13). It has not yet been tried in Africa, but seems promising. Assuming that full adaptation would make the migrant indistinguishable from the local population, Goldlust and Richmond suggest that characteristics of the migrant, his experience at his destination and characteristics of the receiving society must be taken into account. The migrant who is skilled, has some experience of urban life (often in a smaller town), who is young, not too tied to his family, eager to do well, knows the local language and has help from kinsmen or friends in getting established is likely to find his entry to the town fairly simple. The receiving society, on the other hand, makes things easiest for the newcomer if it is fairly balanced demographically, if its level of urbanisation leaves room for the informal social interaction to which he is accustomed, if it provides work for him to do and if government policies and the ethnic and economic stratification systems do not discriminate against him.

Once he has arrived, adaptation is likely to be highly correlated with length of stay, if only because those who cannot adjust usually go home. But it will also be affected by his economic success and consequent social mobility, his taking on aspects of local culture (language, religion, food), the nature of

(70) Mitchell 1973.   (71) Amachree 1968, pp.234–5; Caldwell 1969, pp.152–64.

his social networks and participation in formal organisations and local political activities. These four aspects can be objectively measured; the subjective aspects (changing attitudes) are harder to measure. To what extent does he identify with his new residence? Has his socialisation resulted in internalisation of new beliefs and values or merely outward behavioural conformity? How satisfied is he with his present position in relation to the position of indigenes, other migrants and the people at home? None of these factors works alone, though some are more important for one migrant than for another. The end result for the majority of African migrants is partial adaptation; those who belong (or whose children belong) fully to the receiving society are rare, as this often involves a change of ethnic or subethnic identification.[72]

Effects of migration on town and country
Many opinions have been expressed but little data have been collected on precisely how migration affects social life in the areas from which the migrants come.[73] Myths of the 'peaceful, prosperous countryside' and the 'evil, disorganised town' are often visible behind the rhetoric. A more objective view seems to be that migration has both positive and negative effects, but that it continues because positive effects overbalance negative ones; migrants and their families are not irrational. Negative effects include loss of cash crops (food crops are seldom lost because women do the food farming in many areas); disruption of family relations, with young people no longer helping their parents on the farm, wives separated from their husbands, or children left with grandparents while their parents are in town; and increased independence of young people and women, who have an easy way of escaping from the authority of the elders. (This is a negative feature for the elders, but not for the migrants.)[74]

On the other side, money and consumer goods supplied by the migrants often raise the standard of living in their villages and pay for better housing, school fees and amenities such as schools and health centres. Caldwell[75] estimated that migrants sent or brought home 2.3% of the Ghanaian national income in the early 1960s. Mabogunje[76] complained that migrants often provide amenities for their villages which are not justified by the size of the population and suggested that development capital might be better invested elsewhere. Farmers working in more fertile areas than their own contribute more to national growth. Migrants meet people from other areas and other countries and new ideas are brought into the villages so that they are less

(72) Nelson 1976 provides a comparative study of the effects of cityward migration in Africa, Asia and Latin America. (73) Hance 1970, pp.192–7. (74) Gugler 1969, p.138. (75) 1967b, p.142. (76) 1968.

culturally separated from the towns; this may aid the development of national unity. The rural social system can be continued in spite of land shortages if the excess population migrates to the towns but maintains its ties with kinsmen at home.[77]

The effects are different for short than for long-distance migrants and for emigrants than for those migrating within their own country. Short-distance migrants tend to go home frequently, so that family relationships suffer little disruption; they can easily be called on for aid if needed and are responsible for considerable diffusion of urban values. Long-distance migrants are often ill-equipped to do any but the the lowest paid work; they can seldom visit their homes and have little or no surplus cash to send home. They more often leave their wives and children behind and so are denied a stable family life. If they are emigrants, another country profits from their productivity and the development of their own country may be slowed.[78] However, if their country has few natural resources other than manpower (as has been the case with Upper Volta and Rwanda) the cash they send or bring home may at least compensate for their absence and the few who learn new skills may add something to the indigenous labour force which would not have been available had they not migrated.

Seasonal or short-term migration is less disruptive of village life than long term migration in that migrants generally remain oriented toward village ways. Those who have been away a long time may require considerable readjustment on their return, either because they have become accustomed to new ways while village life has gone on as before or because they expect village life to be as before whereas it has changed considerably in their absence. (It is a mistake to assume that migrants are always either change agents or upholders of the *status quo*; some fall into each category and many are both.)[79]

The effects of migration on towns and rural receiving areas may like-wise be seen as both positive and negative. Strangers arriving in a rural area make life easier for the indigenes, who get a share of the crop for allowing them to farm otherwise unused land or who get help with the hard work in return for a relatively low wage. On the other hand, conflict may arise if 'outside' traders are felt to be making undue profits, over cultural differences, or over women. The large numbers of migrants going to the towns, which some have characterised as overurbanisation, result in greater demands for housing, water, and other amenities than hard-pressed local governments can provide. However, most holders of high-level jobs as well as many of the unemployed are migrants. They provide skills as well as muscle to run the

(77) Van Velson 1961; Skinner in Kuper 1965; Smock 1971; Hart in Amin 1974.
(78) Sangre and Sawadogo in Amin 1974.   (79) Skinner in Kuper 1965.

government, the factories, the railways, etc.

In addition to being moulded by the town, they shape it to their needs. Nearly three fifths of Caldwell's urban Ghanaian migrants[80] reported that town life had lived up to their expectations. Pons[81] found that many residents of Kisangani saw urban life as a welcome escape 'from the harsh authority of tribal chiefs, from sorcery, from drudgery of work in the fields, from obligations to demanding kinsmen and from the hostilities and jealousies of the village.' (LaFontaine and Lux report similar fear and suspicion of kinsmen at home among migrants in other parts of Zaire.)[82] The city gave them and their children an opportunity for social mobility, 'an enjoyable social life and a material standard of living unattainable in tribal areas'. In exchange, they gave up the relative social and economic predictability of the village to participate in a large-scale, cash-based society. (The security of village life is often overstressed by those who forget the multiple causes of crop failure.)

Associations

The impersonal aspect of social life which is often seen as the most important factor differentiating urban from rural life is most visible in formal organisations. Government and industry enforce bureaucratic norms and even recreation is more structured than in the village by the formation of numerous voluntary associations. While it is possible for low-status migrants to live in town but have very little contact with formal organisations of any sort because they rely on self-employment, form no associations and take no part in politics, most migrants who stay for any length of time make some contact with the organisational life of the town, if only through agents of social control such as tax collectors and the police. The most meaningful participation in formal organisations, for both indigenes and migrants, is probably through membership in voluntary associations. While the role of voluntary associations has been over-rated (people spend far more time in informal recreation than in associational activities), they represent an aspect of urban social life which is both easy to study and indicative of behavioural and attitude changes taking place in the urban population.

Voluntary associations are usually more formal than primary groups, though the small ones (such as drinking or savings societies with less than a dozen members) may be both. Generally, associations can be distinguished from sets of people who meet for informal recreation by the presence of a

(80) 1969, p.180. (81) 1969, p.51. (82) 1970, p.150; 1973, p.444.

leadership hierarchy, specific goals, rules indicating the expected performance of members and a clear identity, symbolised by a name.[83]

Thus, a Senior Service Club or National Union of Teachers has officers and a constitution proclaiming the reason for its existence and who may be considered for membership. Smaller home town associations or drinking clubs also have these features, but the rules may be treated somewhat more casually. Religious and social groups often put considerable emphasis on rules of behaviour, clearly differentiating the standard expected of members from what is allowed to outsiders. Little[84] has reported in considerable detail the type of rules laid down by various groups and action taken against those who break them.

The level of participation differs considerably from one individual to another. If these associations are to perpetuate themselves, they must keep the interest of members; this may be difficult where there are many competing ways of spending one's spare time. One way of maintaining interest is by providing prestige-enhancing roles as officers and members of committees. Banton[85] found that young people's associations in Freetown usually had large numbers of officers. One club of ninety members had forty-five officers – far too many people to run an organisation efficiently. Active management is usually in the hands of a few. But holding office makes people feel that they are important to the association and that their status in the wider community is enhanced.

Regular participation in the association is often limited to office-holders, though the inactive members may be called on for special activities. The activists may have been attracted because they had a greater need for the services of the association or for some status-enhancing activity. The rank and file find other activities sufficiently satisfying or the association only marginally rewarding, and so are content to participate only occasionally. Although this may leave the field clear for a few leaders, there are often conflicts over leadership because status and power over even a small group seem worth competing for, especially if the association can be used as a base for a wider political role.[86]

Individuals vary in the use they make of associations; people have different needs and no one association can fill them all. By examining the level of membership and types of associations preferred by people in different social categories, a broader picture can be given of the place of these organisations in urban society. Fortunately, many studies have been made in various parts of Africa, so people of differing background living in many cities can be compared. The discussion will focus on the functions of various types of

(83) Edwards and Booth 1973, p.3.   (84) 1965, p.97.   (85) 1957.   (86) Wolpe 1974.

associations: communal, occupational and special interest (church, recreation and savings).

Communal

Associations based on primary ties (ethnic, clan, family, or hometown) have been frequently reported and attract large numbers of migrants in many towns though, according to Epstein,[87] they are rare in Central Africa. Their influence elsewhere appears to be declining as more migrants are educated and able to either get the help they need from kinsmen who are settled in town or to depend on relatively secure wage employment. Associations based on categorical similarity which might be used politically have become increasingly unpopular with national governments. The Mali Government banned regional associations,[88] the Nigerian military government proscribed large tribal unions and the Ugandan Government forbade meetings based on ethnicity. On the other hand, associations based on a common home place have generally been seen as useful for mutual aid and development and hence tolerated.

In a metropolis such as Lagos or Nairobi, the number of active members tends to be only a small fraction of those who might belong. This relative lack of interest can be examined from two points of view. First, people's social background influences their attraction to associations of this type, inclining some to be far more likely to form and participate in them than others. Second, associational life is more rewarding to some individuals than others, and these tend to participate more intensively.

Based on his studies of associations in Kampala, Southall[89] suggests that participation in communal associations is affected by the numbers, residential distribution, socio-economic standing and attitude towards urban residence of potential members; the traditional structure of the group; and the distance between their home and the town in which they are living. People belonging to customary non-centralised societies who migrate to Kampala in substantial numbers from a medium distance, settle down in the same part of the town and attain a measure of occupational security are most likely to belong to ethnic associations. Banton[90] found that the Kru and Yako in West Africa, also politically uncentralised societies, showed a propensity to form associations. Parkin [91] suggests that

> Urban migrants from uncentralized tribes may attempt to reconcile conflicting egalitarian and hierarchical systems by establishing a hierarchy of associations in a traditional framework, and that migrants from

(87) 1967, p.278.   (88) Meillassoux 1968, p.70.   (89) In Lloyd 1966, p.352.   (90) 1957, p.195.   (91) 1966b, p.94.

centralized tribes tend to continue to act in their rural or traditional hierarchy, or at least find little difficulty in integrating this in the urban status system, and so have less need to establish associations.

This is supported by the relative lack of interest in ethnic associations among the Ganda in Kampala and the Akan in Ghana.

However, there is conflicting evidence which shows that other factors must be taken into account. Other peoples, at all levels of centralisation, demonstrate both high and low participation in communal associations. The Ibo of Nigeria and the Frafra of Ghana migrate about equal distances to Lagos and Accra respectively. Both come from uncentralised societies. But while most of the Ibo belong to a primary association (and often more than one), these associations have never been successful among the Frafra. At the other extreme, the Hausa obtain support from Islam and their strong sense of hierarchy and seem to have no need for communal associations, but the Yoruba, for whom centralisation and hierarchy are also important, have found communal associations useful in maintaining subgroup and family solidarity, in restructuring lineages, and in forwarding the political interests of subgroups and of the Yoruba as a whole. Thus, the political background may foster or hinder the initial impetus to form associations, but other factors are probably more important in long-term development.

This is partly a question of alternative opportunities for getting the support provided by primary associations. The host community (the Ganda in Kampala, Yoruba in Lagos, or Ga in Accra) may be able to control local government sufficiently so that they do not need a special pressure group, or their basic concerns over land ownership may best be handled by family associations; if the town is clearly theirs, they may feel no need for an ethnic association. Other groups may find that a tribal headman or chief can handle the problems of new migrants more adequately and fill the role of lobbyist to the government over a long period more satisfactorily than an association which attracts support only in times of crisis. Small groups of temporary migrants maintain primary ties without the formality of an association.

It might be hypothesised that, other things being equal, groups will form communal associations in heterogeneous towns where they feel threatened but fail to form associations in towns which are homogeneous or where they do not stay long enough in town to do so (Kiga and Ankole migrants to Kampala),[92] because they can satisfy their needs in other ways or hold values inimical to associational activity (the Frafra),[93] or because the civic structure of the town inhibits such activity.[94] They may be under governmental suspicion or prohibition because of possible ties to political movements. A

(92) Southall in Lloyd 1966, p.357.   (93) Hart 1971, p.29.   (94) Epstein 1967, p.278.

comparative study of six towns in Ghana and Nigeria found that membership of ethnic associations was highest in Aba, a provincial town whose population is 98% Ibo, and Kakuri, a suburb of Kaduna where seventy different ethnic groups were located. It was lowest in Ashaiman, an heterogeneous suburb of Tema and in Abeokuta, a provincial town which is 98% Yoruba. Thus, the ethnic mixture of the town seems to be much less important than local pressures to belong and the rewards obtainable from such associations.[95]

There has been a tendency in many towns for people from the same area to settle near each other. This provides opportunities for them to use their own language, patronise sellers of their preferred foods and drinks and participate in communication networks. If a primary association is wanted, it can best flourish where members live fairly close together, because dispersement all over town makes it expensive and time-consuming to attend meetings. Potential members who live on the outskirts are least likely to join or to participate if they do join. For the same reasons, associations in towns such as Lagos are likely to have a lower level of membership than associations in towns where the potential members are all known. In the latter case, it is easier to sanction non-members by getting their kinsmen at home to put pressure on them to cooperate.

Distance is important chiefly for its influence on the number of potential members. Transportation and communications are now much easier than they were twenty years ago, but nearby towns and villages are more likely to be well represented than places several hundred miles away. If there are few representatives of an ethnic group or village in the town, they may join other people from the same area to form an association. This is particularly true of aliens, who feel a common need to protect their position as strangers in the local society. Nigerians living in Ghana in 1968 had a Nigerian Association; they would have belonged to separate ethnic or hometown associations in Nigeria, but found it useful to associate as one group while abroad.

In the early days of urban growth, adaptation to urban life was probably much more difficult than it is for the average migrant today. Hence, mutual aid and support functions directed toward new migrants were probably the most important reason for joining a communal association, but even then many migrants got sufficient help from kinsmen to feel no need for a formal association. Today, migrants tend to get their initial aid from kinsmen already established in town. Okediji[96] suggests that socialisation to urban life of those without kinsmen was and is more often carried out through institutionalised social networks than through associations. Mutual aid is still important for those with a low income and many migrants support the

(95) Barnes and Peil, 1977. (96) 1975.

association because it symbolises the value of ties with home, but associations are increasingly used to exercise political influence at home and/or in the town.

They had this function to a certain extent from the first; young migrants could band together to get more attention from the elders than they would have received at home. As the migrant community has grown and aged, middle-aged men who are beginning to think about retirement are increasingly in control. Men who have not been notably successful in the wider society may seek prominence in a primary association, hoping to improve their status in the village when they go home. The core members of the association will be quickly notified of events in the village and will make frequent visits home if the distance is not too great) so that their views will be represented. This concern with power on the part of experienced migrants tends to decrease participation of young men and of women, who feel that the association no longer fills their needs and is only concerned with their contributions. (Men may not join until they have spent five or ten years in town and women are seldom active members.) It is in the nature of voluntary associations that people will discontinue membership if they find it unrewarding. Thus, associations may vary considerably in size over time, as new leadership and activities draw in new members or as enthusiasm wanes because a leader has moved on to other interests.

The Ibo are an extreme case in their support of primary associations. Smock[97] shows that hometown associations were far more important to most Ibo than the Ibo Union, and that both levels have had an important political role. The Ibo she studied saw political participation as primarily a group activity, since in their experience groups could put more effective pressure on the government than individuals. This 'in unity there is strength' motif is particularly important for trade unions. Where formal communal organisations are compatible with the customary social structure, the shift to the patterns required by post-independence political institutions can be relatively easy.

Well organised associations can contribute considerably to hometown development and be influential in hometown affairs. One of the associations Smock studied provided effective local government for the village over several years as well as building and running a primary and two secondary schools. Another contributed little directly to village development but was able to exercise political influence to the extent of getting government support for several projects.

The enthusiasm of hometown developers may be of less benefit to the

(97) 1971.

country as a whole than it is to their home. Regardless of whether the association invests directly in schools, health centres, roads, etc., or puts pressure
on the government to do so, resources may be used which benefit fewer
people than they should; one small village with ardent supporters and/or a
loyal M.P. may be much better served with amenities than a town with far
more people but less local enthusiasm. Investments in large houses for
prestige and retirement may be a much less efficient use of capital from the
national point of view than an equal amount of money spent on housing in
cities where it is usually in very short supply. National planners might at least
suggest that new schools and hospitals which the government provides be
built in areas where they are most needed. However, it seems worth encouraging the provision of local amenities by the people themselves whenever possible, since the contribution in labour and careful use of funds is
likely to make the project far less costly than one financed by central or
regional authorities; in addition, an amenity provided by the community
itself is likely to be more fully appreciated and used than one in which the
people had no part.

Occupational
People of similar occupation often find it useful to band together to promote
their common interest, organise to control prices and negotiate with the local
authority on market conditions and to build up their capital through joint
saving. In societies where crafts were passed down from father to son, craftsmen had family ties and needed no further organisation, but craftsmen not
following the hereditary principle have often organised guilds to control
apprenticeship, quality and prices.[98] These guilds still function, but they appear to have greatly diminished influence in large cities except among long
established crafts such as goldsmithing. Koll[99] found members of only
twenty-one guilds among over 14,000 Ibadan craftsmen and only a third of
the Lagos craftsmen contacted in another study said they were guild members; over half reported that there was no guild for their craft.

Trade unions attract large numbers of wage employees in most countries,
though as in other types of associations the proportion of members who are
active may be low. The first African trade unions seem to have been the
Nigerian Long Service Union (1912) and the Outdoor Officers' Union,
founded by customers officers in Sierra Leone in 1913. Civil servants, miners
and teachers led the way in founding unions, as there were enough of them in
one place to make the need for organisation evident and there were literates
to provide leadership. Some of the early unions were the Nigerian Railway

(98) Lloyd 1953. (99) 1969, p.36.

Workers' Union and the Nigerian Union of Teachers (1931), the Gold Coast Mine Workers' Union (1934) and the Gambia Labour Union (1935).[100] The settlers in East and Central Africa made it much more difficult to organise unions there. The prevailing assumption was that Africans were incapable of running complex formal organisations; leaders were categorised as communists and a danger to the society.[101] Although racial prejudice was evident, the difficulties of these unions are often remarkably similar to early struggles of unions in Britain and America. The fundamental conflict of interest between employer and worker which gives rise to unions is affected by local culture, but is found throughout the world.

Trade union ordinances in various countries during the 1930s and 1940s gradually made it easier to organise and the growing numbers of workers who settled down in the towns for an extended period meant that there was more interest in improving wages and conditions than in the past. Pressure from the British Labour Government after World War II, changing employment conditions and rises in the cost of living provided considerable impetus for union growth, with all the difficulties which any new organisation must face.[102] The chief problems of trade unions are due to size, the nature of the labour force, and their politics and leadership.

Although workers are generally more committed to a long stay than they were in the past, there is still considerable turnover and this interferes with union organisation. To be successful, voluntary associations must be based on interest and trust. The worker who expects to stay only a year or two is not concerned with long-term prospects; he will not be eligible for promotion or a pension. The union leader may have to make frequent calls for higher wages in order to keep up membership and spend considerable time educating new members who may leave the union when they change jobs. The workers have little opportunity to get to know the leaders and understand their role. This situation is gradually improving as time on the job lengthens, but an unstable economic situation means that many workers are declared redundant and must start again elsewhere.

In addition, the majority of firms are too small to organise efficiently. Many are family concerns, with most of the workers either related to the boss or dependent on him in a patron/client relationship. A formal organisation such as a union has no place in such a primary group. Other small firms under Asian or Lebanese ownership often pay below the minimum wage but provide jobs for people who would otherwise be unemployed and

(100) Roper 1958; Yesufu 1962. (101) Davies 1966, p.78; Sandbrook and Cohen 1975, Part I. (102) Epstein's 1958 study of the African Mine Workers' Trade Union on the Copperbelt is a comprehensive study of the problems faced by unions developing in this period. See Burawoy 1972a for a later report on this union.

who can easily be replaced if they show interest in a union. The union organisers lack the time to visit these small firms and encourage the workers and the pay-off for them in terms of increased membership would be small.

Lubeck and Remy[103] show that factory owners in northern Nigeria have found it fairly easy to use worker insecurity to break up unions. Strikes must be short because workers have no reserve funds and cannot afford to lose their jobs; management has only to wait until the movement collapses. This technique has been used in many parts of Africa, but it is usually limited to small-scale indigenous firms today. Multi-national corporations are watched by the government and must conform to labour legislation; their managers are experienced in dealing with unions and tend to take them for granted rather than fearing them as a challenge to their authority.

African unions have often been ineffective because of their small size. Many have less than 100 members and few over 5 000. Even if all the members pay their dues (and this is seldom the case), there is usually a shortage of funds to pay leaders, provide benefits and cover the rent on an office. There is no correlation between the total size of the union movement and the size of the average union. There are often a few very large unions (teachers, public employees, miners and plantation workers), which account for a third to half the membership, and a large number of tiny unions which take in about half of the rest. Small unions are typical of the early stages of union development. It takes time to master the skills of holding a large association together, and local organisations may provide more effective service than national ones when communications are difficult. Many unions are based on a single firm, which gives employers more control over their workers than if they belong to a wider union. As firms grow in size and workers become more conscious of their common goals, they may find it easier to join together into larger unions. This has been inhibited in some areas by union leaders who find their positions rewarding and are unwilling to give way to a larger organisation in which they might have no place. This has been a particular problem in Nigeria, where unions may be started as a business venture, one man running several.

The Ghana Government handled the size problem by decreeing in 1958 that all unions must merge into twenty-four industrial unions (later reduced to ten). Union dues were to be deducted from wages, so that all workers automatically belonged. The Trade Union Congress became a branch of the Convention People's Party and the union movement lost its autonomy. This led to a considerable disinterest in unions, which took some time to revive after the coup of 1966. Some unions have regained their independence, but

(103) In Sandbrook and Cohen 1975.

most of the large industrial unions remain intact.

Relations between the unions and the government are important because they often lead to conflict between the good of certain groups of workers and the good of the society as a whole. Unions were often active in the independence movement, as they provided large urban groups which could be recruited for demonstrations. Strikes against the government (the major employer) or expatriate firms were seen as blows for liberty. However, after independence many governments have tried to stop strikes because wage increases in the public sector leave less money for development and new investment will not be attracted if the labour market seems unstable or relatively expensive. Trade unions are generally consumptionist (emphasising better wages and conditions for their members) whereas the government is productionist (stressing that everyone should contribute to national development).

It is often difficult to separate normal trade union activity from politics; workers striking for higher wages can be accused of trying to bring down the government and may in fact be doing so. African governments employ a larger proportion of the labour force and have a greater influence on wage rates than is the case in more industrialised countries. Workers demanding their share of the 'national cake' are seen as a threat to elite privilege and can be accused of being already overprivileged in comparison to their subsistence farming fellow citizens.

Problems of union leadership have already been mentioned. Much of the dynamism of the early union movement came from men who found other outlets for their talents limited by colonialism. With independence, many left to go into politics and opportunities for higher pay and more security in the civil service or on the management side tempted many who would otherwise have made effective union leaders. Many of the difficulties of union leaders have resulted from their relative lack of education and experience; training in bookkeeping, doing the research necessary for successful negotiations and running a large organisation has been available only to a minority. Officers sometimes hold the union together by means of charismatic authority and entrepreneurial ability, which means that the union may cease to exist if the leader leaves it. Officers of larger unions often live well at union expense. The rank and file expect this and see it as contributing to their prestige, but the more class-conscious workers want leaders who identify with them rather than with the elite.[104] While the check-off system brings more money into the union, it may allow the leaders to become cut off from members because they are no longer so dependent on continuing

(104) Peace 1974.

interest. The appointment of top union officials by the Tanzanian Government in 1964 brought complaints by the workers, who saw this as denying their right to democratic control from below.[105] Where corrupt officers make deals with employers at the workers' expense or use their position to forward their own interests or those of their ethnic group, the interest of the members who do not benefit is quickly lost. However, the growing stability of the labour force and the union movement should encourage change from entrepreneurial leadership (the union is a business to bring its 'owner' as much profit as possible) to bureaucratic leadership (concern with the organisation and one's career in it).

Special interests

A majority of urban residents build a satisfactory social life from informal contacts with family and friends. However, many at one time or another join an association promoting some special interest. This may be a group sponsored by a church (such as a Bible society or singing band); a recreation society for those who want to join together for drinking, dancing, playing football, or other sports; or a savings society for those interested in building up capital or obtaining a loan at reduced interest rates. These special interest associations may bring together people of different ethnicity and social background, but often they are homogeneous because their interest is related to common background or because membership involves certain costs which only certain types of people can afford. Since many associations fill social and mutual aid functions, membership in one may be a substitute for membership in another; i.e., people who are active in a church society often feel no need to belong to a communal association and *vice versa*.

Young unmarried migrants and members of the elite are the chief patrons of formal recreation. Sometimes this is provided commercially (drinking bars and hotels, bands and concert parties, prostitution). Powdermaker and Skinner[106] have described the social activities centred on attendance at cinemas. But there are also voluntary associations based on similar recreational interests. These may be small and of simple organisation, such as the drinking society in Kisangani described by Pons [107] or more formal, as the Ambas Geda dancing groups in Freetown.[108] They may be sporting clubs whose members play in a league or support the local team, Old Boy groups of ex-students from a secondary school who meet formally only once or twice a year, or branches of international associations such as the Red Cross, the Boy Scouts, etc.

The elite often belong to several clubs and use them as opportunities to

(105) Sandbrook and Cohen 1975, p.132.   (106) 1962, pp.254–72; 1974, pp.285–8.
(107) 1969.   (108) Banton 1957.

interact with other important people. Businessmen meet government officers in a friendly atmosphere and upwardly mobile individuals have an opportunity to get to know people who can be useful to them. The membership fee for an elite club is often high, and drinking there is likely to be expensive. This allows the club to discriminate against the less successful without officially doing so, establishing a social boundary around its members. Other elite clubs may limit membership to people in certain roles, such as senior staff. For example, Grillo[109] compares the Railway African Club, which is open to all railway workers for a small fee, and the Gymkhana Club, which allows only the upper grades of workers to belong and charges a monthly fee which low-level workers cannot afford. As well as providing useful contacts, members find such clubs status-reinforcing in that they are encouraged to see themselves as superior to non-members.

Recreation clubs for young migrants fill other needs. They make new friends, are socialised into the norms of urban life, and may find a spouse if they are not committed to marrying someone from home. It seems likely that this type of association is less important now than twenty years ago, when migrants had less education and information about urban life. Since young people often drop this type of activity when they marry, recreational associations often last only a short time.

Credit and savings societies (known as *esusu, susu, dashi, ikelemba, igub, itshilimba,* etc.) help to provide financial aid and security to poor people throughout the world. The members put in a certain amount each week or month and they take turns drawing out the full amount. This provides a means of forced saving for people who would otherwise find it hard to save. Banks are often uninterested in small sums, and people need to save for school fees, major purchases such as bicycles or sewing machines, or capital for trading. They tend to decline in popularity with increased education, as better educated people have enough income to use banks. However, they often run loan schemes with lower interest than could be obtained elsewhere, and this attracts members who could save on their own.

Some savings societies are so large that they are in effect collection agencies; members never interact as a group.[110] However, the danger of the organiser defecting with the collection or of members dropping out after they have received their share means that most savings societies are based on trust among friends. They seldom exist where close social ties have not been established, as among recent migrants in an heterogeneous urban area. Geertz[111] argues that these associations are important in socialising their members into new patterns of behaviour. They are based on particularistic,

(109) 1973, p.94.   (110) Yusuf 1975, pp.170–1.   (111) 1962, p.439.

affective ties and yet function universalistically to aid their members to achieve their goals in the new society. Thus, they may be an important factor aiding adjustment to change.

This section on associations can be summarised by examining more generally the role which they play in present-day African cities and the factors which promote or inhibit membership.[112] Socio-economic status is relevant in that some individuals are economically so marginal that all their energies must be given to subsistence. At the other extreme, the elites probably participate in associations much less than in industrialised societies because there are fewer associations for them to join and because their relatively small number makes formal associations less important. Middle- and lower-status people are often under considerable communal pressure to participate in primary and church associations, where these are functioning, and find in these associations opportunities for improving their status which the wider society has denied them. Members of the elites may be active in such associations if the contacts made are likely to further their career (i.e., politicians and businessmen).

The structure of the town and culture of the various people living there both affect the nature of associational activity. Certain peoples, such as the Ibo, the Ewe and the Luo, have been notable for their energy in establishing associations wherever they migrate. However, this activity may be a response to the deprivation of opportunities for political participation in the towns where they are living. When one belongs to a minority group, joining to- gether may be seen as the only way to make an impression on local politi- cians and hometown politics may be the only feasible outlet for political interests. Changes in local government so that strangers are allowed equal rights with indigenous people and the participation of all is encouraged may result in considerable loss of interest in primary associations, at least on the part of the more secure and established migrants. However, this depends on the nature of political competition. Wolpe[113] shows that political conflict in Port Harcourt was based on primary associations because politicians saw that the communal ties most likely to provide them with the power they desired were most easily mobilised through associations.

The life cycle of individuals and of associations is also important. Young people are most interested in recreational associations. Participation is low for both men and women in the early years of marriage, when the new family claims their attention. As the length of residence in town and commitment to stay increase, people tend to become more active in associations. Men turn to primary or religious associations; women favour religious groups, or

(112) Barnes and Peil 1977. (113) 1974.

occupational or savings societies if they are employed. Associational activity is more segregated by sex after marriage than among the young people. Migrants thinking of returning home often become active in hometown associations to renew ties and improve their status in the home community.

Associations also have cycles. The presence of a good leader can lead to a surge of activity, followed by a period of dormancy when he or she goes on to other interests. External factors may also be important. A period of competitive politics may give rise to many associations[114] which cease to exist when the military or a one party state is in control. The government may also outlaw some types of associations, such as ethnic unions, when they seem to be taking political roles or fostering conflict within the society.

If primary associations were ever effective in socialising new migrants into urban life, this appears to be no longer necessary, as the job can be done by kinsmen and friends who preceded them. Communal associations are not very efficient in this task because they emphasise the maintenance of customary norms and attachment to traditional values rather than the acceptance of new norms and behaviour patterns. In addition, most members (at least in Ghanaian and Nigerian towns) do not join until they have been in town for some years and participate, at most, only once or twice a month. Other aspects of urban life affect them more directly and regularly. Although associations are an important part of the social life of many urban residents, other less formal activities are more significant for the majority.

Conclusion

Urbanisation is a social phenomenon which has been more notable in Africa in the past thirty years than almost anywhere else in the world, because Africa has been the least urbanised continent and is beginning to catch up. Cities are growing at rates hitherto considered impossible, and the urban way of life is spreading to the countryside through mass communications, the return of migrants, transfers of service and administrative personnel, etc. This does not mean the takeover of a completely new culture; the traditional culture continues to influence urban society and this influence has probably grown since independence. But generally cities are seen as the source of what is new and the young especially are open to what can be learned there.

The difference between urban and rural life may be small or great, depending on the aspect of life and the town or part of town which is being examined. Wage employment and formally organised recreation are more characteristically urban than many aspects of family life or casual relaxation; cities which predate the colonial period tend to provide more opportunities

(114) Wallerstein 1964; Skinner 1974.

for maintaining customary ways than new industrial towns. However, even where differences are least marked, urban or rural origin or residence may be a useful variable for sociological analysis. The differing social structure and opportunities available make size of place an indicator of education, occupation, potential social mobility, completed family size, amount of political participation and many other variables, though the strength of the relationship differs from one place to another. These relationships need much more careful study as urbanisation spreads.

Large numbers of people, especially young adults, migrate every year. It is now possible for most migrants to travel relatively swiftly to their destination and to stay with, or at least meet, kinsmen or people from home when they arrive. This eases the migration and acculturation processes and increases the chances that migration will continue to increase. Migrants are mainly motivated by a desire to improve their standard of living and they tend to stay longer than in the past, though most still intend to return home eventually. Migration brings both advantages and disadvantages to the areas of origin and destination, but on balance both sides tend to see the benefits as outweighing the drawbacks.

The increasing commitment to long-term urban residence means that most migrants participate actively in the social life of the towns. The young and unmarried make the most opportunities for formal and informal recreation, but others also join various types of voluntary associations. Many maintain contacts with home through hometown associations; others find valuable contacts in church, occupational, savings, or recreational associations. Nevertheless, these associations should not be over-emphasised; informal contacts with family and particularistic social networks are more important to the social life of most urban dwellers than participation in formal organisations.

Many references have been made to studies of individual towns, and an attempt has been made to compare different types of towns and towns in different parts of Africa. Our understanding of urbanism is severely hampered by the lack of comparative studies, where several towns are examined from the same point of view. Since we have no way of knowing how typical the towns studied so far are of their area, size and time, it is difficult to decide whether differences observed are due to a unique situation or real social, cultural, or administrative differences. Studies of the differences between towns of varying size and functions within a single country and between towns of the same size and functions in different countries would provide valuable information on the effect of variables such as size, density, heterogeneity, communalism, rate of growth and nature of administrative control on the social interaction of urban residents. This, in turn, would give us a much better understanding of what 'urbanism as a way of life' really means.

Suggested reading and discussion topics
There is a large number of books and articles dealing with specific African cities and towns. Read one or two of the following, looking for themes which have been discussed in this chapter and for points of comparison between the city being reported and other cities or towns you know well. Where both are avilable for the same city, books have been listed before articles. Hance (1970, Chapter 5) presents a brief historical and geographical introduction to fourteen African cities, with maps and pictures, which is a good starting point for comparisons.
Accra: Acquah 1958; Kilson 1974.
Addis Ababa: Shack 1973.
Bamako: Meillassoux 1968.
Blantyre: Chilivumbo in Parkin 1975.
Dar es Salaam: Leslie 1963.
Freetown: Banton 1956.
Ibadan: Lloyd *et al* 1967; Mabogunje 1968; Cohen 1969.
Jinja: Sofer and Sofer 1955.
Jos: Plotnicov 1967, 1965.
Kampala: Southall and Gutkind 1957; Parkin 1969; Southall in Miner 1967.
Kano: Paden 1973.
Kinshasa: Barnard 1968; La Fontaine 1970.
Kisangani: Pons 1969.
Kita: Hopkins 1972.
Lagos: Marris 1961; Mabogunje 1968; Baker 1974.
Livingstone: McCulloch 1956.
Luanshya: Mitchell 1954; Powdermaker 1962.
Lunsar: Gamble 1963.
Mansa: Kay 1960.
Mbale: Jacobson 1973; Hanna and Hanna 1967.
Mombasa: Stren in Hutton 1972.
Monrovia: Fraenkel 1964.
Nairobi: Bujra 1973; Ross 1973, 1975.
Oshogbo: Bascom in Kuper 1965.
Ouagadougou: Skinner 1974.
Port Harcourt: Wolpe 1974.
Sekondi/Takoradi: Busia 1950.
Timbuctoo: Miner 1953.
Umuahia: Hanna and Hanna 1967.
Zinder (also Niamey and Maradi): Van Hoey 1968.

9 **Social Problems**

Early interest in sociology in Britain and America was based on concern for the poor – with the social causes and effects of poverty, ill-health, poor housing, unemployment, crime, etc. Thus, interest in social problems has a long history. These problems are easily found in any large city, and considerable opposition to urban life is based on the difficulties which residents face. However, the presence of social problems in rural areas must not be ignored, just because they are less visible and less documented. If there were no rural poverty, there would be far fewer migrants to the towns.

In approaching the study of social problems, it is important to seek objective evidence, because in the absence of data assumptions often take the place of carefully tested hypotheses; these assumptions tend to owe more to ideology than to science. Ask where and when the study was made, how representative and large the sample was and whether there is supporting or contrary evidence from other studies. Case studies of individuals can be fascinating, but they may be very misleading as to the condition or attitudes of the majority. This chapter will discuss some of the findings on unemployment, housing and the maintenance of social control in order to introduce some of the research problems and possibilities in this field.

Unemployment

Official unemployment rates in Africa tend to be relatively low (6% in Ghana in both 1960 and 1970, 4% in Tanzania in 1965 and 4.5% 'seeking work' in Zambia in 1963). Moreover, the number of reported unemployed declined or remained fairly stable in many countries in the late 1960s and early 1970s in spite of a 2–3% annual population growth rate.[1] Similarly, although there have been reports of urban unemployment as high as 50%,[2] surveys tend to return figures of between 7 and 15%,[3] which appear to change little over time. Adult male unemployment in Nairobi was reported as 12%

(1) I.L.O. 1974.　(2) Pfeffermann 1968, p.43 on Dakar.　(3) Gugler and Flanagan 1977.

in 1968 and 1970.[4] Sample census results for males in a suburb of Tema in Ghana were 14% in 1968 and 10% in 1970. The Nigerian Government estimated 35% adult unemployment in Abeokuta in 1963. A 1972 survey found 1.8% of the men and 0.8% of the women in Abeokuta to be unemployed; the Labour Office had almost no applicants. Thus, it seems highly unlikely that 'within the next five to ten years, up to 35% of all able-bodied males between the ages of fifteen and fifty-five, resident in Africa's major urban areas, will be classified as unemployed.'[5] Urban unemployment is serious, but it is not as catastrophic as many authors suggest. It is probably lower than in many other parts of the developed and underdeveloped world.

However, there are many difficulties in producing accurate statistics on unemployment. Government statements are usually estimates with little data to back them up because the personnel, computing and recording resources necessary for careful studies are not available. An extreme case of the lack of statistical precision was a headline in the Ghanaian *Daily Graphic*[6] proclaiming, '22,530 Persons Unemployed: 600,000 have no work'. Whenever quantative statements on the extent of unemployment are made, check the source of the figures, method of collection, inclusiveness of the sample and definitions used. Did interviewers go from house to house or only to the factory gates and other public places? Is this a small sample from one part of a town or an attempt to locate all the unemployed in one or more towns? Is 'unemployed' defined as lacking wage employment, seeking employment of any sort, registration as unemployed, having little or no income, or self classification?

Governments often report the number of people registered at employment exchanges, but in most countries this is a minority of the unemployed; it may also include many people who are self-employed but interested in finding a wage job. Another method is to count the difference between the numbers reported in wage employment and the estimated number of adult men in the town; this means that employees in small firms unknown to the government, the large numbers of self-employed in the 'informal sector', students and others unable to work are included among the unemployed. The 1963 Zambian census included subsistence farmers, unpaid family workers and children among the unemployed.[7]

If unemployment is defined as being willing and able to work but having no source of pay or profit over a specified period (one week or one month), a definition sometimes used in national censuses, the position is clearer, but between censuses it is difficult to find and count these people. The definition also implies a clear boundary between employment and unemployment,

(4) I.L.O. 1972, p.56.   (5) Gutkind 1967, p.384.   (6) 30 January 1970.   (7) Ohadike 1969, p.118.

whereas substantial numbers of urban residents are difficult to categorise. Craftsmen may have several jobs one week and none the next.[8] Other men who move from one opportunity to another (thief, speculator, trader, labourer) may also be continually in and out of wage employment.[9] Women may move into the labour force when it is convenient and drop out whenever something else claims their time without ever being technically unemployed.[10]

Differential rates

The unemployed can be divided into those who have had previous employment (they have voluntarily or involuntarily lost their previous job) and those who are looking for their first job (or first urban job); these are sometimes called the pre-employed. Both categories must be separated from the underemployed, those who have some work to do which keeps them busy only part time and/or pays them less than a living wage or less than their efforts should be worth given their level of education, training, or skill. Underemployment is endemic in both rural and urban areas, but is extremely difficult to measure objectively. A Tanzanian labour force survey estimated that underemployment in 1965 was equivalent to over 500 000 additional workers, who could have made a considerable contribution to national development.[11]

Finding the first job tends to be considerably more difficult than finding another. Unemployment declines with age (see Table 12) because older workers have better contacts (enabling them to locate openings more quickly), are more experienced (have more to offer a potential employer) and are more stable (having family responsibilities, they are less likely to leave a job voluntarily). Also, an older migrant who finds himself unemployed and likely to remain so is more likely than the new arrival to either go home or go into self-employment. Because they constitute a majority of the unemployed and because their difficulties seem likely to increase rather than decline, most of the attention has been given to the unemployed school-leaver looking for his first job. While the uneducated tend either to stay on the farm or to enter some form of self-employment (craftsman, trader, supplier of services),[12] school-leavers often resist this because they (and their parents) believe that more will be gained by persistent pursuit of wage employment; this provides much greater stability, even if sometimes a

(8) Peil 1969.   (9) Hart 1973.   (10) Handwerker 1973.   (11) Ray 1966, p.60.
(12) Hutton 1973, p.63 suggests that young men without education do not migrate to Kampala because they know that only the educated have a chance of wage employment. Very few of the unemployed she interviewed had any work experience. Those who hung on despite long unemployment usually lacked access to land for farming and needed cash to establish a household.

lower income than self-employment and, in the past at least, a better chance for upward mobility.

School-leavers face three major difficulties:

1 Total wage employment has often declined or remained fairly stable; nowhere has it grown to the same extent as the output of the schools. The wage increases which have made urban employment seem so much more attractive than farming have also made capital investment more economic than employing large numbers of unskilled workers. The large building programme and expansion of the civil service which accompanied independence are now virtually over.

2 Educational expansion has occurred at upper as well as lower levels; this and the shortage of new posts have led to an upgrading of requirements so that jobs formerly obtainable by primary school-leavers are now saved for those with secondary qualifications. (King[13] reports that this happened within a year or two in Kenya.) Migrants from educationally less advanced areas are sometimes unaware of the devaluation of their certificates.

3 Rapid promotions have put young men in positions of authority from which they will not retire for many years; thus, the present cohort's chances of upward mobility (leaving room at the bottom for newcomers) are limited. Satisfaction with finding a job must be balanced against dissatisfaction with its prospects and envy of the preceding cohort, which seems to have monopolised all the best positions.

Table 12 compares unemployment rates in six towns of Ghana and Nigeria, showing the considerable variation which can be found. Abeokuta has the lowest rate. It has so few opportunities for wage employment that young people migrate soon after leaving school. Many of the Abeokuta unemployed, therefore, are living in places like Ajegunle. The high rates in Ghana are due to the poor economic climate at the time of the study and the fact that many migrants were drawn to the Tema factories even though they were doing little hiring; the building industry had also slowed drastically. In two towns (Kakuri and Aba), the female rate is close to the male rate; in most of the rest, men are at least twice as likely as women to be unemployed. This is largely because married women without work classify themselves as housewives; they generally enter the labour force without experiencing unemployment, whereas men take some time to find formal employment.

Unemployment is highest in every case for those under twenty-five, many of whom were recent migrants and school-leavers. Although older men are much less likely to be unemployed, significant numbers of them were without work in Tema and Ashaiman; unemployment is more likely

(13) 1974, p.46.

Table 12 Percent unemployed by Background Characteristics, Town and Sex[a]

| | Nigeria, 1972 | | | | | | | | Ghana, 1968 | | | |
| | Ajegunle | | Kakuri | | Abeokuta | | Aba | | Tema | | Ashaiman | |
	M	F	M	F	M	F	M	F	M	F	M	F
Age												
15–24	28 (239)	6 (333)	12 (428)	10 (208)	5 (56)	3 (111)	9 (254)	7 (221)	18 (224)	14 (226)	21 (249)	6 (153)
25–34	6 (364)	2 (187)	2 (262)	1 (123)	2 (111)	0 (112)	5 (256)	3 (151)	8 (365)	1 (227)	11 (411)	1 (166)
35+	2 (216)	1 (97)	5 (62)	0 (33)	0 (133)	0 (171)	1 (218)	0 (106)	8 (280)	1 (167)	12 (228)	0 (107)
Education												
None	3 (94)	2 (191)	6 (79)	4 (241)	1 (80)	0 (222)	3 (99)	2 (124)	8 (162)	4 (332)	9 (346)	1 (350)
Primary, Muslim	12 (376)	4 (288)	8 (582)	8 (135)	1 (86)	2 (56)	3 (456)	5 (215)	17 (53)	4 (54)	11 (115)	6 (33)
Middle[b]	6 (224)	8 (59)	2 (40)	0 (8)	0 (45)	3 (33)	12 (75)	5 (39)	13 (425)	12 (192)	18 (394)	10 (42)
More	13 (225)	11 (28)	8 (87)	0 (11)	2 (124)	2 (46)	11 (108)	14 (51)	6 (195)	0 (79)	23 (35)	50 (2)
Migrants[c]	9 (788)	3 (443)	6 (728)	5 (326)	2 (309)	1 (335)	5 (666)	2 (381)				
Non-migrants[c]	14 (132)	8 (133)	22 (65)	8 (71)	0 (26)	4 (26)	5 (78)	26 (47)				
Total	9 (981)	4 (608)	5 (829)	5 (409)	2 (392)	1 (395)	5 (821)	4 (473)	11 (835)	6 (657)	14 (890)	3 (427)

Sources: Sample surveys of the total population of randomly selected houses. Ajegunle is a suburb of Lagos near the port and industrial centre of Apapa. Kakuri is an industrial suburb of Kaduna. Abeokuta and Aba are provincial towns. Ashaiman is a suburb of Tema, a new port and industrial town. (Peil 1969).

[a] Numbers in parentheses are bases for the percentages, i.e., 28% of 239 males aged 15–24 in the Ajegunle sample were unemployed.

[b] In Nigeria, Standard 6 and 7, Secondary Modern 1–3 and Secondary Grammar 1–3. In Ghana, middle school.

[c] As Tema and Ashaiman were new towns and had very few non-migrants, they have been omitted from the table.

to be a traumatic experience for them because of their family commitments. There is a tendency for unemployment to increase with education, but opportunities obviously vary from one place to another. Men with more than six years of primary school but less than completed secondary school did fairly well in Ajegunle and Kakuri; some were older men who found their jobs when secondary education was rare and others profited by being somewhat better educated but willing to take jobs for which primary leavers might otherwise have been hired. Prospects do not look promising for the increasing numbers of secondary leavers, though their job aspirations are gradually declining as did the aspirations of primary leavers some years earlier.

While it might be expected that migrants would have a harder time finding work than indigenes, the opposite was true of women in all four towns and of men in Ajegunle and Kakuri; there was no difference for men in the two provincial towns. This is partly because the non-migrants tended to be the children of migrants, young, educated and new to the labour force. But two other factors enter in. Migrants tend to go home or try another town if they cannot find work, whereas non-migrants may have nowhere else to go. Also, young people who are living with their parents feel less pressure to find work than those who are seeking to be independent; they take unemployment less seriously because they are assured of family support.

The usual pattern is for the school-leaver to set off after earning his certificate or after the harvest, when money is available to sponsor his attempt. He goes to stay with a close kinsman who feeds him and provides a place to sleep; he may also receive some pocket money. The kinsman will try to help him find work, if only to make him independent of further support. After six to twelve months as an 'applicant' or 'job-seeker', the unsuccessful usually either return home, try another town, try some form of training (an apprenticeship or typing course) if the fees can be found, or locate some form of at least part-time self-employment. Only a few hang on completely unemployed for two or three years. These may have to move from one kinsman's house to another or share a room with several unemployed friends. (In this case, members of the group usually take turns doing casual labour to earn enough for the group to survive.) Some move to the outskirts of the town and work for a farmer in exchange for room and board.[14]

Many migrants who come to town to try their luck rather than because they reject farming go home if they are unsuccessful. Generally, the more education a migrant has the longer he is willing to wait and the longer his

(14) Callaway 1963; Peil 1972b; Hutton 1973; King 1974.

family is willing to support his pursuit of an urban wage. Those who return home may make further trips to town whenever they hear of new projects offering employment. Eventually, members of each cohort are absorbed into the rural or urban labour force, though often not in the role they aspire to.

Effects

Unemployment has important effects on both the individual and the society. It is a hard psychological blow to discover, after many years of study and anticipation, that no one wants to hire you. At first a young man may have no interest in manual work, considering himself fit only for a clerical post, but he soon learns that he must be willing to do any work which is offered. His relationship with his kinsmen may be badly strained if unemployment is prolonged.[15] The older, married man may have to rely on his wife for support, a sad plight in a male-dominated society. He has usually saved little from better times, and finds it very difficult to find cash for clothes, food and bribes. A man who suffers long-term unemployment may lose the habit of work and find it hard to keep a job if he does find one. This lowers his chances of finding work still further. Social networks tend to contract with prolonged unemployment, because it is impossible to maintain norms of reciprocity.

The economic effects are visible in the increased poverty of households where one worker must support one or more 'applicants' in addition to a wife and children and in a slower rate of development because so many able adults contribute nothing to the gross national product. The educational system is affected by parents refusing to send their children to school[16] and by greater demands for secondary places because primary education is known to be of little use in obtaining employment. The assumptions and practices of the educational system may be questioned. There may be new demands for vocational education in some quarters, but parents and pupils tend to push for more academic education (see Chapter 5). Attempts to satisfy the social demand for education lead to more government expenditure than planners have forecast, and money spent on schools is not available for capital investment in industry, which might produce more jobs.

Political effects arise from the nepotism and corruption which surround the recruitment process in a situation of job scarcity and the potential for political protest from the large numbers of young men roaming the streets. The tendency to favour kinsmen and people of common origin is natural in a family-oriented society, but it generally becomes less common with

(15) Duodu 1967 suggests that conflict may arise in the rural areas as well as in town if school-leavers hang about without any work to do.   (16) This has been questioned by Blakemore 1974.

industrialisation and bureaucratisation because of the need for technical competence. However, the lack of employment opportunities means that individuals are under severe pressure to make appointments on particularistic grounds. Employers and/or personnel officers sometimes demand substantial bribes and supervisors may demand regular payment to ensure against dismissal. This effectively lowers wages and gives rise to dissatisfaction with the government, which is accused of not being sufficiently active against these evils and even fostering them. Nepotism and corruption in employment also contribute to the atmosphere of corruption in the society as a whole (see below).

Fears of mass protest by the unemployed have so far proved unfounded because of turnover, competition and cross-cutting ties. Unemployment is rather like a train or passenger lorry; a large number of people are always riding, but individuals change fairly often. Therefore, there is not time for a cohesive group to develop. Men may congregate outside the labour exchange or the gates of large factories, but because each is in competition with the others there is little incentive to unite. A few associations of the unemployed have arisen, but they have been short-lived. The government either finds jobs for or deals harshly with the leaders and the movement collapses. But even without this action, the social diversity and cross-cutting interests of the unemployed would make it difficult to maintain enthusiasm. King[17] found that particularistic recruitment encouraged job-seekers in Nairobi to continue even though their qualifications were inadequate because if they found the right contact their lack of certificates would not be a hindrance. They saw no reason to join with other unemployed against the rich and powerful because the latter were seen as their best source of help. On the other hand, unequal access to employment by various ethnic groups, especially to high-level employment, can easily become a political issue because applicants at this level are better able than the ordinary unemployed to get political support for their demands.

Urban unemployment, and especially the school-leaver problem, results from aspirations for a higher standard of living and the perception that this is more likely to be achieved in town than at home. Sending beggars and the unemployed home has proved useless; those with no access to an adequate rural income return as soon as it seems safe to do so. Serious attempts to improve rural conditions and agricultural income are likely to be more successful in the long run, but these will probably require that a considerably smaller proportion of the population than at present is employed in the rural areas; the rest must somehow make their living in town. Meanwhile, govern-

(17) 1974, pp.49, 61.

ment support or at least tolerance of a wide range of self-employment seems likely to contribute most to cutting down unemployment.

Housing

Inadequate housing is usually the result of poverty, but the problem is compounded by very rapid urban growth. Urban housing can be roughly divided by ownership into employee housing, public housing and private housing and the latter into houses on authorised and unauthorised plots. Low-grade and overcrowded housing is found in both urban and rural areas; when concentrated in slums, it may give rise to many social problems. The layout of houses and the density, heterogeneity and continuity of the population have important effects on the social life of the community.

Types of provision

When mining towns and plantations were being established, colonial government regulations often required European employers to provide housing for their employees. Since at that time most workers were young, single men who stayed only a short time, this housing was often a barracks-type dormitory or row of small rooms which several workers were expected to share. Housing built later, when employers were more interested in a stable labour force, is often much sought after because of its convenience and relatively low rent, but most private employers now leave their workers to find rooms for themselves rather than providing housing. Exceptions are universities and some secondary schools and government housing for senior civil servants, the army, police and railway workers.[18] A major problem with this type of housing is that the worker who loses his job must find another place to live.

Many governments have also been active over the past forty years in providing public housing at subsidised rents. Attempts were made in southern Africa to house a substantial proportion of the urban population, but migrants always came in greater numbers than public funds could provide for. Further north, housing estates have usually been token gestures or catered for a special situation such as the Accra earthquake victims or those displaced by urban renewal. Increased building costs have made this type of development even less economic than in the past.

A basic difficulty is that planners set too high a standard. Electricity and running water in every house and a separate house for every family are worth

(18) Grillo 1973; van den Berghe 1973.

aspiring to, but the average urban resident would rather not pay a quarter of his income in rent; other things are more important. Estate housing 'for the workers' often goes to middle-level people because the rents charged are more than low income households can pay. The size and arrangement of rooms also makes estate housing more acceptable to those who prefer some segregation from their extended families.[19] Relatively well educated people, in good jobs, can afford the rent and do not object to regulations against visitors, animals, trading, extra buildings, etc. The rest of the population usually finds private housing more to its taste and pocketbook.[20] This means, however, that those most able to house themselves receive government subsidies while the poorest must pay the full market price for what they get.

A partial solution is the site and service scheme, where roads, water and electricity are provided and each householder must build his own house. An early version of this is the Majengo village layout scheme in Mombasa, established in 1927. The government subdivided the area into small plots and required only semi-permanent houses meeting minimum standards. Although leases must be renewed annually, eviction appears to be rare.[21] Pons[22] describes another scheme, with greater formal security of tenure, in Kisangani. Recent schemes have provided more services than these, but this has necessarily raised the cost per plot holder. These schemes are also very costly in government funds for the small numbers who are accommodated.

An important advantage of private over public housing is that the former can be owned. Ownership of housing is by no means limited to those with a large income, and anyone who can manage to acquire a house through inheritance, family support, business success, or careful long-term planning has a source of lifetime income and considerable prestige in the community.[23] While the elites tend to live in single family houses, the rest of the population usually share; landlords have a steady income from renting out some of their rooms. This gives them a secure income after retirement, making it possible to stay in town rather than returning home. Urban house ownership is the best predictor of commitment to urban residence[24]

(19) Marris 1961; Bienefeld and Binhammer in Hutton 1972; Bujra 1973.
(20) Wober 1967 reports that residents of a housing estate in Sapale were younger and in higher occupational categories and had higher aspirations and smaller families than the rest of the work force. Their style of life was seen as 'cool' and quiet compared to the 'hot' life of the town.   (21) Stren 1972.   (22) 1969, p.38.
(23) Barnes 1976.   (24) Mitchell 1969b, p.479 found that residents of private housing in Zambian mining towns had lived in town longer than residents of employee or local authority housing. The study was made in the early 1950s, when private housing was much more limited than it is today, but those who planned a long stay in town often felt more secure and less regimented in private housing.

There are several types of private housing: the palatial manor of a member of the elite; the large family house of urban indigenes; the wide variety (in size and quality) of houses erected by private builders; the packing case, tin sheet shack or thatch-roofed, traditionally constructed dwelling on the outskirts. Access to land in new areas is often available in exchange for a small gift to the indigenous owners; later, land prices rise in value so that only the wealthy can acquire the remaining plots in a well-filled area. House owners sometimes allow poorer kinsmen or tenants to put up small houses behind their own[25] and tenants usually have a lower income than the landlord. Thus, in areas of private housing families of widely different income often share the same neighbourhood; this is quite unlike employer or public housing, which is usually stratified by rent. Frequent contacts slow the development of class identification, which is more likely in the economically homogeneous government estates.[26]

When the landlord lives on the property or nearby, he (or she) takes an interest in the tenants and often has a position similar to a family elder, arbitrating quarrels and giving advice and aid. The Hausa term *maigida* refers to a landlord who is also a business and political leader. His ability to house clients, clerks, servants and his mallam as well as his family is an important component of his success.[27] At the other extreme are non-resident landlords (individuals or companies) who speculate in housing because of the high profits it can provide. Such landlords often exploit their tenants, constructing cheap buildings and charging as high rents as the market will bear. Rents are highest where the government restricts access to land for housing. Muench[28] found higher rents for lower quality housing in Kampala than in Ibadan because the supply of rooms for rent was much greater in Ibadan.

As governments become increasingly interested in urban planning, another distinction has become important, between authorised and un-authorised or squatter housing. True squatting implies deliberately building on land for which no permission has been obtained and against the owner's explicit or implicit wishes. Unauthorised or uncontrolled settlements may have the permission of the traditional owners of the land but lack government permission or approval, or they may be built on publicly owned land which is not being used for anything else. Where customary permission has been obtained, social norms have been observed and the problem is intrinsically political. All forms are usually grouped together in official statistics, since from the government's point of view they are equally illegal, but there

(25) Fraenkel 1964, p.50; Pons 1969, p.32.   (26) Solzbacher 1970, p.50. See also Chilivumbo in Parkin 1975.   (27) Hill 1966; Cohen 1969, Chapter 3.
(28) 1972, p.36.

is usually stronger pressure against squatters than against settlers who have, from their point of view, obtained tenure.

Independent governments are sometimes more and sometimes less tolerant of unauthorised settlements than the colonial governments which preceded them. They tend to expand wherever they are permitted, partly depending on the rate of population increase, the availability of land and controls exercised over building in officially approved areas.[29] 'Informal' settlements housed 20% of the Lusaka population in 1957, when the colonial government tried to keep these to a minimum; greater tolerance after independence brought the figure to 42% by 1973.[30] Squatters have remained a fairly constant 45% of the Nairobi population during the recent years of rapid growth and also contribute about 45% of the Blantyre population.[31] It has been estimated that uncontrolled settlements housed 30% of the Dakar population in 1969 and 36% of the population of Dar es Salaam in 1967.[32] M. A. Cohen[33] reports that very high building standards set for Abidjan led to 'vast bidon-villes of "spontaneous housing" ' on the outskirts for 'more than half the city's population'.

These people have considerable insecurity, since the government may decide at any time to tear down their houses. This may actually help to develop a sense of community (cohesion in the face of conflict with out-siders), but interferes with long term commitment to the area and the self-help improvements which would accompany such an attitude. Any sign that the government is interested in improving the area, however, is enthu-siastically welcomed; the community spirit may then be directed to local development. Van Velson[34] suggests that 'spontaneous housing' is a solution rather than a problem. It houses about 40% of the Zambian population, in small towns as well as cities, and allows residents to choose their housing style and limit their costs. Antagonism toward squatter areas on the part of civil servants and well-paid workers may be an aspect of class conflict; newcomers flooding into the cities compete for urban jobs and services which the well established might prefer to keep for themselves.

Most squatter areas lack roads, water, electricity, sanitation, schools, clinics – amenities which are seen as characteristic of urban life. Settlers often put considerable effort into acquiring these, partly for themselves and partly because they represent government acceptance of responsibility for the area, implicitly recognising their claim to the land.[35] Solzbacher[36] quotes a resi-dent of Kibuli, on the outskirts of Kampala, 'Kibuli is becoming a village of the town.' This recognises that amenities make for urbanisation, but that the

(29) Peil 1976a.   (30) Development Planning Unit 1974.   (31) Norwood 1975, pp.122, 124.   (32) World Bank 1972, p.82   (33) 1974, p.35.   (34) In Parkin 1975.   (35) Ross 1973.   (36) 1970, p.50.

communalism characteristic of a village has so far been maintained, as it has in parts of most towns.

Many low-income areas, authorised and unauthorised, are categorised as slums. The major criteria for this derogatory designation are poor physical conditions, lack of effective social organisation and self-perception as a slum.[37]

Outsiders who see poor physical conditions tend to assume that these are accompanied by unemployment, social isolation, family disruption, crime and other types of social disorganisation, but research has shown that this assumption is often unwarranted. Norwood[38] points out that over 90% of the squatters in Blantyre, Nairobi and Lusaka are employed and their production makes a considerable contribution to the urban economy. Unemployment is at about the same level in Ajegunle and Ashaiman, which are categorised as slums (see Table 12); a third of the Tema labour force lives in Ashaiman.

The crime rate may be high (Ajegunle has been called 'Tiger Town'), but strong social control is maintained in some slums (see below). Sanctions against deviants are easiest to enforce when the community is relatively small.[39] Resident landlords often play an important part in taking responsibility for the behaviour of their tenants and arbitrating conflicts. Active party cells may also play this role, depending on the stability of their leadership.

Residents of low-income private housing are less likely to belong to formal associations than the better educated and more affluent residents of housing estates, but this does not mean that they are anomic or friendless. The lively social life of these areas is obvious to anyone walking through them. Stren[40] found slightly lower participation in associations and civic activity among residents of Majengo (a slum area of Mombasa) than among residents on a housing estate, but felt that this was due largely to the lower level of education and income in Majengo rather than to the social or physical environment. Religious participation was higher in Majengo and few of its residents were socially isolated. The same applies to Pumwani in Nairobi.[41] Comparison of residents in estate housing in Tema and private housing in Ashaiman found that the latter had a more active social life. Two fifths of the Ashaiman respondents, but only a tenth of those in Tema, said they sat and talked frequently with more than ten friends; half the Tema respondents and over four fifths of those in Ashaiman sat and talked with co-tenants. Thus, people living in these areas have more opportunities than estate residents for getting to know well individuals who might otherwise have been avoided as

(37) *Ibid.*   (38) 1975.   (39) Quarcoo 1966; Ross 1973.   (40) 1972, p.166.   (41) Bujra 1973.

strangers.

The self-esteem of slum residents is lowered by the realisation that they live in an area generally recognised as substandard. Knowing that an address in Ajegunle, Chiwama, Kisenyi, Nima, or Pumwani indicates low status and implies possible moral degradation makes it more difficult for those who live there to feel part of the wider society. However, while most residents readily admit to the poverty of their environment, most can add something to their self-esteem by pointing to other parts of the town which are worse than their own, or at least by pointing out that the majority of their neighbours do not fit the stereotype. Given the prevalence of poverty, it is well to remember that most people living in physical slums are socially and morally average citizens.

Beyond having protection from rain and a place to sleep and keep their belongings safely, most Africans place a low value on housing and prefer to spend their money on other things. Thus, while elites and planners often look on slums as unworthy relics which should be cleared, many migrants find in them housing at a price they can afford to pay and a social life not too unlike home.[42] This gives them a base from which to launch themselves on the path of urban social mobility. Many migrants never manage to move out of the slums (and many indigenes of varying wealth continue to live in them), but without them life in town would be impossible for the former and highly valued social life would be missed by the latter. Lagos' experience of slum clearance[43] should be a warning that such programmes often cause more problems than they solve.

Co-tenant interaction

The layout of the house and the heterogeneity and density of tenancy also affect the social life of residents. Three basic floor plans can be distinguished for houses serving several households: a row of rooms opening on the street, a double row of rooms opening on a corridor, and rooms opening on a courtyard. The first offers the least contact among residents; each may come and go without meeting the others. Many housing estates are of this type, which is European in inspiration. The second is a common form of residential accommodation in all parts of Africa. There is sometimes an open space at the back for cooking, bathing, water supply and latrine. Residents meet in the hallway and around the common services. Interaction is even more likely in buildings centred on a courtyard, which are larger but otherwise similar to those found in many rural areas. Children can play safely while their

(42) Chilivumbo in Parkin 1975.   (43) Marris 1961, 1967.

mothers cook, wash clothes and plait hair, and adults have space to sit out talking in the evenings. The social importance of this orientation is evident in that prostitutes and shopkeepers who rent rooms facing the street rather than the centre are much less known to the other tenants.

Economic heterogeneity in housing was discussed above. Although most towns have an ethnically mixed population, heterogeneity generally increases with size; it is greatest in primate cities and industrial towns and least in provincial administrative and marketing centres. Areas within the town also differ in the amount of heterogeneity. An area settled by indigenes may have relatively few outsiders because it was already densely populated by the time urban growth got under way. Early migrants sometimes established separate wards; some of these have maintained their ethnic character, as in Monrovia and Addis Ababa.[44] The tendency for people to congregate where the road from home enters the town has often been noted; this appears to be less common today because migrants are better prepared for urban life and the housing shortage has meant that they must be willing to move wherever a room can be found. Certain areas were reserved for strangers in West African towns: a *sabon gari*, *zongo*, etc. These tend to have mixed populations, but they have often developed a culture based on the largest or most prestigious group (often the Hausa).[45]

Generally, there is considerable mixing of ethnic groups and/or subgroups within houses and in most parts of cities, especially in low-income private housing. Schildkrout[46] noted that ethnic mixing is the norm in the Kumasi *zongo* and Peil reports[47] that only 19% and 7% respectively of the houses sampled in Ajegunle and Kakuri were ethnically homogeneous; 62% and 52% included tenants from more than one of Nigeria's three major regions. Stren[48] found that the Majengo area of Mombasa was ethnically more heterogeneous and religiously more balanced than the Tudor Housing Estate; the latter had very few Muslims (see Table 13). This heterogeneity is socially important because it provides opportunities for residents to meet people of differing background, breaking down stereotypes and increasing tolerance. Acceptance of this opportunity varies; some people prefer a tight-knit community of 'people like us' while others choose more open networks. But friendships tend to be more mixed where opportunities are greater.

Table 13 shows that residents of the more heterogeneous Majengo had more friends of different ethnicity and religion than residents of the Tudor Estate, most of whom were Christian and where fewer ethnic groups were represented. Residents of two low-income suburbs in Nigeria were as likely as those in Majengo to have friends of another religion, but less likely to have

(44) Fraenkel 1964, p.52; Shack 1973, p.256. (45) Dinan 1975. (46) 1974.
(47) 1975b, p.115. (48) 1972, p.103.

Table 13 Ethnicity and Religion of 3 Friends, by Place and Sex, Kenya and Nigeria*

Per cent of friends having the same	Mombasa, Kenya Tudor Estate	Majengo	Nigeria Ajegunle (Lagos) M	F	Kakuri (Kaduna) M	F
Ethnicity	64 (666)	42 (841)	66 (394)	82 (112)	69 (393)	55 (107)
Religion	92 (636)	69 (820)	57 (404)	68 (112)	57 (370)	60 (104)

Source: Stren 1973, p. 103; three best friends, males only. Peil, survey data; first three friends listed; not all listed three.
*The numbers in parenthesis are the bases for the percentages.

interethnic friendships. This may be due to the level of interethnic conflict in Nigeria, or merely to linguistic difficulties. English and Yoruba in Lagos and Hausa in Kaduna are less widely known than Swahili in Mombasa, but the high level of interethnic friendships among Kakuri women suggests that Hausa provides an easier means of communication for women than English or Yoruba. The Ajegunle women were more likely than the men to limit friendships to people of similar background, even though they were more often educated and employed than the Kakuri women.

The density of population in African cities is often considerably higher than in European cities, even though far more buildings in the latter than in the former have more than one storey. Such densities are only achieved when there are a large number of houses for the land area, a large number of small rooms per house and/or a large number of persons per room. Often all three exist together because the average household has more than two people and most households have only one room.

Table 14 shows that more than a third of the households in many towns have three or more people sharing each room and that over half of the households in most towns occupy a single room. Houses were less overcrowded in Abeokuta than elsewhere because a majority of the population live in large family houses, in which rooms are often left empty for returning migrants. Kisenyi and Mulago households were seldom overcrowded even though they had only one room because the migrants living there had often left their families at home. Although the worst cases of crowding are found among the poor, wealthy households are also often crowded because they must accom-

Table 14 Household Density on Two Standards, by Town (Percentages)

Country, Town and Year of Survey	Three or More Persons/Room	Occupying One Room or Less
Ghana: Accra 1960	42	78
Ashaiman 1968	47[a]	81
Kumasi 1967	55[a]	83
Sekondi/Takoradi 1967	38[a]	67
Tema 1968	42[a]	54
Kenya: Nairobi 1962	52	n.a.
Nigeria: Aba 1972	54[a]	58
Abeokuta 1972	12[a]	37
Ajegunle (Lagos) 1972	40[a]	81
Kakuri (Kaduna) 1972	30[a]	83
Uganda: Kisenyi (Kampala) 1954	15	75
Mulago (Kampala) 1954	8	60
Zambia: Lusaka 1969	54	b

Sources: Ghana: Ghana 1960, Vol. VI, Table B13; Peil 1972, p. 165; survey
    data (1968).
    Kenya: Bloomberg and Abrams 1964, p. 15.
    Nigeria and Ghana 1968: survey data.
    Uganda: Southall and Gutkind 1957, pp. 233–8.
    Zambia: Ohadike 1971, p. 192.
[a]2.6 or more persons per room, children under 5 counted as half.
[b]68% in one or two rooms.

modate visiting kinsmen, clients and servants. Ohadike[49] reports that upper-
and middle-income households in Lusaka average 2.3 and 2.4 people per
room, compared to 3.0 for lower-income households. He also found that
70% of the households in several villages near Lusaka had three or more
people per room; villagers are more likely than urban dwellers to have more
than one room, but are not necessarily less crowded. The 1960 Ghana Census
found rural Ghanaians were only slightly less crowded than those in towns;
35% of households had three or more persons per room and 47% lived in a
single room.

(49) 1971, p.192.

While people have differing cultural norms for crowding (some societies value privacy much more highly than others), concentration of people tends to increase the level of conflict because of the high pressure on resources and space. There are often too many people for the standpipes (with consequent fights over water), latrines, schools, buses, and so on. Children may have to sleep out of doors or wait until adults are ready to sleep, which can leave them too tired to do well at school. There is seldom space for them to study quietly. Conflicts over noise and the behaviour of children can easily arise. At the same time, many urban residents enjoy having large numbers of people around and reject the low density of higher-income areas as 'European'.[50]

Social control and deviance

All societies have rules governing the behaviour of their members and measures of social control to encourage observance of these rules. These include the socialisation of new members so they will be aware of the norms and sanctions against those who deviate. The word deviance can have various meanings. It is most often used in a moral sense, referring to an action which is considered to be against societal norms and therefore wrong. But it may also be used in a neutral sense for actions which are merely different. In a society in which almost every woman marries, a woman who remains single is deviant (different); if she is single because she is a prostitute, she may be defined as deviant (morally wrong). There are also various responses to deviance. Minor differences are usually tolerated and may even be approved (social change is essentially deviating from former ways); crimes which violate the mores of the society are severely punished.

Agents of social control

Agents of social control include parents, kinsmen, employers and fellow workers, community elders, neighbours, local leaders, government officers, the courts, the police and the army. Considerable social control is exercised within the family, as parents socialise their children into proper behaviour and punish them for deviance and kinsmen press for conformity to community norms.[51] Community elders often deal with offenders even though they have been deprived of the courts they formerly ran. People come to them for the settlement of disputes and abide by their decisions. Local gossip

(50) Wober 1967; Bujra 1973.   (51) For example, Colson (1953) shows how public opinion, obligations to the local community and crosscutting kinship ties are used to maintain social control and public order in rural Tonga society.

also serves to make many people conform. In the towns and cities, these informal agents of control still operate, but it is easier for those who reject their authority to escape. Zarr's report on Liberia[52] applies in varying measure to cities elsewhere: 'In the urban areas the cohesiveness increasingly gives way to individualism and the vacuum created by the decline in family and tribal authority has only been filled by the impersonal sanctions of the law.' The lower efficiency of these formal sanctions is evident in the growing crime rates reported by Clinard and Abbott.[53]

Informal social control usually remains strong in indigenous areas of towns[54] and operates in other neighbourhoods with a relatively stable population or where a cohesive community has developed. For example, Quarcoo[55] describes a new suburban community near Accra where the leader was able to maintain strong social control over residents in the early years. They even established a Volunteer Town Guard to reduce crime. Volunteers who distinguished themselves at communal labour were given awards and derogatory songs were sung about those who failed to cooperate. However, as the town grew, those who lived on the outskirts and worked elsewhere often showed a lack of communal spirit, which weakened the leader's position.

Parkin[56] shows how gossip provides a framework for socialisation into proper urban behaviour and sanctions against deviants in a Kampala housing estate. This is important to the women, who have little else to do and seldom leave the neighbourhood, but much less important to the men, who spend most of their time elsewhere. Gossip among friends involves evaluation of norms as well as retelling of 'facts'; implicit in this is the control which the group exercises over the activities of those who wish to remain members of it.[57] Participation in the group also means accepting arbitration of conflicts. Ampene[58] reports that members of ethnic associations who take their disputes to outside courts rather than having them solved by the leaders of the association are considered a threat to group solidarity; such an act may lead to withdrawal from the group or ostracism by the group.

Formal social control is in the hands of the police and the courts. During the colonial era, the police were often seen as instruments of alien oppression, though on the criteria of relative education and income they had fairly high prestige.[59] Tamuno[60] reports that the chief complaints of the Nigerian public against their policemen, both before and after independence, have been 'ruthlessness, brutality and the use of violence'. While there is some gratitude

(52) 1969, p.194.   (53) 1973, pp.12–13.   (54) Bamisaiye 1974, p.75.   (55) 1966.
(56) 1969, p.64.   (57) Epstein in Mitchell 1969a.   (58) 1967, p.79.   (59) Mitchell in Lloyd 1966, p.267.   (60) 1970, pp.253, 268.

toward them insofar as they help to maintain public order, too often they appear to put state interests or their own private interests above those of the general public, whom they are supposed to be serving. Many see their job in terms of a personal career rather than a public service; their willingness to drop charges in exchange for a bribe and to use their power to extort bribes when no offence has been committed has made them unpopular in many areas. It was notable that the 1966 Ghana coup, carried out by the army and police, greatly increased army prestige but had little effect on police prestige. Efforts are being made to improve training and salaries, but this problem is by no means confined to Africa and a quick solution seems unlikely. The combination of considerable power and authority, relatively moderate qualifications and income and wide scope for individual decisions almost inevitably means that some individuals are recruited who make the most of their opportunities.[61]

There is a wide variety of courts, from customary courts run by local chiefs and their elders to civil courts run by lay magistrates and high courts under professional judges. Where judges have remained above politics, their prestige is generally high, but magistrates known to take bribes may meet with public derision. Lack of understanding of laws and the manipulations of imported judicial procedures have been (and continue to be) major problems. Post and Jenkins[62] report the reactions of many rioters tried in Ibadan in 1958: 'The morality of the issue was fought out by lawyers in courts where the judges wore wigs and spoke English, where it became clear that "the truth" would be punished, and where the purchase of conflicting evidence could often gain one his release.' A 1966 study of eastern Nigerian villagers[63] showed that only 8% of the Ibo and 54% of the non-Ibo thought they would have a good chance of getting justice if they were involved in a court case.

Traditional courts aimed at restoring community solidarity rather than strict justice. For those accustomed to this system, it is difficult to accept the idea that the same fine should be imposed regardless of circumstances or that a man who is obviously in the right could lose his case on a point of law. Skinner[64] reports that Ouagadougou judges tend to take local customs into account and react sympathetically when individuals have been unwittingly caught by the law, but this adaptability is often missing elsewhere, especially for those who cannot afford a bribe or a lawyer. Thus, courts are much less effective agents of social control than they might be because they act as agents of oppression. Disputants usually prefer to take their case to local leaders, in the expectation that they will judge according to communal

(61) See Potholm 1969.   (62) 1973, p.441.   (63) Smock 1971, p.228.   (64) 1974.

norms and personal knowledge of the contestants.[65]

Deviance: goals and means

To a considerable extent, deviance is the creation of society. Whatever a society or a group within a society define as deviant is so treated by its members. Activities which are acceptable or even highly rewarded in one society may be deviant in another. This is particularly notable with 'civil deviance'; people in various countries are expected to drive on the right or the left, to pay certain taxes, attend school, carry identity papers, avoid certain types of behaviour, etc. However, there are also certain types of behaviour which are defined by all or almost all societies as deviant (murder, incest, theft), even though the precise definition may vary from one society to another and justification may be accepted in certain circumstances. Killing an outsider may not be defined as murder and ritual murder on the death of a chief or jural murder of someone who has committed a serious crime (in many societies, this includes theft) may be permitted or even approved of.[66] But outside institutionalised boundaries there is universal condemnation because such behaviour is seen as threatening the continuance of the group.

In a heterogeneous, plural society, there may be considerable ambiguity as to what 'normal' behaviour is and what deviance is. This usually results in tolerance of many kinds of behaviour which might be considered deviance in a more homogeneous society, especially civil deviance. Clinard and Abbott[67] made comparative studies of people living in two low-income areas of Kampala and of offenders and non-offenders. They found that fighting, beer-brewing and prostitution were less often considered wrong in Kisenyi (which has a high crime rate) than in Namuwongo (which has a low rate), but that stealing was considered equally wrong by young and old in both places. Thus, there was more ambiguity about civilly-defined offences which are, at best, weakly opposed by traditional norms, than about offences which are strongly condemned by societal norms. The offenders (in goal, often for theft) tended to justify theft from the rich, drunkenness and prostitution, but they showed the same attitudes towards beer-brewing, bribery and wife-beating as the non-offenders.

Thus, there is general agreement on some norms but less consensus on others; societies also differ considerably in their consensus on societal goals and the means of obtaining them. (Consensus and conflict theorists differ on the level and nature of agreement, but most concede that societies have some common values plus considerable scope for a diversity of opinions on other

(65) See Lowy 1974 for a discussion of the Ghanaian use of courts and local leaders for conflict resolution, and Ross 1974 for a report on conflict resolution in a Nairobi suburb. (66) Bohannan 1960, pp.232–3. (67) 1973, pp.164, 209.

aspects of behaviour, the areas where deviance is considered neutral or easily tolerated. The question then becomes what are the variations in acceptance of means and goals and what are the implications of this variance for the society?)

Merton[68] has proposed a typology to clarify these differences. The behaviour of members of a society will depend on their acceptance of the goals of that society and the institutionalised means to reach these goals (see Figure 14). If, for example, material success is a major goal of a society, rules which encourage people to seek success and reward those who achieve it will be generally approved by citizens. In such a society, people who do not seek material success will be considered deviants, but it is also possible to seek success in ways not approved of by the rules; these may or may not be considered deviant in a moral sense.

Type	Culture goals	Institutionalised means
Conformity	+	+
Innovation	+	−
Ritualism	−	+
Retreatism	−	−
Rebellion	±	±

Figure 14 A typology of modes of adaptation *(Source: Merton 1957, p.140)*

Conformity (acceptance of both goals and means) is prevalent in stable societies. It could be argued that where there is general acceptance of both goals and means, where most people conform to what is expected of them, the society is likely to be relatively stable. Change brings in new goals and new means, making agreement more difficult and less likely. Deviance will be greatest when social control is weakened by mobility or changing community norms. Merton regards the four other types of adaptation as in some sense deviant. Where certain goals are held up as relevant to and attainable by all members of the society while at the same time these goals are not in fact reachable by the majority, various forms of deviance are likely to occur.

The innovator accepts the goal (wealth, popularity, power), but rejects the institutionalised means (hard work, service to others, election). He may, instead, seek wealth through theft or power through violence. If this individual is successful in attaining his goal, he may be considered deviant

(68) 1957, pp.140–57.

by those who reached the goal in more normal ways but not by others who share his orientation (deny that only the institutionalised means are acceptable) or who feel that they have no chance of reaching the goal if they stick to the institutionalised means.

Ritualism, like innovation, may be due to imperfect socialisation; the individual accepts part but not all of the cultural package. The ritualist lowers his goals to something he can more easily reach (a small house in his village rather than a large mansion in town) but accepts the means so fully that no possible deviation from them can be considered. This is the 'typical' bureaucrat, who knows and applies all the rules even when this interferes with fulfilling the organisation's goals; he never competes, never takes a chance and trains his children to be similarly law-abiding. Few members of the society see him as a deviant; he never does anything 'wrong'. Only the outside observer notes that his lack of success is tied to a lack of striving.

Retreatism, the rejection of both goals and means, is uncommon. Merton argues that the retreatist is not really a member of society because he does not share its values, but this may be too harsh. People who retreat into defeatism, drugs, or quiet resignation to their lot have often been frustrated in their attempts to reach societal goals and are unable to use illegitimate means, but they may still feel that the goals are all right for other members of the society (denying them only for themselves) and the very fact that they consider some means illegitimate implies participation in a society which establishes norms for behaviour. However, there are also people who fit into no community. Often they are mentally ill, having retreated from society into a private world of their own. Others may merely seem to wander about with no particular goals, just surviving somehow. That these are recognised as deviants is an indication of the level of general consensus on societal goals.

Rebellion characterises the revolutionary. He not only rejects the goals and means of the majority (like the retreatist), but seeks to substitute new goals and means to make a new society. He aims to bring together all those who are frustrated because they have found the goals unreachable, to convince them that the institutionalised means are unfair and favour some over others, and to help them to make basic changes in the social structure of their society. Typically, it is not the least advantaged members of the society (who tend to be conformists or ritualists) but those whose conditions have improved somewhat who rebel. Many young people go through a period of rebellion. Their aspirations are very high and they lack patience and become easily frustrated. At the same time, they are often more receptive to new ideas than older people and therefore more likely to be interested in substitution of new goals and/or means and less willing to accommodate to society as they find it.

As with other ideal types, these patterns are seldom found in pure form in real life. Rather than accepting or rejecting *all* goals or *all* means, people generally pick and choose. Many adolescents who rebel by migrating to the city instead of staying home to help with the farming continue to strongly value family life to the extent of sending money home, visiting regularly and helping kinsmen when called on; in this they are conformists. Even gangs of thieves who have adopted their own special language and way of life may be 'law-abiding' when not on a job, paying for rent, meals and cinema tickets and courting in the customary way.

Crime

To be considered a crime, behaviour must be contrary to one of the society's formal laws rather than just deviating from custom. The study of criminology raises some questions which differ from those of deviance, but there are many continuities. For instance, the differential opportunity theory suggests that some members of a society have less access to societal goals and therefore must use illegitimate means to obtain them. It is also often suggested that individuals are socialised to crime by others who are already part of the system; just as conformists are socialised to accept societal values, deviants are socialised to reject them.

A distinction must be made between crime involving civil laws and crime which indicates rejection of community norms. A migrant to the city may easily fall foul of traffic regulations which he has never heard of and sees no reason for. Skinner[69] reports that riding a bicycle without headlights is the most common traffic violation in Ouagadougou. Cyclists see no need for lights on lighted city streets when none are used on the dark roads at home. Beer brewing is against the law in many cities, but since it is taken for granted in the rural areas and fills a social need, the law is usually safely ignored as long as the brewer breaks another law by giving periodic bribes to the police.[70] On the other hand, theft is condemned as against both the civil and the moral law. Neighbours may beat up a thief rather than turning him over to the police because they are concerned with reforming him or chasing him out of their neighbourhood and fear that the law will be too lenient.

Crime rates are usually highest in low-income areas, but this is not necessarily the case. Bamisaiye[71] found that areas of Ibadan where middle- and high-income immigrants lived had higher crime rates than low-income indigenous areas. The important factor here is the effective social control in indigenous Ibadan, which inhibits both delinquency and adult crime; offenders are handled without turning them over to the police. People living in the

(69) 1974, p.350.   (70) Ross 1973.   (71) 1974.

more impersonal immigrant areas have much less control over deviants and are more likely to use police services.

Clinard and Abbott also found significant differences in crime rates within the low-income sector of Kampala society. Where community elders continue to maintain their authority and are able to promote cohesiveness, crime rates are likely to be low even though the area has a transient population; the elders provide continuity and newcomers find their place within a living community. Where this cohesiveness does not exist, leaving everyone to compete on his own, crime rates are likely to be much higher:

> Factors such as physical conditions, socioeconomic status, or population stability do not distinguish between slum communities with high and low crime rates. The low crime community appears to have a much higher degree of unity, expressed by a higher incidence of visiting, participation in local organisations, restricted friendship patterns, and stability in family relationships. By cultural homogeneity and strong emphasis on tribal ties and kin ties members of the low crime community manage to evade the heterogeneity, impersonality, and anonymity that prevailed in areas of high crime. The predominance of primary bonds in a neighbourhood reduced the propensity to steal from a neighbour and made the unnoticed entrance of a stranger less likely. Older persons demonstrated a critical capacity to maintain the unity of the population and helped to enforce compliance to community rules.[72]

Similarly, one distinguishing characteristic of offenders when compared with non-offenders was their relative isolation from urban society. Offenders were more likely to have migrated to Kampala from a village and either to lack kinsmen in town to whom they could turn for help or to ignore them and spend their time with friends of other ethnic groups. Surprisingly, the offenders were slightly more likely than non-offenders to visit their homes, to own land there and to say that they planned to return home eventually. This suggests that young men who get into trouble with the police have found adjustment to urban life difficult. Rural ties provide a sense of security which they miss in town; with greater support from older migrants, fewer would become deviants.[73]

Even when crime is correlated with slum conditions, this does not prove that the poor either commit or endure the most crime. Criminal statistics are notoriously unreliable because crimes are often unreported and because of the considerable leeway given police in defining when a crime has been committed. Crimes may be unreported because no one is aware that a crime

(72) Clinard and Abbott 1973, pp.256–7.   (73) *Ibid.,* pp.125–7, 256.

has been committed, because people handle the matter themselves (by telling no one or by family or communal punishment of the delinquent), or because they have no faith that the police will be able or willing to take appropriate action (recover the stolen goods, find and punish the offender). Therefore, the number of crimes reported (especially minor crimes) is a gross underestimate. The statistics provide even less information on the level of crime when they refer to offenders who have been caught and punished; this is rather an index of police activity. Increases from year to year are as likely to mean an increase in the size of the police force or its level of activity as an increase in the crime rate. One reason there appears to be little rural crime is that in rural areas most deviant activities short of murder are handled through informal social control; villages seldom have a police post to which the victim could report.

The presence of policemen also increases the crime rate because it is often their definition which classifies an activity as a crime. If there were no policemen, no one would be arrested for begging, 'wandering and having no place of abode', or 'being exposed to physical and moral danger'; the last two are frequent causes of children being brought to court.[74] Skinner[75] reports that the Ouagadougou municipal authorities expected a substantial income from fines, so policemen were ordered to crack down on traffic offences which they might otherwise have ignored.[76] Police selectivity also accounts for some of the differential in crime rates between rich and poor. A well-dressed son of a minister is less likely to be fined for reckless driving than an illiterate lorry driver and the poor are more often arrested 'on suspicion' than the rich. It is sometimes argued that everyone commits crimes but only the poor get caught. This is an overstatement, as the majority of both poor and rich are essentially law-abiding. The poor probably have both greater opportunity and greater need to commit crimes, though the most innovative criminals are by no means the poorest members of society. The poor man's theft becomes the rich man's embezzlement.

The majority of crime is committed by young males. Only 4% of arrests in Kampala and 3% of convicted persons in Sekondi/Takoradi were women.[77] These low rates are related to the narrower social field and greater support which females receive. Busia remarks that girls are much less likely than boys to become juvenile delinquents because they are busy helping their mothers and have little time to roam the streets. Young boys whose fathers are dead or away can easily get out of control. Women rarely commit

(74) Busia 1950, pp.92–3. (75) 1974, p.351. (76) It is encouraging to know that Ouagadougou drivers can be arrested for excessive horn blowing. There are many other towns whose residents would be grateful for such a law. (77) Clinard and Abbott 1973, p.94; Busia 1950, p.107.

murder[78] and when they do it tends to be associated with mental illness.[79] Women are mainly involved in domestic institutions, especially in rural areas, whereas men face a wider variety of situations in which conflict can occur and also have greater access to lethal weapons.

Young men are particularly likely to get into trouble because they migrate in the largest numbers and must face most fully the discontinuities brought about by social change. Traditional ceremonies symbolising adulthood and full membership in the community have either been discontinued or seem less meaningful; the schools have socialised them to expect independence and wage employment; and they are often faced with unemployment or low income in a society which glorifies material possessions and power, two things they manifestly lack. Young gangs, reported in many towns, are a response to the need for companionship and support and an attempt to obtain the material goods their members value; their criminal activities mainly involve theft.

Skinner[80] reports considerable cooperation between Ouagadougou gangs, with a sharing out of territories to minimise conflict. Gang leaders are usually better educated and better dressed than members and maintain strict discipline within the group. New members are carefully taught their 'trade'. The social as well as criminal activities of the gang develop solidarity and provide young migrants with a satisfying way of life for a few years, until they are able to find regular employment. Those who get caught may be taught a trade in a borstal or reform school, improving their chances of employment over those of their colleagues who remained free.

Table 15 gives an indication of the common types of crimes. Theft, robbery and burglary, and assault and battery accounted for 70% of the arrests of Kampala males, 68% of the Kampala female arrests and 48% of the Ouagadougou cases. Busia[81] reported that 52% of those convicted by the Sekondi Magistrates' Court over a six-month period were guilty of stealing, house-breaking or 'being on premises for unlawful purposes'. Opportunities for theft are much greater in towns than in villages. The chance of getting caught is relatively small (especially if one works as part of a well-organised gang) and much less guilt is felt when stealing from strangers, especially the rich, than over theft from kinsmen or friends. Embezzlement, forgery, smuggling (contrabanding) and fraud are also used in attempts to get rich quickly, by making the most of any opportunities. Hart[82] argues that most of these activities attract little opprobrium in Nima (a slum area with a bad reputation among residents of other parts of Accra). Successful confidence tricksters such as money-doublers build up considerable local prestige.

(78) Bohannan 1960, p.240.　(79) Asuni 1969, p.1106.　(80) 1974, p.355.　(81) 1950, p.106.　(82) 1973, pp.74–6.

Table 15 Crimes in Kampala and Ouagadougou (percentages)

Type of crime	Kampala 1968 Males	Females	Ouagadougou 1963
Persons			
Assault and battery	29·3	53·4	15·1
Murder, attempted murder, manslaughter	0·7	0·5	3·7
Breach of trust	—	—	9·3
Insulting or evading officer of the law	0·3	0·3	5·4
Rape and other sexual offences	0·8	1·6	—
Other[a]	—	—	2·7
Property			
Robbery, theft, burglary and attempted burglary	40·6	14·4	32·8
Receiving, possession of stolen property	5·2	2·1	8·0
Forgery, fake pretences, counterfeiting, fraud	2·4	1·6	3·4
Arson, malicious damage	2·8	4·0	—
Embezzlement	—	—	1·1
Contrabanding	—	—	0·6
Corruption	0·3	—	—
Other			
Vagrancy, juvenile delinquency, idle and disorderly	6·5	7·7	8·2
Illegal possession of arms, illegal hunting	—	—	4·0
Traffic violations	—	—	2·9
Lack of permit	—	—	1·7
Miscellaneous	—	—	1·7
Total	100·0	100·0	100·0
N	8 827	375	754

Sources: Kampala: Clinard and Abbott 1973, p. 94; refers to arrests.
   Ouagadougou: Skinner 1974, p. 384; refers to cases heard at First Degree Court. Some of these have been referred from rural areas.
[a]Contributing to accidents through violation of labour ordinances, sorcery and abandoning the home. Many other cases of abandoning the home are heard by the Customary Court, which deals with divorces.

Whereas crimes against property are usually planned, crimes against persons are often accidental: a man starts beating his wife and goes too far, drunks fight, someone strikes in anger or to protect his property from a thief. The high proportion of women arrested for assault and battery is due to their lack of participation in other crimes rather than aggressiveness, though women do occasionally strike out at their husbands or children. (As conflict theory suggests, the need to repress conflict within kin groups may mean a more violent expression eventually than if grievances could more easily be expressed when they occurred.) Women are less willing to be submissive in town than in the country, and resentment at their husband's treatment may be channelled into aggression. More often, however, it leads to their leaving him; the town provides a chance of independence.

Homicide and assault are also far more characteristic of low- than of high-status individuals. This is not just a case of selective enforcement of the law; Asuni[83] suggests that people of high status have other outlets for their aggression (dominating clients, running a business) and thus have less need for homicidal acts. Homicide is frequently a domestic matter; killer and victim are usually either kinsmen or well known to each other. This is because conflicts serious enough for homicide are built up over a long period; other cases tend to be accidents or due to mental illness.[84] Study of the most common relationships between killer and victim indicates stress patterns in the society just as accusations of witchcraft and sorcery do.

Corruption is seldom a court matter, however widespread it may be in the society. Highly publicised corruption trials after a military coup are more often a political gesture to gain popularity for the new government than a serious attempt to root out corruption from public life. Individuals caught taking bribes may be sacked or taken to court, but this is probably because they are considered unsatisfactory in other respects rather than for corruption *per se*. (Smith[85] shows that this pattern has a long history among the Hausa.) Corruption is often condemned as a deviation from the norms of public morality, but the norms are ambiguous; in practice it is often difficult to draw a line between expected behaviour and corrupt behaviour.

If corruption can be used in a neutral rather than a pejorative sense, there are occasions when the norms prescribe behaviour which might be considered by outsiders to be corrupt.[86] For example, elected officials who give no special consideration to their constituents when they have jobs, contracts, or other favours to dispense are seen by many as betraying a trust. Similarly, the man who refuses to help his kinsmen under any circumstances is often considered selfish rather than incorrupt. O'Brien[87] shows that the

(83) 1969, p.1106.   (84) Bohannan 1960, pp.242–5.   (85) 1964.   (86) Leys 1965.
(87) 1975, p.198.

redistribution of wealth gained by corrupt religious leaders has important advantages for illiterate and powerless Senegalese farmers:

Corruption does not work solely to the advantage of the already privileged: indeed the total eradication of corruption from the Senegalese state (admittedly a remote eventuality) might well leave the peasants altogether defenceless before a technically qualified bureaucracy.

Ottenberg [88] suggests that local authority corruption involves four value conflicts:

1 The nature of governmental authority. The colonial government established rational-legal authority, but the people expect traditional patterns to be maintained.

2 The status and role of elders. Young men often have power but old men continue to hold authority in the community.

3 Achievement motivation. The norm is that personal achievement should be shared with one's family.

4 Relations with outsiders. Where the norms provide for trust only between kinsmen or friends, giving and accepting a bribe may provide the basis for personalising a relationship.

Corruption can be divided into three types of decreasing acceptability: service or welfare, taxation or business and power.

The provision of services for kinsmen and clients is widely expected and condoned. Prestige in the community often depends on it. The informal taxation of businessmen and scholars which enriches so many civil servants is tolerated where it has not become excessive because those who pay the bribes generally gain far more than their investment. They pay a fairly standard price and receive a valuable service in return. However, this arrangement is seen as exploitation by those who cannot afford to pay and is resented if the officer keeps the money for himself rather than sharing it liberally with kinsmen and people at home. Those who use power to maintain power, most clearly seen in election rigging, are despised by the ordinary people, though they often feel helpless to do anything about it. Power corruption tends to lead to social unrest and demands to reform or replace the government practising it.[89]

Other types of crime, accounting for about 7% in Kampala and 18% in Ouagadougou, are mainly the result of civil regulations and often have little meaning to the general population. Like laws against corruption, enforcement is seldom regular or consistent and bears more harshly on low- than

(88) 1967, pp.33–6.   (89) Peil 1976b, Chapter 3.

on high-status people. Such laws encourage corruption, because neither offenders nor officers of the law see much harm in evading them. The high proportion of cases of insulting or evading the police in Ouagadougou shows another effect; attempting to enforce laws which are unpopular or not understood lowers the status of the police, who are seen as oppressing the people.

Conclusion

Unemployment, poor housing and social control or deviance are all topics with political and economic as well as social implications. Government decisions to act or not to act and local and international economic conditions affect their prevalence. They are of specifically sociological interest not because sociologists as such can do anything about them but because study of those affected provides important clues to the nature of man in society. Social problems are the product or cause of conflict, and the way they are handled tells us something about what holds men together as well as about their divisions.

Strong patterns of family ties are demonstrated in the support given during unemployment and the social control exercised to prevent deviance. The nature of social interaction found in different types of houses and the style of housing built by those who have a choice indicate responses to spatial constraints and changing expectations about family life. Study of heterogeneous houses and neighbourhoods suggests patterns of inter-group social exchange which may later spread through the society as heterogeneity becomes more common. The rate of increase in crime and delinquency (for all the inadequacy of the statistics) provides some indication of how members of the society are coping with social change. It may also suggest where the strains are greatest and therefore where there is the most need for governmental action. So far, traditional norms remain a strong force for minimising deviance and the effects of migration and unemployment.

Suggested reading and discussion topics

1. What parts of the city you live in are known as slums? Do the presumed characteristics of these places differ from one place to another? To what extent are these stereotypes based on evidence rather than rumour?
2. Investigate the statistics available on local unemployment. What definition is used? On what sample are they based? How often are they revised? How might they be improved?
3. Read Leys 1965, Ottenberg 1967, or Smith 1964 and discuss the social aspect of corruption in Africa.
4. Look for all references to crime in the local newspaper over the past

month. Draw up a table showing the number of cases for each type of crime and whether they took place in (a) the capital, (b) other towns, or (c) rural areas. To what extent is this table representative of crimes which actually took place during this period?

10 Social Change

Much of this book has been concerned with the changes which have taken place in African societies during the past fifty years. This chapter provides an opportunity to examine various theories of social change, to see how they can be applied to the data we have been studying and to discuss the factors in-involved in the acceptance or rejection of innovations.

All societies experience a certain amount of change in their social structure and culture over time, and explanations of the causes and nature of this change have been part of the sociologist's task from the beginning of the discipline. Societies cannot remain stable because they are in contact with other societies which do things somewhat differently; ideas, norms and institutions spread from one society to another. Even the most isolated society must have some change from time to time as its members adjust to varying environmental conditions (such as prolonged drought) or invent new ways of doing things.

Because of the interdependence of the various institutions of a society, change in one area tends to lead to change in other areas, just as a pebble thrown into water sets off a series of ripples. Take the introduction of motor transport. The vehicles needed roads rather than footpaths, so people had to be organised to build these roads. New jobs were introduced, such as driver or fitter. Goods and people could now move more easily from place to place; this aided centralisation, government control and the development of cash crop farming. This, in turn, affected the roles of men and women within the family because the cash crop was usually the prerogative of the men.[1] Easier travel encouraged migration, and thus a more extensive mixing of people and the spread of ideas, language and material culture (food, cloth-ing styles, music) from one group to another. Whole villages moved nearer to the road, and villages with good access to motor transportation often grew into towns. This involved changes in the way of life of villagers; they had less time for festivals, took on new jobs, improved their standard of living, built larger and better houses and travelled more from place to

(1) Boserup 1970.

336

place.[2] Each of these effects could be followed to show more changes. The car/lorry is only one of the causes of these changes, but without it many of them would not have happened or would have happened only much later.

Social change may be studied as a short-term or as a long-term phenomenon (the Industrial Revolution, over fifty or a hundred years, or the response of a nomadic group to a two-year drought). We can focus on changes in cultural patterns (religious values, symbols of status), in social structure (family adjustment to the absence of migrant fathers), in aggregated attributes (the proportion of the population which is illiterate or engaged in farming), or in rates of behaviour (increased crime, decreased self-employment). Two or more of these variables may be combined. We want to know under what conditions change will take place and what sort of changes should be expected in response to various pressures.[3] Some decision must be made as to the start and finish of the period to be studied in order to keep the project within manageable proportions. It is best to concentrate on the proximate causes of this particular change and the more immediate reactions to it rather than trying to trace out all the antecedents and effects over an indefinite period, because the data for such an expanded treatment are almost never available.

Change may be examined from the point of view of the social system (the whole society) or from the view of the individual. Mitchell[4] calls the first historical or processive change and the second situational change. The major theories of change have been concerned with historical change, the evolution of institutions over time and the processes by which societies move from one type to another. Much less attention has been given to change as experienced by individuals or groups within a society, except by modernisation theorists, and even these have based their ideas on abstractions developed to account for societal change. Mitchell's suggestion that individuals are responding to the situation in which they find themselves is helpful in isolating some of the factors involved in individual change, but it seems to rule out the possibility of permanent assimilation of new norms, values, or behaviour patterns which are then carried from one situation to another. Individuals do not just respond to urban or rural life, to factory employment or the experience of studying at a university at the moment; their attitudes and behaviour in a situation are the product of all of their experiences up to that time. This is why two men in the same situation react in different ways.

There is a tendency to see change as inevitably bringing improvement (or, for pessimists, of always bringing misfortune). However, change only means that attitudes, behaviour, technology, or social institutions are different

(2) Lawson 1972.   (3) Smelser 1968, pp.200–1.   (4) 1966.

from what they were yesterday or last year or twenty years ago. Much of the emphasis in studies of social change has been on major societal changes such as the industrial and urban revolutions, which involved the development of new patterns in all four variables mentioned above. But there are also many more minor changes which are worth investigating. New words are added to the language and old words are given new meaning; the spread of material possessions such as radios, cars, or motor scooters increases the geographical area with which individuals are in contact and thus influences their attitudes on who is an 'outsider'; changes in the educational curriculum and an increase in the proportion of the population attending primary school lead to changed ideas about the world and about one's place in it (aspirations); new voluntary associations are inaugurated and old ones cease to function; networks of friends take in new members and lose others. Many of these minor changes affect only a small number of people, but they may make a significant difference to the people concerned. A full conception of social change must include them.

A problem arising from the chain effect of social change is that change in one part of a system is not automatically geared to change in another part. Ogburn has called this differential rate of change 'cultural lag'.[5] He argued that material culture (especially technology) changes much faster than non-material culture (beliefs, values, norms, social organisation). For example, the streets of many towns are full of cars, but people still think of streets as places for trading, walking and playing. Where people accept that cars are a useful addition to society but do not accept that the streets should be left free for the movement of cars, a dangerous situation is created. Wherever there is a lag, there is pressure for adjustment. Sometimes this becomes a conflict between those who accept the changes and those who think the old ways are best; sometimes there is a demand for institutional change. In this case, there may be calls for new laws to keep people out of the streets or to limit access of cars to certain streets.

Another type of lag exists when one institution develops more rapidly than another, as has been the case of education and industry in many countries. The spread of education has led to demands for more jobs for the products of the schools or, given unemployment of school-leavers, for a curriculum more suited to the needs of the students. Ogburn's theory was not well enough developed to be tested (rates of change are very difficult to measure and material and non-material culture are so interrelated that it is almost impossible to separate them completely), but it does serve to alert us to change as a process of adjustment and especially to the necessary links

(5) Chinoy 1967, pp.490–1.

between changes in technology and social structure.

Theories of change

The type of theory one develops (or accepts) depends on the sort of questions one asks (What is it we want to explain?) and one's underlying model of society (What are the most fundamental institutions and social processes?). Some theorists are most concerned with how social change begins; others take it for granted that change is more or less continuous in all societies and are more interested in explaining how people react to various pressures for change. Those who see economic or political institutions as the most basic are likely to explain change as coming from and being resolved by actors in these areas. Those who think of society as basically integrated look for a return to integration after a period of disturbance; those who emphasise societal conflict concentrate on the continuing strains and division as pressure for further change. Finally, there is a long-standing allegiance to the idea of progress, development, modernisation, etc., which implies a continuous movement towards a better society.

Theorists have often sought a single cause of change; technology, ideas, economics, conflict and the interaction between cultures have been suggested. Change can be caused by all these factors, but none of them is a necessary and sufficient cause for all change. For example, the idea that aliens are a danger to the society can change the way these people are treated and lead to their expulsion from the country. In this case, the idea was sufficient to cause the change (the charge may not be true), but it was not necessary. The change might have come about in some other way, such as improved technology which made these workers superfluous to national needs. If changes in the economic structure of the society are responsible for other changes in other sectors, as Marxists hold, the ultimate cause of change is not economic but whatever caused the economic changes. There are also many changes which do not have an economic component, though a Marxist might argue that these are not fundamental. However, this merely leads to the impossible task of defining fundamental change. It seems better to accept that social change has many causes rather than just one and to find out which causes are most important in the instance of change being studied.[6]

Evolution and differentiation
Early sociologists were concerned chiefly with the origins of society and the

(6) Cohen 1968, pp.179–207.

transformations necessary to reach the type of society they were experiencing. Since Darwin's ideas of biological evolution were gaining acceptance at this time, the theory of societal evolution also became popular. Comte, Marx, Spencer and Ward all thought of society as progressing from primitive beginnings to an eventual perfection, though the exact nature of this perfection differed. Evolutionary theories got into difficulty because of their methodological weaknesses, especially as more data on a variety of societies became available. First, they were carrying over into sociology ideas from biology, and the models often did not fit. It is possible to trace the evolution of animals from very simple forms (such as the amoeba or worm) to more complex animals and, finally, to man. But societies do not become increasingly complex in the same way. A society which seems in many ways to be simple may at the same time have a very complex kinship or religious system.

Second, there is little evidence about societies of the distant past; theorists must rely on guesses and observation of people now living who seem to have retained a 'primitive' way of life. But these people represent a history as long as our own; we do not know whether they lived in the same way 500 or 5000 years ago or have changed just as we have. It is highly likely that some changes have taken place, and unlikely that they have been as ordered as the evolutionists suggest. While it is very likely that hunting and gathering preceded settled agriculture (i.e., that the Bushmen of Namibia and the Hadza of Tanzania represent an earlier stage of development than neighbouring agricultural peoples) and that this necessarily precedes the development of industry, similar stages cannot be postulated for the development of family or religious institutions. (The Arusha of Tanzania have changed from a pastoral to an agricultural way of life, but many of their social institutions have remained identical to those of the Masai, from whom they separated.[7]) Third, because of these difficulties, evolutionists do not agree on the order of development or what characterises societies at various stages of development. Evolutionism has been largely discredited, but has reappeared in theories of modernisation. These will be discussed below.

Theories of structural differentiation take us somewhat further than the evolutionism from which they are derived. They originated in the work of Spencer and Durkheim, and have been further developed by Parsons and Smelser.[8] The basic idea is that as societies develop there is an increasing separation and specialisation of institutions, which must then be reintegrated into a new whole. In a simple society, the family is responsible for religious, political and economic aspects of life as well as the reproduction and socialisation of new members. Increasing size of population and the uniting

(7) Gulliver 1969.   (8) 1968, pp.243–54.

of groups into a larger society makes more specialisation necessary and, as a result, various institutions attain a separate existence; we now have many governmental, religious and economic institutions which are to a greater or lesser extent interdependent.

Whereas Spencer and Durkheim were principally concerned with the fact of differentiation, later theorists have emphasised the process of change from a less to a more differentiated social structure. The impetus for change comes from dissatisfaction with things as they are. Individuals or groups who are dissatisfied express their hostility in various ways and engender conflict within the society between themselves and those who favour the *status quo*. Various agents of social control attempt to 'handle and channel' the disturbance, partly by repression and partly by trying to improve conditions to remove the cause of the difficulty; this latter may involve introducing new ideas or institutions. As these are integrated into the social system, it settles into a new, more differentiated form – until the next episode of dissatisfaction.

This model poses several problems. First, as the new system is likely to be to the disadvantage of some groups just as it is to the advantage of others, the society may never actually 'settle down', but leaders may have to continue handling and channelling social discontent. Second, authorities may be ineffective agents of social control, especially if they are strong supporters of the *status quo* and hence try to repress all demands for change. The society may go into a period of long-term social decline, or there may be a revolution or military coup which gains legitimacy and acceptance by the mass of the people because they see it as the only way to right their grievances. In this event, the society may undergo a long period of disruption, followed by considerable social change within a short period.

The end result may be further differentiation, or a consolidation and centralisation which does away with some specialisation, or relatively little fundamental change in social structure. In any case, there are likely to be some members of the society who are dissatisfied, so the process can be expected to continue. This theory is useful for describing the development of increasingly complex types of social organisation which accompanied and facilitated industrialisation,[9] but it needs further development before it can adequately handle the problems of why and when dissatisfaction arises and how the newly differentiated institutions are integrated into the society. These problems have also interested the equilibrium and conflict theorists.

(9) Smelser 1968, Chapter 4; Worsley 1970, pp.385–6.

The basic functionalist model is of a society in equilibrium, tending towards stability but reacting to change by adjusting so as to restore the equilibrium. These pressures for change can be exogenous (coming from outside the system, as war or international economic influence) or endogenous (from within the system, as new inventions or demands of the poor for more say in government). If the society is as united by consensus as strong functionalists hold, then we would expect that most pressures for change would be exogenous; members of a society would be satisfied with stability and tend to resist change. Conflict would arise mainly during the process of adjustment to forced change, when consensus is imperfect, or among people who were inadequately socialised so that they do not fully share the consensus of the majority. While it can be shown that conflict is more widespread than this theory assumes, it is also evident that relatively homogeneous, integrated societies may adjust more quickly and easily to change than societies which are split by conflicts. For example, integrated villages had little difficulty accepting the principle of electing government officials, whereas towns where factionalism was well established often experienced election violence.

Equilibrium theory is better for explaining gradual, long-term change such as the Industrial Revolution and changes applying to the society as a whole than in accounting for the more sudden political revolution and smaller endogenous changes where conflict often plays an obvious part. However, van den Berghe[10] suggests that the theory can be expanded once it is accepted that adjustment to change does not necessarily lead to immediate return to equilibrium. If, instead, reactions are dysfunctional and the situation gets worse and worse, it may require violence or even revolution to return the society to a new state of relative balance.

In this case, the relative balance is between institutions; if the economic system has become dominant over the political system (or vice versa), the new balance gives each a more equal part. Van den Berghe suggests that revolution is most likely if opposing groups refuse to compromise, have little communication and deny each other's legitimacy. This can be seen where the increasing isolation and repression of political leaders have led to military coups in some countries. However, revolution is often forestalled or at least delayed because members of conflicting groups have cross-cutting ties or play interdependent roles in the society or because the ruling group is able to control the expression of opposition. A society with many cross-cutting ties tends to be relatively open to change. If no one insists on conformity because heterogeneity of norms is widely accepted, change agents

(10) 1963, pp.698–9.

can easily introduce new ideas and people can get used to them gradually, without pressure for immediate acceptance or rejection. On the other hand, leaders who must maintain their position and control societal conflict by force cannot allow change because it might directly challenge their rule. In this case, revolution may be the only route to change.[11]

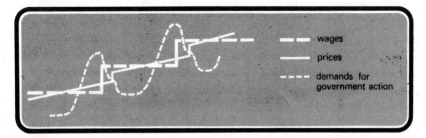

Figure 15 Dynamic equilibrium

Another adaptation of this theory is to look for dynamic rather than stable equilibrium. This accepts that the society does not return to the same position as before, but still looks for a relative balance on each adjustment to change. Figure 15 suggest a series of changes in the relationships between wages and prices. As prices climb relative to wages, the workers demand that the government raise the minimum wage. The government appoints a commission, and eventually establishes a new rate, at which time pressure on it drops. Prices jump in response to the wage rise (sometimes even in advance of it), then continue to go up slowly (a period of relative equilibrium). The general rise in the cost of living makes the workers less satisfied than they might have been with their wage increase, so they continue to press the government for adjustments. This pressure is initially low, because many workers are pleased with the increase they have achieved, but it grows in strength as prices continue to rise until the government has to respond by appointing another commission and granting another increase (a new and higher equilibrium). None of the three variables returns to its previous position, but the pattern of change and the relative balance between wages and prices may remain fairly regular. (In some situations, prices may get seriously out of balance due to rapid inflation, changing the pattern at least temporarily and perhaps precipitating a major change.)

Conflict theorists, following Marx, have seen change as arising largely from within the system, based on the opposition of ideologies, institutions, or groups. Marx taught that conflict of interests is an historical necessity which must inevitably lead to the revolutionary overthrow of a system which

(11) Coser 1956.

will not change of its own accord. As the economic system is most fundamental to society, it must change from capitalism to communism, after which other institutions such as the state and social classes can be disgarded as no longer necessary. More generally, conflict theorists argue that the pressures for change in society are ubiquitous as various interest groups struggle for power and resources. They often follow Dahrendorf[12] in shifting from the economic to the political system as the prime focus of conflict, since the struggle tends to emphasise replacing the ruling group. However, Worsley's assertion[13] that the 'overthrow of the ruling group will result in the introduction of new value-systems' overstates the case; many African coups have changed personnel at the top but had little or no effect on values because the new rulers have the same values as the rest of the society. Where the military try to introduce new values, as in Benin, they may face considerable opposition from the general public unless clear advantages of the new goals can be demonstrated.

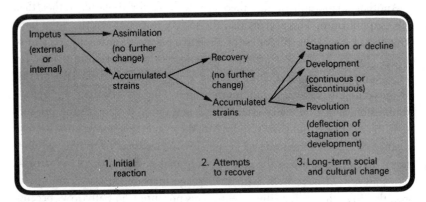

Figure 16 Phases of social change (adapted from Smelser 1968, p.277)

Figure 16 shows a model of change as a combination of conflict and consensus. At each phase, the society may react by adjusting to the impetus or showing strains and tensions which must be resolved in another phase. These strains, pressures for change, are often expressed as conflicts over whether change should take place and, if so, the form it should take.

Smelser[14] suggests that the effect of a change impetus in the first phase will depend on
1 its extent. A flood usually has fairly local effects which are handled within a short period, whereas a three-year drought over a wide area has more prolonged effects for far more people.

(12) 1959.   (13) 1970, p.387.   (14) 1968, pp.269-70.

2 whether it happens suddenly and unexpectedly or builds up gradually. A coup generates more pressure for change than gradually increasing unemployment.

3 the population's reaction to change. Some individuals and peoples find it easier to adjust to change than others, partly because of the level of psychological support they get from the society and its leaders. Those who feel secure can often accept changes more easily than those who feel threatened, while others willingly accept change because they have nothing to lose.

4 the level of structural specialisation. Societies which have highly differentiated and interdependent institutions are more subject to chain reactions of change than those where differentiation has not progressed so far. This can be shown most easily in terms of area specialisation. If each part of the country grows most of the food it needs, a breakdown in transportation such as a strike by railway workers or lorry drivers will be relatively unnoticed by the majority of the people. But if they depend on transport for an important part of their food supply (such as yams, plantains or rice), then the strike will cause much more widespread reaction and there will be demands for a quick solution, by innovation in industrial relations if necessary.

If the impetus is assimilated in the first phase, there is no further effect from this impetus. (The society returns to the relative equilibrium of its former state or to a new balance which incorporates the effects of the impetus. For example, the strike is over, and the workers go back to work, under the same or new wages and conditions.) However, there are often continuing strains and conflicts, which serve as the impetus for further change in phase 2. The result of this may be recovery (again, some sort of relative balance), or the persistence of conflicts (either old ones which have not been resolved or new ones in reaction to the society's attempts to handle and channel earlier dissatisfaction). Whether the society will be able to recover in the second phase depends on how extensive the strain is, how disruptive responses to it have been, the availability of communal resources to handle conflict and the ability of those in authority to handle socially disruptive behaviour and mobilise people and resources to overcome societal conflicts.

Finally, if the society does not recover at phase 2, the accumulated strains are passed on, with the expectation that some long-term social and/or cultural change will occur. The result also depends on the amount of strain and resources available to those who favour or oppose change to organise collective action. Political authorities, other leaders and social organisations may act either as change agents or in the interests of maintaining the *status quo*. The result (at least for this cycle of change) may be the stagnation and decline of the society, as the ancient kingdoms of Ghana and Songhai declined. It may lead to development of the society, either by further differentiation and specialisation of institutions on the same basic framework (continuous development) or by a more radical change in cultural norms and values which indicate a considerable change in direction, as with the widespread imposition of European norms on African societies during the colonial period.[15]

This process of discontinuous change was examined by Malinowski.[16] His work among the Trobriand Islanders of the Pacific led him to study the conflict, compromise and cooperation resulting from attempts of an 'impinging culture' to dominate indigenous cultures and the forces of tradition and reaction by which they respond. These ideas need to be brought up to date by including data from the last thirty years, when the response to Western culture (especially in Africa) has been both more vocal and more organised.

In the third phase, continued conflict may lead eventually to revolutionary overthrow of the government, as Marx predicted. This may halt the process of stagnation and decline or change the direction of development. The new government will have its own way of handling and channelling strains. As far as this episode of change is concerned, the process is complete. There will, of course, be new episodes and other pressures for change which are still in earlier phases. While a society experiences major and minor forces for change simultaneously, the social scientist concentrates on one episode at a time in order to clarify the processes involved.

The Agbekoya ('farmers are suffering') Rebellion in Nigeria's Western State[17] is an example of an episode of social change. The impetus was a rise in taxation and arrest of defaulters coupled with a price for cocoa which was far below the world cocoa price at the time. The poor farmers tried to right their grievances through peaceful channels (initial reaction), but the bureaucracy in the capital refused to listen (accumulated strains). Populist leaders then organised open conflict, burning the property of wealthy farmers and corrupt traditional leaders (*obas* and *bales*) who had profited from local politics and threatening the lives of tax collectors and other village officials. Attempts to recover (phase 2) included police action, the appointment of a commission, and announcements by the Governor designed to calm tempers. Relative quiet lasted about six months (a new balance), but no attempt was made to meet demands for lower taxes and the withdrawal of local council officials.

New attempts to collect taxes by force brought more riots and an attack on the Ibadan jail to free prisoners. The government finally capitulated to the extent of lowering taxes somewhat, withdrawing the local council staff

(15) Smelser 1968, pp.271–6.   (16) 1945.   (17) Williams 1974, pp.126–31; Beer 1977.

346

from the villages and promising amnesty to farmers who had been arrested unless the charge was murder. At this point, the rebellion was officially over (a new balance), though some continuance of strains can be seen in a new revolt (on a much smaller scale) in 1972, when the state attempted to return officials to the villages.

What long-term changes resulted from this episode? It is still too soon to be sure, but they seem to be best classified as development. This was not a revolution, or meant to lead to one. Beer reports that the farmers wanted to correct abuses, not destroy the system which was potentially beneficial to them. They wanted changes in local government so that it was directed to their needs, and were willing to challenge state authority to attain this end. By their continued pressure, they have signalled a willingness to take violent action in defence of their interests; the state government has had to accept that peace cannot be maintained if farmers' interests are ignored. The government has maintained control so far by co-opting leaders into official positions, but new leaders arise if the grievances are great enough. A study of long-term changes in local government in the area will have to include this and similar episodes as indicators of conflict and its resolution.

Modernisation

Theories of modernisation are a current form of evolutionism stemming from the ideas of progress and social engineering which assume that change means improvement of social conditions. They are also a product of Euro-American ethnocentrism which draws its conception of change from its own experience and therefore expects that 'modernising' or 'developing' societies will eventually come to resemble its own. While it is sometimes useful or even necessary (for lack of a better word) to refer to contemporary behaviour and attitudes as 'modern' and to social practices which have continued for a relatively long time as 'traditional', these words have also taken on an ideology and meaning for many people which is much more complex than their use in ordinary speech. Modernisation theorists tend to see only the front end of the process of social change (what the modern society should look like) and ignore the tradition side of their dichotomy. They pay little attention to the wide differences between traditional societies and the processes by which these societies are accommodating to external and internal pressures for both stability and change, often significantly modifying imported social institutions to better suit their needs. Nevertheless, some attention must be given to modernisation theories because they are so prevalent and because they alert us to ways of examining long-term change.

Like other forms of change, modernisation can be studied at the societal and the individual level. Ideal types of simple and complex societies were outlined at the beginning of Chapter 2, and it was pointed out that all societies have some characteristics of both these extremes. The interesting point for empirical study, therefore, is the mixture which operates in a particular social situation and the degree of consensus with which certain norms are supported. For example, if people generally accept that civil servants should treat them as individual clients, the use of universalistic principles in the appointment of civil servants will not affect the particularistic way they carry out their task. If people begin to demand that civil servants should not be bribed, this may serve as an impetus for change to a more universalistic orientation on the part of these men.

Pressure for modernisation is seen as coming from an increase in societal scale. Societies grow when they take in a larger territory and increase the size and density of their population. This provides the impetus for increased urbanisation, interdependence and centralisation of economic and political power. Self-sufficient units and locally based segments (extended families and ethnic subgroups) give way to national interest groups; class replaces status as the prime means of stratification. Political institutions become differentiated from kinship and religious institutions. The society is democratised, at least in the sense that governments feel they must have formal measures for the expression of popular opinion. The mass media and national culture replace local sources of information and culture.[18] These trends have been observed in certain highly industrialised societies, but the assumption that all 'less modern' societies will change to this form is highly questionable.

Bendix[19] shows the fallacy of the argument that all societies will follow the pattern of change experienced by European societies during the Industrial and Democratic Revolutions. Given communications and interdependence between societies, once a change has taken place in one society it cannot happen in another society in exactly the same way because 'follower' societies can learn from the experience of the 'leader' society. While changes in family life, the division of labour, bureaucratic and democratic development may appear to be internal to the society concerned, they are in fact also externally influenced as well, and this influence differs for each society just as the background culture and social structure to which these innovations are added also differs for each society. Thus, the expectation that industrialisation will have the same effects in every society, and that every society will eventually be 'modernised' to an identical version of the leaders is bound to be disappointed. Certain features may be found everywhere (such as elections, secularised and bureaucratised authority, an increasing division of labour, etc.), but the use to which various societies put these features may make them

(18) Hopkins and Wallerstein 1967, pp.37–8.   (19) 1967, pp.324–9.

function quite differently from place to place. One cannot predict what societies now industrialising will be on the basis of a single historical precedent.

Whitaker[20] provides an example of how the leaders of one society, the Hausa/Fulani of northern Nigeria, accommodated the innovations of independence so that they strengthened rather than changed the traditional political structure. He points out that change is seldom as eurhythmic as theorists have conceived it; the acceptance of one innovation does not necessarily mean that the society buys the whole modernisation package, that it must inevitably shift from one side of a dichotomy to the other. Through indirect rule, Hausa/Fulani rulers were able to maintain control over their people during the colonial period. They collected taxes, controlled judicial and legal institutions and selected those who would advance within the hierarchy. The few who achieved significant Western education were largely sons of the traditional elite, so it merely gave them an additional claim to be best able to govern. With the approach of independence, they saw the need for organising a political party, and through the Northern People's Congress (NPC) maintained their hold on the mass of the people.

The use of patron/client relationships and penalising members of opposition parties enabled the NPC to achieve a monopoly of power and authority in most parts of the north. Democracy had been assimilated with relatively little effect on the traditional political system. Whitaker suggests[21] that by remaining flexible, the northern leaders formed a new system which was 'neither purely traditional nor purely modern, yet that was conspicuous for its relative lack of strain and friction.' This system continues to undergo change, but any radical change to the 'modern' bureaucratic form of Weber's ideal type seems a long way off.

The second level of modernisation is the individual. Inkeles[22] has been among the most persistent in proclaiming that individual modernisation necessarily accompanies (and may be responsible for) societal modernisation. He conceives this modernity as a set of attitudes, values and behaviour which fits men for life in modern society and has made a comparative study of men in six nations (including Yoruba in Nigeria) to prove that such a set exists. The 'themes' included in his study were openness to new experiences, knowledge and opinions on national and international topics, an orientation towards the present and future rather than the past, a belief in planning and science, trust in and respect for other people, and preferring achievement to ascription. Using a highly selective sample, he found sufficiently high correlations between these variables to be able to differentiate more modern

(20) 1970.   (21) *Ibid.*, p.460.   (22) 1969, 1975.

from less modern men. Education was the characteristic most highly correlated with modernity,[23] followed by employment in large factories.

In a somewhat earlier study of modernity in East Africa, Doob[24] used some of the same measures but emphasised political attitudes, claiming that this was how local people saw modernity. His exclusive reliance on students leaves open the question of how his results apply to the rest of the population (as does Inkeles' main reliance on factory workers; his other samples were very small and unrepresentative). Mitchell's work in Central Africa[25] suggests that urban workers there see modernity in terms of the acceptance of European customs, though this seems to refer mostly to material culture (such as clothing) and life style, which are more available to the educated with relatively high incomes than to the poor.

Armer and Youtz[26] studied young men in Kano with varying levels of schooling and found that education was strongly related to some value orientations assumed to be included in modernity, especially independence from the family, empiricism (preference for scientific rather than religious medicine) and concern about the future. Other values, including receptivity to change, did not show the expected relationships. This suggests that some information is assimilated in school and some opportunities are more available to those completing various amounts of schooling (hardly surprising), but that accommodation to social change varies from one individual to another independently of education; it therefore raises important questions for modernisation theory.

The characteristics of modernity also appear to vary considerably from one country to another. Inkeles[27] reports that 96% of the better educated Yoruba respondents but only 6% of Israelis and Bengalis belonged to two or more organisations. How then can it be argued that such characteristics will produce identical societies? It would seem more fruitful to examine the attitudes and behaviour which are characteristic of various categories of people within a single country or neighbouring countries and then to analyse how these patterns are the result of accommodation to the social changes taking place around them and to what extent they are modifications of patterns inherited from the past (continuous rather than discontinuous change). Insofar as this can be done without making value judgments, attempts should be made to measure which patterns (and which categories of people) seem to have made the most successful accommodation to change – in terms of a relative absence of strain, alienation, or dissatisfaction. (Discontent may not necessarily indicate that change has not been assimilated. Aspiration for upward social mobility is part of the Euro-American

(23) Inkeles 1973.   (24) 1967.   (25) 1956.   (26) 1971.   (27) 1969, p.218.

modernity complex and many 'traditional' societies also promote a need for achievement which may be expressed as dissatisfaction with one's present position.)

The aim, therefore, should be to study syntheses, the varying ways in which social continuity and change have been blended by members of different societies into something which is 'modern' but uniquely their own. For instance, the Ghanaian factory worker participates in Ghanaian society, and his attitudes and behaviour are a product of these two socialising agents, not just of the factory experience.[28] The Abidjan civil servant who can afford to be polygynous sees no reason why he should not use income from a 'modern' job to procure enjoyment and prestige within the 'traditional' sphere. Similarly, his educated wife may accept a 'traditional' means (polygynous marriage) in order to attain a 'modern' end (equality and independence of action). The role of senior wife to a wealthy man provides some women with power which women in 'modern' countries might well envy.[29]

Christiansen[30] reports that most Fante have little difficulty in combining Christianity with their own 'polytheistic and pluralistic' religion; the new addition merely gives them better protection against life's hazards. Thus, the product of social change cannot be prejudged, but prediction is more likely to be accurate if it builds on a sound knowledge of local culture. Skinner[31] writes:

> The people of Ouagadougou have accommodated and adapted to change by manipulating their traditional values and institutions; by utilising a mixture or syncretization of traditional and modern traits when they could do so; by adopting and adapting modern European traits or institutions when possible; and by attempting to de-Westernize these traits in an attempt at psychological accommodation. This process has not been easy. . . . The resulting behaviour is far from normative, but neither is it normless.

This raises another point, the increased prestige of 'traditional ways' in the post-independence period. Pride in doing things 'the African way' has meant a return to favour of customs which were becoming uncommon, at least in the towns, in the scramble to appear 'civilised'. This applies more to the elite than to ordinary people, but it also means that those who go through university today need to undergo much less 'modernising' in the Westernising sense than their predecessors of twenty years ago.

Some customs are much more easily kept than others, and this also varies from one place to another. For example, the Ghanaian 'cloth', worn like a

(28) Peil 1972a, p.236.   (29) Clignet and Sween 1969.   (30) In Bascom and Herskovits 1959, p.270.   (31) 1974, p.447. See also Mboya in Gulliver 1969.

toga, is much less convenient for wear in a factory or office than the smock, buba, kaftan or dashiki worn by other peoples. Religious customs which can be performed anywhere, such as pouring libation, are more likely to continue than those which are limited in place and personnel. Large-scale celebrations which attract tourists and therefore change from completely participant to largely spectator events are likely to be modified in many ways. Study of social change seems more likely to be fruitful if it concentrates on examining the factors involved in continuity and synthesis rather than looking for the total rejection of the old and acceptance of the new.

How does such a society-by-society or social group by social group approach fit in with the scientific ideal of generalising to as large populations as possible? It is certainly important to theorise as to the probable direction of change and to conduct studies designed to test these theories, but the differences as well as the similarities must be thoroughly analysed and generalisations should be limited to the evidence available.

Researchers are under considerable pressure from their colleagues and their publishers to talk about Africa when they have only studied Ibadan, and to talk about the Third World when they have only studied East Africa. Comparative studies in several nations are an attempt to solve this problem, but so far they have not succeeded in coming to grips with the cultural and societal differences which underlie seeming similarities or variances. If the same behaviour can have a different meaning in Monrovia from the one it has in Blantyre, one should not put too much confidence in the finding that factory workers in both places give similar answers to a series of questions. Certain behavioural and attitudinal patterns do seem to accompany the introduction of large-scale manufacturing (workers expect to work a set number of hours and do not expect to supply their own tools or know all their workmates, for example), but as yet we know far too little about the process of synthesis to analyse the data properly. It would probably be better, as Bendix suggests,[32] to wait until a longer period has elapsed before assuming what form 'modernisation' will take in each society; evolution should be measured in centuries rather than decades. People of the eighteenth century also considered themselves modern.

Response to change

Acceptance or rejection of change is particularly important to officials promoting development, because their schemes often collapse in the face of

(32) 1970, p.311.

disinterest or opposition. This leads to stereotyping villagers as conservative, but Hutton and Cohen[33] suggest that the fault is often with the bureaucrats rather than the peasants. While some societies and individuals are more open to change and adapt more easily to it than others, there are usually good reasons why a particular innovation is rejected.

Sources of resistance

People resist change for many reasons: fear, morality, aesthetics and especially perceived advantage to themselves. Innovations are often initiated by foreign 'experts' who know little about local customs and give no thought to the effect the innovation might have on the society. Many schemes are introduced which have not been carefully thought out and for which very little advance planning has been done. Those who are supposed to welcome the change are often in a better position than bureaucrats in the capital to judge whether the innovation will be in their long-term interests; they may have already learned from experience that innovations tend to be more useful to politicians and wealthy city people than to themselves. Other changes merely make no sense to them; they provide nothing these people want or need.

People who resist change are accused of being conservative or traditional (defined as the opposite of modern). They are said to think first of the family, to distrust outsiders, to lack empathy (an ability to put themselves in another's position), to be unwilling or unable to plan and save for the future, and to accept fatalistically whatever life brings them. In short, from the point of view of the planner, they are not rational. Given the conditions of rural life, where medical aid is hard to get and the weather unpredictable, there may be little point in long-term plans which can so easily be wiped out by disease, accidents, flood, drought, faulty technology, or the actions of others. It seems more reasonable to celebrate when times are good and endure when they are bad. As to empathy, most people have difficulty understanding conditions they have not experienced themselves. The civil servant who grew up in town has as much difficulty putting himself in the position of the illiterate, isolated farmer as the other way round; if this were not so, civil servants would have a clearer idea of why their proposals are being resisted.

A farmer may not want to try a new seed because his family might starve if it fails and his neighbours might accuse him of using supernatural forces to harm their crops if it succeeds and his harvest is better than theirs. The familiar acquires a value just because it is known, no matter how disadvantageous it might seem to the outsider. This makes it especially hard for

(33) 1975.

elderly people to change; they have less to gain and more to lose from abandoning old ways. In addition, societal norms have a moral value which helps to sustain them; people who have been socialised to observe these norms may object to changes as morally wrong. If, for example, one grew up with the conviction that 'good' women remain in the house and are not seen by men outside their family, the idea that girls should attend co-educational schools and women should work in factories would be greeted with some shock. People also acquire, as part of their socialisation, preferences in food, clothing, music, smells, etc. There was considerable complaint in Tanzania when rice imported from a new source did not taste the same as the rice people were used to. Thus, what seem to be minor changes often meet with considerable resistance. Young people are quick to take up new fashions in music and clothing, but tend to be remarkably conservative when it is suggested that major changes be made in the educational system.

No one will willingly accept a change which he sees as seriously damaging his long-term interests. Anyone faced with a demand for change makes a rational calculation of what it will mean to him. As leaders tend to have a vested interest in the *status quo*, central authorities often find that representatives made responsible for the adoption of innovations often sabotage their directives; they have the most to lose if change takes place. The resistance may be based on economic or status interests. Skilled workers often oppose the introduction of new technology which would lessen the value of their skill. Members of hereditary elites in many places ignored or resisted the introduction of Western education in their area, some because they thought it irrelevant to status in their society and others because they saw it as a threat to their power. However, where there was considerable competition among the elite (as in Buganda), education was accepted as enhancing their opportunities.[34] Marginal members of the society and the upwardly mobile are generally much more eager to accept new ideas because they have relatively little to lose and much to gain. Because of their implications for status, changes tend to be diffused downward through a society (see p. 105). People are more likely to accept innovations of which their leaders approve and to resist ideas which come from below.

If innovations tend to be introduced by individuals who are marginal to the society but are most likely to be accepted if promoted by elites whose interests usually lie in the *status quo*, how is it that so many changes are successfully assimilated? Partly, this is because the elites are not unified, so ideas may be taken up and promoted by some leaders though they are rejected by others. Chiefs and other traditional leaders have opposed changes

(34) Maas 1970.

354

which were strongly supported by political or educated elites. However, traditional leaders cannot maintain their position by opposing all change, and they have not done so. It may be customary (as in Ghana) for the chief to be seen as a conservative force while his assistants promote change with his approval. This pattern gives the chief an opportunity to moderate the effects of change (to keep things from going too far by exerting control when necessary) and at the same time relieves him of the official responsibility if things go wrong. He maintains his authority and prestige by representing stability but at the same time helps his people to progress by fostering fruitful change. National leaders and top managers of large corporations often use the same principle when they send assistants for negotiations rather than going themselves. If negotiation fails, the top leader is not responsible. If it succeeds, he comes in at the last minute and takes credit for the success.

Hutton and Cohen[35] suggest that an adequate understanding of response to change requires examination of the economy, social structure and value system of the society before contact with European colonialism, how the society was affected by this contact, and the relationship of the local people with national and regional authorities at the time the innovation is proposed. Where colonialism was experienced as a gradual and fairly continuous change to a higher standard of living and greater opportunity for self-fulfilment and where present authorities are seen to be concerned about the community's best interests, change is likely to be accepted with little question. Where colonial domination was seen as harsh and a force for discontinuous change and where present authorities have done little to build trust, innovations will probably be resisted. In most cases, some accommodation will be reached between the planners' model and the people's method.

Examples

Acceptance and resistance to change take many forms. Some of these will be demonstrated with case studies of pastoralists, Ujamaa villagers, Ghanaian parents and Ibo farmers. The environment, social structure and culture, norms, values and goals at the time the change is introduced all affect the response.

1 Pastoralists

Pastoral people have often been accused of resisting change, but Gulliver[36] shows that this is a response to the threat which change poses to their generally precarious way of life. As with other pastoralists, the Masai economy was geared to the limited potential of their environment. Their

(35) 1975, p.120. (36) 1969.

customs and values preserved a balance with nature which was necessary for survival. In these circumstances, innovations which were helpful to their cultivator neighbours were rejected as against Masai interests. On the other hand, changes which aided the cattle economy, such as treatment for cattle diseases and improvements in water supplies, were welcomed because these served Masai interests as they saw them. Pastoralists in Mali have faced much the same difficulty with change agents from the government attempting to control the size and movement of their herds; the new regulations probably increased the disaster of the drought of the early 1970s.

2 Ujamaa villagers

The contributors to Proctor's booklet[37] enumerate many ways in which settlers who moved to Ujamaa villages were disappointed in their contact with government officials. They were often promised food and housing, which either did not materialise or were insufficient for their needs. They were expected to obey orders blindly and then blamed when things went wrong. Some officials were in too much of a hurry to wait for volunteers, so they rounded up the jobless and criminals, yet the proposed village was infested with mosquitoes, and considerable goodwill was necessary to make a success of it. Potential volunteers got the impression that joining a new village was to be considered only as a last resort; those who had enough land asked why they should share in the poverty of others and were answered only in terms of a socialism they did not yet understand.[38] The Regional Development Committee, composed exclusively of 'intellectuals and expert technical officers',[39] saw no reason to consult the settlers or even the field officer in the settlement. Thus, the settlers were denied an opportunity for the self-reliance which they had been told was so necessary.

In one instance, the settlers showed themselves more favourable to change than the planners. The latter directed that houses should be on acre plots, and thus scattered, as is customary in this area. The settlers demanded a more 'modern' village layout, with houses close together so that they could have more contact with each other and support the Ujamaa spirit.[40]

The large number of 'drop-outs' from the villages studied show that many problems of economy, values and social structure remain to be solved. Some settlers were not prepared for the insecurity of a new project; others missed the companionship of family and friends and the communal ceremonies of their home village; some were unwilling to work. Careful attention to leadership among the settlers and to fruitful contacts with field and regional officers is vital. Where leaders of the Village Development Committee are

(37) 1971.   (38) *Ibid.*, Mboya, p.65.   (39) *Ibid.*, Bakula, p.29.   (40) *Ibid.*

authoritarian or paternalistic, the people work through fear rather than taking up their socialist responsibilities. Extension workers may not be effective change agents because they are better paid than the villagers and committed to the government rather than to the village.[41]

As might be expected, the changeover from independent to Ujamaa farming encountered more resistance where successful cash crop farming was well established than among farmers who barely covered their subsistence needs. Bakula[42] found that 80% of the settlers joined the village he studied in the hope of improving their income, whereas Mboya and Ntirukigwa report that relatively wealthy farmers (many of whom worked very hard on their farms) opposed Ujamaa as against their interests.

Feldman[43] shows how successful farmers in Ismani had an influential role as mediators between the government and the rest of the population. They often had personal contact with the bureaucracy through educated children and kinsmen. In addition, they acted as community leaders by holding office in TANU and the cooperative society, and thus were able to affect the political message which reached the rest of the community. Their interpretation of government policy, that amenities and aid to agriculture would be provided by the government if people would live and farm together, was intended to lead only to small-scale communal work, not to the expropriation of large farms. The forcible collectivisation of land in Ismani in 1970 led to violence; many large farmers left the area. Although there was no evidence of class-consciousness in Ismani,[44] wealthy farmers gradually became aware that their interests were threatened by government policy, and acted to resist these changes.

3 Ghanaian parents

An analysis of varying enthusiasm for formal education in Ghana shows the usefulness of examining community as well as individual response to change. Blakemore compared three villages having high, medium and low proportions of children enrolled in primary school. He found that they differ considerably in their perception of the value of schooling and their 'strategy for dealing with the "outside world" '.[45]

Almost all the Kpetoe children attend school. Education is so well established that it is taken for granted, as is the strong possibility that school leavers will migrate for work. Young people visit home fairly frequently and work at home during periods of unemployment, so they are not considered a loss to the community but an extension of it. Ko is a much poorer community than Kpetoe; about half the children get some schooling. The

(41) *Ibid.*, Mashauri, p.55.   (42) *Ibid.*, p.25.   (43) 1975.   (44) *Ibid.*, p.171.
(45) Blakemore 1975, p.251.

community is ambivalent as to the value of education; it can help members to overcome their poverty, but because the towns providing economic opportunities are so far away educated sons are often lost to their families. Thus, it pays not to send all one's sons to school so as to ensure that one of them will farm at home and look after his parents in their old age.

Only about 10% of Savelugu children are sent to school, and many local schools were closed for lack of pupils. This resistance can be seen as a product of governmental neglect in providing education in the area, but also as representing a low valuation of this education. Savelugu parents complain that educated children are less 'sociable' than those who have not been to school; they set themselves somewhat apart from the rest of the community and spend less time on visiting, ceremonies and community affairs. This can be recognised as a familiar pattern wherever education is new; when it becomes common, school-leavers revert to being ordinary members of the community. The Savelugu community values Islamic education and would prefer that Western education followed the same pattern – one could 'give' a child to study and live with the teacher rather than making the child combine the two worlds of school and home. As there are varying opportunities for attaining status in the Savelugu community (chieftaincy and large-scale farming as well as Islamic and Western education), community strategy lies in diverse training according to the aptitude of each child rather than in wholesale acceptance of a single approach.

Within each community, there were also differences from one family to another in attitudes towards schooling. The most notable of these was between fathers who continued to practise an indigenous religion and those who had adopted either Christianity or Islam. For the former, education often seemed irrelevant to their goals; sons should follow their father on the farm and become socialised for full membership in the community, including its ritual. This is in part a criticism of the curriculum, which gives too little attention to local history, culture and practical skills. Muslims have often resisted the introduction of Western education (especially in northern Nigeria, Senegal and Mali), because they have seen it as drawing children away from strongly held values, but in Savelugu prominent Muslims were more likely than other parents to send at least some of their children to school. They were committed to a world religion based on literacy, and found it quite acceptable to allow a promising child to combine state schooling with after-hours Islamic schooling. This compromise has also gained acceptance in southern Nigeria. Western schooling is seen as valuable in adult life, especially in the towns, and once the danger of conversion is removed resistance based on religion tends to disappear.[46]

4 Ibo farmers

Ottenberg[47] reminds us that continuous change is much easier than discontinuous change. The Ibo were receptive to innovations of the colonial period because these fitted in so well with their basic social expectations and goals. With the exception of respect for age (an almost inevitable casualty in a period of rapid social change), Ibo behavioural patterns have remained remarkably stable. The Ibo are comparable with the Kikuyu in being politically uncentralised in the pre-contact period and quick to take up opportunities for education and employment. However, there were no white settlers to block Ibo advancement, as there were in Kenya, so acceptance of innovations was much better rewarded. Their emphasis on individual achievement of leadership and social status, with consequent social mobility, required only slight modification to use the new means (education and civil service employment) for the attainment of long established goals. Similarly, patterns of village democracy, communal cooperation and hostility towards outsiders proved useful in dealing with political innovations. Village improvement associations for migrants were a logical addition to a rich associational life at home.

Ottenberg's hypothesis that the flexibility and range of choice available in Ibo culture made it easier for them than for peoples with a more rigidly structured social and political system to assimilate change needs to be more adequately tested.[48] We have seen that individuals within the same society often differ considerably in their receptivity to change, either because of the nature of their primary socialisation or because of their position within the social system. Historical factors such as the early introduction of schooling or isolation from trade routes may also put communities having the same basic culture in widely differing positions with respect to social change. Nevertheless, in examining response to change it is important to include an assessment of whether the innovation is seen as a modification of familiar patterns or something completely different. That radical changes are more threatening and therefore more likely to be resisted is confirmed in the strong opposition of Ibo women to the introduction of oil mills which deprived them of considerable income and thus threatened their family position.[49]

(46) See also Peshkin 1973.   (47) In Bascom and Herskovits 1959.   (48) See Henderson 1966. Colson and Scudder in Parkin 1975 show that Zambian farmers with the same culture reacted quite differently to resettlement, reflecting their previous agricultural experience and the opportunities available to them in their new villages. See also Colson 1976.   (49) Okigbo 1956, p.130. See Long 1968 for a study of the varying responses of Zambian farmers to social change.

Responses to change can be summed up as

1 completely passive or negative
2 active and organised resistance
3 adaptability
4 transformation.

A group which completely rejects change, either actively or passively, may undermine the basis of its own continued existence. Given the interdependence of nations and of people within nations, it is no longer possible to remain aloof from changes taking place all around one. Attempts to re-emphasise long established (and sometimes partly forgotten) rituals and symbols or to refuse to be integrated into a new national culture have little or no chance of success. This is not to say that customary ways must be completely abandoned, only that adaptation and/or modification are called for. Leaders who will not compromise are generally replaced by others who can, whereas leaders who are able to shape innovations to their needs may not only continue but increase their authority and status. The Nigerian emirs actively assimilated changes into the established structure and integrated the old and new spheres of life so that their influence could permeate the whole; in this way, their position remained largely intact.

Adaptability often requires considerable tolerance of ambiguity and flexibility; new norms and symbols must be accepted, sometimes with little initial understanding of the new culture which is developing. Transformation requires something more than just adaptation, a fostering of new institutions. Both resisting and transforming leaders vary in the amount of coercion they exert over their followers. A dominant group may try to restructure the whole society to suit their ideology, aiming at a new political, economic and social order with which the whole nation is identified. Generally, the more coercive the leaders the less they tolerate individual differences and the more they emphasise unity in values, behaviour and ideology. Military and religious leaders tend to be more coercive than elites who owe their position to democratic processes.[50]

Conclusion
Social change is continuous in all societies, though some changes are more notable than others. Improved technology and communications mean that the pace of change has speeded up; there is a steady stream of new ideas being introduced and inventions in one part of the world are quickly passed on to other parts. Thus, it is important for anyone who seeks to understand the structure and functioning of society to study social change.

(50) Eisenstadt 1973, p.329.

Change is a product of the interaction of consensus and conflict, of pressures leading to the acceptance or rejection of innovations. Some changes increase conflict in the society; others reduce it. Most are considered an improvement by some members of the society (those who benefit) and worthless by others (those who lose). An outsider may be able to make a more objective assessment, but in many cases the manifest and latent results are so mixed that the conclusions are strongly affected by one's values. Most people have some idea of the society they would like to live in, based largely on their primary socialisation, education, socio-economic position and life experiences. One individual may gladly accept innovations which another strongly resists. Accusation of ignorance or lack of understanding are often made by people who are themselves ignorant of the norms and values of others. Careful study of the society and the interaction of people within it should help to ease the process of social change and enable innovators to better predict its course; this is the goal of sociology as a science of society.

Suggested reading and discussion topic
Select one instance of social change in your area and read any analysis of it which is available.
(a) List as many effects as you can.
(b) What conflicts arose while the change was taking place or as a result of it?
(c) How were these conflicts resolved?
(d) How useful are the various theories of social change for explaining what happened? For predicting future changes of this type?

Bibliography

Books and articles have been selected which are within the competence of first or second year undergraduates and are accessible, at least in the part of Africa to which they refer. Where several items cover similar material, an attempt has been made to give relatively equal coverage to the main geographical areas.

Abernethy, D. B. (1969) *The Dilemma of Popular Education: An African Case*, Stanford University Press, 1969.

Achebe, C. (1960) *No Longer At Ease*, Heinemann, London 1960.

Achebe, C. (1964) *Arrow of God*, Heinemann, London 1964.

Acquah, I. (1958) *Accra Survey*, University of London Press, 1958.

Addo, N. O. (1971) 'Migration and Economic Change in Ghana', (mimeo), Demographic Unit, Department of Sociology, University of Ghana, Legon, 1971.

Allen, V. L. (1972) 'The meaning of the working class in Africa', *Journal of Modern African Studies*, **10**, 1972, pp. 169–89.

Aluko, J. A. (1974) 'Academic Achievement of Nigerian University Students', unpublished M.Soc.Sc. dissertation for Birmingham University, 1974.

Amachree, I. T. D. (1968) 'Reference group and worker satisfaction: studies among some Nigerian factory workers', *Nigerian Journal of Economic and Social Studies*, **10**, 1968, pp. 229–38.

Amin, S. (ed.) (1974) *Modern Migrations in Western Africa*, Oxford University Press for the International African Institute, London, 1974.

Ampene, E. (1967) 'Obuasi and its miners', *Ghana Journal of Sociology*, **3**, 1967, pp. 73–80.

Anderson, C. A. (1970) 'The sorcerer's apprentice: education in developing countries', *Comparative Education*, **6**, 1970, pp. 5–18.

Armer, M. J. (1968) 'Intersociety and intrasociety correlations of occupational prestige', *American Journal of Sociology*, **74**, 1968, pp. 28–36.

Armer, M. J. and Youtz, R. (1971) 'Formal education and individual modernity in an African society', *American Journal of Sociology*, **76**, 1971, pp. 604–26.

Aronson, D. R. (1971) 'Ijebu Yoruba urban-rural relationships and class formation', *Canadian Journal of African Studies*, **5**, 1971, pp. 263–79.

Aryee, A. F. (1967) 'Christianity and polygamy in Ghana: the role of the church as an instrument of social change', *Ghana Journal of Sociology*, **3**, 1967, pp. 98–105.

Asuni, T. (1969) 'Homicide in Western Nigeria', *British Journal of Psychiatry*, **115**, 1969, pp. 1105–13.

Baeta, C. G. (1962) *Prophetism in Ghana*, SCM Press, London, 1962.

Baeta, C. G. (ed.) (1968) *Christianity in Tropical Africa*, Oxford University Press for the International African Institute, London, 1968.

Baker, P. (1974) *Urbanization and Political Change: The Politics of Lagos 1917–1967*, University of California Press, 1974.

Bamisaiye, A. (1974) 'The spatial distribution of juvenile delinquency and adult crime in the city of Ibadan', *International Journal of Criminology and Penology*, **2**, 1974, pp. 65–83.

Banton, M. (1956) 'Adaptation and integration in the social system of Temne immigrants in Freetown', *Africa*, **26**, 1956, pp. 354–67. (Reprinted in Wallerstein 1966 and Middleton 1970.)

Banton, M. (1957) *West African City*, Oxford University Press for the International African Institute, London, 1957.

Banton, M. (1965) *Roles*, Tavistock Publications, London, 1965.

Barnes, S. (1976) 'Migration and land acquisition: the new landlords of Lagos', (mimeo), 1976.

Barnes, S. and Peil, M. (1977) 'Voluntary association membership in five West African cities', *Urban Anthropology*, **6**, 1977.

Barth, F. (ed.) (1969) *Ethnic Groups and Boundaries: The Social Organization of Culture Difference*, Allen and Unwin, London, 1969.

Barrett, D. B. (1968) *Schism and Renewal in Africa*, Oxford University Press, Nairobi, 1968. (Summarised in Baeta 1968.)

Barrett, S. R. (1974) *Two Villages on Stilts: Economic and Family Change in Nigeria*, Chandler, London 1974.

Bascom, W. (1955) 'Urbanization among the Yoruba', *American Journal of Sociology*, **40**, 1955, pp. 446–54.

Bascom, W. (1959) 'Urbanization as a traditional African pattern', *Sociological Review*, **7**, 1959, pp. 29–43.

Bascom, W. (1962) 'Some aspects of Yoruba urbanism', *American Anthropologist*, **64**, 1962, pp. 699–709. (Reprinted in van den Berghe 1965.)

Bascom, W. and Herskovits, M. J. (eds.) (1959) *Continuity and Change in African Cultures*. University of Chicago Press, 1959.

Beckett, P. A. and O'Connell, J. (1972) 'Social characteristics of an elite-information: Nigerian university students,' (mimeo), Department of Government, Ahmadu Bello University, Zaria, 1972.

Beer, C.H. (1977) *The Farmer and the State in Western Nigeria*, University of Ibadan Press, 1977.

Beidelman, T. O. (1974) 'Social theory and the study of Christian missions in Africa', *Africa*, **44**, 1974, pp. 235–48.

Bendix, R. (1967) 'Tradition and modernity reconsidered', *Comparative Studies of Society and History*, **10**, 1967, pp. 292–346. (Reprinted in R. Bendix, *Embattled Reason: Essays on Social Knowledge*, Oxford University Press, New York, 1970, and in Tuden and Plotnicov 1970.)

Bennett, F. J. (ed.) (1973) *Medicine and Social Sciences in East and West Africa*, Nkanga Editions No. 7, Makerere Institute of Social Research, Kampala, 1973.

Berg, E. J. (1965) 'Education and manpower in Senegal, Guinea and the Ivory Coast' in F. Harbison and C. A. Myers (eds.) *Manpower and Education*, McGraw-Hill, New York, 1965.

Bernard, G. (1968) *Ville Africaine, Famille Urbaine: Les Enseignants de Kinshasa*, Mouton, Paris, 1968.

Bharati, A. (1965) 'A social survey' in D. P. Ghai (ed.) *Portrait of a Minority: Asians in East Africa*, Oxford University Press, Nairobi, 1965.

Bibby, J. (1973) 'The social base of Ghanaian education: is it still broadening?', *British Journal of Sociology*, **24**, 1973, pp. 365–74.

Bibby, J. and Peil, M. (1974) 'Secondary education in Ghana: private enterprise and social selection', *Sociology of Education*, **47**, 1974, pp. 399–418.

Birmingham, W., et al (eds.) (1967) *A Study of Contemporary Ghana: Some Aspects of Social Structure*, Allen and Unwin, London, 1967.

Blakemore, K. P. (1975) 'Resistance to formal education: its implications for the status of school leavers', *Comparative Education Review*, **19**, 1975, pp. 237–51.

Blau, P. M. (1956) *Bureaucracy in Modern Society*, Random House, New York, 1956.

Blau, P. M. (1964) *Exchange and Power in Social Life*, John Wiley and Sons, New York, 1964.

Bloomberg, L. N. and Abrams, C. (1964), *United Nations Mission to Kenya on Housing*, United Nations Department of Economic and Social Affairs, Nairobi, 1964.

Bohannan, P. (1960) *African Homicide and Suicide*, Princeton University Press, 1960.

Bohannan, P. (1969) *Social Anthropology*, Holt, Rinehart and Winston, London, 1969.

Boissevain, J. and Mitchell, J. C. (eds.) (1973) *Network Analysis: Studies in*

Human Interaction, Mouton, The Hague, 1973.

Bonacich, E. (1973) 'A theory of middleman minorities', *American Sociological Review*, **38,** 1973, pp. 583–94.

Boserup, E. (1970) *Women's Role in Economic Development*, Allen and Unwin, London, 1970.

Bott, E. (1957) *Family and Social Network*, Tavistock Publications, London, 1957.

Boudon, R. (1974) *Education, Opportunity, and Social Inequality: Changing Prospects in Western Society*, John Wiley, New York, 1974.

Breese, G. (ed.) (1969) *The City in Newly Developing Countries*, Prentice-Hall, Englewood Cliffs, 1969.

Brain, J. (1969) 'Matrilineal descent and marital stability: a Tanzanian case', *Journal of Asian and African Studies*, **4,** 1969, pp. 122–31.

Broom, L. and Selznick, P. (1970) *Sociology*, 4th edn., Harper and Row, New York, 1970.

Brown, G. N. and Hiskett, M. (eds.) (1975) *Conflict and Harmony in Education in Tropical Africa*, Allen and Unwin, London, 1975.

Bujra, J. M., *et al* (1973) *Pumwani: The Politics of Property: A Study of an Urban Renewal Scheme in Nairobi, Kenya,*' (mimeo), Social Science Research Council, London, 1973.

Burawoy, M. (1972a) 'Another look at the mineworker', *African Social Research*, **14,** 1972, pp. 239–87.

Burawoy, M. (1972b) *The Colour of Class on the Copper Mines*, Zambian Papers No. 7, University of Zambia Institute of African Studies, Lusaka, 1972.

Busia, K. A. (1950) *Report on a Social Survey of Sekondi-Takoradi*, Crown Agents for the Colonies, London, 1950.

Caldwell, J. C. (1965) 'Extended family obligations and education: a study of an aspect of demographic transition amongst Ghanaian university students', *Population Studies*, **19,** 1965, pp. 183–99.

Caldwell, J. C. (1966) 'The erosion of the family: a study of the fate of the family in Ghana', *Population Studies*, **20,** 1966, pp. 5–26.

Caldwell, J. C. (1967a) 'Fertility differentials in three economically contrasting rural regions in Ghana', *Economic Development and Cultural Change*, **15,** 1967, pp. 217–38.

Caldwell, J. C. (1967b) 'Migration and urbanization' in W. Birmingham *et al.* (eds.), *A Study of Contemporary Ghana: Some Aspects of Social Structure* Allen and Unwin, London, 1967.

Caldwell, J. C. (1968a) 'Determinants of rural-urban migration in Ghana', *Population Studies*, **22,** 1968, pp. 361–77.

Caldwell, J. C. (1968b) *Population Growth and Family Change in Africa*, Australian National University Press, Canberra, 1968.

Caldwell, J. C. (1969) *African Rural-Urban Migration: The Movement to Ghana's Towns*, Australian National University Press, Canberra, 1969.

Callaway, A. (1963) 'Unemployment among African school leavers', *Journal of Modern African Studies*, **1**, 1963, pp. 351–71.

Callaway, A. (1964) 'Nigeria's indigenous education: the apprentice system', *Odu*, **1**, 1964, pp. 62–79.

Chinoy, E. (1967) *Society*, 2nd edn., Random House, New York, 1967.

Clignet, R. (1967) 'Environmental change, types of descent and child rearing practices' in H. Miner (ed.), *The City in Modern Africa*, Pall Mall Press, London, 1967.

Clignet, R. (1970) 'Inadequacies of the notion of assimilation in African education', *Journal of Modern African Studies*, **8**, 1970, pp. 425–44.

Clignet, R. and Foster, P. (1964) 'Potential elites in Ghana and Ivory Coast: a preliminary comparison', *American Journal of Sociology*, **70**, 1964, pp. 349–62.

Clignet, R. and Foster, P. (1966) *The Fortunate Few*, Northwestern University Press, Evanston, 1966.

Clignet, R. and Sween, J. (1969) 'Social change and type of marriage', *American Journal of Sociology*, **75**, 1969, pp. 123–45.

Clinard, M. B. and Abbott, D. J. (1973) *Crime in Developing Countries*, John Wiley, London, 1973.

Cohen, A. (1969) *Custom and Politics in Urban Africa: A Study of Hausa Migrants in Yoruba Towns*, Routledge and Kegan Paul, London, 1969.

Cohen, A. (1974) *Urban Ethnicity*, Tavistock Publications, London, 1974.

Cohen, M. A. (1974) *Urban Policy and Political Conflict in Africa: A Study of the Ivory Coast*, University of Chicago Press, 1974.

Cohen, P. S. (1968) *Modern Social Theory*, Heinemann, London, 1968.

Cohen, R. (1972) 'Class in Africa: analytical problems and perspectives' in R. Miliband and J. Savile (eds.), *The Socialist Register*, The Merlin Press, London, 1972.

Cole, M. *et al* (1971) *The Cultural Context of Learning and Thinking: An Exploration in Experimental Anthropology*, Tavistock Publications, London, 1971.

Colson, E. (1953) 'Social control and vengeance in Plateau Tonga society', *Africa*, **23**, 1953, pp. 199–211. (Reprinted in Skinner 1973.)

Colson, E. (1970) 'The assimilation of aliens among Zambian Tonga', in R. Cohen and J. Middleton (eds.), *From Tribe to Nation in Africa*, Chandler Publishing Co., Scranton, 1970.

Colson, E. (1976) *The Social Consequences of Resettlement*, Manchester University Press, 1976.

Coser, L. A. (1956) *The Functions of Social Conflict*, Routledge and Kegan Paul, London, 1956.

Court, D. (1974) 'Village polytechnic leavers: the Maseno story', *Rural Africana*, **25**, 1974, pp. 91–100.

Court, D. and Ghai, D. (eds.) (1975) *Education, Society and Development: New Perspectives from Kenya*, Oxford University Press, Nairobi, 1975.

Crawford, J. R. (1967) *Witchcraft and Sorcery in Rhodesia*, Oxford University Press for the International African Institute, London, 1967. (Partially reprinted in Marwick 1970.)

Currie, J. (1974) 'Has the die been cast? A study of Ugandan secondary school recruitment patterns before and after independence', *Rural Africana*, No. 25, 1974, pp. 47–63.

Dahrendorf, R. (1959) *Class and Class Conflict in Industrial Society*, Routledge and Kegan Paul, London, 1959.

Davies, I. (1966) *African Trade Unions*, Penguin, Harmondsworth, 1966.

Davis, K. (1955) 'The origin and growth of urbanization in the world', *American Journal of Sociology*, **60**, 1955, pp. 429–37.

Davis, K. (1969) *World Urbanization 1950–1970: Basic Data for Cities, Countries, and Regions*, University of California Institute of International Studies, Berkeley, 1969.

Davis, K. and Moore, W. E. (1947) 'Some principles of stratification', *American Sociological Review*, **10**, 1947, pp. 242–9. (Reprinted, with comments by M. M. Tumin and rejoinders of 1953 in R. Bendix and S. M. Lipset (eds.), *Class, Status, and Power*, 2nd edn., Free Press, New York, 1966.)

Development Planning Unit (1974) 'The Measurement of Absorption in Lusaka 1957–1973', (mimeo), Development Planning Unit, London, 1974.

Dinan, C. (1975) 'Socialization in an Accra suburb: the zongo and its distinct subculture' in C. Oppong (ed.), *Legon Family Research Papers*, No. 3: *Changing Family Studies*, University of Ghana Institute of African Studies, Legon, 1975.

Doob, L. W. (1967) 'Scales for assaying psychological modernization in Africa', *Public Opinion Quarterly*, **31**, 1967, pp. 414–21.

Dore, R. (1970) 'Social planning for the family' in R. Apthorpe (ed.), *People, Planning and Development Studies*, Frank Cass, London, 1970.

Dore, R. (1976) *The Diploma Disease: Education, Qualification and Development*, Unwin, London, 1976.

Doudu, C. (1967) *The Gab Boys*, Andre Deutsch, London, 1967.

Drucker, P. F. (1961) 'The educational revolution' in A. H. Halsey, J. Floud, and C. A. Anderson (eds.), *Education, Economy, and Society*, Free Press, New York, 1961.

Durkheim, E. (1915) *The Elementary Forms of the Religious Life* (trans. J. W. Swain), Allen and Unwin, London, 1915.

Durkheim, E. (1938) *The Rules of the Sociological Method*, University of Chicago Press, 1938.

Edwards, J. N. and Booth, A. (eds.) (1973) *Social Participation in Urban Society*, Schenkman Publishing Co., Cambridge, Mass., 1973.

Eisenstadt, S. N. (1973) *Tradition, Change, and Modernity*, John Wiley and Sons, New York, 1973.

Ekeh, P. P. (1974) *Social Exchange Theory*, Heinemann, London, 1974.

Elkan, W. (1976) 'Is a proletariat emerging in Nairobi?' *Economic Development and Cultural Change*, **24**, 1976, pp. 695–706.

Elliott, K. (1970) *An African School*, Cambridge University Press, 1970.

Epstein, A. L. (1957) *Politics in an Urban African Community*, Manchester University Press, 1957.

Epstein, A. L. (1961) 'The network and urban social organization', *Rhodes-Livingstone Institute Journal*, **29**, 1961, pp. 29–61. (Reprinted in Mitchell 1969.)

Epstein, A. L. (1967) 'Urbanization and social change in Africa', *Current Anthropology*, **8**, 1967, pp. 275–95. (Reprinted in Breese 1969 and Wilmott 1973, Vol. 2.)

Fallers, L. A. (1954) 'A note on the "trickle effect" ', *Public Opinion Quarterly*, **18**, 1954, pp. 314–21. (Reprinted in Fallers 1973 and in Bendix and Lipset 1966 – see Davis and Moore above).

Fallers, L. A. (1957) 'Some determinants of marriage stability in Busoga', *Africa*, **27**, 1957, pp. 106–24.

Fallers, L. A. (ed.) (1964) *The King's Men*, Oxford University Press for the East African Institute of Social Research, London, 1964.

Fallers, L. A. (1965) *Bantu Bureaucracy*, University of Chicago Press, 1965.

Fallers, L. A. (1973) *Inequality: Social Stratification Reconsidered*, University of Chicago Press, 1973.

Feldman, R. (1975) 'Rural social differentiation and political goals in Tanzania' in I. Oxall, T. Barnett and D. Booth (eds.), *Beyond the Sociology of Development*, Routledge and Kegan Paul, London, 1975.

Fiawoo, D. K. (1968) 'From cult to "church": a study of some aspects of religious change in Ghana', *Ghana Journal of Sociology*, **4**, 1968, pp. 72–87.

Field, M. J. (1960) *Search for Security: An Ethno-psychiatric Study of Rural Ghana*, Northwestern University Press, Evanston, 1960.

Fisher, H. J. (1973) 'Conversion reconsidered: some historical aspects of religious conversion in black Africa', *Africa*, **43**, 1973, pp. 27–40.

Fortes, M. (1953) 'The structure of unilineal descent groups', *American Anthropologist*, **55**, 1953, pp. 17–41. (Reprinted in Ottenberg 1960.)

Fortes, M., Steel, R. W. and Ady, P. (1947) 'Ashanti survey, 1945–46: an experiment in social research', *Geographical Journal*, **90**, 1947, pp. 149–79.

Foster, P. (1963) 'Secondary schooling and social selection in a West African nation', *Sociology of Education*, **37**, 1963, pp. 150–71.

Foster, P. (1965) *Education and Social Change in Ghana*, Routledge and Kegan Paul, London, 1965.

Foster, P. (1966) 'The vocational school fallacy in development planning' in C. A. Anderson and M. J. Bowman (eds.), *Education and Development*, Cass, London, 1966.

Fraenkel, M. (1964) *Tribe and Class in Monrovia*, Oxford University Press for the International African Institute, London, 1964.

Frankenberg, R. (1969) 'Man, society and health: towards the definition of the role of sociology in the development of Zambian medicine', *African Social Research*, **8**, 1969, pp. 573–87.

Gamble, D. (1963) 'The Temne family in a modern town (Lunsar) in Sierra Leone', *Africa*, **33**, 1963, pp. 209–25.

Gamble, D. (1966) 'Occupational prestige in an urban community (Lunsar) in Sierra Leone', *Sierra Leone Studies*, New Series No. 19, 1966, pp. 98–108.

Garlick, P. C. (1971) *African Traders and Economic Development in Ghana*, Clarendon Press, Oxford, 1971.

Gay, J. and Cole, M. (1967) *The New Mathematics and an Old Culture*, Holt, Rinehart and Winston, New York, 1967.

Geertz, C. (1962) 'The rotating credit association: a "middle-rung" in development', *Economic Development and Cultural Change*, **10**, 1962, pp. 241–63. (Reprinted in Wallerstein 1966.)

Ghana (1960) *1960 Population Census of Ghana*, published 1962–71, but referred to in text as Ghana 1960, Central Bureau of Statistics, Accra, 1962–71.

Ghana (1970) *1970 Population Census of Ghana*, published 1972, but referred to in text as Ghana 1970, Central Bureau of Statistics, Accra, 1972.

Gibbs, J. L. (ed.) (1965) *Peoples of Africa*, Holt, Rinehart and Winston, New York, 1965.

Gluckman, M. (1955) *Custom and Conflict in Africa*, Basil Blackwell, Oxford, 1955.

Gluckman, M. (1960) 'Tribalism in modern British Central Africa', *Cahiers D'Etudes Africaines*, **1**, 1960, pp. 55–70. (Reprinted in van den Berghe 1965.)

Goldlust, J. and Richmond, A. H. (1974) 'A multivariate model of immigrant adaptation', *International Migration Review*, **8**, 1974, pp. 193–224.

Goode, W. (1963) *World Revolution and Family Patterns*, Free Press, New York, 1963.

Goody, E. (1962) 'Conjugal separation and divorce among the Gonja of Northern Ghana' in M. Fortes(ed.), *Marriage in Tribal Societies*, Cambridge University Press, 1962.

Goody, E. (1966) 'The fostering of children in Ghana', *Ghana Journal of Sociology*, **2**, 1966, pp. 26–33.

Goody, E. (1970) 'Kinship fostering in Gonja' in P. Mayer, ed. *Socialization*, Tavistock Publications, London, 1970.

Goody, E. (1971) 'The Varieties of Fostering', *New Society*, **18**, 1971, pp. 237–9.

Goody, J. (1957) 'Anomie in Ashanti?', *Africa*, **27**, 1957, pp. 356–63.

Goody, J. (1971) 'Class and Marriage in Africa and Eurasia', *American Journal of Sociology*, **76**, 1971, pp. 585–603.

Goody, J. (ed.) (1975) *Changing Social Structure in Ghana*, International African Institute, London, 1975.

Goody, J. and Watt, I. (1963) 'The Consequences of Literacy', *Comparative Studies of Society and History*, **5**, 1963, pp. 304–45. (Reprinted in J. Goody (ed.), *Literacy in Traditional Societies*, Cambridge University Press, 1968.)

Gouldner, A. W. (1960) 'The norm of reciprocity: a preliminary statement', *American Sociological Review*, **25**, 1960, pp. 161–78.

Grillo, R. D. (1973) *African Railwaymen*, Cambridge University Press, 1973.

Grindal, B. (1972) *Growing Up in Two Worlds: Education and Transition among the Sisala of Northern Ghana*, Holt, Rinehart and Winston, New York, 1972.

Gugler, J. (1969) 'On the theory of rural-urban migration: the case of sub-Saharan Africa' in J. A. Jackson (ed.), *Migration*, Cambridge University Press, 1969.

Gugler, J. (ed.) (1970) *Urban Growth in Subsaharan Africa*, Nkanga Editions No. 6, Makerere Institute of Social Research, Kampala, 1970.

Gugler, J. (1972) 'The second sex in town', *Canadian Journal of African Studies*, **6**, 1972, pp. 289–301.

Gugler, J. and Flanagan, W. G. (1976) *Urbanization and Social Change in West Africa*, Cambridge University Press, 1976.

Gulliver, P. H. (1969) *Tradition and Transition in East Africa*, Routledge and Kegan Paul, London, 1969.

Gutkind, P. C. W. (1967) 'The energy of despair; social organization of the unemployed in two African cities, Lagos and Nairobi', *Civilizations*, **17**, 1967, pp. 186–214 and 380–405.

Gutkind, P. C. W. (ed.) (1970) *The Passing of Tribal Man in Africa*, special issue of *Journal of Asian and African Studies*, 5, 1970. (Reprinted by E. J. Brill, Leiden, 1970.)

Hance, W. A. (1970) *Population, Migration and Urbanization in Africa*, Columbia University Press, 1970.

Handwerker, W. P. (1973) 'Kinship, friendship, and business failure among market sellers in Monrovia, Liberia, 1970', *Africa*, **43**, 1973, pp. 288–301.

Hanna, W. J. and J. L. (1967) 'The integrative role of urban Africa's middle-places and middlemen', *Civilisations*, **17**, 1967, pp. 12–27.

Harrell-Bond, B. E. (1975) *Modern Marriage in Sierra Leone*, Mouton, Paris, 1975.

Hart, K. (1971) 'Migration and tribal identity among the Frafras of Ghana', *Journal of Asian and African Studies*, **6**, 1971, pp. 21–36.

Hart, K. (1973) 'Informal income opportunities and urban employment in Ghana', *Journal of Modern African Studies*, **11**, 1973, pp. 61–89.

Hastings, A. (1973) *Christian Marriage in Africa*, SPCK, London, 1973.

Hastings, A. (1976) *African Christianity*, Geoffrey Chapman, London, 1976.

Hauser, P. M. (1965) 'Urbanization: an overview' in P. M. Hauser and L. F. Schnore (eds,) *The Study of Urbanization*, John Wiley and Sons, London, 1965.

Henderson, R. N. (1966) 'Generalized cultures and evolutionary adaptability: a comparison of urban Efik and Ibo in Nigeria,' *Ethnology*, **5**, 1966, pp. 365–91.

Heyneman, S. P. (1976) 'A brief note on the relationships between socio-economic status and test performance among Ugandan primary school children', *Comparative Education Review*, *20*, pp. 42–7, 1976.

Hill, P. (1966) 'Landlords and brokers: a West African trading system', *Cahiers D'Etudes Africaines*, **6**, 1966, pp. 349–66.

Hill, P. (1968) 'The myth of the amorphous peasantry: a northern Nigerian case study', *Nigerian Journal of Economic and Social Studies*, **10**, 1968, pp. 239–60.

Hill, P. (1969) 'Hidden trade in Hausaland', *Man*, **4**, 1969, pp. 392–409.

Hill, P. (1972) *Rural Hausa*, Cambridge University Press, 1972.

Hodge, R. W., Trieman, D. J. and Rossi, P. H. (1966) 'A comparative study of occupational prestige' in R. Bendix and S. M. Lipset (eds.), *Class,*

Status, and Power, Free Press, New York, 1966.

Homans, G. C. (1950) *The Human Group*, Harcourt, Brace and Co., New York, 1950.

Hopkins, A. G. (1966) 'The Lagos strike of 1897: an exploration in Nigerian labour history', *Past and Present*, **35**, 1966, pp. 133–55.

Hopkins, N. S. (1972) *Popular Government in an African Town: Kita, Mali*, University of Chicago Press, 1972.

Hopkins, T. K. and Wallerstein, I. (1967) 'The comparative study of national societies', *Social Science Information*, **6**, 1967, pp. 25–58.

Horowitz, D. L. (1975), 'Ethnic Identity' in N. Glazer and D. P. Moynihan (eds.), *Ethnicity: Theory and Experience*, Harvard University Press, 1975.

Horton, R. (1967) 'African traditional thought and western science', *Africa* **37**, 1967, pp. 50–71 and 155–87. (Abridged in Marwick 1970.)

Horton, R. (1971) 'African conversion', *Africa*, **41**, 1971, pp. 85–108.

Horton, R. (1975) 'On the rationality of conversion', *Africa*, **45**, 1975, pp. 219–35 and 373–99.

Human Resources Research Unit (1973) *Socio-Economic Background of Nigerian University Students*, Bulletin No. 1/001, University of Lagos, 1973.

Hurd, G. E. and Johnson, T. J. (1967) 'Education and social mobility in Ghana', *Sociology of Education*, **40**, 1967, pp. 55–79. (See also comments by P. Foster in *Sociology of Education*, **41**, pp. 111–15 and reply by Hurd and Johnson in *Sociology of Education*, **41**, pp. 116–21.)

Hutton, C. (1969) 'Unemployment in Kampala and Jinja, Uganda', *Canadian Journal of African Studies*, **3**, 1969, pp. 431–40.

Hutton, C. (1973) *Reluctant Farmers? A Study of Unemployment and Planned Rural Development in Uganda*, East African Publishing House, Nairobi, 1973.

Hutton, C. and Cohen, R. (1975) 'African peasants and resistance to change: a reconsideration of sociological approaches', in I. Oxall, T. Barnett and D. Booth (eds.), *Beyond the Sociology of Development*, Routledge and Kegan Paul, London, 1975.

Hutton, J. (ed.) (1972) *Urban Challenge in East Africa*, East African Publishing House, Nairobi, 1972.

Imoagene, S. O. (1967a) 'Mechanisms of immigrant adjustment in a West African urban community', *Nigerian Journal of Economic and Social Studies*, **9**, 1967, pp. 51–66.

Imoagene, S. O. (1967b) 'Psycho-social factors in rural-urban migration', *Nigerian Journal of Economic and Social Studies*, **9**, 1967, pp. 375–86.

Imperato, P. J. (1974) 'Traditional medical practitioners among the Bambara of Mali and their role in the modern health-care-delivery system', *Rural Africana*, **26,** 1974, pp. 41–53.

I.N.A.D.E.S. (1964) *Cours de Sociologie*, Institut Africain pour le Développement Economique et Social, Abidjan, 1964.

Inkeles, A. (1969) 'Making men modern: on the causes and consequences of individual change in six developing countries', *American Journal of Sociology*, **75,** 1969, pp. 208–25.

Inkeles, A. (1973) 'The school as a context for modernization', *International Journal of Comparative Sociology*, **14,** 1973, pp. 163–79.

Inkeles, A. (1975) *Becoming Modern: Individual Change in Six Developing Countries*, Heinemann Educational Books, London, 1975.

I.L.O. (1972) *Employment, Incomes and Equality: A Strategy for Increasing Productive Employment in Kenya*, I.L.O., Geneva, 1972.

I.L.O. (1974) *Yearbook of Labour Statistics*, I.L.O., Geneva, 1974.

Irvine, S. H. and Sanders, J. T. (eds.) (1972) *Cultural Adaptation within Modern Africa*, Teachers College Press, New York, 1972.

Jacobson, D. (1973) *Itinerant Townsmen: Friendship and Social Order in Urban Uganda*, Cummings Publishing Co., Menlo Park, Calif., 1973.

Jahoda, G. (1954) 'Social background of a West African student population', *British Journal of Sociology*, **5,** 1954, pp. 355–65, and **6,** 1954, pp. 71–81.

Janzen, J. M. (1974) 'Pluralistic legitimation of therapy systems in contemporary Zaire', *Rural Africana*, No. 26, 1974, pp. 105–22.

Jolly, R. (ed.) (1969) *Education in Africa: Research and Action*, East African Publishing House for the African Studies Association of the U.K., Nairobi, 1969.

Kapferer, B. (1972) *Strategy and Transaction in an African Factory*, Manchester University Press, 1972.

Kay, G. (1960) *Social and Economic Study of Fort Roseberry*, Rhodes-Livingstone Communications No. 21, Rhodes-Livingstone Institute, Lusaka, 1960.

Kaufert, J. and Peil, M. (1976) 'Selectivity ratios and mobility through education: a research note', *International Journal of Comparative Sociology*, **17,** 1976, pp. 103–6.

Kilson, M. (1974) *African Urban Kinsmen*, C. Hurst, London, 1974.

King, K. (1974) 'Kenya's educated unemployed', *Manpower and Unemployment Research in Africa*, **7,** 2, 1974, pp. 45–63.

Kluckhohn, C. (1951) 'Values and value-orientations in the theory of action: an explanation in definition and classification' in T. Parsons and E. A. Shils (eds.), *Toward a General Theory of Action*, Harvard University Press,

1951.

Koll, M. (1969) *Crafts and Cooperation in Western Nigeria*, Bertelsmann Universitätsverlag, Freiburg, 1969.

Kuper, H. (ed.) (1965) *Urbanization and Migration in West Africa*, University of California Press, 1965.

Kuper, L. and Smith, M. G. (eds.) (1969) *Pluralism in Africa*, University of California Press, 1969.

LaFontaine, J. S. (1969) 'Two types of youth group in Kinshasa', in P. Mayer (ed.), *Socialization*, Tavistock Publications, London, 1969.

LaFontaine, J. S. (1970) *City Politics: A Study of Leopoldville 1962–63*, Cambridge University Press, 1970.

Lawson, R. M. (1972) *The Changing Economy of the Lower Volta 1954–67*, Oxford University Press for the International African Institute, London, 1972.

Lemarchand, R. (1966) 'Power and stratification in Rwanda: a reconsideration,' *Cahiers d'Etudes Africaines*, **6**, 1966, pp. 592–610. (Reprinted in Skinner 1973.)

Lenski, G. (1954) 'Status crystalization: a non-vertical dimension of social status', *American Sociological Review*, **19**, 1954, pp. 405–13.

Lenski, G. (1956) 'Social participation and status crystalization', *American Sociological Review*, **21**, 1956, pp. 458–64.

Leslie, J. A. K. (1963) *A Survey of Dar es Salaam*, Oxford University Press for The East African Institute of Social Research, London, 1963.

Levine, D. N. (1965) *Wax and Gold: Tradition and Innovation in Ethiopian Culture*, University of Chicago Press, 1965.

LeVine, R. A. (1966) *Dreams and Deeds: Achievement Motivation in Nigeria*, University of Chicago Press, 1966.

LeVine, R. A., Klein, N. H. and Owen, C. R. (1967) 'Father-child relationships and changing life-styles in Ibadan, Nigeria', in H. Miner (ed.), *The City in Modern Africa*, Pall Mall Press, London, 1967.

Levi-Strauss, C. (1956) 'The Family' in H. L. Shapiro (ed.), *Man, Culture and Society*, Oxford University Press, New York, 1956.

Leys, C. (1965) 'What is the problem about corruption?', *Journal of Modern African Studies*, **2**, 1965, pp. 215–30.

Little, K. (1965) *West African Urbanization*, Cambridge University Press, 1965.

Lloyd, B. B. (1969) 'Yoruba mothers' reports of child-rearing' in P. Mayer (ed.), *Socialization*, Tavistock Publications, London, 1969.

Lloyd, P. C. (1953) 'Craft organization in Yoruba towns', *Africa*, **23**, 1953, pp. 30–44. (Reprinted in Wallerstein 1966.)

Lloyd, P. C. (1959) 'The Yoruba town today', *Sociological Review*, **7**, 1959, pp. 45–63.

Lloyd, P. C. (ed.) (1966) *The New Elites of Tropical Africa*, Oxford University Press for the International African Institute, London, 1966.

Lloyd, P. C. (1967) *Africa in Social Change*, Penguin, Harmondsworth, 1967.

Lloyd, P. C. (1968) 'Divorce among the Yoruba', *American Anthropologist*, **70**, 1968, pp. 67–81.

Lloyd, P. C. (1974) *Power and Independence: Urban Africans' Perception of Social Inequality*, Routledge and Kegan Paul, London, 1974.

Lloyd, P. C., Mabogunje, A. L. and Awe, B. (eds.) (1967) *The City of Ibadan*, Cambridge University Press, 1967.

Long, N. (1968) *Social Change and the Individual: A Study of the Social and Religious Responses to Innovation in a Zambian Rural Community*, Manchester University Press, 1968.

Lowy, M. J. (1974) 'Me Ko court: the impact of urbanization on conflict resolution in a Ghanaian town,' in G. Foster and R. Kemper (eds.), *Anthropologists in Cities*, Little, Brown, Boston, 1974.

Lucas, D. (1973) 'Nigerian women and family resources' in C. Oppong, (ed.) *Family Research Seminar*, (mimeo), University of Ghana Institute of African Studies, Legon, 1973.

Luckham, R. (1971) *The Nigerian Military*, Cambridge University Press, 1971.

Lux, A. (1971) 'The network of visits between rural wage-earners and their kinsfolk in western Congo', *Africa*, **41**, 1971, pp. 109–28.

Lux, A. (1973) 'Gift exchange and income redistribution between Yombe rural wage-earners and their kinsfolk in western Zaire', *Africa*, **42**, 1973, pp. 173–91.

Maas, J. van L. (1970) 'Educational change in pre-colonial societies: the cases of Buganda and Ashanti', *Comparative Education Review*, **4**, 1970, pp. 174–85.

Mabogunje, A. L. (1962) *Yoruba Towns*, Ibadan University Press, 1962.

Mabogunje, A. L. (1968) *Urbanization in Nigeria*, University of London Press, 1968.

McClelland, D. C. (1961) *The Achieving Society*, Van Nostrand, Princeton, 1961.

McClelland, D. C. (1963) 'The achievement motive in economic growth' in UNESCO (ed.), *Industrialization and Society*, Mouton, The Hague, 1963. (Reprinted in G. D. Ness (ed.), *The Sociology of Economic Development*, Harper and Row, London, 1970.)

McCulloch, M. (1956) *A Social Survey of the African Population of Livingstone*,

Rhodes-Livingstone Paper No. 26, Rhodes-Livingstone Institute, Lusaka, 1956.

McEwan, P. J. M. and Sutcliffe, R. B. (eds.) (1965) *The Study of Africa*, Methuen, London, 1965.

MacLean, U. (1971) *Magical Medicine: A Nigerian Case-Study*, Penguin, Harmondsworth, 1971.

Magid, A. (1976) *Men in the Middle: Leadership and Role Conflict in a Nigerian Society*, Manchester University Press, 1976.

Mair, L. (1974) *African Societies*, Cambridge University Press, 1974.

Malinowski, B. (1945) *The Dynamics of Culture Change*, Yale University Press, 1945. (Excerpts in Wallerstein 1966.)

Mangin, W. (ed.) (1970) *Peasants in Cities*, Houghton Mifflin Co., Boston, Mass., 1970.

Marris, P. (1961) *Family and Social Change in an African City*, Routledge and Kegan Paul, London, 1961.

Marris, P. (1967) *African City Life*, Nkanga Editions No. 1, Transition Books, Kampala, 1967.

Marris, P. and Somerset, A. (1971) *African Businessmen: A Study of Entrepreneurship and Development in Kenya*, Routledge and Kegan Paul, London, 1971.

Marsh, R. M. (1967) *Comparative Sociology*, Harcourt, Brace and World, New York, 1967.

Marwick, M. (ed.) (1970) *Witchcraft and Sorcery*, Penguin, Harmondsworth, 1970.

Masemann, V. (1974) 'The "hidden curriculum" of a West African girls' boarding school', *Canadian Journal of African Studies*, **8**, 1974, pp. 479–94.

Mauss, M. (1925) *The Gift*, (trans. I. Cunnison,) Cohen and West, London, 1925. (Excerpts in Wilmot 1973, Vol. 1.)

Mayer, P. (1961) *Townsmen or Tribesmen*, Oxford University Press, Cape Town, 1961.

Mayer, P. (1962) 'Migrancy and the study of Africans in town', *American Anthropologist*, **64**, 1962, pp. 576–92.

Mbilinyi, M. J. (1969) *The Education of Girls in Tanzania*, Printpak, Dar es Salaam, 1969.

Mbiti, J. S. (1969) *African Religions and Philosophy*, Heinemann, London, 1969.

Meillassoux, C. (1968) *Urbanization in an African Community: Voluntary Associations in Bamako*, University of Washington Press, Seattle, 1968.

Meillassoux, C. (1970) 'A class analysis of the bureaucratic process in Mali', *Journal of Development Studies*, **6**, 1970, pp. 97–110.

Melson, R. and Wolpe, H. (eds.) (1971) *Nigeria: Modernization and the Politics of Communalism*, Michigan State University Press, 1971.

Merton, R. K. (1957) *Social Theory and Social Structure*, Free Press, Glencoe, Ill., 1957.

Middleton, J. (ed.) (1970) *Black Africa: Its Peoples and Their Cultures Today*. Collier-Macmillan, London, 1970.

Miner, H. (1953) *The Primitive City of Timbuctoo*, Doubleday, New York, 1953.

Miner, H. (1967) *The City in Modern Africa*, Pall Mall Press, London, 1967.

Mitchell, J. C. (1954) 'African urbanization in Ndola and Luanshya,' Rhodes-Livingstone Communication No. 6, Rhodes-Livingstone Institute, Lusaka, 1954.

Mitchell, J. C. (1956) *The Kalela Dance*, Rhodes-Livingstone Paper No. 27, Manchester University Press for the Rhodes-Livingstone Institute, 1956.

Mitchell, J. C. (1957) 'Aspects of African marriage on the Copperbelt of Northern Rhodesia', *Human Problems of British Central Africa*, **22**, 1957, pp. 1–30.

Mitchell, J. C. (1966) 'Theoretical orientations in African urban studies' in M. Banton (ed.), *The Social Anthropology of Complex Societies*, Tavistock Publications, London, 1966.

Mitchell, J. C. (1969a) *Social Networks in Urban Situations: Analyses of Personal Relationships in Central African Towns*, Manchester University Press, 1969.

Mitchell, J. C. (1969b) 'Urbanization, detribalization, stabilization and urban commitment in southern Africa: a problem of definition and measurement' in P. Meadows and E. H. Mizruchi (eds.), *Urbanism, Urbanization, and Change: Comparative Perspectives*, Addison-Wesley, London, 1969. (An earlier version appeared in UNESCO, 1956b.)

Mitchell, J. C. (1973) 'Distance, transportation and urban involvement in Zambia', in A. Solihull (ed.), *Urban Anthropology*, Oxford University Press, 1973.

Mitchell, J. C. and Epstein, A. L. (1959) 'Occupational prestige and social status among urban Africans in Northern Rhodesia', *Africa*, **29**, 1959, pp. 22–40. (Reprinted in van den Berghe 1965.)

Moock, J. L. (1973) 'Pragmatism and the primary school: the case of a non-rural village', *Africa*, **43**, 1973, pp. 302–15. (Reprinted in Court and Ghai, 1975.)

Moore, W. E. (1963) 'But some are more equal than others', *American Sociological Review*, **28**, 1963, pp. 13–9.

Morgan, R. W. (1965) 'Occupational prestige ratings by Nigerian students', *Nigerian Journal of Economic and Social Studies*, **7**, 1965, pp. 325–32.

Morrill, W. T. (1963) 'The Ibo in twentieth century Calabar', *Comparative Studies in Society and History*, **5**, 1963, pp. 424–48. (Reprinted in L. A.

Fallers (ed.), *Immigrants and Associations*, Mouton, The Hague, 1967.)

Muench, L. H. (1972) 'Town planning and the social system' in M. Koll (ed.), *African Urban Development*, Bertelsmann Universitätsverlag, Freiburg, 1972.

Muhsam, H. V. (1971) 'The population factor in the demand for education', (mimeo), *ECA African Population Conference*, Accra, 1971.

Nadel, S. F. (1952) 'Witchcraft in four African societies', *American Anthropologist*, **54**, 1952, pp. 18–29. (Reprinted in Marwick 1970 and in Wilmot 1973, Vol. 2.)

Nelson, J. M. (1976) 'Sojourners versus new urbanites: causes and consequences of temporary versus permanent migration in developing countries', *Economic Development and Cultural Change*, **24**, 1976, pp. 721–57.

Nigeria (1971) *Statistics of Education in Nigeria*, Federal Ministry of Education, Lagos, 1971.

Norwood, H. C. (1975) 'Squatters compared', *African Urban Notes*, Series B, No. 2, 1975, pp. 119–32.

Nyerere, J. (1967) *Education for Self-Reliance*, Government Printer, Dar es Salaam, 1967.

Nyerere, J. (1974) 'Education and liberation', Address to IDS/Dag Hammarskjold Seminar in Dar es Salaam, *Development Dialogue*, Uppsala, **2**, 1974, pp. 46–52.

O'Brien, D. C. (1975) *Saints and Politicians: Essays in the Organisation of a Sengalese Peasant Society*, Cambridge University Press, 1975.

Ohadike, P. O. (1969) 'The nature and extent of urbanisation in Zambia', *Journal of Asian and African Studies*, **4**, 1969, pp. 107–21.

Ohadike, P. O. (1971) 'Aspects of domesticity and family relationship: a survey study of the family household in Zambia', *Journal of Asian and African Studies*, **6**, 1971, pp. 191–204.

Okediji, F. O. (1967) 'Some social psychological aspects of fertility among married women in an African city', *Nigerian Journal of Economic and Social Studies*, **9**, 1967, pp. 67–79.

Okediji, O. O. (1975) 'On voluntary associations as adaptive mechanisms in West African urbanization: another perspective', *African Urban Notes*, Series B, No. 2, 1975, pp. 51–73.

Okigbo, P. (1956) 'Social consequences of economic development in West Africa', *Annals of the American Academy of Political and Social Science*, **305**, 1956, pp. 125–33. (Reprinted in van den Berghe 1965.)

Olusanya, P. O. (1969) *Socio-Economic Aspects of Rural–Urban Migration in*

Western Nigeria, Nigerian Institute of Social and Economic Research, Ibadan, 1969.

Omari, T. P. (1960) 'Changing attitudes of students in West African society toward marriage and family relationships', *British Journal of Sociology*, **11**, 1960, pp. 197–210.

Omari, T. P. (1963) 'Role expectation in the courtship situation in Ghana', *Social Forces*, **42**, 1963, pp. 147–56. (Reprinted in van den Berghe 1965.)

Oppong, C. (1967) 'Local migration in northern Ghana', *Ghana Journal of Sociology*, **3**, 1967, pp. 1–16.

Oppong, C. (1970) 'Conjugal power and resources: an urban African example', *Journal of Marriage and the Family*, **34**, 1970, pp. 676–80.

Oppong, C. (1974) *Marriage among a Matrilineal Elite: A Family Study of Ghanaian Senior Civil Servants*, Cambridge University Press, 1974.

Ottenberg, S. (1967) 'Local government and the law in southern Nigeria', *Journal of Asian and African Studies*, **2**, 1967, pp. 26–43. (Reprinted in Middleton 1970.)

Ottenberg, S. and P., (eds.,) (1960) *Cultures and Societies of Africa*, Random House, New York, 1960.

Paden, J. N. (1973) *Religion and Political Culture in Kano*, University of California Press, 1973.

Parkin, D. J. (1966a) 'Types of urban African marriage in Kampala', *Africa*, **36**, 1966, pp. 269–85.

Parkin, D. J. (1966b) 'Urban voluntary associations as institutions of adaptation', *Man*, **1**, 1966, pp. 90–5.

Parkin, D. J. (1969) *Neighbours and Nationals in an African City Ward*, Routledge and Kegan Paul, London, 1969.

Parkin, D. J. (1972) *Palms, Wines, and Witnesses*, Intertext Books, London, 1972.

Parkin, D. J. (1975) *Town and Country in Central and Eastern Africa*, International African Institute, London, 1975.

Parsons, T. (1951) *The Social System*, Free Press, Glencoe, Ill., 1951.

Parsons, T. (1954) 'A revised analytical approach to the theory of stratification' in T. Parsons, *Essays in Sociological Theory*, revised edn., Free Press, Glencoe, Ill., 1954.

Parsons, T. (1970) 'Equality and inequality in modern society, or social stratification revisited' in E. O. Laumann (ed.), *Social Stratification: Research and Theory for the 1970s*, Bobbs-Merrill, Indianapolis, 1970.

Parsons, T. and Platt, G. M. (1974) *The American University*, Harvard University Press, 1974.

Peace, A. (1974) 'Industrial protest in Nigeria' in E. de Kadt and G. Williams (eds.), *Sociology and Development*, Tavistock Publications, London, 1974.

Peel, J. D. Y. (1968) *Aladura: A Religious Movement among the Yoruba*, Oxford University Press for the International African Institute, London, 1968. (One section reprinted in Wilmot 1973, Vol. 2.)

Peil, M. (1965) 'Ghanaian university students: the broadening base', *British Journal of Sociology*, **16**, 1965, pp. 19–28.

Peil, M. (1968) 'Aspirations and social structure: a West African example', *Africa*, **38**, 1968, pp. 71–8.

Peil, M. (1969) 'Unemployment in Tema: the plight of the skilled worker', *Canadian Journal of African Studies*, **3**, 1969, pp. 409–19.

Peil, M. (1970) 'The apprenticeship system in Accra', *Africa*, **40**, 1970, pp. 137–50.

Peil, M. (1971) 'The expulsion of West African aliens', *Journal of Modern African Studies*, **9**, 1971, pp. 205–29.

Peil, M. (1972a) *The Ghanaian Factory Worker*, Cambridge University Press, 1972.

Peil, M. (1972b) 'Male unemployment in Lagos', *Manpower and Unemployment Research in Africa*, **5**, 2, 1972, pp. 18–24.

Peil, M. (1975a) 'Female roles in West African towns' in J. Goody (ed.), *Changing Social Structure in Ghana*, International African Institute, London, 1975.

Peil, M. (1975b) 'Interethnic contacts in Nigerian cities', *Africa*, **45**, 1975, pp. 107–22.

Peil, M. (1975c) 'Social aspects of religion in West African towns', *African Urban Notes*, Series B, No. 2, 1975, pp. 95–104.

Peil, M. (1976a) 'African squatter settlements: a comparative study', *Urban Studies*, **13**, 1976, pp. 155–66.

Peil, M. (1976b) *Nigerian Politics: The People's View*, Cassells, London 1976.

Peil, M. and Lucas, D. (1972) *Survey Research Methods for West Africa*, Human Resources Research Unit, University of Lagos, 1972.

Peshkin, A. (1972) *Kanuri Schoolchildren: Education and Social Mobilization in Nigeria*, Holt, Rinehart and Winston, New York, 1972.

Peshkin, A. (1973) 'Social change in northern Nigeria: the acceptance of western education' in U. G. Damachi and H. D. Seibel (eds.), *Social Change and Economic Development in Nigeria*, Praeger, New York, 1973.

Pfeffermann, G. (1968) *Industrial Labor in the Republic of Senegal*, Praeger, New York, 1968.

Plotnicov, L. (1965) 'Nigerians: the dream is unfulfilled', *Trans-Action*, **3**, 1965, pp. 18–22. (Reprinted in Mangin 1970.)

Plotnicov, L. (1967) *Strangers to the City: Urban Man in Jos, Nigeria*, University of Pittsburgh Press, 1967.

Plotnicov, L. and Tuden, A. (eds.) (1970) *Essays in Comparative Social Strati-fication*, University of Pittsburgh Press, 1970.

Pons, V. (1969) *Stanleyville*, Oxford University Press for the International African Institute, London, 1969.

Population Reference Bureau (1975) *World Population Data Sheet*, Population Reference Bureau, Washington, D.C., 1975.

Post, K. W. J. and Jenkins, G. D. (1973) *The Price of Liberty: Personality and Politics in Colonial Nigeria*, Cambridge University Press, 1973.

Potholm, C. P. (1969) 'The multiple roles of the police as seen in the African context', *Journal of Developing Areas*, **3**, 1969, pp. 139–58.

Powdermaker, H. (1962) *Copper Town*, Harper and Row, New York, 1962.

Prewitt, K. (ed.) (1971) *Education and Political Values: an East African Case Study*, East African Publishing House, Nairobi, 1971.

Price-Williams, D. R. (1962) 'A case study of ideas concerning disease among the Tiv', *Africa*, **32**, 1962, pp. 123–31. (Reprinted in Skinner 1973.)

Proctor, J. H. (ed.) (1971) *Building Ujamaa Villages in Tanzania*, Tanzania Publishing House, Dar es Salaam, 1971.

Prothero, R. M. (1968) 'Migration in tropical Africa' in J. C. Caldwell and C. Okonjo (eds.), *The Population of Tropical Africa*, Longmans, London, 1968.

Quarcoo, A. K. (1966) 'Social control in Madina', Ghana Journal of Sociology, **2**, 2, 1966, pp. 8–14.

Radcliffe-Brown, A. R. (1952) *Structure and Function in Primitive Society*, Cohen and West, London, 1952.

Radcliffe-Brown, A. R. and Forde, D. (eds.) (1950) *African Systems of Kinship and Marriage*, Oxford University Press for the International African Institute, London, 1950.

Rado, E. R. (1972) 'The relevance of education for employment', *Journal of Modern African Studies*, **10**, 1972, pp. 459–75.

Ray, R. S. (1966) *Labour Force Survey of Tanzania*, Ministry of Economic Affairs and Development Planning, Dar es Salaam, 1966.

Read, M. (1959) *Children of their Fathers: Growing Up among the Ngoni of Nyasaland*, Methuen, London and Holt, Rinehart and Winston, New York, 1959.

Redfield, R. (1947) 'The folk society', *American Journal of Sociology*, **41**, 1947, pp. 293–308.

Richards, A. I. (1954) *Economic Development and Tribal Change*, Heffer and Son, Cambridge, 1954.

Riesman, D. *et al* (1950) *The Lonely Crowd*, Yale University Press, 1950.

381

Roper, J. I. (1958) *Labour Problems in West Africa*, Penguin, London, 1958.

Ross, M. H. (1973) *The Political Integration of Urban Squatters*, Northwestern University Press, Evanston, 1973.

Ross, M. H. (1974) 'Conflict resolution among urban squatters'. Urban Anthropology, **3**, 1974, pp. 110–37.

Ross, M. H. (1975) *Grass Roots in an African City: Political Behaviour in Nairobi*, MIT Press, Cambridge, Mass., 1975.

Rotberg, R. (1961) 'The Lenshina movement of Northern Rhodesia', *Rhodes-Livingstone Journal*, No. 29, 1961. pp. 63–78,

Salamone, F. A. (1975a) 'Becoming Hausa: ethnic identity change and its implications for the study of ethnic pluralism and stratification', *Africa* **45**, 1975, pp. 410–24.

Salamone, F. A. (1975b) 'The Serkawa of Yauri: class, status or party?', *African Studies Review*, **18**,1, 1975, pp. 88–101.

Sanday, P. R. (1973) 'Female status in the public domain' in M. Z. Rosaldo and L. Lamphere (eds.), *Woman, Culture and Society*, Stanford University Press, 1973.

Sandbrook, R. and Cohen, R. (eds.) (1975) *The Development of an African Working Class*, Longman, London, 1975.

Schildkrout, E. (1970) 'Strangers and local government in Kumasi', *Journal of Modern African Studies*, **8**, 1970, pp. 251–69.

Schildkrout, E. (1973) 'The fostering of children in urban Ghana: problems of ethnographic analysis in a multi-cultural context', *Urban Anthropology*, **2**, 1973, pp. 48–73.

Schildkrout, E. (1974) 'Ethnicity among first and second generation Mossi immigrants in Ghana', in A. Cohen (ed.), *Urban Ethnicity*, Tavistock Publications, London, 1974.

Shack, W. A. (1973) 'Urban ethnicity and the cultural process of urbanization in Ethiopia', in A. Southall (ed.), *Urban Anthropology*, Oxford University Press, 1973.

Shack, W. A. (1976) 'Occupational prestige, status and social change in modern Ethiopia', *Africa*, **46**, 1976, pp. 166–81.

Shils, E. (1957) 'Primordial, personal, sacred and civil ties', *British Journal of Sociology*, **8**, 1957, pp. 130–45.

Simmel, G. (1950) 'The stranger' in *The Sociology of George Simmel* (ed. and trans. K. H. Wolff), Free Press, New York, 1950.

Sjoberg, G. (1955) 'The preindustrial city', *American Journal of Sociology*, **60**, 1955, pp. 438–45. (Reprinted in P. K. Hatt and A. J. Reiss (eds.), *Cities and Society*, revised edn., Free Press, New York, 1963.)

Sjoberg, G. (1960) *The Preindustrial City*, Free Press, New York, 1960.

Skinner, E. P. (1958) 'Christianity and Islam among the Mossi', *American Anthropologist*, **60,** 1958, pp. 1102–19. (Reprinted in L. Schneider (ed.), *Religion, Culture and Society*, John Wiley and Sons, New York, 1964.)

Skinner, E. P. (1960) 'Labour migration and its relationship to socio-cultural change in Mossi society', *Africa*, **30,** 1960, pp. 375–99.

Skinner, E. P. (1963) 'Strangers in West African societies', *Africa*, **23,** 1963, pp. 307–20.

Skinner, E. P. (1973) *Peoples and Cultures of Africa*, Doubleday Natural History Press, New York, 1973.

Skinner, E. P. (1974) *African Urban Life: The Transformation of Ouagadougou*, Princeton University Press, 1974.

Skinner, E. P. and Shack, W. A. (eds.) (1977) *Strangers in African Societies*, University of California Press, 1977.

Smelser, N. J. (1967) 'Sociology and the other social sciences' in P. Lazarsfeld, W. H. Sewell and H. L. Wilensky (eds.), *The Uses of Sociology*, Basic Books, New York, 1967. (Reprinted in Smelser 1968.)

Smelser, N. J. (1968) *Essays in Sociological Explanation*, Prentice-Hall, Englewood Cliffs, 1968.

Smith, M. G. (1959) 'The Hausa system of social status', *Africa*, **29,** 1959, pp. 239–52.

Smith, M. G. (1964) 'Historical and cultural conditions of political corruption among the Hausa', *Comparative Studies of Society and History*, **6,** 1964, pp. 164–98.

Smith, M. G. (1966) 'Pre-industrial stratification systems' in N. J. Smelser and S. M. Lipset (eds.), *Social Structure and Mobility in Economic Development*, Routledge and Kegan Paul, London, 1966.

Smock, A. (1971) *Ibo Politics: The Role of Ethnic Unions in Eastern Nigeria*, Harvard University Press, 1971.

Sofer, C. and R. (1955) *Jinja Transformed*, East African Institute of Social Research, Kampala, 1955.

Solzbacher, R. M. (1970) 'East Africa's slum problem: a question of definition' in J. Gugler (ed.), *Urban Growth in Subsaharan Africa*, Nkanga Editions No. 6, Makerere Institute of Social Research, Kampala, 1970.

Southall, A. (1959) 'An operational theory of role', *Human Relations*, **12,** 1959, pp. 17–34.

Southall, A. (ed.) (1961) *Social Change in Modern Africa*, Oxford University Press for the International African Institute, London, 1961.

Southall, A. (1970) 'Stratification in Africa' in L. Plotnicov and A. Tuden (eds.), *Essays in Comparative Stratification*, University of Pittsburgh Press, 1970.

Southall, A. and Gutkind, P. C. W. (1957) *Townsmen in the Making: Kampala and Its Suburbs*, East African Institute of Social Research, Kampala, 1957.

Soyinka, W. (1965) *The Interpreters*, Andre Deutsch, London, 1965.

Stren, R. (1972) 'A survey of lower income areas in Mombasa' in J. Hutton (ed.), *Urban Challenge in East Africa*, East African Publishing House, Nairobi, 1972.

Sundkler, B. G. M. (1948) *Bantu Prophets in South Africa*, Oxford University Press for the International African Institute, London, 1948.

Tamuno, T. N. (1970) *The Police in Modern Nigeria, 1861–1965*, Ibadan University Press, 1970.

Tiger, L. (1966) 'Bureaucracy and charisma in Ghana', *Journal of Asian and African Studies*, **1**, 1966, pp. 13–26.

Timasheff, N. S. (1955) *Sociological Theory: Its Nature and Growth*, Random House, New York, 1955.

Trieman, D. J. (1975) 'Problems of concept and measurement in the comparative study of occupational mobility', *Social Science Research*, **4**, 1975, pp. 183–230.

Troeltsch, E. (1931) 'Sect-type and church-type contrasted' in *The Social Teaching of the Christian Churches* (trans. O. Wyon), Allen and Unwin, London. (Reprinted in L. Schneider (ed.), *Religion, Culture and Society*, John Wiley, London, 1964.)

Tuden, A. and Plotnicov, L. (eds.) (1970) *Social Stratification in Africa*, Collier-Macmillan, London, 1970.

Twumasi, P. A. (1975) *Medical Systems in Ghana*, Ghana Publishing Corporation, Accra, 1975.

Uchendu, V. C. (1965) *The Igbo of Southeast Nigeria*, Holt, Rinehart and Winston, New York, 1965.

Udo, R. K. (1975) *Migrant Tenant Farmers of Nigeria*, African Universities Press, Lagos, 1975.

Ulin, P. R. (1974) 'The traditional healer of Botswana in a changing society', *Rural Africana*, No. 26, 1974, pp. 123–30.

United Nations (1974) *Demographic Yearbook 1973*, United Nations, New York, 1974.

U.N.E.S.C.O. (1956a) 'African elites', *International Social Science Bulletin*, **8**, 1956, pp. 413–88.

U.N.E.S.C.O. (1956b) *Social Implications of Industrialization and Urbanization in Africa South of the Sahara*, UNESCO, Paris, 1956.

van den Berghe, P. L. (1963) 'Dialectic and functionalism: toward a theoretical synthesis', *American Sociological Review*, **28**, 1963, pp. 695–705.

van den Berghe, P. L. (1965) *Africa: Social Problems of Change and Conflict*, Chandler Publishing Co., San Francisco, 1965.

van den Berghe, P. L. (1968) 'An African elite revisited', *Mawazo*, **1**, 4, 1968, pp. 57–71.

van den Berghe, P. L. (1973) *Power and Privilege at an African University*, Routledge and Kegan Paul, London, 1973.

van den Berghe, P. L. and Nuttney, C. M. (1969) 'Some social characteristics, of University of Ibadan students', *Nigerian Journal of Economic and Social Studies*, **11**, 1969, pp. 355–76.

vanden Driesen, I. H. (1971) 'Some observations on the family unit, religion and the practice of polygyny in the Ife Division of Western Nigeria', *Africa*, **42**, 1971, pp. 44–56.

Van Hoey, L. (1968) 'The coercive process of urbanization: the case of Niger' in S. Greer *et al.* (eds.), *The New Urbanization*, St. Martin's Press, New York, 1968.

van Rensburg, P. (1974) *Report from Swaneng Hill*, Dag Hammarskjold Foundation, Uppsala, 1974.

Van Velson, J. (1961) 'Labour migration as a positive factor in the continuity of Tonga tribal society', *Economic Development and Cultural Change*, **8**, 1961, pp. 265–78. (Reprinted in Southall 1961 and Wallerstein 1966.)

Wallace, T. (1974) 'Educational opportunities and the role of family background factors in rural Buganda', *Rural Africana*, No. 25, 1974, pp. 29–46.

Wallace, T. and Weeks, S. G. (1974) 'How to scale occupations', *Manpower and Unemployment Research in Africa*, **7**, 1, 1974, pp. 9–13.

Wallerstein, I. (1964) *The Road to Independence: Ghana and the Ivory Coast*, Mouton, Paris, 1964.

Wallerstein, I. (ed.) (1966) *Social Change: The Colonial Situation*, John Wiley, New York, 1966.

Ward, B. E. (1956) 'Some observations on religious cults in Ashanti', *Africa*, **26**, 1956, pp. 47–60.

Weber, M. (1930) *The Protestant Ethic and the Spirit of Capitalism*, (trans. T. Parsons), Allen and Unwin, London, 1930.

Weber, M. (1946) *From Max Weber: Essays in Sociology*, (trans. and ed. H. H. Gerth and C. W. Mills), Oxford University Press, New York, 1946.

Weber, M. (1947) *The Theory of Social and Economic Organization*, (trans. T. Parsons and A. M. Henderson), Free Press, Glencoe, Ill. 1947.

Weber, M. (1953) 'The three types of legitimate rule' (trans. H. Gerth), *Berkeley Journal of Sociology*, 1953. (Reprinted in A. Etzioni (ed.), *Complex Organizations*, Holt, Rinehart and Winston, New York, 1961.)

Weber, M. (1958) *The City*, (trans. and ed. D. Martindale and G. Neu-wirth), Free Press, New York, 1958.

Welbourn, F. B. (1961) *East African Rebels: A Study of Some Independent Churches*, SCM Press, London, 1961.

Whitaker, C. S. (1965) 'Three perspectives on hierarchy: political thought and leadership in Northern Nigeria', *Journal of Commonwealth Political Studies*, **3**, 1965, pp. 1–19. (Reprinted in E. A. Nordlinger (ed.), *Politics and Society*, Prentice-Hall, Englewood Cliffs, 1970. Also in Wilmot 1973, Vol. 2.)

Whitaker, C. S. (1970) *The Politics of Tradition, Continuity and Change in Northern Nigeria, 1946–66*, Princeton University Press, 1970.

Williams, G. (1974) 'Political consciousness among the Ibadan poor' in E. de Kadt and G. Williams (eds.), *Sociology and Development*, Tavistock Publications, London, 1974.

Williamson, S. G. (1965) *Akan Religion and the Christian Faith*, K. A. Dickson (ed.), Ghana Universities Press, Accra, 1965.

Wilmot, P. F. (ed.) (1973) *Sociology in Africa: A Book of Readings*, Sociology Department, Ahmadu Bello University, Zaria, 1973.

Wilson, M. H. (1951) 'Witch-beliefs and social structure', *American Journal of Sociology*, **56**, 1951, pp. 307–13. (Reprinted in Marwick 1970.)

Wirth, L. (1938) 'Urbanism as a way of life', *American Journal of Sociology*, **44**, 1938, pp. 1–24. (Reprinted in P. K. Hatt and A. J. Reiss (eds.), *Cities and Society*, revised edn., Free Press, New York, 1963.)

Wober, M. (1967) 'Individualism, home life and work efficiency among a group of Nigerian workers', *Occupational Psychology*, **41**, 1967, pp. 183–92.

Wolpe, H. (1969) 'Port Harcourt: Ibo politics in microcosm', *Journal of Modern African Studies*, **7**, 1969, pp. 469–93.

Wolpe, H. (1974) *Urban Politics in Nigeria: A Study of Port Harcourt*, University of California Press, 1974.

Wood, A. W. (1974) *Informal Education and Development in Africa*, Mouton, Paris, 1974.

World Bank (1972) *Urbanization* (Sector Working Paper), World Bank, Washington, D.C., 1972.

Worsley, P. *et al* (1970) *Introducing Sociology*, Penguin, Harmondsworth, 1970.

Yesufu, T. M. (1962) *An Introduction to Industrial Relations in Nigeria*, Oxford University Press for the Nigerian Institute of Social and Economic Research, London, 1962.

Young, A. (1974) 'The practical logic of Amhara traditional medicine',

Rural Africana, No. 26, 1974, pp. 79–89.

Yusuf, A. B. (1974), 'A reconsideration of urban conceptions: Hausa urban-isation and the Hausa rural-urban continuum', *Urban Anthropology*, **3**, 1974, pp. 200–221.

Yusuf, A. B. (1975) 'Capital formation and management among the Muslim Hausa traders of Kano, Nigeria', *Africa*, **45**, 1975, pp. 167–82.

Zarr, G. H. (1969) 'Liberia' in A. Milner(ed.), *African Penal Systems*, Routledge and Kegan Paul, London, 1969.

Zeller, D. L. (1974) 'Traditional and western medicine in Buganda: co-existence and complement', *Rural Africana*, No. 26, 1974, pp. 91–104.

Index

For Ghana, Kenya, Nigeria, Sierra Leone, Tanzania and Zambia, see also references under various towns and ethnic groups shown on Maps 1 and 2. Cities and countries mentioned only on pp. 255–6 are not indexed.

Aba, 248n, 255, 292, 307–8, 320
Abbott, D. J., 267, 322, 324, 328, 329n, 331n
Abeokuta, 124, 248n, 255, 277n, 292, 305, 307–8, 319–20
Abernethy, D. B., 175n, 181n, 195, 208n
Abidjan, 148–9, 195, 255, 315, 351
Abrams, C., 320n
Abure people, 55
Accra, 86, 97, 105, 162, 191, 195, 253, 255, 273, 276, 280–1, 291, 303, 312, 320, 322, 330
acculturation, 281–7; see also adaptation
Achebe, C., 90n, 142
achievement, 15, 93, 100, 110, 183, 196–8, 333, 350
Acquah, I., 303
adaptation, 118–19, 121, 126, 274, 277, 285, 292, 328, 337, 360
Addis Ababa, 255, 275, 303, 318
Addo, N. O., 275n
adolescence, 54, 58, 330
Agbekoya Rebellion, 346
Ajegunle, 248n, 307–9, 316–18
Akan people, 105, 145–6, 160, 167, 214, 264, 291; see also Asante people
alienation, 41, 183, 267
aliens, 118–20, 274, 292
Allen, V. L., 97n
Aluko, J. A., 191n
Americo–Liberian people, 123
Amhara people, 234
Amin, S., 273, 275n
Ampene, E., 322
Anderson, C. A., 176n
Anderson, J. E., 180, 202n

Angola, 255, 278
Ankole people, 291
anomie, 115, 237–8, 267
apprenticeship, 53, 158, 174, 187–8
Armer, M. J., 88n, 350
Aronson, D. R., 97
Arusha people, 340
Aryee, A. F., 148n, 223, 249n
Asante people, 106, 139, 154, 168, 215, 220, 237–8
Ashaiman, 248n, 292, 307–8, 316, 320
Asian people, 118–19, 123, 226, 232, 295
associations, 18, 95, 119, 127, 236, 271, 288–301, 311, 316
Asuni, T., 332
authority, 6, 34–7, 42, 55, 64, 92, 95, 183, 240–2; see also leadership

Baeta, C. G., 236n
Baker, P., 120n, 303
Bakula, B. B., 356n
Bamako, 175, 255, 275, 303
Bamisaiye, A., 327
Banjul, 255, 275
Banton, M., 12n, 127, 131, 227n, 289–90, 298n, 303
Barkan, J., 183–4
Barnard, G., 162, 303
Barnes, S., 292n, 300n, 313n
Barth, F., 125n
Barrett, D. B., 36n, 243–4
Barrett, S. R., 164n
Bascom, W., 253n, 261n, 263, 303
Becker, H., 28
Beckett, P. A., 191n, 192
Beer, C. H., 346, 347
Beidelman, T. O., 224n, 240

beliefs, 116, 227–39
Bemba people, 129
Benedict, B., 122n
Bendix, R., 348, 352
Benin, 106, 118, 255, 344
Benin City, 253, 255
Berg, E. J., 188n
Bete people, 55
Bienefeld, M. A., 313n
Bharati, A., 119n
Bibby, J., 190n, 192n, 197–8n, 200n
Binhammer, H. H., 313n
Blakemore, K. P., 180, 194–5n, 310n, 357n
Blantyre-Limbe, 167, 255, 303, 315–6
Blau, P., 37, 63–4
Bloomberg, L. N., 320n
Bohannan, P., 23n, 95n, 136n, 213n, 230n, 324n, 330n, 332n
Bolgatanga, 258n
Bonacich, E., 118n
Booth, A., 289n
Booth, C., 1
Boserup, E., 160n, 336n
Boswell, D. M., 75
Botswana, 202n, 236, 255
Bott, E., 69
Boudon, R., 210
Brain, J., 155
Broom, L., 47n, 239n
Brown, G. N., 174–5n, 211
Bujra, G. M., 19n, 303, 313n, 316n, 321n
Burawoy, M., 85, 115n, 122–3, 295n
bureaucracy, 37–41, 100–01, 103, 108, 201–03, 240, 254, 326, 333, 346–7, 353, 356–7
Bushmen people, 16, 79, 148, 340
Busia, K. A., 129n, 143n, 303, 313n, 329–30

Caldwell, J. C., 150, 156, 167, 171, 273n, 279–81, 285n, 286, 288
Callaway, A., 159n, 188n, 309n
Cameron, J., 175n
Cameroon, 160, 255
Cape Coast, 191, 255
change, 7–8, 30, 35, 40, 82, 107, 163–71, 178–9, 219–24, 226, 237–8, 250, 287, 321, 325–6, 330, 337–61
charisma, 35–6, 239–41, 245
child rearing, 55–8, 196, 229; fostering, 157–8

Chilivumbo, A. B., 167, 303, 314n, 317n
Chinoy, E., 338n
Christianity, see religion
Christiansen, J. B., 351
civilisation, 12, 85, 351
class, 81–5, 96–103, 315, 357
Clignet, R., 55, 88n, 148–50n, 151–2, 162n, 182n, 187n, 195, 197, 322, 351n
Clinard, M. B., 267, 324, 328, 329n, 331n
Cohen, A., 59, 110, 125n, 127n, 218n, 219, 303, 314n
Cohen, M. A., 315
Cohen, P. S., 41n, 43n, 338n
Cohen, R., 100n, 102, 127, 295n, 298n, 353, 355n
Colson, E., 126n, 321n, 359n
communalism, 124–31, 147, 202, 290–4, 300–01
community, 19, 218, 245, 270–2, 283, 315, 328, 357–8
comparative method, 21–4, 113
Comte, A., 1, 340
concept, 9–10
conflict, 13–15, 71, 76, 102, 117, 120, 131, 136–7, 200–01, 218, 229–30, 270, 321, 342–7; conflict theory, 41–4, 81–2, 98, 122, 245, 324–6, 332
consensus, 41–3, 200, 218, 324–6, 342–6, 348
conversion, 219–24
Cooley, C. H., 30, 257
corruption, 59, 98, 101, 115, 298, 311, 327, 332–4
Coser, L. A., 43, 44n, 343n
Court, D., 175n, 187, 188n
Crawford, J. R., 230
Creole people, 86, 106, 117, 123, 131, 152n
crime, 327–34
culture, 10–12, 80, 174n, 223, 243–4, 250, 338, 346
Currie, J., 192, 194–5n

Dahrendorf, R., 81n, 344
Dakar, 98, 256, 304, 315
Dar es Salaam, 86, 184, 253, 256, 280, 303, 315
Darwin, C., 1, 340
Davies, I., 295n
Davis, K., 80n, 252n–3n, 256n
demography, 8, 170–1, 253–7, 272,

279–81, 319–20
development, 11, 340, 345–7
Developing Planning Unit, 315n
deviance, 50, 58, 267, 321, 324–7
Dinan, C., 318n
Dinka people, 220
divorce, 152–6
Doob, L.W., 350
Dore, R., 172, 176n, 202n
Dorjahn, V. R., 148
Drucker, P. F., 187
Durkheim, E., 21, 28, 61, 214–5, 237n, 340–1

East London, 73, 268
education, 2, 17, 21, 56, 86, 99–100, 107, 112, 118, 122, 143, 166–7, 171, 174–212, 244, 280–1, 283, 306–10, 350, 357–8; see also literacy
Edwards, J. N., 289n
Eisenstadt, S. N., 24, 360n
Ekeh, P. P., 24n, 60
elites, 57, 74–5, 85, 99, 101–10, 128, 150–1, 156, 162, 166–8, 183, 190, 192–3, 196–7, 264, 298, 300, 351, 354
Elkan, W., 98n
entrepreneurship, 49, 118–20, 225–6
Epstein, A. L., 68, 74, 88n, 105, 113n, 263n, 279n, 283n, 290, 291n, 295n, 322n
equality, 79–80, 82, 92, 95, 100, 114, 200–01
Ethiopia, 88n, 104, 234, 242, 255, 275, 277, 303, 318
ethnic group, 125; ethnicity, 98, 125, 152, 286, 290, 319
ethnocentrism, 11, 22, 116–31, 347
evolutionism, 23–4, 27, 164, 339–41, 347
Ewe people, 234, 300

Fallers, L. A., 79n, 94, 95n, 105, 109n, 155
family, 56, 133–73, 334; see also kinship
Fante people, 106, 351
Feldman, R., 357
Faiwoo, D. K., 234, 237n
Field, M. J., 236n
Fisher, H. J., 177n, 220, 222–3
Flanagan, W. G., 304n
folkways, 16, 50
Forde, D., 135n

Fortes, M., 134n, 168
Foster, P., 88n, 175n, 186, 187n, 188, 190n, 195, 197
Fraenkel, M., 12n, 85, 162n, 303, 314n, 318n
Frafra people, 97, 114, 136, 170, 264, 291
Frankenberg, R., 235n
Frazier, J. G., 214
Freetown, 86, 127, 256, 289, 298, 303
Freud, S., 50
friendship, 74–5, 86, 138, 269, 318–9
Fulani people, 93–4, 264n, 283, 349
function, 5, 19–21; functionalism, 80, 88, 122, 201, 342
Furnival, J. S., 122

Ga people, 146, 160, 264, 276, 291
Gambia, 91, 104, 255, 275, 295
Gamble, D. P., 56, 88n, 303
Ganda people, 86, 93–4, 109, 117–18, 126, 167, 176, 180, 192, 234, 253, 291, 354
Gao, 253
Garlick, P. C., 119n
Geertz, C., 299
Ghai, D., 175n
Ghana, 1, 16, 36, 65, 88, 109–10, 113, 116, 118–20, 140–1, 148–50, 153, 156, 169, 171, 175n, 178, 180, 190, 192, 197, 223, 229, 247, 254, 274–5, 286, 288, 295–6, 301, 304, 357–8
Gisu people, 86, 180
Gluckman, M., 43–4, 155, 281
Godfrey, E. M., 188n
Goldlust, J., 284n, 285
Gonja people, 154, 158
Goode, W., 163–4n
Goody, E., 154, 158n
Goody, J., 92, 143, 179n, 232, 238
Gouldner, A.W., 60
Grillo, R. D., 74, 86–7, 276n, 299, 312n
Grindal, B., 54
group, 18–19, 34, 96, 103–4; primary, 30–3, 44, 51, 135, 229, 234; reference, 52–3, 85, 103, 105, 118, 271; solidarity, 116, 119, 123, 125, 322
Gugler, J., 284, 286n, 304n
Guinea, 35, 169, 255, 274
Gulliver, P. H., 125n, 340n, 355
Guru people, 155
Gusii people, 160
Gutkind, P. C.W., 125n, 265n, 303,

305n, 320n
Gwari people, 230

Hadza people, 340
Hance, W. A., 286n
Handwerker, W. P., 306n
Hanna, W. J. and P. L., 303
Harrell-Bond, B. E., 152n
Harries-Jones, P., 75
Hart, K., 96–7, 115n, 226, 258n, 287n, 291n, 306n, 330
Hastings, A., 140, 148n, 236n
Hausa people, 49, 59, 65–6, 93–4, 110, 124, 127, 158, 218–19, 247, 260n, 264, 283, 291, 314, 318–19, 332, 349
Hauser, P. M., 254n, 261
healing, 88, 233–9
Henderson, R. N., 95n, 359n
Heyneman, S. P., 197
Hill, P., 92n, 114n, 137n, 158n, 249n, 314n
Hiskett, M., 174–5n, 211
Hodge, R. W., 88n
Homans, G. C., 18, 62–4
Hopkins, A. G., 102n
Hopkins, N. S., 44n, 303
Hopkins, T. K., 348n
Horowitz, D. L., 126n
Horton, R., 219–22, 231, 241n
household, 114–17, 164
housing, 99, 259, 312–21
Human Resources Research Unit, 192n
Hurd, G. E., 190n, 192n
Hutton, C., 276n, 278n, 306n, 309n, 353, 355n
Hutu people, 90

Ibadan, 57, 59, 110, 127, 151, 191, 218–19, 234, 247, 255, 294, 303, 314, 323, 327, 346
Ibo people, 49, 90, 93, 95, 114, 160, 162, 170, 202n, 264, 278, 291–3, 300, 323, 359
ideal type, 27, 30, 38, 260
Idoma people, 14n
Ijaw people, 155
Ila people, 264n
Ile-Ife, 148–9, 191, 253, 255, 278
Imoagene, S. O., 279, 283
Imperato, P. J., 235
ILO, 304–5n
INADES, 222n
industrial workers, 63–4, 71, 74–5, 83,

86–8, 97–8, 100, 102, 113, 123, 149, 258, 273, 276, 281, 350–2; see also trade unions
influence, 34, 64, 72, 107, 109
Inkeles, A., 179, 349–50
institution, 17, 338, 345–6
Irvine, S. H. 174n
Islam, see religion
Ivory Coast, 55, 88n, 118, 148–9, 152, 162, 187–8, 195, 197, 255, 273–5, 315, 351

Jacobson, D., 74, 271n, 276n, 303
Jahoda, G., 190–1n, 229
Janzen, J. M., 235n
Jenkins, G. D., 323
Jinja, 123, 303
Johnson, T., 190n, 192n
Jos, 258, 303

Kabwe, 63
Kaduna, 256, 292, 308n; Kakuri-Makera, 248n, 292, 307–9, 318–20
Kampala, 58, 74, 86, 184, 253, 256, 265, 268, 271, 290–1, 303, 306n, 314–5, 319–20, 322, 324, 328–31, 333
Kanema, 258
Kano, 175, 218, 252, 256, 260n, 263, 303, 350
Kanuri people, 177, 180, 204
Kapferer, B., 63–4, 69–71
Katsina, 252, 256
Kaufert, J., 190–2n, 195
Kay, G., 303
Kenya, 74, 122, 175, 180, 184, 187, 190, 274
Kiga people, 291
Kikuyu people, 149, 276, 359
Kilson, M., 303
Kimbanguism, 227
King, K., 159n, 188n, 200n, 202n, 309n, 311
Kinshasa, 58, 162, 256, 303
kinship, 90, 93, 97–8, 105, 133–8, 145, 147, 158, 164, 167–8, 229–30, 262, 279, 288, 291–2, 309–10, 333; see also family
Kisangani, 256, 288, 298, 303, 313
Kita, 44n, 303
Kluckhohn, C., 15
Koll, M., 294
Kru people, 119, 127, 273, 290
Kumasi, 19, 124, 143, 158, 253, 255,

258–9, 278, 281, 318, 320
Kuper, L., 122n

LaFontaine, J. S., 58, 288, 303
Lagos, 123–4, 137, 147, 162, 178, 180–1,
    192–4, 248n, 253, 255, 261, 265, 268,
    290–2, 294 see also Ajegunle
Lala people, 75
language, 11–12, 48, 174n
law, 16–17, 108, 322–3
Lawson, R. M., 337n
leadership, 33–41, 91–2, 94, 107–10, 114,
    227, 246, 289, 297–8, 341, 345, 347,
    354–5, 360; see also authority
Lebanese people, 118, 295
Legon, see Accra
Lemarchand, R., 90n
Lenski, G., 87
Leslie, J. A. K., 280, 303
Levine, D. N., 104n, 118n, 183n
LeVine, R. A., 49, 57, 95n, 114n, 151,
    160
Levi-Strauss, C., 24, 62, 141
Levy-Bruhl, L., 214
Leys, C., 332n
Liberia, 12, 65, 85, 104, 106, 119, 123,
    127, 162, 166, 255, 273, 277, 303,
    318, 323
literacy, 176–9, 221, 232, 241, 247, 294
Little, K., 289
Livingstone, 303
Lloyd, B. B., 57, 147n, 196n
Lloyd, P. C., 97, 100, 103n, 107, 127n,
    155, 167, 259, 294n, 303
LoDegaa people, 126
Long, N., 226n, 359n
Lowy, M. J., 324n
Luanshya, 256, 303
Lubeck, P. 296
Lucas, D., 113, 162
Luckham, R., 105, 125n
Luhya people, 126
Lukhero, C., 167
Lunsar, 56, 258, 303
Luo people, 118, 127, 149, 167, 170,
    273, 276, 278, 300
Lusaka, 75, 145, 149, 152, 256, 263,
    266, 315–6, 320
Luvale people, 129
Lux, A., 168, 288

Maas, J. van L., 354n
Mabogunje, A. L., 263n, 286, 303

McClelland, D. C., 49
McCulloch, M., 303; see also Fraenkel
McEwan, P. J. M., 227n
MacIver, R. M., 28
Maclean, U., 234, 235n
magic, 214, 228–9, 232–3, 236
Magid, A., 14n
Maine, H., 28
Malawi, 53, 126, 140, 167, 240, 255,
    278, 283, 303, 315–16
Mali, 44n, 101, 103, 175, 235, 253, 255,
    261, 263, 264n, 274–5, 290, 303, 356,
    358
Malinowski, B., 346
Mande (Mandingo) people, 247
manpower, 184–9
Mansa, 303
Maquet, J., 90n
Maradi, 303
Marghi people, 91n
Margoli people, 170
marriage, 90, 92, 98–9, 128, 138–63,
    183; see also kinship, polygyny
Marris, P., 119n, 130n, 137n, 226, 265n,
    268, 303, 313n, 317n
Marsh, R. M., 23n
Marwick, M., 228–30n
Marx, K., 81, 83–4, 343, 346; Marxism,
    97, 339–40
Masai people, 264n, 340, 355
Mashauri, R. K., 357n
mass communications, 51
Mauritania, 166, 177, 255
Mauss, M., 59, 61
Mayer, P., 73, 268
Mbale, 74, 261, 303
Mbilinji, M. J., 178n
Mbiti, J. S., 227n
Mboya, G. R., 356n, 357
Mboya, T. J., 115n, 351n
Mead, G. H., 50
medicine, see healing
Meillassoux, C., 91n, 101, 103n, 275,
    290n, 303
Melson, R., 128
Mende people, 131
Merton, R. K., 14, 20, 39n, 52n, 106,
    267, 325–6
migration, 19, 73–4, 120, 138, 142, 145,
    167–8, 258–9, 269, 272–88, 292, 309,
    319,328
Miner, H., 261, 303
Mitchell, J. C., 65, 67, 73, 85, 88n, 92n,

113n, 121n, 124, 126, 129–30, 143, 153–4, 262, 281–3, 285n, 303, 313n, 337, 350
modernisation, 104, 179, 347–52
Mogadishu, 253, 256
Mombasa, 253, 255, 258, 303, 313, 316, 318–9
Monrovia, 85, 123, 255, 303, 318
Moock, J. L., 190n
Moore, W. E., 80n
Moreno, J. L., 65
mores, 16, 50
Morgan, R.W., 88n
Morrill, W. T., 95n, 119n
Mossi people, 124, 143, 158, 223
Muench, L. H., 314
Muhsam, H. V., 186n
Murdock, G. P., 24
Mutiso, G.-C. M., 188n
Mwingira, A. C., 182n

Nadel, S. F., 103, 230
Nairobi, 98n, 105, 149, 167, 255, 257, 263, 266, 271, 290, 303–4, 311, 315–6, 320, 324n
Namibia, 255, 340
Ndebele people, 129
Ndola, 74, 256
neighbourhood, 58, 99, 247, 269, 328
Nelson, J. M., 286n
Ngoni people, 53–4, 129
Niger, 254, 274–5, 303
Nigeria, 11, 35, 75, 88n, 98, 104–5, 109, 116, 119–20, 128–9, 131, 140, 142–3, 161, 164n, 183, 189, 195, 221, 237, 241, 249, 254, 273, 280, 295–6, 301, 322, 358, 360
Nkrumah, K., 36
norm, 16–17, 48, 50, 52–3, 73–6, 115, 138, 324, 327, 332; of reciprocity, 60–1, 101, 310
Norwood, H. C., 315n, 316
Ntirukigwa, E. N., 357
Nuer people, 44, 136, 220
Nupe people, 230
Nuttney, C. M., 191n
Nyasa people, 126
Nyerere, J., 176, 182n

O'Brien, D. C., 332
O'Connell, J., 191n, 192
Ogburn, W. F., 338
Ohadike, P. O., 145, 149, 152, 280n, 305n, 320

Okediji, F. O., 167n
Okediji, O. O., 292
Okigbo, P., 359n
Olusanya, P. O., 277n, 279n
Omari, T. P., 141, 150
Oppong, C., 105, 145, 156, 161–2, 167, 273n
organisation, 13, 17, 27–46, 201–5, 239–49
Oshogbo, 256, 303
Ottenberg, P. V., 160
Ottenberg, S., 333, 359
Ouagadougou, 124, 256, 303, 323, 327, 329–31, 333–4, 351
Oyo, 256, 265, 277n

Paden, J. N., 124, 218, 303
parenthood, 157–9
Parkin, D. J., 58, 74, 125n, 127, 129n, 149, 167, 226, 268, 271n, 273n, 290, 303, 322
Parsons, T., 24, 29, 80n, 202n, 203, 217, 340
patron/client relations, 69, 75, 90, 94, 102, 295, 349
pattern variables, 29
Peace, A., 97, 102, 297n
Peel, J. D.Y., 36n, 219, 241, 245, 247
Peil, M., 41n, 88n, 96n, 109n, 112n, 113, 119–20n, 127n, 129–30, 143n, 149n, 159–60n, 162n, 168n, 188n, 190–2n, 195n, 197–8n, 200n, 207n, 248n, 261n, 276n, 279–81n, 292n, 300n, 306n, 308–9n, 315n, 318–20n, 333n, 351n
Perlman, M. L., 95n
Peshkin, A., 177, 180, 204, 359n
Pfeffermann, G., 98, 304n
Platt, G. M., 202n, 203
Plotnicov, L., 89n, 279n, 303
pluralism, 122, 239
polygyny, 92, 99, 137, 146–52, 154, 164, 169, 223, 245–6, 249, 351
Pons, V., 288, 298, 303, 313, 314n
Population Reference Bureau, 256n
Port Harcourt, 20, 256–7, 300, 303
Post, K.W. J., 323
Potholm, C. P., 323n
Powdermaker, H., 298, 303
power, 33–4, 63, 95, 101, 161–3, 293, 333
prejudice, 116–17
prestige, 95, 105, 113, 178, 208–9, 330,

333; occupational, 87–8, 94, 113; of
    teaching, 208–9; *see also* status
Prewitt, K., 182–3, 195n, 195–6n, 201n
Price-Williams, D. R., 230n
Priestley, M., 106
Proctor, J. H., 356
profession, 205–6
Prothero, R. M., 273n
Pygmy people, 79

Quarcoo, A. K., 316, 322

racism, 120–3
Radcliffe-Brown, A. R., 23–4, 137n,
    216, 224n
Rado, E. R., 187n
Ray, R. S., 306n
Read, M., 53
reciprocity, *see* norm, social exchange
religion, 19–20, 92, 110, 127, 148, 181,
    194, 213–51, 278, 319; Christianity,
    139–40, 151, 155, 169, 175, 351;
    Islam, 124, 129, 139, 175, 177, 211,
    218, 283, 291, 358
Remy, D., 296
research, 4, 8, 22–4, 73, 84, 302, 304–5,
    337, 350–2; *see also* statistics
Rhodesia, *see* Zimbabwe
Richards, A. I., 126n
Richmond, A. H., 284n, 285
Riesman, D., 50–1
ritual, 39, 215–7, 222
role, 12–15, 29, 64, 79–81, 136, 156–63,
    268–9
Roper, J. I., 295n
Ross, M. H., 105, 167, 271, 303, 315n,
    324n, 327n
Rotberg, R., 241n
Rwanda, 90, 254, 256, 273, 287

Salamone, F. A., 126–7, 221
Salisbury, 167, 256
sanction, 13, 16
Sanday, P. R., 161n
Sandbrook, K. R. J., 102, 295n, 298n
Sanders, J.T., 174n
Sangre, A., 287n
Sapele, 313n
Sawadogo, J. M., 287n
Schildkrout, E., 19, 119n, 124n, 125,
    129n, 138n, 143, 158n, 318
science, 2–6, 231–3, 236
Scudder, T., 359n

Schwab, W. B., 85, 99n, 267
sect, 236–7, 239–49
Sekondi/Takoradi, 143, 255, 257, 259,
    281, 303, 320, 329–30
Selznick, P., 47n, 239n
Senegal, 91, 98, 256, 275, 315, 333, 358
Shack, W. A., 88n, 275, 303, 318n
Shils, E., 32
Shona people, 230
Sierra Leone, 88n, 119, 257, 274, 283,
    294
Simmel, G., 43, 117–18, 266–8
Sisala people, 54–5
Sjoberg, G., 264
Skinner, E. P., 118–19n, 124, 223, 282n,
    287n, 298, 301n, 303, 323, 327,
    329–30, 331n, 351
Smelser, N. J., 6n, 13n, 17n, 25n, 337n,
    340, 341n, 344, 346n
Smith, M. G., 89n, 92n, 94n, 122n, 332
Smock, A., 202n, 287n, 293, 323n
social control, 16, 32, 51, 71, 270, 316,
    321–34, 341
social distance, 129–30
social exchange, 59–64, 162
social mobility, 52, 94–5, 99, 110–16,
    166, 189–201, 207, 229, 307
social network, 64–76, 138, 245, 268,
    284, 310, 318
social order, 41–4
social sciences, 7–9
socialisation, 47–59, 165, 176, 179–84,
    201, 225, 292, 299, 301, 322, 326–7,
    354
society, 4–5, 27–30, 44
Sofer, C. and R., 123, 303
Soga people, 155
Solzbacher, R. M., 314–15n
Somalia, 11, 127, 253–4, 256
Somerset, A., 119n, 198, 200n, 204, 226
South Africa, 73, 122, 131, 226, 242,
    244, 258, 268, 273, 275
Southall, A., 12–13n, 88n, 92n, 263,
    265n, 268, 290, 303, 320n
Soyinka, W., 106
Spencer, H., 1, 340–1
statistics, 253n, 305, 328–9
status, 59, 63, 81, 85–9, 114, 118, 144,
    147, 152–4, 161, 207, 226, 230, 235,
    269, 299; *see also* prestige
Steward, J. H., 24
strangers, 19, 117–20, 218, 232, 287,
    300, 333

stratification, 17, 79–110, 203–4; caste, 80, 85, 90–1, 111; slavery, 85, 89–90, 93
Stren, R., 303, 313n, 316, 318–19n
structure, 13, 24, 60, 67, 80, 134, 230, 345
Sudan, 44, 136, 220, 278
Sumner, W. G., 16–17
Sundkler, B. G. M., 226, 242n
Sutcliffe, R. B., 227n
Swahili, 11, 253, 319
Sween, J., 148–50n, 151–2, 351n
symbols, 62, 70, 102

Tallensi people, *see* Frafra
Tamuno, T. N., 322
Tanzania, 11, 76, 101, 175n, 178n, 182–4, 189, 196, 201, 257, 298, 304, 306, 354, 356–7
teachers, 80, 109, 113, 205–09, 278, 294
Tema, 248n, 253, 255, 258, 281, 292, 305, 307–8, 316, 320
Temne people, 57, 127, 131
Thoden Van Velzen, H. U. E., 76
Tiger, L., 36
Timasheff, N. S., 27n
Timbuctoo, 252, 261, 263, 303
Tiv people, 93, 95, 135–6, 230
Toennies, F., 28
Tonga people, 126, 321n
Toureg people, 264n
trade unions, 87, 98, 102, 206, 294–8
Treiman, D. J., 87n, 112–13n
Troeltsch, E., 239n
Tuden, A., 89n
Tutsi people, 90
Twa people, 90
Twaddle, M., 86n, 180n
Twumasi, P. A., 234n, 236n
Tylor, E. B., 213–14

Uchendu, V. C., 90n, 95n
Udo, R. K., 273n, 274, 276n, 278
Uganda, 75, 113, 120, 131, 140, 148, 182, 184–6, 191, 197, 236, 273–4
Ulin, P. R., 236n
Umuahia, 303
UNESCO, 103n
unemployment, 304–11
United Nations, 256n
Upper Volta, 119, 124, 223, 256, 273, 275, 283, 287, 303, 323, 327, 329–31, 333–4, 351
urbanisation, 148–9, 196, 252–73

value, 4, 15–16, 23
van den Berghe, P. L., 40, 81n, 128, 191n, 312n, 342
vanden Driesen, I. H., 148–9, 278
Van Hoey, L., 303
van Rensburg, P., 202n
Van Velson, J., 287n, 315
variable, 2–3, 16
Vaughan, J. H., 91n
Veblen, T., 39

Wallace, T., 113, 194n
Wallerstein, I., 301n, 348n
Ward, B. E., 237–8
Ward, L., 340
Warner, W. L., 86
Watt, I., 179n, 232n
Weber, M., 4, 23, 33–6, 38, 81, 83, 84n, ' 225, 270–1, 349
Weeks, S. G., 113
Welbourne, F. B., 242n
Weppa-Wano people, 155
Whitaker, C. S., 104n, 349
White, L. A., 24
Williams, G., 97n, 103n, 346n
Williamson, S. G., 238n
Wirth, L., 260, 262
witchcraft, 57, 71, 76, 154, 228–30, 234, 238, 270
Wober, M., 313n, 321n
Wolpe, H., 19–20, 98n, 128, 289n, 300, 303
Wood, A. W., 189
World Bank, 256n, 315n
Worsley, P., 9, 37n, 43n, 341n, 344

Xhosa people, 73, 268
Xydias, N., 88n

Yako people, 290
Yao people, 283
Yesufu, T. M., 294n
Yombe people, 168
Yoruba people, 49, 55–7, 97, 100, 103, 114, 117, 124, 126, 146, 151, 154–5, 158, 160, 167, 247, 259, 263–6, 277n, 291, 319, 349–50
Young, A., 234
Youtz, R., 350
Yusuf, A. B., 65–6, 260n, 299n

Zaire, 58, 88n, 118, 162, 168, 227, 235n, 253, 256, 273–4, 278, 288, 290–2, 298, 303, 313
Zambia, 65, 85, 88n, 113, 122–3, 143, 148, 240–1, 253–4, 257–8, 261, 273–4, 278, 280, 304–5, 313n, 350
Zanzibar, 253

Zaria, 191, 252, 256
Zarr, G. H., 322
Zeller, D. L., 234n
Zimbabwe, 85, 122, 167, 230, 253, 256, 267
Zinder, 303
Zulu people, 226, 244